Global Population in Transition

Jo. M. Martins · Fei Guo
David A. Swanson

Global Population
in Transition

 Springer

Jo. M. Martins
Department of Marketing and Management
Macquarie University
Sydney, NSW
Australia

David A. Swanson
Department of Sociology
University of California Riverside
Riverside, CA
USA

Fei Guo
Department of Marketing and Management
Macquarie University
Sydney, NSW
Australia

ISBN 978-3-319-77361-2   ISBN 978-3-319-77362-9   (eBook)
https://doi.org/10.1007/978-3-319-77362-9

Library of Congress Control Number: 2018934437

Printed on acid-free paper

This Springer imprint is published by the registered company Springer International Publishing AG part of Springer Nature
The registered company address is: Gewerbestrasse 11, 6330 Cham, Switzerland

Preface

Purpose

Population growth and transition are of major concern to policy makers, managers in the public and private sectors, academics and students, as well as to the population at large. The purpose of this book is to provide insights into the multifaceted nature of issues related to population growth conditioned by the environment in which people live, and the on-going evolution of human activity that changes not just social and economic relationships and organisation but also living conditions and the environment.

Organisation

The chapters in the book are organised to offer complementary perspectives of the world's population transition as it affects societies in regions with different and evolving population characteristics at various stages of development. It deals with population growth and the evolving nature of human activity, which affect social relationships, organisation and also work, standards of living and the environment.

The first chapter provides an overview of human development as it evolved on the planet, population growth, activity and development.

The following six chapters examine the diversity of views, notions, concepts and theories that have emerged to explain population and socioeconomic change and related concerns. These chapters deal with the basic elements of population dynamics, namely fertility, survival and migration, and some aspects of their manifestation in the settlement of the growing population in urban settings and population ageing.

Then, two social questions of importance and consequence are discussed. The first is concerned with gendered differences in human behaviour and social organisation, and the evolving nature of gender inequalities is examined.

Discussion of deviance in the form of departure from social conventional norms and criminal behaviour follows. The innovative nature of some deviant behaviour as an element in social change is reviewed, as well as the individual and social costs of criminal behaviour.

Then follows two chapters that examine socioeconomic activity and its effect on living conditions and the environment. Socioeconomic development through time and its effect on social and economic organisation are examined, with emphasis on the evolving and growing importance of human capital, and implications to changes in employment, productivity, inequalities in the sharing of productivity gains, as well as the changing nature of consumer priorities. The impact of human activity on the environment is then considered. The effects on the three major environmental domains of land, water and air are reviewed. The uncertainties of the outcome of continuing current economic practices regarding emissions from power generation and other energy use are considered, as well as the problem of reconciling private and social interests.

Finally, the last chapter is an agenda of challenges to be faced in the future arising from the inevitable future growth in population, the needs of a larger number of people in an already crowded planet, and the continuing lags and gaps of the living conditions of people in countries at different stages of development.

Use

The book is of interest to practitioners concerned with population change, such as those involved in social and economic policy analysis and development, business and human resources management, education and public health, and to academics with similar interests. It is also pertinent to students in population-related studies such as applied demography, human geography, sociology, economics, human resources management, political sciences and public health.

Sydney, Australia   Jo. M. Martins
Sydney, Australia   Fei Guo
Riverside, USA   David A. Swanson

Contents

List of Figures

List of Tables

List of Boxes

Chapter 1
Population: Survival and Growth

1.1 Earth, Life and Humans in Context

1.1.1 Recent Arrival of Humans

Early humans evolved some five to six million years ago, and from the last common grandmother of humans and chimpanzees around 2.5 million years ago, the genus homo arose with the development of stone tools (Harari 2015). This is late in Earth's chronology that is thought to go back about 4,600 million years ago. The surviving Homo sapiens are believed to have evolved even more recently about 150,000 years ago (Harari 2015). Human origins and evolution are controversial and the factors that led to the relatively recent appearance of human life are still being debated. New technologies have helped and new findings have added to current knowledge but have not eliminated the uncertainty that surrounds the appearance and evolution of the human genus. Homo sapiens being the last of the genus could be considered ominous.

1.1.2 Earth's Formation

Current consensus suggests that the Earth's origins go back to the creation of the solar system from a gas and dust nebula that collapsed under gravity. It formed a system of planets around the Sun including the inner rocky planets of Mercury, Venus, Earth and Mars some 4,600 to 4,000 million years ago (MYA) during Hadean times (Box 1.1). At some stage, this accretion consolidated into Earth's solid inner and a liquid outer *core* enveloped by a *mantle* where hotter material rises to the surface and colder material falls to lower depths of the mantle. Flows between the mineral core and the rocky mantle are said to have affected changes in the magnetic polarity of the Earth over time. Eventually, a colder *crust* was formed that

© Springer International Publishing AG, part of Springer Nature 2018
Jo. M. Martins et al., *Global Population in Transition*,
https://doi.org/10.1007/978-3-319-77362-9_1

at times has sunk back into the mantle and added to by mantle emissions. The early history of Earth was characterised by violent asteroid and meteorite bombardment, volcanic activity with molten emissions, tumultuous climate changes, and a cooling crust that formed shifting tectonic plates. The Moon may have been created by a major collision of a large space object with Earth (Palmer et al. 2012).

Over the eons, oceans and land masses changed continuously due to mantle upwellings and volcanic emission, subduction of the crust into the mantle and drift of continental plates. Large land masses were formed such as Gondwana, Laurentia, Baltica, Siberia, Euramerica, Eurasia, Australia, Antarctica, and supercontinents such as Rodinia (*mother of all continents*), Pannotia and Pangea came together and then broke up (Zhao et al. 2004; Palmer et al. 2012). Land mass movements could be classified as *collisional* or *accretionary* in nature. The first tended to create new geological features while the second added to the periphery of other land masses, in the process they might also affect changes in the oceans (Murphy et al. 2009). Land mass compression from these movements in more recent times created some of the present mountain ranges such as the Himalayas, the Alps and Pyrenees. Cooler temperatures have been associated with low levels of carbon dioxide concentration in the atmosphere, and glaciation at even lower concentration levels; while warmer temperatures were found at higher levels of carbon dioxide (Royer 2006). Atmospheric conditions and climate were also affected by mantle emissions, cosmic material impact, plant photosynthesis that led to the oxidation of the oceans and the atmosphere. Emissions, subduction and continental drift changed oceans and their currents. Geological features formed from such movements such as mountain ranges have effected climate. Evolving conditions led to either glaciation or warmer climates, or a mixture of both.

1.1.3 Human Essentials: Water and Oxygen

The formation of large masses of water and the oxidation of the atmosphere basic to human and other forms of life are a matter of conjecture. A number of possibilities have been suggested regarding the origins of water on Earth. One notion is that a hydrogen-rich atmosphere might have prevailed early and that was oxidised by iron oxides to produce water. This view may not fit the time scale of the appearance of water on Earth. Another possibility is that ice from the comet bombardment early in the planet's existence might have carried water to Earth. This was discounted earlier because the ice composition of comets was different from the water on Earth. More recently, however, a comet was detected to have a similar composition to water on the planet. Nevertheless, this idea does not seem to fit with the number of comets required to produce the mass of water on Earth. It is currently more accepted that water is the result of the accretion of the planet from its elements and the condensation of water vapour that took place early in the planet's history (Dauphas and Morbidelli 2014).

A major element in evolution of organic life was the Great Oxidation Event (GOE) that started during Archean times (Box 1.1) some 2,400-2,200 MYA. The oxidation of the oceans and atmosphere is suggested to have arisen from photosynthesis by micro-organisms. Before then, the atmosphere was likely to have been anoxic and had greenhouse conditions dominated by methane and hydrogen that led sometimes to cooling and glaciation. It is posited that oxygenic photosynthesis by cyanobacteria freed oxygen from water and also led to the reduction of carbon dioxide. Oxygen in its stable molecular form of dioxygen (O_2) was released in water and the atmosphere. It is thought that the separation of oxygen from other elements in water and the reduction of carbon dioxide was associated with the escape of hydrogen into space and the burial of carbon in organic sediments. In turn, dioxygen in the atmosphere led to its two-atom form being split by ultraviolet and by combination ($O_2 + O$) into ozone (O_3) that protects living organisms from ultraviolet, which until then were shielded from it by living in water. The GOE led to the extinction of much anaerobic life and enhanced opportunities for aerobic organisms (Noffke et al. 2013; Catling 2014).

1.1.4 Early Life

Biospheric evolution during Hadean times resulted in oceans and continental crusts, climate and other conditions compatible with the existence of life, in spite of the late heavy cosmic bombardment (Abramov and Mojzsis 2009). However, there are no known manifestations of it during the Hadean. The bombardment, subduction of the crust into the mantle and volcanic activity may have destroyed any evidence of life. The available evidence points to the appearance of life in Archean (*beginning*) times (Box 1.1). Although the possibility of earlier vestiges of life have been discussed, stromatolites found in Pilbara area of Western Australia are thought to be the oldest traces of life on Earth (Summons and Hallmann 2014). These sedimentary structures arose from microbial mats that lived in an aquatic environment going back some 3,480 MYA (Noffke et al. 2013). The origins of life on Earth may have come from favourable conditions in hydrothermal vents in the oceans that led to the synthesis of proteins (made up of amino acids) with nucleotides and other elements. The possible function of RNA (*ribonucleic acid*) in a RNA-world that preceded the origin of life continues to be a source of conjecture (Copley et al. 2007). The end of the Great Cometary Bombardment experienced during the Hadean and the Great Oxidation Event that began towards the end of the Archean led to major changes in the atmosphere and life during Proterozoic (*earlier life*) times (Box 1.1) some 2,500 to 541 MYA (Palmer et al. 2012).

1.1.5   From Single Cell to More Complex Life

Early life was characterised by single cell organisms (*prokaryotes*) such as cyanobacteria with asexual reproduction. Early Proterozoic fossils of living organisms are mostly of this nature. It is late in the Proterozoic that fossils of more complex organisms with a nucleus (*eukaryotes*) became relatively more abundant. Most of these cells reproduce sexually and are oxygen dependent (*aerobic*). How these came into being is uncertain but it may have been the result of symbiosis of two or more prokaryotes. Fossils of wormlike multicellular life (Ediacara type fauna) found in Australia have been dated to about 670-545 MYA. It is suggested that this phase marks a major step in the evolution of multicellular organisms in the form of plants, animals and fungi (Palmer et al. 2012).

1.1.6   Great Oxidation, Ozone and Aerobic Life

The appearance of living organisms with photosynthetic capacity affected the composition of the oceans and the atmosphere that favoured aerobic organisms and had a deleterious effect on anaerobic ones. The creation of the ozone layer allowed living organisms to leave the protective ocean environment. The evolution from single-cell organisms mostly of anaerobic nature with asexual reproduction to multi-cell organisms that reproduced sexually and mostly of an aerobic nature were major steps that took place in Precambrian times and forebode the dramatic evolution of life diversity that followed during Phanerozoic (*visible life*) times (Box 1.1) from 541 MYA to the present.

1.1.7   Vertebrates and the First Life Mass Extinction

During the Cambrian period (Box 1.1: 541-490 MYA) carbon dioxide levels were said to be rather high and there was no notable glaciation. Ocean levels rose. This was a time of life explosion and evolution of living forms. In the following Ordovician period (Box 1.1: 490-440 MYA), hard-shelled and organisms with skeletons appeared in the form of worms and fish (Cartmill and Smith 2009). Towards the end of that period of major life diversification, carbon dioxide levels declined and glaciation took place. This may have led to lower ocean levels that were associated with the first identified mass extinction of life (Palmer et al. 2012).

1.1.8   Life on Land and the Second Life Mass Extinction

Life seems to have migrated from water to land for the first time during the Silurian period (Box 1.1: 440-420 MYA) in plant form (possibly green algae) followed, most likely, by invertebrate animals. The Devonian period (Box 1.1: 420-360 MYA) was a time of major plant evolution on land with the appearance of tall treelike plants and changes in soil conditions. It was also the period when the first four legged vertebrates appeared (*tetrapods*) in the form of fish with legs, lungs and gills. Internal fertilisation in animals might have taken place (Cartmill and Smith 2009). During this period the second recorded mass extinction of life took place with major oxygen depletion of the ocean. A meteorite impact may have contributed to it (Palmer et al. 2012).

Box 1.1 The Earth's geological age

Earth's evolution continues to be a mixture of science and conjecture. To facilitate scientific discussion, the International Commission on Stratigraphy (ICS) issued a guide on terminology and nomenclature. Different aspects of the properties of rocks provide insights into aspects of the Earth's evolution:

- *lithostratigraphy* is concerned with the layers in which rocks are found
- *biostratigraphy* deals with the fossil content of rocks
- *magnetostratigraphy* assesses changes in the magnetic orientation of rocks
- *chronostratigraphy* is based on the time of rock formation

All of them play a role in the study and classification of rocks and iden-tification of their place in Earth's history. These properties lead to a multi-classification of a complementary nature. However, some of these classifications may not be applicable in some instances.

Chronostratigraphic units are the most reliable in the time sequence of the Earth's history. The ICS has adopted geochronologic units to give boundaries to the sequence of time in the formation of bodies of rocks in terms of:

- *Eons*
- *Eras*
- *Periods*
- *Epochs*
- *Age*
- *Sub-age*

These units have no time uniformity and have been applied to the history of Earth from its earliest times. Geochronology consists of three eons:

- *Archean (ancient life)*
- *Proterozoic (earlier life)*
- *Phanerozoic (visible life)*

An earlier time to the Archean eon is the *Hadean* (from Hades of the Underworld). The chronological boundaries of these eon and their eras gives the extent of Earth's history

- *Hadean* >4,000 million years ago
- *Archean* 4,000-2,500 million years ago (about 1,500 million years)

  - Eo-archean 4,000-3,600
  - Paleo-archaen 3,600-3,200
  - Meso-archean 3,200-2,800
  - Neo-archean 2,800-2,500

- *Proterozoic* 2,500-541 million years ago (about 1,959 million years)

  - Paleo-proterozoic 2,500-1,600
  - Meso-proterozoic 1,600-1,000
  - Neo-proterozoic 1,000-541

- *Phanerozoic* 541 million years ago—present (about 540 million years)

  - Paleozoic 541-252
  - Mesozoic 252-66
  - Cenozoic 66-Present

The earlier eons are the *Precambrian* times. The *Cambrian* is the early period of the Paleozoic era in the Phanerozoic eon. It was followed by Ordovician, Silurian, Devonian, Carboniferous and Permian periods in the Paleozoic era. The Mesozoic period started with the Triassic period that preceded the Jurassic and Cretaceous periods. The Cenozoic era is made up of the Paleogene, Neogene and the Quaternary periods.
(Cohen et al. 2013; Murphy and Salvador Undated).

1.1.9 Plant and Animal Reproduction on Land

During the Carboniferous period (Box 1.1: 360-300 MYA) seed plants evolved on land and large trees and ferns were abundant. Animal life also evolved with fish developing jaws and some tetrapods loosening their gills. Amphibious reproduction that required water to bring egg and sperm together was complemented by eggs with a tougher membrane that could cope with land conditions and sperm being implanted into the egg in the female reproductive system (Cartmill and Smith 2009; Palmer et al. 2012).

1.1.10   Mammal-Like Animals and the Third Life Mass Extinction

Forests grew in less arid conditions and mammal like reptiles are presumed to have evolved during the Permian period (Box 1.1: 300-250 MYA) (Palmer et al. 2012). A characteristic of mammals is that the female carries the egg internally and the developing foetus is fed by the mother's placenta. Major volcanic activity seems to have led to the third mass extinction of life (250 MYA), especially marine life in oxygen starved oceans. An estimated 80–96% of marine life became extinct and much of terrestrial life also ceased to exist (Sahney and Benton 2008).

1.1.11   Recovery and Fourth Life Mass Extinction

Plants and animals evolved and climate diversity led to plant zonation in the Triassic period (Box 1.1: 250-200 MYA). Life recovery from the Permian disaster was associated with the evolution of reptiles, birds, mammals and dinosaurs late in the period. A fourth life mass extinction took place towards the end of this period (200 MYA) without known causes (Palmer et al. 2012). It affected about 80% of species including much marine life and amphibian vertebrates. This mass extinction might have been caused by the impact of comets and meteorites on Earth (Spray et al. 1998) or volcanic activity (Galli et al. 2005).

1.1.12   Dinosaurs and Other Life Prosper and the Fifth Life Mass Extinction

Plankton is propounded to have made its appearance and changed the ocean chemistry and invertebrate organisms in the sea and land (e.g. insects) prospered during the Jurassic period (Box 1.1: 200-145 MYA). This is the period when dinosaurs that had survived the Triassic life mass extinction became the most conspicuous vertebrates on Earth. However, birds, reptiles and mammals also prospered. Plant life evolved and flowering plants are presumed to have appeared during the Cretaceous period (Box 1.1: 145-66 MYA). However, volcanic activity and possibly meteoritic impacts are assumed to have led to the fifth life mass extinction that wiped out the dinosaurs and some 75% of life on Earth (66 MYA) (Palmer et al. 2012).

1.1.13   New Life from Mammals to Primates

This major catastrophe was the harbinger of further changes in the Cenozoic era
(*new life*) (Box 1.1: 66 MYA to the present). Land masses consolidated. India
impacted into Asia, European and Asian land masses came together and continental
drifts led to plate compressions that formed the Himalayas, the Alps, Pyrenees and
many other mountain ranges. The Panama isthmus linked North and South
America, Australia moved away from Antarctica and Africa that had broken from
South America earlier moved further apart from it. These led the oceans largely
taking their present shape. Carbon dioxide levels continued to be at lower levels but
temperatures continued to oscillate and influenced by geological features and ocean
currents. Periods of high glaciation and lowered ocean levels occurred with complementary land expansion. They alternated with warmer periods when ocean and
land areas reversed. Weather and regional conditions led to the formation of
grasslands in some areas and forests in wetter places, and animal life evolved to
take advantage of these conditions. Mammal and other megafauna developed in the
ocean (e.g. whales) and land (e.g. mastodons). Much of the land megafauna is now
extinct, possibly due to later human activity. Primates evolved from other mammals
according to fossil evidence some 65 MYA. Early primates are extinct. Primates
evolved as temperatures changed. They became more noticeable some 55-35 MYA
(Palmer et al. 2012). However, mitochondrial DNA studies indicate that the primate
divergence might have taken place much earlier some 80 MYA (Chatterjee et al.
2009). This would place the common ancestor of primates at a time before the fifth
life mass extinction in the Cretaceous period. Primates are characterised by larger
brain in relation to body size, with hands and some with feet with divergent digits
for enhanced grasping, with nails rather than claws, more forward placed eyes for
binocular vision that give a better sense of depth, less reliance on olfactory capacity,
greater importance on hindlimb for movement, longer gestation with slower foetal
growth and possible longer life span (Stringer and Andrews 2011).

The primate evolution that led to the human genus and the surviving Homo
sapiens continues to be unclear in spite of mitochondrial DNA analysis. It is
apparent that many evolved primates are now extinct (Palmer et al. 2012). The split
of Prosimian and Simian (*Anthropoids*) primates (Fig. 1.1) is estimated to have
taken place some 64 MYA. In turn, the divergence between monkeys and apes in
the Simian family is assessed to have taken place 29 MYA, and the gibbons from
other apes about 22 MYA (Chatterjee et al. 2009). The split of some primates from
common ancestors continues to be studied and discussed as scientific methods
develop. Approximate divergence time indicates that the orangutan divergence
from a common ancestor of the Hominids took place about 13 MYA, the gorilla
about 7 MYA and the Chimpanzee about 6 MYA. The divergence of humans from
the chimpanzee is estimated to have taken place about 5–6 MYA (Glazko and Nei
2003; Andrews 2015). The Prosimians that split earlier are usually characterised by
a wet snout while the Simians have a dry one. Face features are usually also
different with Prosimians having a longer face with a more predominate snout, with

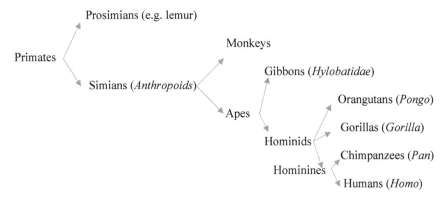

Fig. 1.1 Approximate primate tree
Source Palmer et al. (2012), Stringer and Andrews (2011)

more sideway eyes, while Simians tend to have a flatter face, smaller ears, less
salient snout and eyes that are more forward looking. A feature of the apes is that
unlike monkeys they have no tail. Another feature is that the elbow of the apes
provides for greater flexibility and stability of the arms (Stringer and Andrews
2011). Gibbons are the smallest of the apes with large limbs that make them the
most agile of the apes. They are mostly arboreal and their means of locomotion is
brachiation and leaping. Their diet is mostly of leaves and fruit. They tend to mate
for life in monogamous families that is not common among apes. Orangutans have
large bodies and powerful arms. They are mostly arboreal using four-hand climbing
and brachiation as their most common means of locomotion. They eat mostly fruit
and leaves. They are solitary animals with males living apart from females and
coming together for mating. Like all apes, they have large brains in relation to their
body size but smaller than those of humans. Gorillas are the largest of the apes.
They are part arboreal and part terrestrial, with quadrupedal gait and knuckle
walking. They are mostly vegetarians. They live in groups with a dominant male
and practice polygamy. Chimpanzees and humans are the two Hominine genera.
Chimpanzees are said to share about 95% of human DNA characteristics. However,
their brain size is much smaller than that of humans. Chimpanzee habitat is both
arboreal and terrestrial. They have large arms that enhance brachiation and lead to
their terrestrial knuckle walking like gorillas. They are also mostly vegetarian. They
live in groups with male dominance and bonding. Female transfers from one group
to another (Stringer and Andrews 2011; Srivastava 2009).

1.1.14 Human Evolution

Fossil and other evidence shows that human evolution has continued since the
divergence from other apes. There were transitional species with ape-like and some
modern human features (e.g. Australopithecines). In spite of molecular analysis,

human origins continue to be controversial. Humans differ from their closest relative the chimpanzee by an s-shaped vertebral column to support their erect gait and bipedal walk. They have arms that are shorter than their legs. Other skeletal features such as the pelvis and leg bones, feet with big toes in line with rather opposed to other toes, and longer heels support their bipedal walk. Their skull is rounder with flatter face and protruding nose and chin. The shape of the skull allows for a larger brain. Hands tend to be shorter with straight fingers and writs that enhance dexterity. At least some of the Homo species had hyoid bones that supported the use of language (Wood and Richmond 2000; Stringer and Andrews 2011).

The fossil trail makes it apparent that there were a number of Homo species before the appearance of the surviving Homo sapiens. Some of these species co-existed with others and disappeared without known causes. There is no evidence pointing to a continuous lineage or how they related to each other. Homo habilis is sometimes suggested to be the first of the Homo genus. Habilis existence is dated to 2-1.5 MYA. They had a rounder cranial shape, but a relatively small brain in comparison with modern humans, with facial and body features that some considered to be closer to Australopithecines than modern humans (Wood 2014). Homo ergaster, erectus, heildelbergensis and antecessor were among Homo species that preceded Homo sapiens. The geological time of their recorded existence shows that at least some of them overlapped and co-existed even if in different locations in the last two million years. Their cranial, rib cage, pelvis and limbs characteristics varied with no obvious sequential line. The same applied to assessed brain size in relation to body size. Some had relative brain size similar to modern humans (Wood and Richmond 2000).

Five Homo species are now accepted to have co-existed with Homo sapiens and overlapped with each other before their disappearance: Homo neanderthalensis, soloensis, ergaster, floresiensis and denisova (Harari 2015). The Neanderthals were identified earliest and have been the subject of greater study while Floresiensis and Denisovan have been identified more recently. Floresiensis was found in the island of Flores and has been described as having a small body, possibly due to island dwarfing, and small brain even in relation to body size. However, skull, face, teeth and other skeleton features suggest resemblance with other Homo species. This is strengthened by their use of sophisticated tools and hunting practices (Morwood et al. 1998; Stringer and Andrews 2011). They are found to have existed until about 60,000 years ago (Sutikna et al. 2016). The Neanderthal is recorded to have lived 350,000-30,000 years ago (Palmer et al. 2012). They are seen as having more robust bodies than Homo sapiens and their cranial case was also larger than that of Homo sapiens but somewhat different in shape. They had large noses and small chins. They possessed a hyoid bone that would enhanced the possibility of speech. They had a wide pelvis and leg and foot characteristics that made them strong walkers. They have been found to have lived mostly in Eurasia. They produced a wide range of stone tools, and wooden spears that they used in hunting. They also controlled their use of fire and buried their dead (Stringer and Andrews 2011; Roebroeks and Villa 2011). The Denisovan identification is based on recent and a relatively amount of small bone and teeth material. They lived at least 50,000 years ago (Gibbons 2011). Molecular analysis suggests that Neanderthals and Denisovans not only co-existed with Homo sapiens but that they also interbred (Reich et al. 2011; Paabo 2014). How these overlapping Homo species ceased to exist and Homo sapiens possibly the last presumed to arrive about some 200,000-150,000 years ago survived continues to be a matter of conjecture (Palmer et al. 2012; Stringer and Andrews 2011).

1.1.15   Surviving Modern Humans

Modern humans share features with other Homo species such as a straight gait and skeleton features that enhance bipedal walking, globe-shaped skull and large brain capacity in relation to body size, flat face with protruding nose. However, they tend to have a more forward chin than that of the Neanderthals, and also a less robust body. They also have flatter brow ridges and lower nose. It is likely that, like other apes, modern humans started as vegetarians. Their scavenging, trapping and hunting practices led to a more varied diet from vegetable and animal sources. Tool making and use shared with other Homo species became gradually more sophisticated with the production of such fine tools as needles. Modern humans form families with a wide range of diversity. Some like gibbons are monogamous, others like the gorillas are polygamous, yet others polygynous like the chimpanzees (Stringer and Andrews 2011). A major characteristic of modern humans is their speech capacity. This has given modern humans greater capacity to communicate with each other and the sharing of experiences and passing of knowledge from one individual to another, and from one generation to another, beyond the practice of imitation (Boesch and Tomasello 1998). Modern humans are also characterised by their art in terms of adornments, carvings, drawings and paintings (Palmer et al. 2012). Poston and Bouvier (2017) estimated that since the appearance of modern humans (Homo sapiens) about 117,000 million have lived on Earth.

There are several perspectives regarding the location of the origin of modern humans:

- Out of Africa or replacement
- Multiregional or continuity
- Compromise

The Out-of-Africa view places modern human evolution in a single location—Africa—with migration to other regions where they replaced other earlier human species. An alternative view is that an earlier Homo species spread from Africa to Europe and Asia and that evolution took place separately giving rise to the physical differences that exist today. The compromise view mixes elements of the other two perspectives: there was a flow from Africa but also a regional mix between the new and the older species that preserved some of the regional physical features. Although genetic evidence tends to support the Out-of-Africa notion, this has been contested. Genetic evidence points to the origins of modern humans in Africa, with migration to Asia and then Europe, and to Australia and more recently to the Americas (Palmer et al. 2012; Stringer and Andrews 2011).

Some 11,000 years ago modern humans started to domesticate wild plants such as cereal grains, which they were gradually improved through choice of mutated species and controlled breeding (Diamond 1997). Similar methods were used, to some extent, in the domestication of some animals. The combination of the two considerably changed the ability to produce and store food allowing for more sedentary settlements. The use of irrigation and fertilisation further increased the efficiency of food production and the manner in which humans secured food. The greater settlement of people resulted in more complex social organisation and specialisation of functions of different members of society. It also led to new risks through the contamination of food by animal and human wastes and facilitated the communication of infectious diseases. The first large civilisation developed 7,000 years ago in the Fertile Crescent in Sumer in the present Iraq. Humans moved from a family centred society close to the place where food was available to a diversity of settings, including groups of unrelated people in cities away from the sources of food production, and with occupations unrelated to food production (Boyden 2004; Algaze 2008). Although, natural disasters, such as volcanic eruptions and earthquakes, and epidemics, such as the plague, continued to affect population growth, new food and other technology changes, as well as evolving socioeconomic organisation allowed human population to grow with consequent higher and varied population densities (McNeill 1976; Diamond 1997).

1.2 World Population Growth and Distribution

1.2.1 Growing and Multiplying

The world's population reached 7,383 million in 2015. Roughly, the fitness of a species can be measured by its capacity to survive and reproduce. From this point of view, it could be said that humans have been quite successful to have risen from a few to a population of about 1–10 million by 10,000 BCE (Table 1.1). Given the estimate by Poston and Bouvier (2017) that 117,000 million of the species have existed on earth, the current world population represents about 6% of all persons born.

Box 1.2 Rates of growth and doubling of population

Given two population estimates a few years apart the average annual rate of growth usually follows the compound rate of growth in the equation

$$P_{t+n} = P_t * e^{r*n} \text{ or } e^{r*n} = (P_{t+n}/P_t)$$

P_t Population at the base year t

n   The number of years after t

P_{t+n} Population at base plus n years

e   The mathematical constant 2.7182828

r   The exponential rate of growth

Taking the natural logarithm (LN) to both sides of the equation, it can be simplified to

$$r = LN(P_{t+n}/P_t)/n$$

The estimation of doubling of population given an average annual growth rate follows a similar path where

$$P_{t+n}/P_t = 2 \text{ then } 2 = e^{r*n}$$

and taking LN to both sides of the equation

$$r = 0.69314/n \text{ or } n = 0.693147/r$$

(Yusuf et al. 2014)

Accordingly,

Annual growth rate	Doubling time
%	Years
0.1	693
0.5	139
1.0	69
1.5	46
2.0	35
2.5	28
3.0	23
3.5	20
4.0	17
5.0	14
7.0	10
10.0	7

Estimates of population for earlier years are tentative and have a wide range. The rate of population growth was affected by a relatively low life expectancy from living conditions, recorded famines and epidemics that occurred in Asia and Europe in earlier times. It has been estimated that the average life expectancy was only

Table 1.1 World population growth 10,000 BCE—2015

Year	Population (millions)	Average annual growth rate from preceding date (%)
10,000 BCE	(range 1–10) 5	
5,000 BCE	(range 5–20) 12.5	0.018
1,000 BCE	50	0.035
1 CE	300	0.179
1000	310	0.003
1500	500	0.096
1750	790	0.183
1800	980	0.431
1850	1,260	0.503
1900	1,650	0.539
1950	2,536	0.860
2000	6,145	1.770
2015	7,383	1.224

Note (*BCE*) Before the Current Era or (*BC*) Before Christ, (*CE*) Current Era or (*AD*) After Christ. Estimates of population for early dates are often guess-estimates because of the lack of records and different methods used. The population estimates for the dates before 1 CE are from the US Census based on a number of sources, hence the range of different estimates. Those from 1 CE to 1900 are from UN (1999) and those from 1950 onwards from UN (2017)
Sources USCB (2013), UN (1999, 2017). Computations made by the authors

about 35 years by the time of the late Roman empire (Lancaster 1990) and it continued to be low as plague and other epidemics continued to restrain population growth throughout the Middle Ages (McNeill 1976). The exposure of Amerindians to European invaders led to major devastating population losses and the same applied to Aboriginal people in Australia (McNeil 1976; Lancaster 1990). Gradual improvement in food supplies and public health measures led to higher population growth rates in 1800s and early 1900s, and the population explosion in the later 1900s, when high population growth from the baby-boom of post-World War II in developed countries added to the high fertility of less developed ones, led to more than doubling of the population in only five decades (Table 1.1).

An outcome of this population growth has been an impressive rise in the population density that was below 10 people per square kilometre in 1850 to more than five times that (54 people per square kilometre) in 2015 (Table 1.2). This population pressure has major social and environmental implications.

1.2.2 Regional Distribution

Migration and differences in natural increase rates (difference between birth and death rates) have resulted in varied population growth in different regions of the

Table 1.2 World population density, 1-2015

Year	Population (millions)	Average number of people per square kilometre
1 CE	300	2.2
1000	310	2.3
1500	500	3.7
1750	790	5.8
1800	980	7.2
1850	1,260	9.3
1900	1,650	12.1
1950	2,536	18.6
2000	6,145	45.1
2015	7,383	54.2

Note (*CE*) Current Era or (*AD*) After Christ. Population densities were estimated based on the world's land surface as per UN (2014)
Sources UN (1999, 2014, 2017). Computations made by the authors

globe and uneven distribution of the global population. Asia with the largest proportion of the land mass (23%) has kept more than half of the world's population throughout the period, while Oceania with the smallest proportion of land (6%) has also kept the lowest proportion (less than one percent) of the world's population. Although all regions of the world have experienced population growth in the last three centuries, their share of the total population has changed. A marked shift is the fall in Europe's proportion from about a quarter (25%) in 1900 to about one tenth (10%) in 2015. Northern and Latin America and the Caribbean, in spite of losses due to exposure to European invaders, increased their proportion of the world's population partly due to migration but also to related natural increase. Africa's estimated earlier loss was followed by gains more recently and in 2015 had a larger proportion (16%) than about two and half centuries earlier (13% in 1750) (Table 1.3).

Table 1.3 World population regional distribution, 1750-2015

Region	Year					
	1750	1850	1900	1950	2000	2015
World population (millions)	790	1,260	1,650	2,536	6,145	7,383
Percentage of world population						
Africa	13.4	8.8	8.1	9.0	13.3	16.2
Asia	63.5	64.1	57.4	55.4	60.7	59.9
Europe	20.6	21.9	24.7	21.6	11.8	10.0
Latin Am. and Caribbean	2.0	3.0	4.5	6.7	8.6	8.6
Northern America	0.3	2.1	5.0	6.8	5.1	4.8
Oceania	0.3	0.2	0.4	0.5	0.5	0.5
All regions	100.0	100.0	100.0	100.0	100.0	100.0

Sources UN (1999, 2017). Computations made by the authors

Table 1.4 World population density by region, 1750–2015

Region	Year					
	1750	1850	1900	1950	2000	2015
	People per square kilometre					
World population	5.8	9.3	12.1	18.6	45.1	54.2
Africa	3.5	3.7	4.4	7.5	27.0	39.4
Asia	15.7	25.3	29.7	44.0	116.9	138.5
Europe	7.1	12.0	17.7	23.8	31.6	32.1
Latin Am. and Caribbean	0.8	1.8	3.6	8.2	25.6	30.8
Northern America	0.1	1.2	3.8	7.9	14.4	16.3
Oceania	0.2	0.2	0.7	1.5	3.6	4.6

Note Population densities were estimated based on land surface as per UN (2014)
Sources UN (1999, 2014, 2017). Computations made by the authors

During the population explosion that took place since 1950, population densities grew about five fold in Africa (5.2) and almost four fold in Latin America and the Caribbean (3.8). Northern America and Oceania densities also rose but at a lower rate, with Europe recording the lowest relative increase in population density (1.3) in that period (Table 1.4). Thus, the impact of population growth varied but had in all cases implications to socioeconomic and environmental conditions.

Varying growth and the relative share of the world population living in each region placed different population pressures in each region due to the size of the land mass available in each. The degree of impact was also affected by the disparate pace of change and diverse characteristics of each region, such as areas that lend themselves for forest and agriculture and related water resources from rain fall and streams. In spite of its larger land mass, the average population density of Asia has been more than twice that of other world regions having more than doubled from about 44.0 people per square kilometre in 1950 to 138.5 in 2015. This compares with that of Oceania with a density of only 4.6 people per square kilometre in 2015. However, a large proportion of the land mass in Oceania, Australia, is mostly desert.

Box 1.3 Basic population model and measures of population change
The basic population model expresses the fundamental features of changes in population stocks in a given period of time due to three change flows: births, deaths and migration. It is obvious that from a global perspective migration is nil and that any change in population stocks is due to the difference between births and deaths (natural increase). The term "stock" is used to refer to population size and composition at a given point in time. "Flow" refers to the components of change over the given time period.

$$P_{t0+1} = P_{t0} + B_{t01} - D_{t01} \pm M_{t01}$$

P_{t0} Population stock at base time t0
B_{t01} Births during period t01
D_{t01} Deaths during period t01
M_{t01} Migration (Net) during period t01 (arrivals less departures)
P_{t0+1} Population stock at the end of period t01

When both sides of the equation are divided by the population at time t0

$$P_{t0+1}/P_{t0} = P_{t0}/P_{t0} + B_{t01}/P_{t0} - D_{t01}/P_{t0} \pm Mt_{01}/P_{t0}$$

It leads to a proportional growth model

$$p = \text{growth in population} = 1 + b - d \pm m$$

When P_{t0+1} is not substantially greater than P_{t0} then
b is close to the definition of the *crude birth rate* (Births/average population during t01)
d is close to the definition of the *crude death rate* (Deaths/average population during t01)
m is close to the definition of the *net migration rate* (Net Migration/average population during t01)

$$g = \text{population growth rate} = b - d \pm m$$

Empirical evidence shows that the flows of births and deaths (and to some extent migration) tend to vary with age and that comparisons over time and between different populations need to take that into consideration. Accordingly, the concepts of the *Total Fertility Rate* (TFR) and *Life Expectancy* (Le) have been devised and commonly use, among others. The TFR is defined as the average number of children that a woman has during her lifetime in a given population and the Le is the average number of years that a person in a given population is expected to live. The estimation of these two measures require data for the many decades involved in the reproductive period of women and the life span of people in given populations. To overcome these constraints, synthetic measures of TFR and Le have been devised. TFR estimation is based on the age-specific fertility rates of women in a population in a given period of time, usually one year. Le is estimated based on age-specific survival rates of people, given age-specific death rates, in a population over a given period of time, often one to three years.

Table 1.5 World population by stage of development, 1950–2015

Stage of development	Year				Change 1950–2015
	1950	1970	2000	2015	
World population (millions)	2,536	3,701	6,145	7,383	4,847
Percentage of world population					
More developed	32.1	27.3	19.4	17.0	−15.1
Least developed	7.7	8.3	10.8	13.0	5.3
Other less developed	60.2	64.4	69.8	70.0	9.8
World	100.0	100.0	100.0	100.0	

Source UN (2017). Computations made by the authors

1.2.3 Population and Stage of Development

Implicit in the regional population distribution is the changing of population away from more developed countries and the rising proportion of population in less developed countries, especially other less developed countries where most people live, which include China and India. Although the total population of more developed countries continued to increase their proportion of the world's population fell from 32% in 1950 to 17% in 2015. The share of the population of least developed countries, although smaller, rose considerably from 8 to 13% during that period, while that of other less developed countries increased even more from 60% in 1950 to 70% in 2015 (Table 1.5).

1.2.4 Trends of Recent Population Growth

Population growth in the 65-year period of 1950–2015 is a unique phenomenon when the world's population almost tripled. It will continue to influence future population size and composition. If by nothing else than by the momentum that has been created. Average growth rates for this period mask the timing of the earlier peaks, diversity in time shifts and trends in different parts of the world.

The average annual population growth in the period 1950–2015 was 1.64% per year. As expected from the population estimates already shown, Africa recorded the highest average annual growth rate of 2.54%, while Europe the lowest of 0.46%. Africa was followed by Latin America and the Caribbean (2.03%), Oceania and Asia (1.76%) and Northern America (1.11%). However, the rate of decline was sharper in some cases such as in Europe from a comparatively low annual growth rate of 0.90% in 1950–1970 to an even lower rate of 0.12% in 2000–2015. Africa experienced a shifting trend rising from a higher annual growth rate of 2.36% in 1950–1970 to 2.67% in 1970–2000, before falling (but still to the highest rate) to 2.53% in 2000–2015. The high growth rate of Latin America and the Caribbean

Table 1.6 World population growth by region, 1950–2015

Region	Average annual growth rate (%)			
	1950–2015	1950–1970	1970–2000	2000–2015
World population	1.64	1.89	1.69	1.22
Africa	2.54	2.36	2.67	2.53
Asia	1.76	2.10	1.86	1.13
Europe	0.46	0.90	0.34	0.12
Latin Am. and Caribbean	2.03	2.67	2.01	1.23
Northern America	1.11	1.46	1.01	0.86
Oceania	1.76	2.23	1.53	1.57

Sources UN (2017). Computations made by the authors

kept its downward trend throughout the period. This downward tendency in growth rates was also experienced in Asia, Northern America and Oceania (Table 1.6).

Population growth in the 65-year period is characterised not only by its diversity but also its association with stage of development. Population estimates show an inverse association between the level of development and population growth rates. While the average annual population growth rate of more development countries was below one percent (0.66%) that of the least developed was 2.44%, and that of other less developed 1.88%. The average annual rate of population growth of the least developed countries peaked later in 1970–2000 while those of more and other less developed countries did so earlier in 1950–1970 (Table 1.7). The higher rates of population growth in least and other less developed countries has implications for the additional capacity required, higher pace and effort to raise low standards of living and overcome existing poverty traps.

The levels of average annual population growth of over 1.5% have been at an unprecedented swiftness in recorded history. Although the average global rate of growth has been lower than that voiced by Malthus (Chap. 2) of doubling of the population every 25 years, at about annual growth rate of 3%, some countries in Africa such as South Sudan (3.3% p.a.) and Angola (3.5% p.a.) have experienced this degree of population growth as recently as 2010–2015 (UN 2017). The exceptional pace of recent additions to the world's population is reflected in the

Table 1.7 World population growth by stage of development, 1950–2015

Country stage of development	Average annual growth rate (%)			
	1950–2015	1950–1970	1970–2000	2000–2015
World population	1.64	1.89	1.69	1.22
More developed	0.66	1.07	0.55	0.34
Least developed	2.44	2.29	2.56	2.43
Other less developed	1.88	2.23	1.96	1.25

Sources UN (2017). Computations made by the authors

Table 1.8 World population from one to seven billion people, 1804–2011

Population billions	Year	Interval years
1	1804	
2	1927	123
3	1960	33
4	1974	14
5	1987	13
6	1999	12
7	2012	13

Sources UN (2007, 2013). Computations made by the authors

123 years that took to move from the first billion of the world's population to the second billion (1804–1927) compared to the 33 years from the second to the third (1927–1960); and the momentum gained in reaching the fourth billion in just 14 years (1960–1974). Population momentum has kept the intervening periods between fourth, fifth, sixth and seventh billion at respectively 13, 12 and 13 years in 1987, 1999 and 2012 (Table 1.8). The longer interval between the sixth and the seventh billion is in line with the trend of falling population growth rates experienced more recently, after the peak in 1950–1975, and the downward trend even in the least developed countries in more recent years (Table 1.7).

1.3   Transitional Factors in Population Growth

1.3.1   Engine of Population Growth

Only a substantial excess of births over deaths can explain the large population growth in world experienced since 1950–55 (Box 1.3). A complementary question is whether these considerable population additions are due to high or rising female fertility rates or huge falls in death rates. Estimates for 1950–55 show that there were on average 37 births per thousand people against 19 deaths in the world or a difference of about 18 births over deaths per thousand people and that an excess of birth over death rates has prevailed since then (UN 2017).

   Although variations existed (McCaa 2002), it has been suggested that birth rates of 40 per thousand people and over were common for centuries (Gelbard et al. 1999) with the average number of children per women over their life time (TFR) being between 6 and 8 children. Birth rates per thousand people have fallen since the 1950s worldwide but have remained above 30 births per thousand people among the least developed countries (Table 1.9). Accordingly, a few countries such as Niger (TFR 7.4 children), Burundi (TFR 6.0), Somalia (TFR 6.6) and Angola (TFR 6.0) continued to have considerably high fertility rates in 2010–15

Table 1.9 World crude birth rates by stage of development, 1950–55 to 2010–15

Country by stage of development	Years						
	1950–1955	1960–1965	1970–1975	1980–1985	1990–1995	2000–2005	2010–2015
	CBR						
World	36.9	35.4	31.4	27.9	24.3	20.9	19.6
Least developed	48.3	48.0	46.9	45.5	41.4	37.7	33.5
Other less developed	43.0	41.3	35.7	30.2	25.4	20.9	19.2
More developed	22.3	19.5	16.0	14.4	12.3	11.0	11.1

Note (CBR) is the annual average number of live births per thousand people in a given period
Source UN (2017)

Table 1.10 World fertility rates by stage of development, 1950–55 to 2010–15

Country by stage of development	Years						
	1950–1955	1960–1965	1970–1975	1980–1985	1990–1995	2000–2005	2010–2015
	TFR						
World	4.96	5.03	4.46	3.60	3.02	2.63	2.52
Least developed	6.58	6.72	6.75	6.54	5.76	5.00	4.30
Other less developed	6.00	6.07	5.22	3.88	3.06	2.54	2.37
More developed	2.82	2.66	2.16	1.84	1.67	1.58	1.67

Note (TFR) is the average number of children per woman during her life span
Source UN (2017)

(UN 2017). However, there has been a general trend towards lower fertility throughout the world, even in the least developed countries (Table 1.10).

The world's average total fertility rate (TFR) has fallen from about 5.0 children per woman in 1960–65 to 2.5 in 2010–15 (Table 1.10). The later TFR is still above the population replacement level usually set at 2.1 children per woman. As in the case of population growth rates (Table 1.7), there is an inverse association between the stage of development and fertility; and the timing of the peaks and the start of downward trends are also different in countries at varying stages of development. In more developed countries the peak came earlier with the baby-boom in the immediate post World War II (1950–55), while that of least developed countries took place some two decades later in 1970–75. Other less developed countries were somewhat in-between and peaked in 1960–65. The fertility rate of more developed countries reached replacement level at about 1970–75 and continued at the low level of 1.7 in 2010–15. The biggest fall in fertility was experienced by other less developed countries from 6.0 children per woman to 2.4 children per woman in the period from 1950–55 to 2010–15. The world's average is greatly influenced by fertility in the other less developed countries where most people live (Table 1.10). In turn, this average is affected by those of China (TFR 1.6 in 2010–15) and India

(TFR 2.4 in 2010–15) that are the two most populous countries and together accounted for 36.7% of the world's population in 2015 (UN 2017).

High fertility experienced early in the period and still prevailing in some less developed countries when accompanied by low or falling infant mortality results in the formation of populations with a high proportion of children such as in Nigeria and Ethiopia (UN 2017). This has intergenerational implications that affect overall productivity and places weight on the efforts of the adult population to maintain and invest in the quality of the child population to ensure their's and future society's living standards. Yet, another issue is the "male preference" in fertility that reflects current social attitudes in some societies that have a major impact on female survival and their position in the social and economic fabric (Sen 1999).

The trend of declining fertility shows that countries at different stages of development are at varying transitional fertility levels. The trend in more developed countries below replacement level will continue and may be followed by less developed ones, that will affect population growth, age composition, and related social and economic impact. Caldwell (2002) has raised the possibility that fertility below replacement might be a current phenomenon that may not be sustained in the future. He stated that there are a number of factors that may lead to a stabilisation and even a return of fertility to above replacement level in more developed countries. This includes the perceived threat that actual population reductions might pose to some countries. Further, the present fall in fertility in many countries involves the postponement of births partly because of later age of marriage by females. This may not continue indefinitely, and policies that provide greater opportunities for childcare may encourage fertility of two or more children per woman. This could lead to larger natural increases in population and higher growth rates than those assumed to prevail in the future. This possibility is reflected in the rise of fertility in more developed countries from TFR 1.6 in 2000–05 to 1.7 in 2010–15 (Table 1.10).

1.3.2   Survival and Longer Lives

Death rates were high throughout most of human history and kept population growth at relatively low levels in spite of high fertility rates (Table 1.1). Some pestilences resulted in actual reductions in population. McNeill (1976) mentions possible reductions in the population of China by as much as a quarter between 2 and 742 CE, and by more than 40% in England between 1348 and 1430.

Mortality has declined in more developed countries since the 19th century. Estimates in Sweden and other Scandinavian countries indicate that death rates of 25–30 per thousand people fell to 20–25 per thousand by the 1820s and to about 15 per thousand by the 1901–10. Similar declines were experienced in England and Wales, the Netherlands and Australia (Lancaster 1990). This decline in mortality is part of what has been called the *mortality transition* experienced by more developed countries and that is also being felt in less developed ones. Accordingly, there was a

Table 1.11 World crude death rates by stage of development, 1950–55 to 2010–15

Country by stage of development	Years						
	1950–1955	1960–1965	1970–1975	1980–1985	1990–1995	2000–2005	2010–2015
	CDR						
World	19.1	16.1	12.0	10.1	9.1	8.4	7.7
Least developed	28.1	23.3	20.5	17.0	14.6	11.3	8.3
Other less developed	22.4	18.4	11.8	9.3	8.0	7.4	7.1
More developed	10.6	9.3	9.5	9.7	10.0	10.3	9.9

Note (CDR) is the average number of deaths per thousand people in a given period
Source UN (2017)

dramatic fall in the world death rates from 19.1 per thousand people in 1950–55 to 7.7 in 2010–15. They about halved in the three decades between 1950s and 1980s. These reductions resulted from falls in the rates of less developed countries, while death rates stayed around 10 per thousand in more developed countries (Table 1.11).

The observed crude death rates gloss over differences in age distribution of populations that have a direct impact on the number of deaths in populations because of the varying death rates at different age. A better measure is the average life expectancy (Box 1.3). Survival has risen in countries at all stages of development in the period 1950–55 to 2010–15 and the world's average life expectancy rose by about 24 years. There is a positive association between survival and stage of development, with more developed countries having experienced gains earlier and longer average life expectancy throughout the last six decades. The rises of survival narrowed the gap between more and least developed countries from about 29 years in 1950–55 to about 16 years in 2010–15. Although more developed countries continued to improve their survival years by about 14 years, during that period, other less developed countries, where most people live, gained about 28 years in life expectancy followed by least developed countries with 27 additional years (Table 1.12).

Table 1.12 World life expectancy by stage of development, 1950–55 to 2010–15

Country by stage of development	Years						
	1950–1955	1960–1965	1970–1975	1980–1985	1990–1995	2000–2005	2010–2015
	Le (years)						
World	47.0	51.2	58.1	62.1	64.6	67.2	70.8
Least developed	36.1	40.9	44.3	48.8	51.5	56.4	62.7
Other less developed	42.5	47.0	56.6	61.4	64.6	67.3	70.5
More developed	64.8	69.5	71.1	72.9	74.2	75.6	78.4

Note (Le) is the average number of years people are expected to live during their life span given the age-specific survival rates in a given period
Source UN (2017)

Rising longevity especially in conjunction with low or falling fertility has led to the populations with a high proportion of older people such as Italy and Japan (UN 2017). In addition to issues related to potential changes in productivity, health and quality of life, this change in population composition also poses intergenerational questions of social and economic mechanisms for the implicit transfers from those economically active to those who have retired and may not have sufficient capacity to meet their living needs.

1.3.3 Moving Urge

Migration has been a human trait from early times. Palmer et al. (2012) favour the Out-of-Africa spread of humans that included their migration to Asia some 60,000 years ago, a later move to Europe and Australia about 45,000 years ago, and an even later arrival in the Americas (15,000 years ago). It is presumed that the population of the Pacific islands may have taken place from Melanesia to Polynesia even more recently. Hawaii seems to have been reached around 200 CE and New Zealand at about 800 CE (Kirch 1985). The incursion of people from Asia to Europe has been another feature of human history, as well as the invasion of the Roman Empire by the populations from Northern Europe. More recent migrations took place from Europe to the Americas, and another was the forced migration of African labour to the Americas (Danzer 2000). Australia offer another example of forced and voluntary European migration.

The inter-regional net migration in the six decades 1950–2010 has been relatively small in relation to the size of the population of the various regions. Most migration tends to take place within countries that is not captured in international migration figures considered here (UN 2013). Northern America was the only region that consistently received a large number of people during the period (Table 1.13). Europe, the next large net receiver, lost considerable numbers early in

Table 1.13 World average annual net number of migrants by region 1950–1960 to 2000–2010

Region	Years					
	1950–1960	1960–1970	1970–1980	1980–1990	1990–2000	2000–2010
	Migrants (000s people)					
Africa	−101	−185	−487	−501	−443	−388
Asia	116	12	−319	−294	−1,334	−1,780
Europe	−427	41	414	525	960	−1,866
Latin Am. and Caribbean	−80	−318	−439	−708	−707	−1,155
Northern America	403	324	792	880	1,438	1,282
Oceania	89	126	39	98	87	175

Note Figures may not add up because of rounding
Source UN (2013)

the post-World War II period, but became a net receiver as economic conditions improved in the 1960s. Oceania, mostly Australia and New Zealand, was a much smaller but consistent net receiver. Migration out of Latin America and the Caribbean made it the largest *sender* or loser of population mostly to Northern America, but Asia also lost large numbers of people. During the 1950s and 1960s Asia experienced net gains, partly due to the migration to oil producing countries that has continued. However, from the 1970s onwards, Asia became a net sender of people, as a result of the migration of Turkish workers to Europe in earlier decades, the migration of Indians to more developed countries in Europe and Northern America and the resettlement of refugees (UN 2016).

The pattern of migration is consistently from less to more developed countries (Table 1.14). The rate of migration rose after the 1950s and this has been maintained in the last few decades. Some of the flows of migrants relate to economic inequalities among countries and work opportunities in countries with labour force shortages. However, some are also due to migrants running away from areas experiencing war or civil unrest. Of the estimated stock of 244 million international migrants in 2015 about 19.5 million are classified as refugees. This is the highest level since World War II (UN 2016).

There is a great disparity in the relative importance of migrants in the populations of different countries. In the major receiving countries of Europe, Northern America and Oceania, migrants made up at least 10% of the population in 2015 but they constituted less than 2% in the Africa, Asia and Latin America and the Caribbean (UN 2016). Migration can be mutually convenient for communities with surplus and deficits in the labour force, and to those who migrate to improved living conditions. However, it may also lead to "brain drain" from less to more developed countries. In times of economic contraction, social problems can arise when migrants may be seen as competitors for scarce employment opportunities. Differences in culture between the place of origin and the country of migration have implications to social tolerance and adaptive and adoptive behaviour that may be difficult to attain, especially when social and economic threats arise.

Table 1.14 World average annual net number of migrants by country stage of development, 1950–1960 to 2000–2010

Country by stage of development	Years					
	1950–1960	1960–1970	1970–1980	1980–1990	1990–2000	2000–2010
	Migrants (000s people)					
Least developed	−105	−169	−917	−1,038	−73	−1,210
Other less developed	76	−433	−390	−437	−2,475	−2,246
More developed	29	601	1,307	1,475	2,548	3,455

Note Figures may not add up because of rounding
Source UN (2013)

1.3.4 Speculative Futures

The United Nations population projections offer four hypothetical futures based on different fertility, mortality and migration assumptions. These projections assume a high, medium and low population growth and one variant with fertility being held constant, in view of the uncertainty in the direction that fertility will take place, the latter is the worst scenario (UN 2017). The high growth projection scenario adds another 3,466 million people by 2050 and 9,138 million by 2100 to the 7,383 million in 2015. This is substantially lower than the constant fertility variant that projects a population of respectively 10,942 and 26,329 by 2050 and 2100. The low growth variant adds 1,369 million people to the 2015 population by 2050 and a reduction of 1,477 million people between 2050 and 2100. This would mean that the world population would be lower in 2100 than in 2015. The medium variant envisages an increase of 2,389 million to 9,772 by 2050 and another addition of 1,412 million to 11,184 million in 2100. Three of the variants have below and declining average annual population growth rates from those experienced in 2000–15, in line with the trend in recent decades. The exception is the constant fertility variant (Table 1.15).

The medium growth projections tend to be closer to actual experience than the other scenarios. It would result in average annual growth rates of 0.80% in the 35-year period 2015–2050 and a further decline to 0.27% in the following five decades. This projection would lead to an increase in the population of all regions by 2050, with the exception of Europe that is projected to have a negative rate of population growth. The projections would result in a decline in the population of Asia, Europe and Latin America and the Caribbean in the following five decades to 2100. Substantial gains would occur only in Africa but still with an average annual rate of population growth of 1.14% (Table 1.16).

The projected slow-down of the world's population growth relies on the assumption that fertility will continue to fall to a level just above replacement level (TFR 2.24) by 2045–2050 and will be just below replacement level (TFR 1.97) by 2095–2100. This would mean a major decline in fertility in Africa and a continuing

Table 1.15 Variants of world population projections, 2015, 2050 and 2100

Projection variant	Years				
	2015	2050	2100	2015–2050	2050–2100
	Millions of people			Average annual growth rate (%)	
High	7,383	10,849	16,521	1.10	0.84
Medium	7,383	9,772	11,184	0.80	0.27
Low	7,383	8,752	7,275	0.49	−0.37
Constant fertility	7,383	10,942	26,329	1.12	1.76

Source UN (2017). Computations made by the authors

Table 1.16 World population medium projections by region, 2015, 2050 and 2100

Region	Years				
	2015	2050	2100	2015–2050	2050–2100
	Millions of people			Average annual growth rate (%)	
Africa	1,194.4	2,527.6	4,467.6	2.14	1.14
Asia	4,419.9	5,256.9	4,780.4	0.50	−0.19
Europe	740.8	715.7	653.3	−0.10	−0.18
Latin Am. and Caribbean	632.4	779.8	712.0	0.60	−0.18
Northern America	356.0	434.7	499.2	0.57	0.28
Oceania	39.5	57.1	71.8	1.05	0.46
World	7,383.0	9,771.8	11,184.4	0.80	0.27

Note Figures may not add up because of rounding
Source UN (2017). Computations made by the authors

downward trend in other regions with the exception of Europe and Northern America with slight rises to still under replacement level (Table 1.17).

The projections also assume continuing increments in life expectancy from an average of 70 years in 2010–2015 to 77 and 83 years respectively in 2045–50 and 2095–2100. The assumption of improved survival follows current trends and would lead to major additions in life expectancy in Africa to 71 and 78 years respectively in 2045–2050 and 2095–2100 from about 60 years in 2010–2015. However, the average life expectancy would also rise substantially in all other regions (Table 1.17).

These assumptions would lead to a lower proportion of children and larger proportion of older people in the whole population. They would also have

Table 1.17 World assumed fertility and life expectancy by region, medium variant projection, 2010–2015, 2045–2050 and 2095–2100

Region	Years					
	2010–2015	2045–2050	2095–2100	2010–2015	2045–2050	2095–2100
	TFR			Le		
Africa	4.72	3.09	2.14	60.2	70.9	78.4
Asia	2.20	1.90	1.81	71.8	77.5	83.5
Europe	1.60	1.78	1.84	77.2	82.8	89.3
Latin Am. and Caribbean	2.14	1.77	1.78	74.6	81.3	87.9
Northern America	1.85	1.89	1.91	79.2	84.4	89.9
Oceania	2.41	2.06	1.86	77.9	82.3	87.4
World	2.52	2.24	1.97	70.8	76.9	82.6

Note (*TFR*) Total fertility rate or the average number of children per woman during life span, (*Le*) Life expectancy or the average number of years that people will live during their life span
Source UN (2017)

Table 1.18 World population density by region, 2015, 2050 and 2100

Region	Year		
	2015	2050	2100
	People per square kilometre		
Africa	39.4	83.4	147.4
Asia	138.5	164.7	149.8
Europe	32.1	31.1	28.3
Latin Am. and Caribbean	30.8	38.0	34.7
Northern America	16.3	20.0	22.9
Oceania	4.6	6.7	8.4
World	54.2	71.8	82.1

Sources UN (2014, 2017). Computations made by the authors

significant impact on the transitional phases created by differences in the timing and degree of the fall in fertility of various countries at different stages of development. Some of these changes appear to be inevitable because of the population momentum created by past experiences. However, the degree of presumed change in the rates will also have social and economic implications to productivity and social organisation to ensure the maintenance of standards of living in more developed countries and improvements in the poorest in less developed countries.

Another aspect of the impact of the projected population growth is the pressure on land and its related resources. The projections would increase population density by about one third (32%) in 2050 and about one half (51%) by 2100. The changes would be most felt in Africa with the largest projected rate of population growth but they would also have an incremental effect in Asia that has currently the largest population density, from about 139 people per square kilometre to 165 by 2050. This would decrease to about 150 people per square kilometre in 2100 with the projected reduction in population (Table 1.18). In addition to population pressure on the environment, higher population densities also imply greater crowding with related impact on social organisation and living arrangements.

1.4 Survival and Enterprise

Human survival depended on the ability to secure sufficient food and protection from predators and environmental threats, such as changes in climate. In addition to the evolution of social organisation that enhanced the survival of the group, a major factor in population growth has been improvements in food and other technologies, that in turn led to evolved social and economic organisation, such as the adoption of agriculture and animal husbandry to improve and make food production more reliable.

Estimates of the production of food and other goods and services are tentative, especially for early periods of the world's history. Nevertheless, they provide a sense of the changes in the volume of production that reflect both population

Table 1.19 Growth of the world's gross domestic product, 1–2001

Year	World GDP millions 1990 international dollars	Average annual growth rate from preceding date (%)
1 CE	102,619	
1000	116,787	...
1500	248,308	0.2
1600	330,982	0.3
1700	371,269	0.1
1820	695,346	0.5
1870	1,112,655	0.0
1913	2,732,131	2.1
1950	5,329,719	1.8
1973	16,023,529	4.8
2001	37,193,868	3.0

Note (GDP) is the sum of the total goods and services produced over a specified period, usually one year. Only the goods and services produced in the country are included, thus the "domestic". Expenditures on goods and services to replace the existing stock of capital are included, thus the "gross". (1990 international dollars) are purchasing power parities based on 1990 United Sates dollars. The estimates follow the Geary-Khakis method and rely on a variety of sources and the work of Maddison, after the pioneer methodological work of Gilbert and Kravis. An explanation of the methodology is found in Kravis et al. (1982). *World product and income—International comparison of real gross product*. Baltimore: The Johns Hopkins University Press. (...) mean less than 0.05%
Source Maddison (2003). Growth rates estimated by the authors

growth and changes in productivity. Maddison's estimates of the world's gross domestic product (Table 1.19) show that economic activity grew slowly until the industrial revolution in the 1800s. The rate of growth rose substantially in the post-World War II years to reach 4.8% per year from 1950 to 1973. This was also a period of exceptional population growth and accompanied by the *Green Revolution* (Brown 1970) that, once again, changed food production technology and provided for more than the double the population of the world. Human enterprise has also led to technological changes in the fields of power generation, transport and communication, among others, that led to and enhanced economic activity growth.

By early 1700s, substantial inequality in the goods and services available per head of population was apparent. Europe's GDP per head of population (p.c.) of $859 (1990 international dollars) was more than double that in Africa of $421 and well above the world average of $615. However, by 1820 Europe's GDP p.c. that had risen to $993 was surpassed by the new Offshoots of European countries, mostly the United States of America, that continued to outdo other areas of the world. Asia's average annual GDP p.c. growth reached 3.8% in the 23-year period of 1950–1973 that was well above the world's average of 2.9%, also above those in Europe (3.7%) and the Western Offshoots (2.4%). Africa with the lowest GDP per head of population experienced the lowest rates of economic growth since 1950.

Table 1.20 World growth in gross domestic product per capita by region, 1700–2001

Region	Year						
	1700	1820	1870	1913	1950	1973	2001
GDP p.c. 1990 international dollars							
Europe	859	993	1,521	2,556	3,655	8,568	11,978
Western Offshoots	476	1,202	2,419	5,233	9,269	16,179	26,943
Latin America	527	692	681	1,481	2,506	4,504	5,811
Asia	571	581	558	696	712	1,720	3,861
Africa	421	420	500	637	894	1,410	1,489
World	615	667	875	1,525	2,111	4,901	6,049
Average annual growth rate on previous date (%)							
Europe		0.1	0.9	1.2	1.0	3.7	1.2
Western Offshoots		0.8	1.4	1.8	1.5	2.4	1.8
Latin America		0.2	–	1.8	1.4	2.5	0.9
Asia		–	−0.1	0.5	0.1	3.8	2.9
Africa		–	0.3	0.6	0.9	2.0	0.2
World		0.1	0.5	1.3	0.9	2.9	1.4

Note (GDP p.c.) is gross domestic product per head of population. (1990 Int. $) are 1990 international dollars as in Table 1.18. (…) means less than 0.05%. (Europe) includes the old USSR. (Western offshoots) are Australia, New Zealand, Canada and the United States
Source Maddison (2003). Growth rates estimated by the authors

Latin America had uneven experiences throughout which kept its GDP per head of population at about the world average (Table 1.20).

The decade 2000–2010 includes the great financial crisis of the 2000s that affected Western Europe and the Western Offshoots that include the United States of America. The slower rate of economic growth per head of population in these countries and the upsurge in other regions led to a greater convergence in goods and services available, in some cases, between developed and developing countries but did not diminish to any great extent the inequalities between countries in the regions of the world, with people in Sub-Sahara Africa continuing to have about a daily average of $4 per head compared with $57 in Western Europe and $81 in the Western Offshoots of Australia, New Zealand, Canada and the United Sates (Table 1.21).

These estimates of economic activity raise a number of issues concerned with the increasing intensity of the use of land and stock of other fixed world resources, as a whole, and in different parts of world with varying natural endowments, including different water resources. They point to the implications to social and economic organisation required to raise the rate of production per head of the world's population by about 13 times in the three centuries from 1700 to 2010. They also expose the large inequality in the goods and services available per head of population to people living in different parts of the world, in spite or because the overall growth in production. The projected population growth adds to demands made to address these issues.

Table 1.21 World growth of gross domestic product per capita by region, 2000–2010

Region	GDP p.c. 1990 international $		Region as proportion of world average		2000–2010 average growth p.a. (%)
	2000	2010	2000	2010	
Western Europe	19,315	20,841	3.24	2.64	0.76
Eastern Europe	4,950	8,027	0.83	1.02	4.83
Western Offshoots	27,572	29,581	4.63	3.75	0.70
Latin America	5,848	7,109	0.98	0.90	1.95
East Asia	5,451	9,804	0.92	1.24	5.87
South and SE Asia	2,198	3,537	0.37	0.45	4.76
Mid. East and Nth Africa	4,497	5,743	0.76	0.73	2.45
Sub-Sahara Africa	1,099	1,481	0.18	0.19	2.98
World	5,957	7,890	1.00	1.00	2.81

Note (GDP p.c.) is gross domestic product per head of population. (1990 International $) are 1990 international dollars as in Table 1.18. (p.a.) is per year. (Western Offshoots) are Australia, New Zealand, Canada and the United States. The regions are somewhat different from those in Table 1.19 and the figures of GDP p.c. are for the year 2000 rather than 2001 as in Tables 1.18 and 1.19. The estimates follow the same methodology but the population estimates have been changed slightly
Source Bolt (2014). Computations made by the authors

1.5 Knowledge and Its Transmission

A distinguishing characteristic of modern humans is their capacity for abstract thinking, ability to speak and the sharing of experiences beyond just imitation (Sect. 1.2). This has led to the development of stocks of knowledge in populations and their passing from one generation to another (Harari 2015). Eventually, humans developed the ability to write and use of numerical symbols that improved the storage and transmission of knowledge in a cumulative process. More systematic approaches to knowledge acquisition led to formal education processes. It is posited that literacy and education have both direct and indirect effects on human well-being. They enhance people's enjoyment by giving them a wider field of reference and appreciation of their environment and activities. They provide means to increase skills and organisation with resulting improvements in productivity and work satisfaction. They are also seen to give people a better understanding of ways of improving health, gaining of skills that can reduce income inequality, and enrich lives that result in lower crime rates and greater political stability (van Leeuwen and van Leeuwen-Li 2014).

Estimates of literacy and education are difficult to make especially in earlier years and tend to be more indicative than absolute. Nevertheless, they provide an

Table 1.22 World average years of education, 1850–2010

Year	Average years of education	Additional years since previous date
1850	0.9	
1870	1.2	0.3
1890	1.5	0.2
1910	2.0	0.5
1930	2.5	0.5
1950	3.2	0.7
1970	4.5	1.3
1990	6.1	1.6
2010	7.7	1.6

Source van Leeuwen and van Leeuwen-Li (2014). Computations made by the authors

indication of changes that have taken place in the last three centuries. They suggest a relatively low average level of education in the 19th and early 20th centuries with a world average of 0.9 years of education in 1850 that rose to only 2.5 years in 1930. Greater progress was made after 1950 and the world average years of education rose from 3.2 in 1950 to 7.7 in 2010 (Table 1.22).

The world average glosses over substantial regional differences and attainment of universal enrolment in formal education. In this regard the Western Offshoots of Australia, New Zealand, Canada and the United States achieved full enrolment earlier (1940s) followed by Western Europe. Latin America and East Asia's population with at least basic education progressed considerably in the post-World War II to reach respectively about 94 and 90%. However, populations in South and South East Asia, Middle East and Northern Africa reached less than 80% by 2010 and Sub-Sahara Africa lagged at about 65% in 2010 (Table 1.23).

Table 1.23 World population with basic education by region, 1870–2010

Region	Population with at least basic education (%)				
	1870	1910	1950	1990	2010
Western Europe	60.0	82.6	91.3	99.5	99.8
Eastern Europe	25.1	36.1	97.1	99.7	n.a.
Western Offshoots	82.3	96.7	100.0	100.0	100.0
Latin America	13.5	26.7	54.0	83.3	93.5
East Asia	24.3	32.8	45.8	80.0	89.8
South and SE Asia	1.8	6.3	19.7	53.7	70.3
Mid. East and Nth Africa	4.2	7.1	14.0	55.2	73.8
Sub-Sahara Africa	1.8	3.6	13.4	45.2	65.4
World	23.9	35.6	49.0	71.1	81.5

Note The estimates represent the percentage of the population aged over 15 years who enrolled in formal education
Source van Leeuwen and van Leeuwen-Li (2014)

Although, education is not the only factor influencing gross domestic product per capita there is a high degree of correlation between the average years of education and per capita income (van Leeuwen and van Leeuwen-Li 2014). The existing inequalities in education levels have implications to the capacity of different populations and people within them to improve their standards of living and wellbeing, especially those caught in poverty traps. They also have an implicit effect on the quality of human capital in countries with different levels of education and their ability to catch up with more developed countries. Another important dimension of education inequality is that between females and males. The average years of education in the world was 7.4 for males and 6.0 for females (2002–2012). However, while the size of the gap was 0.2 years in highly developed countries (11.6 vs. 11.8 years), it was 2.0 years in low development countries at a much lower level of education (3.1 vs. 5.1 years) (UNDP 2014).

1.6 Key Dimensions of Human Development

It is understood that people's wellbeing is not determined by economic factors alone. The United Nations Development Program (UNDP) has conceptualised measures that take into consideration what are considered to be three basic dimensions of human development

- long and healthy life
- knowledge
- decent standard of living

The related Human Development Index (HDI) takes into consideration life expectancy at birth, schooling, and gross national income per capita, in purchasing power parities, as surrogates for these three basic aspects of human life. Features and trends of these three factors have been examined in previously (Sects. 1.3–1.5) the HDI brings them together in its assessment of human development (Box 1.4).

The index shows that these three aspects of human wellbeing have risen on average over the 35-year period 1980–2015. Although the gap between those at the highest and lowest level has been reduced somewhat, the large gap between the two levels of development remains. Most gains took place in countries at high and medium levels of development (Table 1.24).

HDI reflects the importance of other than just economic performance in assessing levels of human development and wellbeing among countries. However, it does not give an indication of the degree of inequality within individual countries. To take this dimension into consideration, UNDP has compiled an Inequality-adjusted Human Development Index (IHDI) (Box 1.4).

The inequality-adjustment to the index indicates that inequality is a major factor in human development as defined and that the lower the level of development the higher the importance of inequality becomes. The index loss is about 32% in the

Table 1.24 Human Development Index, 1980–2014

Stage of development	Human Development Index				
	1980	1990	2000	2010	2015
Highest	0.757	0.801	0.851	0.887	0.892
High	0.534	0.592	0.642	0.723	0.746
Medium	0.420	0.473	0.537	0.611	0.631
Low	0.345	0.638	0.404	0.487	0.497
World	0.559	0.597	0.641	0.697	0.717

Note A description of the components of the Human Development Index (HDI) and its estimation is given in Box 1.4
Sources UNDP (2014, 2016)

Table 1.25 Inequality-adjusted Human Development Index, 2015

Stage of development	2015		
	HDI	IHDI	Percentage loss
Highest	0.892	0.793	11.1
High	0.746	0.597	20.0
Medium	0.631	0.469	25.7
Low	0.497	0.337	32.3
World	0.717	0.557	22.3

Note (HDI) *Human Development Index*, (IHDI) *Inequality-adjusted Human Development Index*. A description of the components of each index and estimation is given in Box 1.4
Sources UNDP (2016)

case of countries at the lowest level of development and still 11% for the highest developed countries (Table 1.25).

Box 1.4 Human Development Index

The Human Development Index (HDI) was designed by the United Nations Development Program (UNDP) to focus on people's capabilities and stages of development beyond those reflected in the measurement of the production of goods and services. HDI is concerned with three basic aspects of human life: healthy life, knowledge and standard of living. It is a composite index that uses available proxy variables of these three dimensions: life expectancy at birth, mean and expected years of schooling, people aged 15 years and over, and gross national income (GNI) per capita, in purchasing power parities.

Three indices are combined to arrive at the HDI. The approach taken in each instance is to take the maximum and minimum values set as benchmarks as the denominator and then use the difference between the actual value in the particular country and the minimum value of benchmarks as the numerator.

Dimension index = (actual value − minimum value)/(maximum value − minimum value)

In the health index life expectancy is expressed in years. The index takes 20 years as the minimum value on the understanding that no country has recorded less than that in recent decades. The maximum life expectancy has been set at 85 years, in line with experience. The knowledge (education) index is made up of two indicators: average years of schooling and expected years of schooling. The minimum average years of schooling and expected years of schooling have been set at 0. The maximum mean years of schooling has been set at 15, thought to be the level reached in 2025 and the maximum expected years of schooling is 18, about the years required for a master's degree level. In the standard of living (income) index, the minimum GNI per capita is $100 and the maximum $75,000 per capita. The standard of living (income) index reflects the understanding that as income rises additional income has a smaller effect. In this sense the natural logarithm (ln) of income is used in the index.

Health Index = (actual life expectancy in country − 20)/(85 − 20)

Average years of schooling index = (actual mean years of schooling − 0)/ (15 − 0)

Expected years of schooling index = (actual expected years of schooling − 0)/ (18 − 0)

Education Index = (mean years of schooling index + expected years of schooling index)/2

Income Index = (ln actual GNI p.c.- ln100)/(ln75,000−ln100)

The estimated Human Development Index is the geometric mean of the three indices

$$\mathbf{HDI} = \left(I_{\text{Health}} \cdot I_{\text{Education}} \cdot I_{\text{Income}}\right)^{1/3}$$

The HDI does not capture the degree of inequality from the average within countries. To overcome this an inequality-adjusted HDI has been developed by UNDP. For that purpose, an inequality measure (A_x) is estimated for each variable (x)

$$A_x = 1 - g/p$$

where g is the geometric mean of the distribution and p is the arithmetic mean of the distribution. The inequality-adjusted index for each variable is

$$I_x^* = (1 - A_x) \cdot I_x$$

and the Inequality-adjusted Human Development Index is the geometric mean of the three indices

$$\mathbf{IHDI} = \left(I_{\text{Health}}^* \cdot I_{\text{Education}}^* \cdot I_{\text{Income}}^*\right)^{1/3}$$

Source UNDP (2015).

1.7   Population Growth, Activity and Sustainability

These indicators of human development reflect what could be seen as one of the dimensions of the human condition and efforts to enhance standards of living. However, since ancient times there has been other concerns related to the sustainability of population growth and threats to human existence arising from human activity. Some of these concerns have been given rising attention and the subject of recent debate, such as pollution and climate change from anthropogenic emissions of gases into the atmosphere.

Among others, two indicators of anthropogenic emissions of gases point to the impact of human activity on the environment. Sulphur dioxide emissions can arise naturally such as in the case of volcanic eruptions or from human activity. Anthropogenic emissions from the burning of fossil fuels are now greater than natural emissions. They affect climate by reflecting sunlight and having a cooling effect. They can also take the form of *acid rain* that damages the quality of the soil and water of rivers and lakes, and affects plant and animal life. Sulphur dioxide emissions have risen faster than population and have been associated with growing industrial activity, especially at the time of the industrial revolution in the 19th century. Emissions per head of population rose from about 0.002 of a metric ton in 1850 to 0.033 p.c. in 1970. They have declined since to 0.016 in 2000 (Table 1.26) and also in absolute terms. This has been attributed to a switch of fuels with less sulphur content and technologies to reduce their emission (Goldewijk 2014).

Earth's chronology indicates that human life has coincided with a long period of low carbon dioxide in the atmosphere (Sect. 1.1) and that higher levels of carbon dioxide in the past have been associated with warmer temperatures (Royer 2006).

Table 1.26 World anthropogenic emissions per capita of SO_2 and CO_2, 1850–2000

Year	Emissions p.c. in metric tons		Percentage addition on previous date	
	SO_2	CO_2	SO_2	CO_2
1850	0.002	0.04		
1870	0.004	0.11	100	175
1890	0.008	0.23	100	109
1910	0.017	0.47	113	104
1930	0.019	0.51	12	9
1950	0.022	0.64	16	25
1970	0.033	1.08	50	69
1990	0.023	1.15	−30	6
2000	0.016	1.06	−30	−8
Change 1850–2000	+0.014	+1.02	700	2,550

Note (SO_2) is sulphur dioxide, (CO_2) is carbon dioxide. Emissions are expressed in metric tons (1 ton = 10^3). CO_2 is measured in carbon metric tons
Source Goldewijk (2014). Computations made by the authors

Table 1.27 World anthropogenic emissions per capita of SO_2 and CO_2 by region, 2000

Region	Emissions p.c. in metric tons		Difference from average	
	SO_2	CO_2	SO_2	CO_2
Western Europe	0.019	2.09	+0.003	+1.03
Eastern Europe	0.048	2.55	+0.032	+1.49
Western Offshoots	0.057	5.21	+0.041	+4.15
Latin America	0.016	0.67	–	−0.39
East Asia	0.020	1.12	+0.004	+0.06
South and SE Asia	0.006	0.23	−0.010	−0.83
Mid. East and Nth Africa	0.016	0.98	–	−0.08
Sub-Sahara Africa	0.005	0.30	−0.011	−0.76
World	0.016	1.06		

Note (SO_2) is sulphur dioxide, (CO_2) is carbon dioxide. Emissions are expressed in metric tons (1 ton = 10^3). CO_2 is measured in carbon metric tons
Source Goldewijk (2014). Computations made by the authors

As in the case of sulphur dioxide, carbon dioxide can arise from natural causes but anthropogenic emissions have been the main source of carbon dioxide more recently. These have risen from about 0.04 of a metric ton (carbon) per head of population in 1850 to 1.15 in 1990. They declined to 1.06 tons (carbon) p.c. in 2000 (Table 1.26). However, they continued to grow in absolute terms.

The impact of industrial development on emissions of sulphur and carbon dioxides per head of population are apparent in the association between the level of industrial activity and emissions per head of population of sulphur dioxide and carbon dioxide in 2000. Accordingly, the level of emissions of sulphur dioxide were about 3.6 times in the Western Offshoots than the world average and about 4.9 times in the case of carbon dioxide (Table 1.27). This association raises issues regarding possible increases in emissions as industrial development takes place in less developed countries, this is reflected in the above average emissions per head of population in East Asia that has experienced the largest rate of growth in GDP per capita in recent times (Tables 1.20 and 1.21).

1.8 Transitional and Evolving Setting

In their relatively short existence, human beings have experienced considerable success in raising their number and the attainment of longer lives. The pace of these developments has not been steady. Slow growth in numbers and shorter lives prevailed during most of human history and the spread of humans has been unequal across different parts of the planet. However, population growth accelerated from the 19th century and its pace has further risen since 1950. Uneven migration has also affected population densities in several areas of the world.

Recent developments have been characterised not only by rapid growth but also by inequalities that have affected the characteristics and wellbeing of human populations. A factor in these dynamics has been the ability to accumulate, transfer and use knowledge and the evolution of social organisation to facilitate this and take advantage, or suffer the deleterious consequences, of the outcomes.

Different starting points in the adoption and level of use of knowledge and social organisation have led to populations with disparate levels of technological development that in turn impact on population characteristics and standards of living. This has meant that for a variety of reasons, some populations improved their productivity earlier so that their standards of living were enhanced while others lagged behind, and yet others eventually started to catch up.

An example of this is the revolution in public health. New public health measures prevented or lowered the spread of disease that improved health and reduced mortality. Changes were also taking place in other technologies at about the same time during the industrial revolution in the 19th century. They provided feedback loops that affected social organisation and eventually fertility in what has been described as the *population transition*. However, the adoption of new technologies has not been uniform across populations and has resulted in populations with different characteristics and at varied levels of development and wellbeing, as well as with diverse impact on the planet's fixed resource endowment and the environment.

Among others, inequalities continue to prevail in

- longevity and fertility
- rates of population growth
- proportion of dependent children and aged people
- complementary fraction of economic active people
- social organisation
- access to learning and knowledge
- goods and services available to different populations and within them
- status of males and females and their relative place in family, workplace and society
- environmental conditions

Thus, averages and trends are the result of unequal and often contrasting characteristics and outcomes; and some of the factors that have a bearing on them deserve further examination.

References

Abramov, O., & Mojzsis, S. J. (2009). Microbial habitability of the Hadean Earth during the late heavy bombardment. *Nature, 459*, 419–422.

Algaze, G. (2008). *Ancient Mesopotamia at the dawn of civilization*. Chicago: University of Chicago Press.

Andrews, P. (2015). *An Ape's view of human evolution*. Cambridge, UK: Cambridge University Press.

Boesch, C., & Tomasello, M. (1998). Chimpanzee and human cultures. *Current Anthropology, 39* (5), 591–614.

Bolt, J., Trimmer, M., & van Zanden, J. L. (2014). GDP per capita since 1820. In J. L. Van Zanden, J. Baten, M. M. d'Ercole, A. Rijpma, C. Smith, & M. Timmer (Eds.), *How was life? Global well-being since 1820*. Paris: OECD.

Boyden, S. (2004). *The biology of civilisation*. Sydney: University of New South Wales Press.

Brown, L. R. (1970). *Seeds of change*. New York: Praeger Publishers.

Caldwell, J. C. (2002). The contemporary population challenge. In *Report of the Expert Group Committee meeting on completing the fertility transition*. New York: United Nations.

Cartmill, M., & Smith, F. H. (2009). *The human lineage*. London: Wiley.

Catling, D. C. (2014). The great oxidation event transition. In H. Holland & K. Turekian (Eds.), *Treatise on geochemistry*, Vol. 6: *Atmosphere—History* (pp. 177–195). Amsterdam: Elsevier.

Chatterjee, H. J., Ho, S. Y. W., Barnes, I., & Groves, C. (2009). Estimating the phylogeny and divergence times of primates using a super matrix approach. *BMC Evolutionary Biology, 9*, 259. Retrieved May 16, 2016, from www.ncbi.nlm.nih.gov/pmc/articles?PMC2774700.

Cohen, K. M., Finney, S. C., Gibbard, P. L., & Fan, J.-K. (2013). The ICS international chronostratigraphic chart. *Episodes, 36*, 199–204. Retrieved March 18, 2015, from www.stratigraphy.org/ICSchart/ChronostartChart2014-10.pdf.

Copley, S. D., Smith, E., & Morowitz, H. J. (2007). The origin of the RNBA world: Co-evolution of genes and metabolism. *Bioorganic Chemistry, 35*, 430–443.

Danzer, G. A. (2000). *Atlas of human history*. Ann Arbor: Borders Group Inc.

Dauphas, N., & Morbidelli, A. (2014). Geochemical and planetary dynamic views on the origin of earth's atmosphere and the oceans. In H. Holland & K. Turekian (Eds.), *Treatise on geochemistry. Atmosphere—History* (Vol. 6, pp. 1–35). Amsterdam: Elsevier.

Diamond, J. (1997). *Guns, germs, and steel*. New York: W. W. Norton & Co.

Galli, M. T., Jadoul, F., Bernasconi, S. M., & Weissert, H. (2005). Anomalies in global carbon cycling and extinction at Triassic/Jurassic boundary: Evidence from a marine C-isotope record. *Palaeogeography, Palaeochemistry, Palaeoecology, 216*(3–4), 203–214.

Gelbard, A., Haub, C., & Kent, M. M. (1999). World population beyond six billion. *Population Bulletin, 54*(1), 1–44.

Gibbons, A. (2011). Who were the Denisovans? *Science, 333*, 84–108.

Glazko, G. V., & Nei, M. (2003). Estimation of divergence times for major lineages of primate species. *Molecular Biology and Evolution, 20*(3), 424–434.

Goldewijk, K. K. (2014). Environmental quality since 1820. In J. L. Van Zanden, J. Baten, M. M. d'Ercole, A. Rijpma, C. Smith, & M. Timmer (Eds.), *How was life? Global well-being since 1820*. Paris: OECD.

Harari, Y. N. (2015). *Sapiens: A brief history of humankind*. New York: Harper.

Kirch, P. V. (1985). *Feathered goods and fishhooks; an introduction to Hawaiian archaeology and prehistory*. Honolulu: University of Hawai'i Press.

Kravis, I. B., Heston, A. & Summers, R. (1982). *World product and income—International comparison of real gross product*. Baltimore: Johns Hopkins University Press.

Lancaster, H. O. (1990). *Expectations of life*. New York: Springer.

Maddison, A. (2003). *The world economy: Historical statistics*. Paris: OECD.

McCaa, R. (2002). Paleodemography of the Americas: From ancient times to colonialism and beyond. In R. Seckel & J. Rose (Eds.), *The Backbone of history: Health and nutrition in the western hemisphere* (pp. 94–124). Cambridge: Cambridge University Press.

McNeill, W. H. (1976). *Plagues and people*. New York: Anchor Books.

Morwood, M. J., O'Sullivan, P. B., Aziz, F., & Raza, A. (1998). Fissions-track ages of stone tools and fossils on the east Indonesia island of Flores. *Nature, 392*(6672), 173–176.

Murphy, J. B., Nance, R. D., & Cawood, P. A. (2009). Contrasting modes of supercontinent formation and the conundrum of Pangea. *Gondwana Research, 15,* 408–420.

Murphy, M. A., & Salvador, A. (Undated). *International stratigraphic guide—An abridged version.* International Commission on Stratigraphy. Retrieved March 18, 2015, from www.stratigraphy.org.bak/guide/abgui.hmt.

Noffke, N., Christian, D., Wacey, D., & Hazen, R. M. (2013). Microbially induced sedimentary structures recording and ancient ecosystem in the c.a. 3.48 billion-year old dresser formation, Pilbara, Western Australia. *Astrobiology, 13*(12), 1103–1124.

Paabo, S. (2014). *Neanderthal man: In search of lost genomes.* New York: Basic Books.

Palmer, D., Brasier, M., Burnie, D., Cleal, C., Crane, P., Thomas, B. A., et al. (2012). *Prehistoric life.* New York: DK Publishing.

Poston, D., & Bouvier, L. (2017). *Population and society; an introduction to demography* (2nd ed.). Cambridge: Cambridge University Press.

Reich, D., Patterson, N., Kircher, M., Delfin, F., Nandineni, M. R., Pugach, I., et al. (2011). Denisova admixture and the first modern human dispersals into Southeast Asia and Oceania. *The American Journal of Human Genetics, 89,* 516–528.

Roebroeks, W., & Villa, P. (2011). On the earliest evidence for habitual use of fire in Europe. *Proceedings of the National Academy of Sciences*, 108(13). Retrieved May 22, 2016, from www.pas.or/content/108/13/5209.

Royer, D. L. (2006). CO2-forced climate thresholds during the Phanerozoic. *Geochimia et Cosmochimia Acta, 70,* 5665–5675.

Sahney, S., & Benton, M. J. (2008). Recovery from the most profound mass extinction of all time. *Proceedings of the Royal Society, B, 275,* 759–765.

Sen, A. (1999). *Development as freedom.* New York: Anchor Books.

Spray, J. G., Kelley, S. P., & Rowley, D. B. (1998). Evidence for a late Triassic multiple impact event on earth. *Nature, 392,* 171–173.

Srivastava, R. P. (2009). *Morphology of primates and human evolution.* New Delhi: PHI Learning.

Stringer, C., & Andrews, P. (2011). *The complete world of human evolution* (2nd ed.). London: Thames & Hudson.

Summons, R. E., & Hallman, C. (2014). Organic geochemical signatures of early life on earth. In H. Holland & K. Turekian (Eds.), *Treatise on geochemistry. Organic Geochemistry* (Vol. 12, pp. 33–46). Amsterdam: Elsevier.

Sutikna, T., Tocheri, M. W., Morwood, M. J., Saptomo, E. W., Jatmiko, Awe, R. D., Wasisto, S., et al. (2016). Revised stratigraphy and chronology for Homo floresiensis at Liang Bua in Indonesia. *Nature, 532,* 366–369.

United Nations (UN). (1999). *The world at six billion.* New York.

United Nations (UN). (2007). *World population prospects—The 2006 revision.* New York.

United Nations (UN). (2013). *World population prospects—The 2012 revision.* New York.

United Nations (UN). (2014). *United Nations demographic yearbook.* New York.

United Nations (UN). (2016). *International migration report 2015.* New York.

United Nations (UN). (2017). *World population prospects—The 2017 revision.* New York.

United Nations Development Program (UNDP). (2014). *Human development report 2014.* New York.

United Nations Development Program (UNDP) (2015). *Human Development Report 2015—Technical Notes.* New York. Retrieved August 21, 2016, from http://hdr.undp.org/en/content/human-development-index-hdi.

United Nations Development Program (UNDP). (2016). *Human development report 2016.* New York.

United States Census Bureau (USCB). (2013). *World population—Historical estimates of the world population.* Retrieved May 24, 2016, from www.census.gov/population/international/data/worldpop/table_history.php.

Van Leeuwen, B., & van Leeuwen-Li, J. (2014). Education since 1820. In J. L. Van Zanden, J. Baten, M. M. d'Ercole, A. Rijpma, C. Smith, & M. Timmer (Eds.), *How was life? Global well-being since 1820*. Paris: OECD.

Wood, B., & Richmond, B. G. (2000). Human evolution: Taxonomy and paleobiology. *Journal of Anatomy, 196,* 19–60.

Wood, B. (2014). Fifty years after Homo habilis. *Nature, 508,* 31–33.

Yusuf, F., Martins, J. M., & Swanson, D. A. (2014). *Methods of demographic analysis*. Dordrecht: Springer.

Zhao, G., Sun, M., Wilde, S. A., & Li, S. (2004). A Paleo-Mesoproterozoic supercontinent: Assembly, growth and breakup. *Earth-Science Reviews, 67,* 91–123.

Chapter 2
Population: Notions, Theories and Policies

2.1 Diversity of Views

Diverse views on population have been expressed throughout the ages. Far back in history, Confucius is known to have been concerned with population growth and loss of productivity and Greek philosophers with concepts of optimum population and social welfare. Some thinkers were concerned with numbers and density of human population in relation to their environment, their position in the food chain, and availability of subsistence resources (Cragg and Pirie 1955; Coleman 1985; Yusuf et al. 2014). Some views involve a wider general scope and interest that deal with past and future development of the world's society, while others tend to focus more on demographic factors.

2.2 Population Size and Balance

2.2.1 Some Basic Concepts

Some theories involve animal and or mathematical models concerned with concepts of population oscillation, balance or equilibrium imposed by environmental or biological limits. Three such major concepts have evolved:

- *Stationary population*
- *Maximum population*
- *Minimum population*

© Springer International Publishing AG, part of Springer Nature 2018   43
Jo. M. Martins et al., *Global Population in Transition*,
https://doi.org/10.1007/978-3-319-77362-9_2

2.2.2 Stable and Stationary Populations

The *stationary population* concept relies on a mathematical model that shows if fertility and mortality, and net migration are held constant, then the age distribution of the population will tend towards a *stable-age* population (Swanson et al. 2016). A stationary population is a special case of a stable population where the birth rate is held constant at the level of the death rate and net migration is nil, which yields a population growth rate of zero (Swanson et al. 2016; Yusuf et al. 2014). The concept of *stationary population* is not only a theoretical concept, but also a possible objective that societies and populations could achieve in the time of a few generations. Long-term averages of zero population growth have occurred in history, such as in ancient Egypt, as a result of the combination of population growth and decline over time (Cohen 1995). *Stationary population* scenarios have been modelled using the fertility and mortality experiences of contemporary populations, such as long-term replacement level fertility (Livi-Bacci 1989). *Stationary population* and *stable population* are also expressed in other forms, such as *steady-state* or *stable equilibrium*, achieved through the competing forces of population growth and technology development, over a long period of time in human history (Lee 1986).

2.2.3 Maximum Population

The *maximum population* concept usually depends on an idea of maximum capacity for population growth imposed by the environment in which humans live and its *carrying capacity*. Animal models are sometimes the basis, but food supply has been one of the major constraining variables used. Concerns with other non-renewable resources and pollution have also been variables brought into the models used (Meadows et al. 1972).

2.2.4 Minimum Population

The *minimum population* concept relates to the viability of an isolated population to sustain itself and address the problems associated with inbreeding or even in finding a mate. It has been suggested that a minimum of about 500 with monogamy and 300–400 with polygamy is required (Sauvy 1974).

2.2.5 Optimum Population

By implication the attractive concept of *optimum population* has been developed in contrast to the concept of maximum population. It often carries quality connotations rather than quantity, and to have a welfare concern. Such as the social *stationary state* envisaged by some classical economists (Mill 1970). According to Lewis (1963), from an economic point of view, a country could be said to be over-populated if the output per head increased with a smaller population. Paradoxically, a country could be said to be over-populated if the population is so large in relation to a country's resources that a reduction in population would make no difference to total production.

2.3 Population Regulation

Possibly based on biological and ecological dicta, the notion of *population regulation* has been put forward in relation to human populations. The idea is that there is an equilibrium population size in relation to the resources available and human know-how, and that when populations depart from it, social and institutional practices will push or pull towards equilibrium. This is similar to the precepts of carrying capacity and population size in that context. An underlying view is an understanding that humans have a tendency to reproduce beyond sustainable conditions and lead to population pressure on their ecological environment. Thus, under given ecological circumstances, there is a population equilibrium size K with a r rate of growth equal to zero. If population size is below K, fertility will rise above mortality and r will rise above zero to bring population towards K size. However, if r continues to rises above zero after population size reaches K, equilibrium is broken and social and institutional forces will force the value of r to below zero to bring population to the sustainable K size in accordance with current ecological capacity (Wood 1998). This is a homeostasis concept in relation to human populations. At issue is what are the sensor and stimulus mechanisms that lead to homeostasis seeking behaviour in human populations (Cowgill 1975).

2.4 Technology and Population Growth

One anthropological perspective is the link between population size and technological development. According to this perspective, population growth has been uneven and upsurges have taken place with technological innovations that led to the tool-making revolution, the agricultural revolution and more recently the industrial revolution (Harari 2015). These are also seen as drivers for higher population concentrations and densities (Nag 1973). An economic view put forward by Boserup is that although in the short-term population growth may lead to lower agricultural productivity, in long-term it will force more intensive agricultural production techniques and higher productivity and higher levels of production to feed larger population densities (Marquette 1997). Different views have been stated regarding the *autonomous intensification* of agricultural production and its consequences as a generic model of improved productivity as a response to population growth. A number of reasons such as the impact of rapid population growth, as opposed to slow growth in Boserup hypothesis, and the tendency to mine land for short-term purposes rather than its protection for future use. This can lead to environmental degradation and social factors that affect future agricultural productivity (Lele and Stone 1989).

2.5 Malthus' and Other Classical Propositions

2.5.1 Malthus and Carrying Capacity

The publication of Malthus' *An Essay on the Principle of Population* in 1798 was a major landmark in the debate on population that has taken place since classical times. The Reverend Thomas Malthus was concerned with the effect of Mr. Pitt's "Poor Bill":

> ...his Poor Bill...is calculated to defeat the very purpose which it has in view. It has no tendency that I can discover to increase the produce of the country, and if it tended to increase the population, without increasing the produce, the necessary and inevitable consequence appears to be that the same produce must be divided among a greater number, and consequently that a day's labour will purchase a smaller quantity of provisions, and the poor therefore in general must be distressed. (Malthus 1970: 117)

However, population hypotheses, theories and or perspectives were well advanced before Malthus. In fact, the *Essay* is a debate of views held by a multitude such as M. Condorcet, Mr. Godwin, Dr. Smith and Dr. Price. Malthus put forward two postulata:

- *First, That food is necessary to the existence of man.*
- *Secondly, That the passion between the sexes is necessary and will remain in its present state.* (Malthus 1970: 70)

And followed them with two propositions:

- *Population, when unchecked, increases in a geometric ratio.*
- *Subsistence increases only in arithmetic ratio.* (Malthus 1970: 71)

> Taking the population of the world at any number, a thousand millions, for instance, the human species would increase in the ratio of – 1, 2, 4, 8, 16, 32, 64, 128, 256, 512, etc. and subsistence as – 1, 2, 3, 4, 5, 6, 7, 8, 9, 10, etc. In two centuries and a quarter, the population would be to the means of subsistence as 512 to 10; in three centuries as 4096 to 13, and in two thousand years the difference would be almost incalculable, though the produce in that time would have increased to an immense extent. (Malthus 1970: 77–78)

Malthus concluded that: ...*For I conceive that it may be laid down as a position not be controverted, that, taking a sufficient extent of territory to include within it exportation and importation, and allowing some variation for the prevalence of*

Table 2.1 World indices of food production per head by region, 1974/79—1996/97

Region	1974–76	1979–81	1984–86	1994–96	1996–97
Africa	104.9	100.0	95.4	98.4	96.0
Asia	94.7	100.0	111.6	138.7	144.3
• India	96.5	100.0	110.7	128.7	130.5
• China	90.1	100.0	120.7	177.7	192.5
Europe	94.7	100.0	107.2	102.3	105.0
Nth and Cent. America	90.1	100.0	99.1	99.4	100.0
• USA	89.8	100.0	99.3	102.5	103.9
South America	94.0	100.0	102.8	114.0	117.2
World	97.4	100.0	104.4	108.4	111.0

Source Sen (2000)

luxury, or of frugal habits, that population constantly bears a regular proportion to the food that the earth is made to produce. (Malthus 1970: 87)

Not only did Malthus disagree with M. Condorcet's vision that people may see the wisdom of controlling fertility, but he also disagreed with M. Condorcet on the timing when population might be greater than the subsistence available to keep it at an acceptable level. Malthus saw that the time *...has long since arrived* (Malthus 1970).

Malthus can be criticised in terms of both his propositions. The first is that the *passion between the sexes* may not necessarily lead to high fertility levels. The fertility transition observed in recent times shows that M. Condorcet might have seen the light at the end of the tunnel. Secondly, the production of food, at least in recent times, can and has kept pace with population growth (Table 2.1).

One of the reasons for Malthus' perspective was his not accepting that the behaviour of the masses could be changed. He held the *...view the improbability that the lower classes of people in any country should ever be sufficiently free from want and labour to obtain any higher degree of intellect improvement* (Malthus 1970: 148–149). Although, empirically Malthus has been found wanting, he continued to be influential and his concept of limits to population growth has continued to be pursued in other forms. A major service to society was to bring to the fore the importance of population in social and economic development and foster inquiry into the factors that influence it.

2.5.2   *J. S. Mill and the Stationary State*

John Stuart Mill was an influential classical economist that was not quite certain about Malthus' propositions but accepted them with some modifications. He saw room for population growth but he was concerned about distribution issues and advocated the containment of population growth. He envisaged the possibility of a *stationary state* where one of the features was a steady population:

> It is scarcely necessary to remark that a stationary condition of capital and population implies no stationary state of human improvement… it is questionable if all the mechanical inventions yet made lightened the day's toil of any human being. They have enabled a greater population to live the same life of drudgery and imprisonment, and an increased number of manufacturers and others to make fortunes… but they have not yet begun to effect those great changes in human destiny, which it is their nature and in their futurity to accomplish. (Mill 1970: 116)

As it will be seen, others have promoted the stationary state as an ideal worthwhile pursuing. However, this fine balance between fertility and mortality has not been achieved even in recent decades, when contraception has become more readily available and premature mortality has been reduced.

2.5.3   Marx and Engels and Civilization

Marx's influence continues to pervade thinking about social and economic change. He borrowed a human history model that envisaged three stages before modern times: *For the time being we can generalize Morgan's periodisation as follows: Savagery – the period in which the appropriation of natural products, ready for use, predominated; the things produced by man were, in the main, instruments that facilitated this appropriation. Barbarism – the period in which knowledge of cattle breeding and land cultivation was acquired, in which methods of increasing the productivity of nature through human activity were learnt. Civilization – the period in which knowledge of the further working up of natural products, of industry proper, and of art are acquired* (Marx and Engels 1958: 190). He saw over-population as a problem of the capitalist phase of social development. He did not see such a problem in a socialist society because: *…Mankind are the only beings who may be said to have gained an absolute control over the production of food. The great epochs of human progress have been identified, more or less directly, with the enlargement of the sources of subsistence* (Marx and Engels 1958: 185).

Although Marxism has been highly influential in China's post World War II development and in other countries, China's leadership adopted a one-child per family policy. This has been accompanied by a substantial decline in fertility in that country to below replacement level (UN 2017). However, as Sen (2000) has pointed out similar falls in fertility have been experienced by other developing countries without such policies.

2.6 Demographic Transition

2.6.1 Thompson's A, B and C

Warren Thompson (1929) observed that there were three groups of countries:

- A—Countries with falling birth and death rates, and declining natural increase. For example: northern and western Europe and countries with migrants from these areas.
- B—Countries that were experiencing declines in both birth and death rates but with death rates declining as much or even more than birth rates, and natural increase likely to become large in future. For example: Italy, Spain and central Europe.
- C—Countries that showed no such signs in birth and death rates, but with some countries such as Japan showing some early declines in mortality.

A similar typology could be applied to three groups of countries in accordance to stage of development in the immediate post World War II period:

- *More developed countries* experiencing both declines in fertility and mortality.
- *Other less developed countries* with a decline in mortality and early falls in fertility.
- *Least developed countries* with some small decline in mortality but yet to experience lower fertility.

2.6.2 Kingsley Davis' Explosion and Transition

In the immediate post World War II period, Kingsley Davis (1945) referred to a demographic explosion taking place ...*Viewed in long-run perspective, the growth of the earth's population has been like a long, thin powder fuse that burns slowly and haltingly until it finally reaches the charge and then explodes* (Davis 1945:1). He was referring to countries in different stages of what has become known as the *Demographic Transition*. It involves a decline in mortality that is then followed by a decline in fertility. However, in the interim countries experience high birth rates and declining death rates that lead to large natural increase and population growth. Davis offered the example of Japan as a country that was experiencing a decline in fertility after a decline in mortality. He foresaw that rises in literacy and less dependency on agriculture for employment would allow rapid industrialisation of developing countries to sustain the inevitable population explosion (Davis 1945).

2.6.3   Kingsley Davis' Change and Response

The demographic transition theory was underpinned by the proposition that high fertility was the response to high mortality. This observation in relation to industrialised countries was criticised because it did not lead to great predictability. Kingsley Davis (1963) responded by putting forward a *theory of demographic change and response*. He claimed that the understanding of demographic change had been hindered by seeing demographic behaviour as a response to either a *reproductive urge* and *means of subsistence*, or a function of *traditional culture* and *value system* (Davis 1963: 345). He put forward the thesis that ...*faced with a persistent high rate of natural increase resulting from past success in controlling mortality, families tended to use every demographic means possible to maximize their opportunities and to avoid relative loss of status* (Davis 1963: 362). The measures taken include abortion and sterilisation, where possible, contraception, when available, internal or international migration, postponement of marriage and celibacy. Davis also affirmed that poverty was unlikely to be the motivational link, as in the case of industrialised countries the responses had been accompanied with substantial economic growth.

2.7   Prophets of Doom and Others

2.7.1   Population Growth Views

In the 1960s and 1970s three influential works dealt with population growth

- *Stages of Economic Growth* by Rostow (1962)
- *Population Bomb* by Ehrlich (1969)
- *Limits to Growth* by Meadows et al. (1972).

2.7.2   Stages of Growth

Rostow's five stages of economic growth put some emphasis on the third stage: *The take-off*. This is seen as a watershed leading to stages of maturity, mass consumption and beyond it. Population growth rates of below 1.5% per year are said to be typical of the take-off stage. However, the shaky basis of this proposition is revealed by Rostow's mentioning a range from 0.5 to 2.5%. He claims that the high population rates in the range of 1.5–2.5% then being experienced by developing countries ...*impose a strain and challenge in both aggregative terms, and more narrowly, in terms of the pace of the technological revolution in agriculture* (Rostow 1962: 141). This perceived population induced strain arises to some extent from the implicit use of the Harrod-Domar growth model that will be discussed later. It is also the result of the use of the concept of under-employment in rural societies with a low rate of productivity in agriculture. Rostow's proposition shows the continuing preoccupation of a balance between population and food production in individual countries.

2.7.3 Zero-Population Growth

Ehrlich's population bomb expressed a concern that population growth and over-consumption was stretching the use of resources and altering the composition of the atmosphere. He advocated a return to a stationary state where birth and death rates would be brought into balance (Ehrlich 1969). The zero-population movement has been the source of much controversy and some of the issues are still being debated. The demographic transition experienced by the more developed countries and even some of the less developed countries has gone some way towards Ehrlich's position of a stationary state. However, the over-consumption and atmospheric pollution issues continue to be a source of dispute. This is illustrated by the current debate over *Global Warming* and expressed aims to reduce anthropogenic gas emissions.

2.7.4 Limits to Growth

The work by Meadows et al. (1972) on limits to growth was undertaken at the request of the Club of Rome. It used modelling to assess the impact of exponential growth in production and use of resources and the population carrying capacity of the planet. Like Ehrlich, they could be labelled as neo-malthusian in their approach and concern for the living standards of a growing population. They adopted Ehrlich's proposal that birth and death rates should be equalised and propose that capital additions be equal to depreciation. They followed J. S. Mill in the advocacy of a stationary state and claimed that ...*Population and capital are the only quantities that need to be constant in an equilibrium state* (Meadows et al. 1972: 175). This work has become less influential as some of the projections made have proved to be off the mark. However, the themes pursued in their work continue to be part of the current debate.

2.8 Population and Development Economics

2.8.1 Harrod-Domar Model

Economic development has been one of the major national and global policy issues since World War II, especially after the break-up of the European colonial empires into a large number of less developed countries. Population and its growth have been variables that have been the object of considerable attention. The Harrod-Domar model gained popularity and became a highly influential model in economic planning in the 1950s and 1960s. It promised a simple approach to development based on Keynesian theory of investment, savings and income (Kurihara 1961). In its early form, it read as follows:

$$g = (s/b)$$

g   is the desired rate of income growth ($\Delta Y/Y$)
s   is the savings rate required (S/Y)
b   is the capital: output ratio ($\Delta K/\Delta Y$)

The model provided an easy prescription for economic development and was frequently used in economic planning. Given a certain capital:output ratio, the desired economic growth was dependent on the rate of saving. An early criticism of the model was that it did not take into account population growth. To meet this objection, the model was further developed to incorporate the concept of income per capita growth. If the depreciation of capital is omitted, the reformulation of the model reads as

$$g^* = (s/b) - n$$

g*   is the desired rate of income growth
s   is the savings rate required
b   is the capital:output ratio
n   is the population growth rate

This formulation clearly shows that *ceteris paribus* the greater the rate of population growth the lower the growth rate of income per capita. One of the criticisms is it does not take into account the age distribution of the population, and the relative burden imposed by a higher or lower dependency ratio. Other criticisms could be made of the model. Its level of aggregation glosses over the complementary nature of the various investments including *human capital*—a more recent concept. Another important criticism was raised by Solow that deals with the concept of diminishing returns to Capital and Labour that tends to change the capital:output ratio. The essence of the arguments put forward is that without *technical progress* that increases the capital:output ratio, Capital accumulation must outstrip population growth, but diminishing returns will eventually force a decline in income per capita (Ray 1998).

2.8.2 Human Capital and Technical Progress

In more recent years, economic development models have come to recognise the role that *technical progress* plays in economic growth such as the *green revolution* that led to higher yields of rice production in Asia. In addition, the concept of *human capital* has also evolved to allow for the recognition of investments in humans, through education and health, as important variables in development. This concept provides that investment can be either in physical plant or humans that improve skill and level of performance of the labour force. These investments in people have a cumulative effect. It can be shown that countries with high investment in physical plant without investments in human capital will tend to have lower rate of growths than those that invest in people. It is suggested that the high rate of economic progress in Japan was due to their increasing investment in human capital that made their investment in physical plant more productive (Ray 1998).

2.8.3 Human Capital and Fertility

Empirical studies have indicated that there is a linkage between investments in the education of women and fertility. According to Sen (2000), two factors have been found to be the major explanatory variables for lower fertility in India. They are the degree of female literacy and female participation in labour outside the household. These two variables proved to be more powerful than other indicators of economic wellbeing. The concept of *human capital* was also used in explaining fertility decline after the baby boom generation in the industrialised countries in the late 1950s. Woman's time spent on child rearing does not have the same monetary values as in employment. When more women were encouraged to participate in wage-earning employment outside their households, the time they spent on child rearing would decrease, hence, fertility decreases (Schultz 1986). However, it is unclear whether this concept could still be useful when woman's labour force participation rate and earnings are as high as men (Table 2.2).

Table 2.2 World female literacy and fertility, 2005–13 and 2010–2015

Countries	2005–2013 Female 15–24 literacy percent	2010–2015 TFR
Arab States	86.9	3.2
East Asia and Pacific	98.7	1.9
Latin America and Caribbean	98.0	2.2
South Asia	74.3	2.6
Sub-Saharan Africa	62.7	5.1
Europe and Central Asia	99.3	2.0
Very high human development	...	1.8
High human development	99.0	1.8
Medium human development	82.2	2.6
Low human development	62.7	4.6
World	84.7	2.5

Note (...) denotes close to 100.0
Source UNDP (2015)

2.9   Population Change and Institutions

2.9.1   Search for Explanation of Population Change

While general biological models and economic models have been used to serve as central paradigms in understanding dynamics and structure of populations by many demographers, many others find equally powerful explanations in sociological concepts, especially in institutional frameworks, such as culture, relationship and regulations and interventions.

2.9.2   Determinants of Fertility

It is posited that human fertility is affected by one's biological conditions and individual choices, which are affected by cultural patterns of society and economic and social conditions of people. It has been suggested that the biology, shaped by cultural patterns, determines the *supply of children*. Individual choice of desirable family size, modified by social and economic conditions including regulations, determines the *demand for children*. In turn, factors such as education, female employment, urbanization, and income have modifying effects on the *supply of children* and *demand for children* or fertility regulation costs. In addition to the individual reproductive history, a range of socioeconomic, demographic and biological characteristics, and factors associated with culture and society have also been seen to affect individuals' fertility. Accordingly, institutional and cultural norms and perceptions are perceived as important fertility determinants (Freedman et al. 1983).

2.9.3 Second Demographic Transition

In the recent history of European populations, a number of drastic fertility declines were experienced. It has been advanced that two successive fertility declines in the 1870s and the 1930s marked the process of the *second demographic transition*. It is thought that the first fertility decline in the 1830s was the result of the change in mode of production and the decreased utilitarian value of children in households and the availability of contraception. And the second fertility decline was related to individual attitudes and behaviour toward family, marriage, extramarital sexuality, cohabitation, abortion and women's labour force participation. It is conceived that the pursuit of individual autonomy and occupational advancement discouraged childbearing couples from placing their efforts and hope in their children's future. The institutional factors in affecting the second demographic transition were even stronger in largely Catholic countries (Lesthaeghe 1995; van de Kaa 1987; Caldwell 2004). Other institutional factors are also seen to have contributed to the decline in fertility, such as patriarchy family structure in Mediterranean Europe. This obliged working females to undertake almost all household and childcare tasks without much help from their male partners. Accordingly, increasing labour force participation in in this region directly discouraged women from having a large number of children (McDonald 2000). Although the fertility decline in more developed countries is conceived as largely a spontaneous and socially natural process, in many developing countries this process was notably accelerated by institutional policy interventions. The perceived unifying trend was that the fertility decline process was *a progression of largely inevitable changes* in human history (Caldwell 1997).

2.9.4 Intergenerational Transfer and Fertility

It is suggested that in some societies where fertility is largely high there is no net economic gain to the family from reducing fertility (Arnold et al. 1975). In this type of societies, children over their life time provide their parent with more economic returns than they receive from parents. While in other societies, due to a range of socioeconomic factors, having children or having large number of children is not desirable. In the latter, children receive more resources over their life time from their parents than they provide to them. Therefore, fertility decline occurs when the direction of intergenerational wealth flow changes from favouring parents to favouring children. The reversal of intergenerational transfers within the family is closely associated with improvement in education, shift in employment opportunities from family production to waged labour markets, as well as cultural influence of non-traditional values and ideas (Caldwell 1982).

2.9.5 Ageing and Sustainability

After a long process of demographic transition many countries have moved from
the stage of high fertility and high mortality to one of low fertility and low mortality. One of the consequences of the completion of the transition is population
ageing, and another consequence is slow and eventual negative population growth.
Japan is an example of such transition. The completion of demographic transition
process has resulted in serious demographic consequences in Japanese society.
Sustainability problems have become even more serious in some small and rural
farming communities due to outmigration of people of working age in aged populations (Hara 2015).

A number of more developed countries, like Japan, have started to experience
the challenges of population ageing and negative growth and the world's overall
fertility has fallen and will be projected to fall further. Nevertheless, population
momentum will result in population growth from 7.4 in 2015 to 9.8 billion in 2050
(according to the United Nations medium variant projection). In the next few
decades, population growth will be largely in the developing countries (UN 2017).
This should mean that greenhouse gas emissions in developing countries, where
most people live, will grow faster than in the developed world, which require more
focused efforts on emissions reduction, especially in the larger economies, such as
China, India and Brazil. Sustainability challenges will be more severe in an ageing
society like Japan. As a highly urbanized country, Japan will be affected by the
urban heat in summer season. Rising temperature will make a rapidly ageing society
even more vulnerable (Stern 2007).

Box 2.1 Malthus' and other population curves

The propensity towards systematic analysis of population led to Malthus and
others to express population change in mathematical terms that can be
expressed in curve shapes. Accordingly, Malthus basic propositions were that
population tends to increase at a geometric rate while food increased at an
arithmetic rate. The first can be expressed as an exponential curve and the
second as a straight line (Fig. 2.1).

Others saw that after a period of exponential growth, population would
reach a point of diminishing resources and population growth would be
reduced towards and equilibrium level that would eventually plateau, at level
of equilibrium with resources available. This is similar in shape to the logistic
or S-shaped curve. The United Nations population projections (medium
variant) follow a pattern similar to the logistic curve (Fig. 2.2).

Another concept is that instead of staying on a plateau, population might
fall after reaching a point where resources will decline and population may
actually fall following a dome-shaped curve. The population of Japan and the
United Nations projections for that country to 2100 (UN 2017) follow a
similar shape (Fig. 2.3).

Yet, another population curve is implied in Malthus' understanding of ...*a perpetual oscillation between happiness and misery*... (Malthus 1970: 67) where population would possibly oscillate up and down of an equilibrium value in the shape of a sine or cosine curve.

It might not be a precise oscillation with varying points up or below a given equilibrium level (Fig. 2.4).

Population concepts following these mathematical patterns and curve shapes are often put forward in population studies.

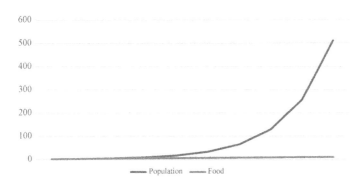

Fig. 2.1 Malthus' arithmetic and geometric curves of population and food growth

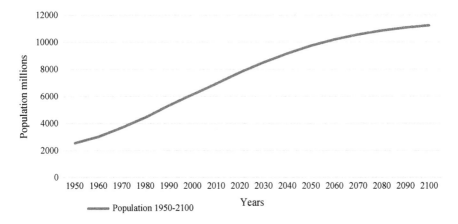

Fig. 2.2 World population and projections 1950–2100

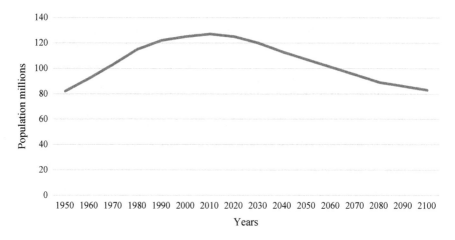

Fig. 2.3 Japan population and projections 1950–2100

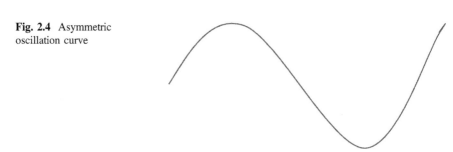

Fig. 2.4 Asymmetric
oscillation curve

2.10 Changing Perceptions and Population Policies

2.10.1 Policies on Population Growth

The fertility and mortality transitions have had different starting points in time and space. At a given point in time, countries have felt varying type of impacts on their population growth and composition depending on the particular phase of these transitions they are experiencing (Chap. 1: Sects. 1.2 and 1.3).

Consequently, it is no surprise that countries have had different perspectives on population growth over time and evolved population policies accordingly. In general terms, the proportion of more developed countries, at advanced stages of the demographic transition, after years of low fertility and mortality, with policies that favour population growth increased from 24% in 1976 to 49% in 2013. The inverse has been the case in least developed countries still with high fertility rates and declining mortality rates. The proportion of these countries with policies to raise population growth have declined from 12% in 1976 to zero in 2013. The proportion of less developed countries, most of which are in the middle of their

Table 2.3 Government policies on rate of population growth, 1976–2013

Population growth policies by stage of development	1976	1986	1996	2005	2013
	Percentage of countries				
Raise					
More developed	24	24	23	35	49
Less developed	17	14	10	8	10
Least developed	12	8	2	0	0
World	*19*	*16*	*13*	*15*	*20*
Maintain					
More developed	0	24	13	17	14
Less developed	0	3	7	16	23
Least developed	0	6	2	8	6
World	*0*	*7*	*8*	*16*	*21*
Lower					
More developed	0	0	2	0	2
Less developed	34	41	48	48	49
Least developed	14	29	55	70	84
World	*26*	*32*	*37*	*36*	*37*

Note The number of countries were 150, 164, 193, 194, and 197 respectively in 1976, 1986, 1996, 2005 and 2013. The percentages do not add to 100. The remainder are countries that had *no intervention* policies
Source UN (2013)

population transition, with policies to raise population growth fell from 17% in 1976 to 10% in 2013. Trends in the proportion of countries with policies to lower their population growth reflect the varying circumstances faced by countries at different stages of development. The proportion of least developed countries with policies to lower their population growth has increased from 14% in 1976 to 84% in 2013. A smaller increase from 34 to 49% over the same period has taken place in less developed countries most of which are experiencing lower population growth. More developed countries with declining proportions of people of working age and facing the possibility of shrinking populations usually have no policies to reduce their population growth (Table 2.3).

2.10.2 Policies on Fertility Levels

Government policies regarding fertility tend to be associated with their stances regarding population growth. Accordingly, the proportion of more developed countries with policies to raise fertility rose from 21% in 1976 to 69% in 2013. The proportion remained close to nil in the least developed countries. However, an upsurge from 5 to 14% to place in less developed countries, during the same period,

Table 2.4 Government policies on fertility levels, 1976–2013

Fertility level policies by stage of development	1976	1986	1996	2005	2013
	Percentage of countries				
Raise					
More developed	21	24	33	50	69
Less developed	5	8	8	10	14
Least developed	2	4	0	0	0
World	*9*	*12*	*14*	*20*	*27*
Maintain					
More developed	21	18	8	17	14
Less developed	10	8	10	16	18
Least developed	5	8	6	6	4
World	*13*	*10*	*10*	*16*	*17*
Lower					
More developed	0	0	2	0	0
Less developed	34	42	56	53	57
Least developed	14	31	65	76	94
World	*27*	*33*	*42*	*40*	*43*

Note The number of countries were 150, 164, 193, 194, and 197 respectively in 1976, 1986, 1996, 2005 and 2013. The percentages do not add to 100. The remainder are countries that had *no intervention* policies
Source UN (2013)

some of which are facing the possibility of lower proportions of people of working age. In a complementary way, the proportion of least developed countries with policies to reduce fertility rose substantially to about 94% in 2013, while more developed countries with similar policies remained about nil. The proportion of less developed countries, at different phases of their transition, with policies to reduce their fertility levels increased from 34% in 1976 to 57% in 2013 (Table 2.4).

2.10.3 Policies on Internal Migration

The process of industrialisation has had an impact on employment opportunities that have favoured urban areas. This has resulted in considerable migration from rural to urban areas in most countries. As migrants are usually young adults with their children, this migration has led to imbalances in the age distribution of rural and urban areas (Hara 2015). High rates of internal migration can also lead to lags between population growth in urban areas and the capacity of existing urban infrastructures to cope with them. These concerns have resulted in government policies aimed at lowering the rate of internal migration from rural to urban areas. This is especially the case of less developed countries experiencing the largest rates

Table 2.5 Government policies internal migration from rural to urban areas, 1976–2013

Internal migration policies by stage of development	1976	1986	1996	2005	2013
	Percentage of countries				
Raise					
More developed	5	5	0	5	2
Less developed	8	3	6	3	3
Least developed	4	0	0	2	0
World	*7*	*3*	*5*	*4*	*3*
Maintain					
More developed	0	5	13	2	2
Less developed	0	5	4	1	2
Least developed	0	4	3	0	0
World	*0*	*5*	*6*	*1*	*2*
Lower					
More developed	60	47	29	61	67
Less developed	44	52	41	73	84
Least developed	41	33	53	78	88
World	*48*	*51*	*38*	*70*	*80*

Note The number of countries were 150, 164, 193, 194, and 197 respectively in 1976, 1986, 1996, 2005 and 2013. The percentages do not add to 100. The remainder are countries that had *no intervention* policies
Source UN (2013)

of population growth and internal migration from rural to urban areas. The proportion of less developed countries with policies aimed at lowering the rate of internal migration rose from 44% in 1976 to 84% in 2013 (Table 2.5).

2.10.4   Government Concerns with Population Ageing

The concerns with population growth and fertility expressed by countries at different stages of their transition are associated with those for population ageing with implications for varying degrees of old-age dependency on the population of working age. Thus, more developed countries with growing proportions of old-age people and declining proportions of people of working age have expressed growing major concern with population ageing from 76% in 2005 to 92% in 2013. Least developed countries with rising proportions of people of working age and low proportions of old-age people had lesser reason to have a major concern with population ageing. However, less developed countries, some of which are still experiencing a demographic bonus in terms of high proportions of people of working age and still low proportions of old-age people, kept about the same degree of major concern about population ageing between 2005 (43%) and 2015 (42%) (Table 2.6).

Table 2.6 Government
concern with ageing of
population, 2005 and 2013

Concern with ageing by stage of development	2005	2013
	Percentage of countries	
Major concern		
More developed	76	92
Less developed	43	42
Least developed	26	18
World	*52*	*55*
Minor concern		
More developed	24	8
Less developed	57	53
Least developed	71	73
World	*48*	*41*

Note The number of countries were 165 and 185 respectively in
2005 and 2013. The percentages do not add to 100. The
remainder are countries that expressed *no concern*
Source UN (2013)

2.11   Towards Greater Ecological Understanding

Biological and other theoretical notions have attempted to explain the regulation of
human population in terms of its size, growth and composition. A common perception is that humans like other living organisms have a tendency to reproduce to
perpetuate their species. This leads to population growth and eventual size and
density beyond ecological sustainability. This conundrum is then resolved through
often mechanistic population checks that bring population back to equilibrium with
resources available. Ecological approaches have evolved to examine the impact of
human populations on both biotic and abiotic features of their environment that in
sequence affect human lives. These tussles have gone some way but have fallen short
to explain population dynamics and their expression in the population transformation of more recent decades. These propositions point to notions of carrying capacity
and human population densities and pressures but also to the role of technological
development. These developments have affected carrying capacity, not only in terms
of food supply but also other production that has changed human life styles and use
of resources. In turn, feedback loops have resulted in changes in social and economic
organisation that also have had an impact on the planet's ecology.

2.12   Perceptions and Reactive Population Policies

Features of population policies related to population growth, fertility, migration and
ageing have varied over time. They have reflected the stage of development and
associated phase of the population transformation that they are experiencing. Least

developed countries with high levels of population growth and fertility have evolved policies aimed at lowering fertility and population growth, but usually have no concerns with population ageing. Usually, more developed countries with fertility below replacement levels, reduced proportion of people of working age, growing proportion of old-age people, and in some cases the prospect of shrinking populations have policies to encourage higher levels of fertility and growth in people of working age. Other less developed countries that are mostly experiencing demographic bonuses with a high proportion of people of working age, lower degrees of dependent children and still low dependency from old-age people tend to have policies to reduce fertility and population growth. They show a moderate degree of concern for population ageing. However, all tend to have policies to lower the level of migration from rural to urban areas as they face the impact of high urban densities and pressure on related infrastructure.

References

Arnold, F. S., Bulatao, R. A., Buripakdi, C., Chung, B. J., Fwacett, J. T., Iritani, T., et al. (1975). *The value of children: A cross-national study.* Honolulu: East-West Population Institute.

Caldwell, J. (1982). *Theory of fertility decline.* New York: Academic Press.

Caldwell, J. (1997). Global fertility transition: The need for a unifying theory. *Population and Development Review, 23*(4), 803–812.

Caldwell, J. (2004). Demographic theory: A long view. *Population and Development Review, 30* (2), 297–316.

Cohen, J. (1995). *How many people can the earth support?* New York: W. W. Norton & Company.

Coleman, D. (1985). Population regulation: A long-range view. In D. Coleman & R. Schofield (Eds.), *The state of population theory.* Oxford: Basil Blackwell.

Cowgill, G. L. (1975). On causes and consequences of ancient and modern population changes. *American Anthropologist, 77*(3), 505–525.

Cragg, J. B., & Pirie, N. W. (1955). *The numbers of man and animals.* Edinburgh: Oliver & Boyd.

Davis, K. (1945). The world demographic transition. *Annals of the American Academy of Political and Social Sciences, 237,* 1–11.

Davis, K. (1963). The theory of change and response in modern demographic history. *Population Index, 29*(4), 345–366.

Ehrlich, P. R. (1969). *The population bomb.* Ballantine.

Freedman, R., Easterlin, R., Menken, J., Willis, R., Lapham, R., & Bulatao, R. (1983). A framework for the study of fertility determinants. In R. Bulatao & R. Lee (Eds.), *Determinants in fertility decline in developing countries* (Vol. 1). New York: Academic Press.

Hara, T. (2015). *A shrinking society: Post-demographic transition in Japan.* Tokyo: Springer.

Harari, Y. N. (2015). *Sapiens: A brief history of humankind.* New York: Harper.

Kurihara, K. K. (1961). *Introduction to Keynesian dynamics.* London: George Allen & Unwin Ltd.

Lee, R. (1986). Malthus and Boserup: A dynamic synthesis. In D. Coleman & R. Schofield (Eds.), *The state of population theory.* Oxford: Basil Blackwell.

Lele, U., & Stone, S. W. (1989). *Population pressure, the environment and agricultural intensification—Variations on the Boserup hypothesis.* World Bank: Washington DC.

Lesthaeghe, R. (1995). The second demographic transition in western countries: An interpretation. In K. M. Oppenheim & A. Jensen (Eds.), *Gender and family change in industrialized countries: 17–62* (pp. 17–62). Oxford: Clarendon.

Lewis, W. A. (1963). *The theory of economic growth*. London: George Allen & Unwin Ltd.
Livi-Bacci, M. (1989). *A concise history of world population*. Malden, MA: Blackwell Publishers Inc.
McDonald, P. (2000). Gender equity, social institutions and the future of fertility. *Journal of Population Research, 17*(1), 1–6.
Malthus, T. R. (1970). *An essay on the principle of population and a summary view of the principle of population*. Harmondsworth: Penguin Books Ltd.
Marquette, C. (1997). *Turning but not toppling Malthus: Boserupian theory of population and environment relationships*. WP 1997:16. Bergen: CHR. Michelsen Institute.
Marx, K., & Engels, F. (1958). *Selected works* (Vol. 2). Moscow: Foreign Language Publishing Houses.
Meadows, D. H., Meadows, D. L., Randers, J., & Behrens, W. W. (1972). *The limits of growth*. London: Pan Books.
Mill, J. S. (1970). *Principles of political economy*. Harmondsworth: Penguin Books Ltd.
Nag, M. (1973). Anthropology and population; problems and perspectives. *Population Studies, 27* (1), 59–68.
Ray, D. (1998). *Development economics*. Princeton: Princeton University Press.
Rostow, W. W. (1962). *The stages of economic growth: A non-communistic manifesto*. Cambridge MA: Cambridge University Press.
Sauvy, A. (1974). *General theory of population*. London: Methuen & Co.
Schultz, T. (1986). The value and allocation of time in high-income countries: Implications for fertility. In D. Kingsley, M. Bernstem, & R. Ricardo-Campbell (Eds.), *Below-replacement fertility in industrial societies: Causes, consequences, policies. Population and development review*, (Supplement 12, pp. 87–108).
Sen, A. (2000). *Development as freedom*. New York: Anchor Books.
Stern, N. H. (2007). *The economics and climate change: The Stern review*. Cambridge: Cambridge University Press.
Swanson, D. A., Tedrow, L., & Baker, J. (2016). Exploring stable population concepts from the perspective of cohort change ratios: Estimating the time to stability and intrinsic r from initial information and components of change. In R. Schoen (Ed.), *Dynamic demographic analysis* (pp. 227–258). Dordrecht: Springer B. V. Press.
Thompson, W. S. (1929). Population. *The American Journal of Sociology, 34*, 959–979.
United Nations (UN). (2013). *World population policies*. New York.
United Nations (UN). (2017). *World population prospects—The 2017 revision* (Vol. I). New York.
United Nations Development Programme (UNDP). (2015). *Human development report 2015*. New York.
Van de Kaa, D. (1987). Europe's second demographic transition. *Population Bulletin, 42*(1), 1–57.
Wood, J. W. (1998). The theory of preindustrial population dynamics—Demography, economy, and well-being in Malthusian systems. *Current Anthropology, 39*(1), 99–121.
Yusuf, F., Martins, J. M., & Swanson, D. A. (2014). *Methods of demographic analysis*. Dordrecht: Springer.

Chapter 3
Fitness Challenge: Too Many or Too Few

> ... *Fertility is the most direct contributor to an organism's fitness (i.e. the number of descents it produces). In fact, all other fitness components, such as mortality, only affect fitness through their effect on fertility (e.g. mortality rates affect fitness by affecting the probability of living to the next reproductive event). All else constant, any increase in fertility increases an organism's fitness.*
>
> Kaplan and Lancaster (2003)

3.1 Life, Reproduction and Evolution

3.1.1 Reproduction and Fitness

Humans are living beings and share some characteristics with other living organisms. Reproduction is one of the features of life. On it depends the survival or demise of species. The reproduction of living organisms such as plants and animals can take many forms. However, it is usually classified as

- *Asexual*
- *Sexual*

Asexual reproduction usually involves the reproduction of offspring with the same genetic composition as that of the parent. Sexual reproduction generally entails the genetic recombination of the parents' attributes that provides a greater diversity and possible adaptation to changing environments. Humans are the offspring of sexual reproduction. Fitness to survive and reproduce sexually is dependent on

- *supply of food to sustain life*
- *protection from environmental hazards*
- *mating*

(Verena 2004).

© Springer International Publishing AG, part of Springer Nature 2018
Jo. M. Martins et al., *Global Population in Transition*,
https://doi.org/10.1007/978-3-319-77362-9_3

The term *fitness* is used in the sense that individuals will survive to reproduce and will have offspring that will ensure survival or growth of the species in following generations.

Some also like to distinguish between *fecundity* and fertility. Fecundity is a biological attribute concerned with the ability to reproduce (Last 1983) while fertility refers to the frequency of reproduction.

3.1.2 Biology: Cells, Genes, Homeostasis and Natural Selection

A number of notions in biology have been postulated over time and continue to have a major influence on the way demographers, sociologists and others deal with fertility. These include the observation that living organisms are made up of one or more cells and that these cells came from cells of previous generations. Another notion is concerned with living organisms' inheritance of attributes from parents, through the passing of genetic material from one generation to another. Yet another notion is that of homeostasis or the propensity towards a stable internal state that allows organisms to function. Also of importance is the notion of the evolution of living organisms through natural selection proposed by Charles Darwin and Alfred Wallace. Four main points arise from the Darwin/Wallace propositions:

- *Living organisms tend to adapt to their environment*
- *Living organisms are characterized by varying attributes*
- *Living organisms tend to reproduce beyond the carrying capacity of their environment*
- *Living organisms vary in their fitness to survive and reproduce and natural selection leads to the survival of the fittest*

(Farabee 2001a).

The concept of *carrying capacity* is similar to and based on Malthus' proposition (Chap. 2) that: at any point in time the number of people is related to the possible production of food, given existing land and its fertility. Any excess population generated above that level leads to unfavourable living conditions and wastage of the population until it returns to the carrying capacity level: a thermostat type of reaction. In more recent times, new technologies and their diffusion have enhanced (or limited) *carrying capacity*.

Errors may occur in the recombination of the parents' genetic material in sexual reproduction. The impact of these errors may be relatively small if they affect the structural or non-coding areas of DNA (deoxyribonucleic acid—the carrier of genetic information for most organisms, excluding viruses), but may have a major effect if they affect the coding material. These errors constitute mutations. They may occur only in relation to one or a few offspring to distinguish them from the rest of the population (*segregating mutation*). As most mutations have a tendency to affect fitness unfavourably, they tend to have a lower survival and or undesirable mating attributes. This *natural selection* may lead to the mutation dying out.

However, the mutation may be spread widely and become *fixed* in the whole population and be transmitted from one generation to another. In small and isolated populations, it is possible that breeding pressure may lead to the mating of mutated and less healthy individuals and the spread of unfavourable genetic material. This may result in a decline in the health of the population and even eventual extinction. Mathematical models indicate that the impact of the mutation is not sudden. It tends to lead to population growth close to the carrying capacity and a plateau in the population numbers, as less fit individuals become a larger proportion of the population. As the proportion of less fit individuals increases by reproduction and there are less healthy individuals to mate, a steep decline in population takes place —*mutational meltdown*—which may lead to the extinction of the population (Verena 2004).

3.1.3 Human Reproduction, Chromosomes and Sex

The human genome[1] has two strings each with a set of genes acquired at random from each parent. There are 44 non-sex determining chromosomes and 2 sex-determining chromosomes that determine the sex of the individual human being: XX for females and XY for males. Other combinations are possible but they constitute abnormalities. The failure of replicated chromosomes to segregate may result in XXY (maleness) or XXX or XO nondisjunctions. Individuals suffering from these abnormalities are generally sterile and underdeveloped in the case of maleness. Other chromosomal abnormalities may lead to harmful conditions such as dwarfism, mental retardation, degeneration of the nervous system, haemophilia, cystic fibrosis and albinism (Farabee 2001b).

3.2 Fertility: Variation and Themes

3.2.1 Fitness-Maximizing and Human Fertility

Observations of living organisms have led to the belief that animals reproduce to maximize fitness to the limits of the carrying capacity. It has been estimated that without the use of contraception and with regular sexual intercourse, on average women could have about 15 children from menarche—at 12 years of age—to menopause—at 50 years of age (McFalls 2003).

---

[1]Genome is the complete set of hereditary traits in the haploid set of chromosomes.

The measurement of fertility around the world indicates that there are considerable variations in average fertility across countries and within them, and also that fertility has declined generally, with some temporary resurgences (UN 2015). Observations of contemporary hunter-gatherer societies (!Kung of Botswana and the Ache of Paraguay) suggested that women had less children on average than would be expected if they were *fitness-maximizing beings*. A study of a contemporary agricultural population (the Dogon of Mali) led to the observation that women also had less offspring than expected if they were in a fitness-maximizing mode (Strassmann and Gillespie 2002).

Fertility surveys have thrown up some challenges. Cross-sectional surveys point to decreasing fertility as household income rises, which is contrary to the notion of fitness-maximization as the carrying capacity of the household rises. While other observations suggest that women follow an adaptive behaviour and fertility falls when economic conditions decline (MacDonald undated), such as the 1930s Depression, and rises again when economic conditions are more favourable as in post-World War II period.

Two major approaches have been taken to examine this phenomenon. One involves the use of frameworks or models that identify the contribution made by different demographic components to the observed changes. Another approach takes a more *evolutionary* path that entails the examination of economic or social factors that influence the observed changes in the component analysis and issuing interaction.

3.2.2   Fertility Determinants

The first approach follows a path covered by Davis and Blake (1956) *intermediate variables* and Bongaarts (1978) *proximate determinants.* Davis and Blake proposed that fertility was dependent on three major variables

- *Access to sexual activity*
- *Contraception*
- *Abortion*

Bongaarts suggested that four proximate determinants accounted for most of the variations in fertility: lactation, contraception, abortion and non-mating.

$$TFR = TR(Ci * Cc * Ca * Cm)$$

TFR   Total Fertility Rate
TR   Maximum potential fertility rate
Ci   Proportion of non-fecund women due to post-partum amenorrhea
Cc   Proportion of women who use contraception

Ca   Proportion of women that terminate a pregnancy
Cm   Proportion of women in child-bearing age not married or in union

When the values of C are equal to one then TFR = TR (Robinson 2003).

A more recent re-iteration of this model makes more explicit the separation of the less controllable biological factors and those that are more dependent on family decisions and socio-economic factors.

$$TFR = IFS(Fu * Fs * Fr * Ft * Fi * Fc)$$

TFR   Total Fertility Rate
IFS   Intended family size
Fu   Unwanted fertility
Fs   Sex preferences
Fr   Replacement effect
Ft   Tempo effect
Fi   Infecundity
Fc   Competition

Some of the variables represent adjustments that are made in light of the intended family size and events that are not known when the decision on the intended family size was made, such as the sex (Fs) or the death (Fr) of an offspring. Infecundity (Fi) is another major issue because it may force unforeseen outcomes, even though therapy and IVF are possible interventions but will have a tempo effect. The postponement of birth (Ft) often has a major downward impact on TFR, as may lead to less offspring than the intended family size. Unwanted fertility (Fu) also has an impact on the TFR. The review of intended family size (Fc) could have a downward or upward impact on TFR. It may be the result of constraints arising from trade-offs between the intended family size and other family objectives such as improved chances for a lower number of offspring, or the lack of personal opportunities (Morgan 2003).

3.2.3 Fertility: Social and Economic Factors and Adaptive Behaviour

The models put forward by Davis-Black-Bongaarts are useful in examining the relative weight of the variables involved in variations in fertility. The more recent elaboration points to other factors that influence the determinants of fertility. *Evolutionary* demographers, sociologists, economists and others have sought to assess the factors that influence the direction and nature of decisions made directly by women and households and indirectly by societies (*implicit policies*) in the determination of the level of fertility and family size.

3.2.4   Fitness-Maximizing and Carrying Capacity

Malthus' proposition that relates fertility to the carrying capacity in terms of food production is an early example of the introduction of boundaries to carrying capacity, in view of the notion that women are fitness-maximizing beings who will reproduce to the level of carrying capacity and beyond. The puzzle posed by the decline of fertility in industrialised countries with greater carrying capacity has challenged many Malthusian notions. The observation that the decline in fertility has been associated with a previous decline in infant mortality is part of the *demographic transition* framework. Further, the association of some variables with fertility, such as women's education and labour force participation, has also raised some questions.

3.2.5   Cohort Size, Price of Labour and Fertility

Answers to the questions raised have been pursued by some, such as Easterlin, by looking at the interaction between fertility and economic factors faced by different cohorts. Easterlin argued that cohort size is an important factor in determining fertility. He emphasised ... *the importance for the study of fertility behaviour of focusing on the economic experience of those in the early childbearing ages.* (Easterlin 1966: 131). He used some of Becker's arguments that ...*a rise in the stock of consumer goods available to husband and wife is an alternative to expanding the size of the family* (Easterlin 1966: 139). Further, following from contributions to consumer theory by Dusenberry, Modigliani, Brady and Friedman, he also put forward the proposition that ...*consumption levels experienced in the parents' households serve, among other things, to shape their current preference in much the same way as a previous higher income level would affect those of given household* (Easterlin 1966: 140).

Easterlin attributed the increase in fertility experienced in the United States during the Baby Boom to the relative small size of the cohort entering the labour force in the late 1940s and their greater income in relation to the previous generation who experienced the Depression in 1930s. In turn, following the decline in fertility in 1960s and the previous large cohort entering the labour force, Easterlin stated ...*a sharp rise in the relative number of young adult workers, has led to deterioration of their relative income position, and through this to a shift towards deferment of marriage, later household formation, and reduced fertility* (Easterlin 1968: 16). Thus, Easterlin linked cohort size, their relative income and desired consumption to fertility.

Easterlin's hypotheses have given stimulus to a large number of empirical studies. Macunovich (1996) found evidence that the difference between relative income and female wage influenced fertility. Thus, while a rise in male relative income led to an increase in fertility, a similar rise in female wages resulted in a decline in fertility in the United States. A review by Pampel and Peters (1995) pointed to a number of conditions that must prevail for the *Easterlin Effect* to be found. The review indicated that the *effect* is more consistently found in countries such as the United States that went through a major Baby Boom in the late 1940s and 1950s, e.g. Canada and Australia, and that it is less apparent in European countries. Some of its application also seems to be less relevant to the 1990s, when major changes have taken place in the role of women in relation to that of their partners. Nevertheless, although cohort size may not be the major factor in the current decline in fertility, a study found evidence of the *Easterlin Effect* among OECD countries for the period 1975–1999 (Jeon and Shields 2005).

3.2.6   Backward Intergenerational Goods and Old Age Security

Others have looked at questions of backward intergenerational goods (BIGs). It has been posited that in more traditional societies, without organised social safety nets, parents look at their children as a source of economic security in their old age. Children could be considered as investments. As the source of economic productivity is often associated with males, this could also lead to the preference for male offspring in some societies. Thus, fertility could be seen as a function of the number of male offspring required to provide parents with an adequate support in their old age. The observed level of infant and child mortality will influence parents' decisions on the desired number of children to attain economic security in old age. Accordingly, the higher the infant and child mortality rate the larger the number of offspring required (Ray 1998). This has been formulated as the *replacement effect* (Palloni and Rafalimanana 1999). The replacement effect could lead to higher fertility in households with lower income that usually have higher rates of infant and child mortality. For instance, a study in Peninsular Malaysia indicated that the number of children born to (ever-married) women aged 40–49 were 40% higher for women in the lowest-income bracket compared with those in the highest. The same study also shows that infant mortality rates were about double in the lowest income brackets (Arshat et al. 1988).

3.2.7   Female Labour Force Participation and the Opportunity-Cost of Children

Becker (1960) proposed that there are costs and benefits of having children and in some cases the costs may outweigh the benefits (Ray 1998). Industrialization has created greater employment opportunities for females in the formal sector of the economy. Situations can arise where the cost of a larger number of children may be greater than the benefits to the household if the female is prevented from gainful employment by the number of children dependent on her care. At a certain point, the female's perception may lead to the curtailment of fertility in favour of higher household income. Some studies have found an association between higher female workforce participation and lower fertility levels (Sen 1999). More recent cross-sectional aggregated data for countries at different stages of development do not show this inverse association, and least developed countries with a higher level of female workforce participation also experiencing higher fertility (UNDP 2015).

3.2.8 Trade-Off Between Quantity and Quality: Human Capital

The concept of human capital has been given considerable weight in social development. There are different nuances in the application of this concept to fertility. One nuance is that women, given the opportunity, will reduce fertility and affect a trade-off between the quality and quantity of children. The lower fertility creates an opportunity to increase the quality of offspring by dividing available household resources among a smaller number, and increase the time dedicated to each child, and improve nutrition and education levels (Becker 1995). Other things being equal, this more intensive investment in each child will raise their future earning capacity and improve the quality of future human capital. The trade-off between quality and quantity has been found in a study of a contemporary traditional agricultural society (Strassmann and Gillespie 2002).

Another nuance is that human capital is cumulative across generations. Therefore, parents with higher education have more and are more capable to pass on the human capital that they have. Consequently, the better educated tend to dedicate more time and resources to fewer children in order to maximize improvements in human capital of their children and the family as a whole. This nuance can be associated with social status and attitudes to upward social mobility. Thus, parents who see an opportunity to improve social and economic status and the possibility of upward mobility will reduce fertility and invest more on a smaller number of children. While parents with low human capital of their own and seeing low possibilities for upward mobility will have no incentive to reduce fertility (MacDonald undated). The negative association between mother's education and fertility is often used as evidence supporting this proposition.

3.2.9 Embodied Human Capital and Trade-Offs

Kaplan and Lancaster (2003) have combined aspects of fitness with trade-offs and the notion of embodied human capital. Fertility decisions involve three major trade-offs between

- *present and future reproduction*
- *quantity and the quality offspring*
- *mating and parental effort*

The first trade-off is concerned with fitness and the energy involved in reproduction: repeated pregnancies can be harmful and lead to negative trade-offs between reproduction in the present and future times. Embodied capital is expressed in terms of

- *strength*
- *speed*
- *immune function*
- *skill*
- *knowledge*
- *other capabilities*

and investments must be made to allow it to grow, develop and be maintained.

The second trade-off involves the long-term survival and success of offspring: the number of offspring may diminish the yield from the investment made in children as it divides available resources among a larger number of children.

The third trade-off relates to the effort made to find a mate in different mating-market conditions and the opportunity cost of those efforts in relation the reproductive effort itself.

Kaplan and Lancaster maintain that four important elements are involved in the timing, rate and each parent investment in reproduction

- *quantum of resources used in reproduction and the method used to obtain them*
- *mortality risk and available ways of reducing mortality*
- *degree of complementarity between the efforts of each parent in offspring production*
- *variability in capacity to produce resources and capital owned by individuals and of individuals over time*

The first element is connected with the investments made in offspring to place them in advantageous position to enhance their capacity to produce the resources involved in the effort of reproduction.

The second element expresses the relationship between the chances of survival and realisation of the investments made in the production of offspring. Thus, the lower the risk of mortality and the capacity to prevent premature death the greater willingness to invest in offspring.

The third element relates to the degree of effort of one parent in relation to the other in the production of offspring. A parent is less likely to invest in the offspring if the other partner's effort can be a substitute for their own. Thus, complementarity that allows for specialization by each parent is likely to lead to greater total investment in offspring.

The fourth element involves the characteristics of different mating-markets and the relative value of the inputs made by males or females in relation to resources for reproduction. Female dominance will tend to result in males having to compete in terms of their traits in gaining acceptance to mate by a female, and may result in single males without a partner. In turn, male dominance will tend to greater male choice in the quality of the female and male competition for the resources needed to exercise such choice.

Further, Kaplan and Lancaster maintained that women have always been caught in the dilemma between the production of resources and efforts involved in reproduction, especially because of the continuing dependence of offspring of different ages. They discerned a pattern of markets for labour that discriminates in favour of human capital based on education and skill. The methods of production based on these attributes rather than physical force have allowed greater participation of females in the labour force, and have also increased the opportunity cost of home work and child rearing against employment outside the home. It also discriminated in favour of embodied capital in terms of female education. Improvements in public health and medicine have also reduced infant and child mortality and enhance the chance that investments made in children will yield better results. These developments have provided incentives in favour of lower fertility. However, these trends have also led to a lower degree of complementarity between male and female efforts in offspring rearing and affected family formation and household type. This reduction in complementarity has led to higher levels of divorce and to single-female-parent households (Kaplan and Lancaster 2003).

3.3 Fertility in Transition

3.3.1 Demographic Transition: Fertility and Mortality

A feature of the *demographic transition* framework is that a decline in mortality in general, and infant mortality in particular, preceded the fall in fertility observed in European and other industrialised countries since the 19th century, and more recently in developing countries (Palloni and Rafalimanana 1999). The effect of the fall in mortality on fertility has been questioned and continues to be controversial. A difficult problem is the sorting out of the influence of the many factors that have accompanied both the mortality and fertility declines, and then establish a consistent relationship that shows the effect of the fall in mortality on fertility.

Studies by Coale (1973) and Van de Walle (1986) did not find *convincing evidence* to support the causal relationship between the fall in mortality and the following decline in fertility. A review of Latin American countries' experience also did not produce statistical evidence of a strong effect (Palloni and Rafalimanana 1999). However, when they revisited early European experiences, Galloway et al. (1998) found supporting evidence of the effect of the fall in infant mortality on fertility. Similarly, evidence from Brazil also indicated the strong effect of infant mortality on fertility, after controlling for the effects of other variables (Potter et al. 2002).

3.3.2 Early Declines in Fertility

Declines in fertility took place in a few countries as early as the later part of the 18th century. It became more accentuated in the 19th century in some European countries and other more developed countries in North America (UN 2002). It was also apparent in Australia in that century (Table 3.1). In some cases, the decline in fertility appeared to be adaptive behaviour in response to economic downturns such as the 1890s and the 1930s.

The downward trend has persisted with some temporary upturns, such as the Baby Boom experienced in the post-World War II period. However, this trend was not apparent early in the 20th century in areas with lower economic development (UN 2002), such as India and Sri Lanka (Table 3.2).

3.3.3 Varying Experiences and Stages of the Fertility Transition

Substantial differences in fertility continue to be experienced in different parts of the world and in countries at varying levels of economic development. Nevertheless,

Table 3.1 Gross reproduction rates Sweden, England and Wales and Australia, 1820s–1964

Year	Gross reproduction rate		
	Sweden	England and Wales	Australia
1821–30	2.28		
1841–50		2.13	
1871–80	2.25	2.35	(1881) 2.65
1901–10	1.82	1.63	(1901) 1.74
			(1911) 1.71
1935–39	0.87	(1936–9) 0.89	(1931) 1.14
1951		(1952) 1.05	1.49
1956	1.10	1.15	1.61
1963		1.39	1.63
1964	1.21		1.53

Note The Gross Reproduction Rate is the average number of female offspring that a woman produces during her reproductive years
Sources Myrdal (1968) early Sweden, England and Wales; CBCS (1968). Australia and later Sweden and England and Wales

Table 3.2 Gross reproduction rate in India and Sri Lanka, 1900–1952

Year (Sri Lanka)	Gross reproduction rate	
	India	Sri Lanka
1901 (1900–02)	2.99	2.40
1911 (1910–12)	3.14	2.11
1921 (1920–22)	2.83	1.91
1931 (1930–32)	2.99	2.04
1941 (1940–42)	2.76	2.16
1951 (1952)	2.70	3.66

Note The Gross Reproduction Rate is the average number of female offspring that a woman produces during her reproductive years
Source Myrdal (1968)

the fertility transition spread to most countries in the second half of the 20th century. The average number of children per female declined by about half in the world during the period from 1950–1955 to 2010–2015. In Asia, Europe Latin America and Caribbean and Northern America the average number of children per female were close to or below the conventional replacement level of 2.1 children per female. Although higher levels of fertility tended to prevail in the 1950s and 1960s, peaks tended to be earlier in Asia and Europe and come somewhat later in Africa, Latin America and Caribbean, Northern America and Oceania (Table 3.3).

The major reductions in the Total Fertility Rate (TFR) took place in Latin America and the Caribbean (−3.7) and Asia (−3.60), but even Africa with the

Table 3.3 World fertility by region, 1950–55 to 2010–2015

Years	Total Fertility Rate						
	Africa	Asia	Europe	Latin America	Northern America	Oceania	World
1950–1955	6.62	5.80	2.66	5.87	3.34	3.84	4.96
1960–1965	6.72	5.81	2.57	5.89	3.28	3.96	5.03
1970–1975	6.71	5.03	2.17	5.03	2.02	3.21	4.46
1980–1985	6.48	3.70	1.88	3.96	1.79	2.60	3.60
1985–1990	6.18	3.50	1.81	3.46	1.88	2.51	3.44
1990–1995	5.72	2.92	1.57	3.06	2.00	2.49	3.02
1995–2000	5.34	2.56	1.43	2.76	1.95	2.46	2.75
2000–2005	5.08	2.41	1.43	2.48	1.99	2.44	2.63
2005–2010	4.89	2.30	1.55	2.26	2.01	2.53	2.57
2010–2015	4.72	2.20	1.60	2.14	1.85	2.41	2.52
Change 1950–1955 2010–2015	−1.90	−3.60	−1.06	−3.73	−1.49	−1.43	−2.46

Note The Total Fertility Rate is the average number of live births a woman produces during her fertile period from menarche to menopause. Latin America includes the Caribbean
Source UN (2017)

highest regional TFR (4.7) in 2010–2015 experienced a reduction in recent decades. Europe that started its fertility transition in the 18th century experienced the lowest decline in fertility in the period (−1.1). However, with an average TFR of 1.6, Europe was the region with the lowest TFR in 2010–2015. It was followed by Northern America with a TFR of 1.9 (Table 3.3). These regional averages gloss over substantial wide ranges in fertility among the populations within them. For instance, Asia had a wide range of fertility levels from 5.9 and 5.3 respectively in Timor-Leste and Afghanistan to 1.2 in both Singapore and Korea. The average in Oceania also reflects a wide range from 3.8 and 4.1 in Papua New Guinea and Solomon Islands to 1.9 and 2.0 in Australia and New Zealand (UN 2017).

As shown earlier (Table 1.10), the analysis of fertility decline by level of development points to a hierarchy of average fertility levels in accordance with development: the higher the level of development the lower the TFR. On average, more developed countries tend to experience fertility rates well below replacement levels while the least developed countries are about twice that level.

The fertility trends observed in countries with different levels of economic development and industrialization are in accordance with notion that the opportunity-cost of female labour has an impact on fertility, this could also be extended to the notion of backward intergenerational goods sought by parents in less economically developed countries.

The sharp decline in fertility in the world since the 1960s was the result of the considerable fall in the proportion of the world population with three or more children per woman that constituted about 78% in 1953 and 19% in 2008, while the proportion below replacement level of 2.1 children per female rose from less than 1% in 1953 to about 48% in 2008 (Table 3.4).

Table 3.4 World population by stage of fertility transition, 1953–2008

Average children per female	Percentage of world population				
	1953	1973	1993	2008	Change 1953–2008
Five or more	66.0	43.5	13.0	9.4	−56.6
3 or less than 5	12.1	30.0	31.9	9.1	−3.0
2.1 or less than 3	21.9	10.5	9.9	33.4	+11.5
1.85 or less than 2.1	0.1	13.8	29.3	14.5	+14.4
1.4 or less than 1.85	–	2.2	12.3	26.2	+26.2
Less than 1.4	–	–	3.5	7.4	+7.4
World	100.0	100.0	100.0	100.0	
Three or more	78.1	73.5	44.9	18.5	−59.6
Less than 2.1	0.1	16.0	45.1	48.1	+48.0

Note Figures may not add due to rounding. Only countries or areas with 90,000 people or more in 2013 are included
Source UN (2013). Computation made by the authors

3.4 Conundrum: Saving the Planet or Reducing the Dependency Burden

3.4.1 Population Growth and Falling Fertility

The importance of fertility levels on population growth is an issue that has engaged people from ancient times to Malthus and many others more recently with the upsurge of fertility after the Second World War (Chap. 2). The rise in fertility in industrialised countries after the decline experienced during the 1930s (Gille 1957) contributed to the substantial increment in population growth in the world during the 1950s and 1960s. This was associated with neomalthusian concerns and perceived need to address them (e.g. Erlich 1969; Meadows et al. 1972). More recently, the fall in fertility below replacement levels in industrialised (and some less developing countries) has raised fears regarding population aging and its possible impact (e.g. Morgan 2003; Demeny 2015; Coleman and Basten 2015). Thus, the world has not experienced the features that characterise stable (and stationary) populations with constant fertility and mortality schedules and a steady rate of population growth that eventually lead to a given age distribution.

The basic population model shows that the population growth rates arise from the difference between birth and mortality rates (natural increase) and the net migration rate (Box 1.3). Obviously, in a closed population such as that of the world as a whole, the rate of population growth is entirely due to natural increase. Another relevant factor is that birth and death rates vary with age and lead to different rate of natural increase depending on the population distribution of the time. Accordingly, differences in population growth rates in the period 1950–2015 reflect not only changes in the age-specific fertility and mortality rates but also their momentum in changing the age distribution at a particular point in time. The total fertility rate (TFR) is useful in this regard, as it controls for age differences and indicates whether fertility is at replacement level (2.1 children per female), above it and contributing to population growth or below it and adding to losses in population.

3.4.2 Rise and Fall in Fertility and Its Momentum

A feature of the period 1950–2015 was that mortality rates declined throughout that time span (Tables 1.11, 1.12 and 3.5). This made changes in fertility above replacement level and their momentum more apparent in their effect on population growth rates, the proportion of people in the conventional working age of 15–64 years and in the dependent ages of 0–14 and 65 years and over.

The rise in the world's average TFR that reached a peak in 1960–65 (5.0 or 3 children per woman above replacement level) led to additions in the proportion in the child population 0–14 years of age from about 34% in 1950 to 38% in 1970.

Table 3.5 World population growth rate and age distribution, 1950–2015

Years of age	1950	1960	1970	1980	1990	2000	2010	2015
Age group as percentage of total population								
0–14	34.3	37.1	37.5	35.4	32.9	30.1	28.0	26.1
15–64	60.6	57.9	57.2	58.8	61.0	63.0	64.7	65.6
65 and over	5.1	5.0	5.3	5.9	6.1	6.9	7.3	8.3
World population (millions)	2,536	3,033	3,701	4,458	5,331	6,145	6,958	7,383
TFR	4.96	5.03	4.46	3.60	3.02	2.63	2.57	2.52
Le	47.0	51.2	58.1	62.1	64.6	67.2	69.1	70.8
Pop. growth p.a. (%)	1.78	1.93	1.95	1.78	1.52	1.25	1.23	1.19
Dependency ratio (%)								
Dependency ratio	65	73	75	70	64	59	55	53
Child Dep. ratio	56	64	66	60	54	48	43	40
Old-age Dep. ratio	8	9	9	10	10	11	12	13

Note (TFR) the average number of children per female during her reproductive life. (Le) the average Life expectancy at birth in years. (Dependency Ratio) is the sum of the Child and Old-age dependency ratios. (Child Dep. Ratio) is the percentage ratio of the population aged 0–14 years to that aged 15–64. (Old-age Dep. Ratio) is the percentage ratio of the population aged 65 and more years to that 15-64. The (TFR), (Le) and (Pop. growth rate p. a. percentage) are for the periods 1950–55…2000–05, 2010 is the average 2005–10 and 2015 is the average 2010–15. Figures may not add up because of rounding
Source UN (2017). Computations made by the authors

The share of the old-age people 65 years of age and over remained about the same at 5%, while that of people in working age fell from about 61 to 57%. The higher fertility experienced, with declining mortality, led to an increment in the average annual population growth rate from 1.8% in 1950–55 to 2.0% in 1970–75 (Table 3.5).

As TFR declined to 2.4 and 1.5 children above replacement level respectively in 1970–75 and 1980–85, the proportion of the child population dropped to 33% in 1990 and that of working-age people rose to 61% with a slight increase in the percentage of the old-age people to 6%. TFR continued to fall to only the equivalent 0.4 children above replacement level in 2010–15 and the proportion of the child population dropped to 26% of the total, but that of the old-age population rose to 8% in 2015. The percentage of the working-age people that had risen to about 65% in 2010 rose slightly to 66% in 2015. Thus, the often-called *demographic bonus* of a rising proportion of working-age people from the momentum created by the initial fertility boom that led to increasing numbers joining the labour force in consequent years rose somewhat in 2010–2015 (Table 3.5).

The analysis of the trends in crude birth and death rates confirms that most of the decline in the rate of population growth in the world from 1950–1955 to 2010–2015 was due to falls in fertility. This is in spite of increases in life expectancy that went a considerable way to diminish the impact of lower fertility but could not stop the rate of natural increase from falling (Table 3.6).

Table 3.6 World crude birth and death rates, natural increase and population growth rates, 1950–1955 and 2005–2010

Rates	1950–1955	2010–2015	Difference 1950–1955 2010–2015
CBR	36.9	19.6	−17.3
CDR	19.1	7.7	−11.4
Natural increase rate	17.8	11.9	−5.9
Population growth p. a. (%)	1.78	1.19	−0.59

Note (CBR) is the crude birth rate or the number of births per thousand people. (CDR) is the crude death rate or the number of deaths per thousand people. (Natural Increase rate) is the difference between (CBR) and (CDR)
Source UN (2017). Computations made by the authors

3.4.3 Fertility and the Dependency Burden

These population dynamics can be translated in terms of changes in the relative social costs of dependency, i.e. the ratio of the child and old-age people to those of working age. The initial rise in fertility led to a larger child dependency ratio from about 56% in 1950 to 66% in 1970, while old-age dependency ratio rose only from 8 to 9%. Thus, the substantial increment in the overall dependency ratio from 65 to 75% was almost entirely due to the upsurge in fertility. The fall in the total dependency ratio to 53% in 2015 was mostly due to a fall in the child dependency ratio (−16%) and to a lesser extent to a counter increase in the old-age dependency ratio (+5%) (Table 3.5).

3.4.4 Shrinking Societies Led by Japan

The world average fertility masks substantial differences between countries, but the trend has been for a decline in TFR throughout the world towards replacement level or below it, as illustrated in the proportion of the world population where an average of 2.1 children per woman prevailed dropped considerably (Table 3.4). In dealing with the impact of declining fertility at an advanced stage, Japan provides an example of what Hara (2015) has called a *shrinking society*. Some European populations have experienced similar declines in fertility. However, they have tended to use immigration to compensate somewhat for lower numbers flowing into working age. Japan has not experienced immigration to any great extent and the impact of lower fertility in Japan is more apparent.

According to Hara (2015), fertility in Japan declined from 5.1 children per female in 1925 to 3.7 in 1950. However, the TFR in 1950 was still the equivalent of

1.6 children above replacement level, and similar to the peak in TFR in the United States, Canada and Australia during their Baby-Boom in the 1950s and 1960s (UN 2017). TFR in Japan fell to about replacement level in the 1960s and the early 1970s, but then dropped and stayed below it. Accordingly, the proportion of children 0–14 fell from about 35% of the population in 1950 to 13% in 2015. However, the earlier higher level of fertility above replacement level led to a demographic bonus in increments to the proportion of people of working age 15–64 years that rose from 60% in 1950 to 70% in 1990. This declined back to 61% in 2015. Over the 65-year period, the proportion of old-age people rose from 5% in 1950 to more than a quarter of the population (27%) in 2015. The consistent low level of fertility below replacement level meant a continuing decline in the population annual growth rate from 1.6% in 1950 to less than 0.1% in 2010, and an eventual reduction in total population from 2010 to 2015. This substantial drop in population growth took place against a trend of considerable rise in life expectancy that added to the proportion of people of old age (Table 3.7).

The demographic bonus from the decline in fertility kept the dependency ratio below 60% in the six decades 1960–2010, as the child dependency ratio fell from 59% in 1950 to 21% in 2010. During the same period, the old-age dependency ratio rose from 9% in 1960 to 36% in 2010 and then to 44% in 2015. The trend is for rising dependency as cohorts flowing into the labour force will be smaller due to low fertility, thus lowering the proportion and number in working age while aging

Table 3.7 Japan population growth rate and age distribution, 1950–2015

Years of age	1950	1960	1970	1980	1990	2000	2010	2015
Age group as percentage of total population								
0–14	35.4	30.2	24.0	23.5	18.2	14.6	13.2	12.7
15–64	59.6	64.1	68.9	67.4	69.7	68.1	63.8	60.6
65 and over	4.9	5.7	7.1	9.1	12.1	17.4	23.0	26.7
Population (millions)	84.1	94.3	104.7	117.1	123.6	126.9	128.1	127.1
TFR	3.65	2.00	2.13	1.75	1.54	1.36	1.39	1.46
Le	61	68	72	76	79	81	83	84
Pop. growth p.a. (%)	1.58	0.92	1.08	0.90	0.42	0.21	0.05	−0.15
Dependency ratio (%)								
Dependency ratio	68	56	45	48	43	47	57	65
Child Dep. ratio	59	47	35	35	26	21	21	21
Old-age Dep. ratio	8	9	10	14	17	26	36	44

Note (TFR) the average number of children per female during her reproductive life. (Le) the average Life expectancy at birth in years. (Dependency Ratio) is the sum of the Child and Old-age dependency ratios. (Child Dep. Ratio) is the percentage ratio of the population aged 0–14 years to that aged 15–64. (Old-age Dep. Ratio) is the percentage ratio of the population aged 65 and more years to that 15–64. The Le is the weighted average of male and female life expectancies and the figure for 2015 is a trend estimate. Figures may not add up because of rounding

Source SBJ (2016). Computations made by the authors

of earlier large cohorts and lower mortality add to the old-age population (Table 3.7).

3.4.5 Inequality in Female Education and Access to Contraception

Japan could be seen as an example of social modernisation associated with the adoption of new technologies, industrialisation and rising levels in education. Of more direct relevance to fertility, Japan has been characterised by high levels of female education (UNDP 2015) and access to contraception (UN 2015). These have been associated with female social and economic empowerment and lower levels of fertility (Sen 1999).

An examination of some of these variables shows a substantial inequality in female literacy and contraception prevalence among countries and an inverse relationship between these factors and TFR levels (Table 3.8). These differences have a bearing on the varying stages of the fertility transition in countries in spite of the trend towards lower levels of fertility.

3.4.6 Migration Replacement

The experience in Europe of lower fertility resulted in a lower number of people entering the work force and led to industrialised European countries changing from being net losers of people to migration to being net gainers (Table 1.13). The net gain expressed a demand for additional labour often at the lower end of the skill range. Other industrialised countries that had gone through an early fertility

Table 3.8 World female literacy and fertility, 2005–13 and 2010–2015

Countries	Female literacy (%)	Contraception prevalence (%)	TFR
Sub-Sahara Africa	62.7	28.4	5.1
South Asia	74.3	58.6	2.5
Latin America and Caribbean	62.7	72.7	2.1
Least developed	65.9	39.5	4.3
World	84.7	63.6	2.5

Note (Female literacy) is for females aged 15–24 years of age in 2005–2013. (Contraception prevalence) is the percentage of married females or in a union aged 15–49 who are using any method of contraception. (TFR) is the average number of children per female during their reproductive years in 2010–2015
Source UNDP (2015), UN (2015), UN (2017)

transition, such as the United States, Canada and Australia, continued their migration programs that enlarged their labour forces, even at the time of resurgence in fertility during the Baby Boom of the 1950s and early 1960s. The effects of compensating migration in European countries have led to social discrimination at times of economic downturns, as illustrated by a higher level of unemployment of foreign-born (OECD 2016).

3.5   Transitional Phases and Challenges

The experience over time of Japan and other countries at what could be called post-transition stage offers insights of the possible pathways and issues to be addressed by other societies at different phases of the fertility transition. Countries that are still experiencing high but falling fertility rates (e.g. India), as Japan was in 1950s and 1960s, could benefit from the demographic bonus of a drop in the proportion of dependent children and a swell in that of people of working age. However, for this potential to be realised investments in human and other capital are complementary factors. They require purposeful action and organisation, if they are to overcome factors associated with low female education, access to contraception and work participation in the formal sector.

Other countries that have reached replacement or lower levels of fertility, as Japan did in 1970s, 1980s and 1990s, face similar requirements of continuing investment in human and other capital and related organisation, but in addition they need to prepare to tackle different generational transfers as the demographic bonus starts to wear out.

In addition to Japan, the post-transitional phase of fertility has affected, for some time, many and diverse European countries such as Germany and Portugal (UN 2017). However, other countries like Korea and Thailand that have rising levels of female education, access to contraception and participation in the formal sector are now also experiencing fertility rates below replacement level (UNDP 2015; UN 2015) and having to meet the impact of the intergenerational transfers, as the demographic bonus becomes smaller or comes to an end.

Inequality in fertility levels and the timing of their decline have led to a diverse world population, at varied phases of the fertility transition with different age compositions and proportion of people in working age to bear the burden of intergenerational dependency. About a fifth of the world population with an average of three or more children per woman have to deal with the dependency of the large proportion of children. Most of the world is experiencing the demographic bonus of past higher but declining fertility rates that are feeding or maintaining a larger proportion of people in working age. The decline in fertility has reduced child dependency without as yet adding to old-age dependency. Yet others, are facing the aftermath of the demographic bonus that has reduced the proportion of people of working age while adding to old-age dependency.

These post fertility transition populations place greater demands on the productivity of people of working age and social mechanisms for intergenerational income transfers to maintain adequate standards of living. Diverse forms of social and political organisation present challenges to realise shifts from the traditional extended family to wider social intergenerational transfers to overcome inequalities in income and sustain adequate standards of living for the growing proportion of old-age people.

References

Arshat, H., Tan, A. T., Peng, T. N., & Subbiah, M. (1988). *Marriage & family formation in Peninsula Malaysia*. Kuala Lumpur: National Population and Family Development Board.

Becker, G. S. (1960). An economic analysis of fertility. In A. J. Coale (Ed.), *Demographic and economic change in developed countries*. Princeton, NJ: Princeton University Press.

Becker, G. S. (1995). *Human capital and poverty alleviation*. HROWP 52, March 1995. Washington DC: World Bank.

Bongaarts, J. (1978). The proximate determinants of fertility. *Population and Development Review, 3*(4), 278–325.

Coale, A. (1973). The demographic transition. In *Proceedings of the of the general population conference* (Vol. 1, pp. 53–72). Liege: International Union of for the Scientific Study of Population.

Coleman, D., & Basten, S. (2015). The death of the west: an alternative view. *Population Studies: A Journal of Demography, 69*(S1), S107–S118.

Commonwealth Bureau of Census and Statistics (CBCS). (1968). *Official year book of the Commonwealth of Australia No.54*. Canberra.

Davis, K., & Blake, J. (1956). Social structure and fertility: An analytical framework. *Economic Development and Cultural Change, 4*(1), 211–235.

Demeny, P. (2015). Sub-replacement fertility in national populations: Can it be raised? *Population Studies: A Journal of Demography, 69*(S1), S77–S85.

Easterlin, R. A. (1966). On the relation of economic factors to recent and projected fertility changes. *Demography, 1*, 131–153.

Easterlin, R. A. (1968). *Population, labor force, and the long swing in economic growth—The American experience*. New York: National Bureau of Economic Research.

Ehrlich, P. R. (1969). *The population bomb*. Ballantine.

Farabee, M. J. (2001a). *Introduction: The nature of science and biology*. Retrieved September 2, 2016, from www.emc.maricopa.edu/faculty/farabee/BIOBK/BioBookintro.html.

Farabee, M. J. (2001b). *Human genetics*. Retrieved September 2, 2016, from www.emc.maricopa.edu/faculty/farabee/BIOBK/Biohumgen.html.

Galloway, P., Lee, R., & Hammel, G. (1998). Infant mortality and the fertility transition: Macro evidence from Europe and new findings from Prussia. In M. Montgomery & B. Cohen (Eds.), *From death to birth: Mortality decline and reproductive change*. Washington DC: National Research Council.

Gille, H. (1957). An international survey of recent fertility trends. In *Demographic and economic change in developed countries*. New York: Columbia University. Retrieved September 9, 2015, from www.nber.org/chapters/c2381.

Hara, T. (2015). *A shrinking society—Post-demographic transition in Japan*. Tokyo: Springer.

Jeon, Y., & Shields, M. P. (2005). The Easterlin hypothesis in the recent experience of higher-income OECD countries: A panel-data approach. *Journal of Population Economics, 18*, 1–13.

Kaplan, H. S., & Lancaster, J. B. (2003). *An evolutionary and ecological analysis of human fertility, mating patterns and parental investment.* National Academy of Sciences. Retrieved January 27, 2016, from http://books.nap.edu.ctalog/10654.html.

Last, J. M. (1983). *A dictionary of epidemiology.* New York: Oxford University Press.

MacDonald, K. (Undated). *An evolutionary perspective on human fertility.* Long Beach CA: California State University. Retrieved January 27, 2016, from www.csulb.edu/~kmacd/fertility.html.

Macunovich, D. (1996). *Social security and retirees—An economist perspective.* Washington DC: National Academy of Social Insurance.

McFalls, J. A. (2003). Population: A lively introduction. *Population Bulletin, 58*(4).

Meadows, D. H., Meadows, D. L., Randers, J., & Behrens, W. W. (1972). *The limits of growth.* London: Pan Books.

Morgan, S. P. (2003). Is low fertility a twenty-first century demographic crisis? *Demography, 40*(4), 589–563.

Myrdal, G. (1968). *Asian drama: An inquiry into the poverty of nations* (Vol. II, 1424). Harmondsworth: Penguin Books.

Organisation for Economic Co-operation and Development (OECD). (2016). *OECD Factbook 2015–2016.* Paris. Retrieved September 12, 2016, from http://dx.doi.org/10.1787/factbook-2015-en.

Palloni, A., & Rafalimanana, H. (1999). The effects of infant mortality on fertility revisited; new evidence from Latin America. *Demography, 36*(1), 41–58.

Pampel, F. C., & Peters, H. E. (1995). The Easterlin effect. *Annual Review of Sociology, 1995*(25), 163–194.

Potter, J. E., Schmertmann, C. P., & Cavenaghi, S. M. (2002). Fertility and development: Evidence from Brazil. *Demography, 39*(4), 739–761.

Ray, D. (1998). *Development economics.* Princeton, NJ: Princeton University Press.

Robinson, W. C. (2003). Demographic history and theory as guides to the future of world population growth. *Genus,* LIX(3-4), 11–41.

Sen, A. (1999). *Development as freedom.* New York: Anchor Books.

Statistics Bureau of Japan (SBJ). (2016). *Statistical yearbook of Japan 2016.* Tokyo: Ministry of Internal Affairs.

Strassmann, B. I., & Gillespie, B. (2002). Life-history theory, fertility and reproductive success in humans. *Proceedings of the Royal Society of London, Series B: Biological Sciences, 269,* 553–562.

United Nations (UN). (2002). *World population prospects: The 2000 revision. Volume III—Analytical report.* New York: Population Division.

United Nations (UN). (2013). *World population prospects: The 2012 revision.* New York.

United Nations (UN). (2015). Trends in contraceptive use worldwide 2015. New York.

United Nations (UN). (2017). *World population prospects—The 2017 revision—Volume I: Comprehensive tables.* New York: Population Division.

United Nations Development Programme (UNDP). (2015). Human development report 2015. New York.

Van de Walle, F. (1986). Infant mortality and the European demographic transition. In A. J. Coale & S. C. Watkins (Eds.), *The decline of fertility in Europe.* Princeton, NJ: Princeton University Press.

Verena, G. (2004). Reproduction. Retrieved March 16, 2016, from http://csep1.phy.ornl.gov/mu/node4.html.

Chapter 4
Survival and Longevity

4.1 Necessity, Endowments, Knowledge and Organisation

Human survival and longevity have changed dramatically over time. The importance of food availability to survival has been the subject of considerable discussion. The influence of genetic endowments in the wider context of natural selection and evolution has also been considered important to survival. In addition, human knowledge, technical progress and social organisation combined to form a complex array of factors that have led to extensive changes in survival and longevity. Thus, a number of aspects needs to be examined to gain a better understanding of the changes that have taken place and their impact on human survival and longevity.

4.2 Nature and Nurture

The survival and growth of any species relies on its ability to reproduce. Humans need to survive for a period of time before they can breed. Thus, in addition to the capacity to reproduce (fecundity), humans need some longevity for their survival as a species. In this regard, there has been interest in the relative importance of genetic and social and environmental determinants on human survival: of nature or nurture. Humans could be described as survival machines, with limited life, for genes that use this vehicle for their replication from generation to generation. However, while individuals inherit genetic characteristics from their parents, characteristics acquired by them during their life time are not genetically transmitted from one generation to another (Dawkins 2006).

Studies of twins have shown that genetic inheritance account for 20–30% of differences in longevity. But the importance of genetic material on longevity rises somewhat with age, as trauma and other external causes of death become less frequent among old people (Herskind et al. 1996; Hjelmborg et al. 2006). It is

© Springer International Publishing AG, part of Springer Nature 2018   87
Jo. M. Martins et al., *Global Population in Transition*,
https://doi.org/10.1007/978-3-319-77362-9_4

apparent that some human characteristics may be more influenced by genetic inheritance than others but that social and environmental factors have a greater influence on longevity.

4.3   Survival and Food

4.3.1   FAD and FEE

Malthus stated the obvious that *food is necessary* for human life. His concern was the imbalance between population and food availability because of their different rates of growth. He posited that the tendency for a higher rate of population growth than food available led to an oscillation pattern of checks on population. This is a reflection of his perception of natural laws of homeostasis that led to a balance between population and food. The feedback mechanisms described by Malthus as misery and vice, and by implication increased mortality, kept population in balance with food available. He also thought that if early marriages prevailed in China and the country had a stationary population, as Adam Smith reported, then infanticide and famines were factors that kept China's population in check (Malthus [1798] 1970). Regardless of the accuracy of Adam Smith's perceptions and Malthus' surmising, famines have been experienced in China and other parts of the world with associated loss of life. Food availability decline (FAD) has often been the result of natural disasters or human-caused events, such as wars (Lancaster 1990). However, famines and hunger may be experienced even when there is sufficient food available to populations as a whole. This can occur when the relative prices of people's labour, commodities or possessions prevent their exchange for food (FEE —failure of exchange of entitlements) (Sen 1981).

4.3.2   Food and Surviving the Population Explosion

The rising pace of population growth since the 1700s was accompanied by improved agricultural practices and food production. The spread of the cultivation of potatoes, maize and tomatoes, among others, from the Americas also widened the range of and fostered the volume of food production. A degree of political stability, increased food production and related nutrition improved the chances of survival of European and Chinese populations. In contrast with Adam Smith's reported perception, China's population almost doubled in the 1800s (McNeill 1998).

The remarkable population growth after the Second World War posed the old Malthusian issue of the balance between population and food production. According to Brown (1970: 6–7) ...*Just prior to World War II, the countries of Asia, Africa and Latin America were exporting grain, mostly to Western Europe,*

Table 4.1 Rises in the production of cereals in India, Pakistan, Sri Lanka and Mexico, 1960–1968

Year	India wheat	Pakistan wheat	Sri Lanka rice	Mexico all cereals
Production per capita 1960 = 100				
1960	100	100	100	100
1968	143	133	123	137

Source Brown (1970). Computations made by the authors

where it earned valuable foreign exchange. After World War II, all these regions became net food importers, principally from the United States. Initially, agricultural surplus in countries such as the United States, Canada and Australia provided some of the relief to meet food deficits in developing countries such as India. However, the response to this challenge was the *Green Revolution* that introduced new seeds from research in the previous decade. The new seeds of rice and wheat required larger amounts of fertilizers but led to dramatic changes in yields and total production of cereals.

The production of wheat per head of population in India increased by about 43% in the 8-year period 1960–1968. Similar rises in production took place in some Asian and Latin American countries (Table 4.1). The food-supply challenge has not gone away, it has been most felt in Africa, where war and civil strife have led to a large number of refugees without their own food supply and disruption of the cultivation of land.

4.3.3 Survival and Food Security

Food security affects survival and longevity both directly and indirectly. Malnutrition often associated with poverty increases the risk of death of mothers and children. It also affects the capacity of children to learn, their physical development and levels of physical and social activity. This has an impact on future productivity, escape from poverty and survival chances (WB 1993).

Box 4.1 Factors influencing food security
Four major factors have been identified of relevance in attaining food security

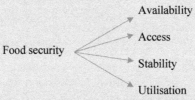

Availability depends on the level of food production, source and diversity of nutritional value. *Access* is related to transport available, relative price of food and related share of the household budget, and the adequacy of food consumption, especially by the poor.

Stability is concerned with the steadiness of sources of food, political stability, and civil order.

Utilization is manifested by the degree of wasting, stunting and under-weight in children, prevalence of anaemia in pregnant women and children, and the degree of deficiency of vitamin A and iodine, among other things, in the population.

Source FAO (2015).

Considerable progress has been made to mitigate malnutrition and, by impli-cation, improve survival and quality of life in recent years. The number of undernourished people in the world continues to be substantial but fell from about 1,011 million in 1990–1992 to 821 million in 2010–2012. This change was influenced by a number of factors that affected people differently in countries throughout the world. Most of the gains were in Asia and the Pacific countries, with some improvements in Latin America and the Caribbean, and Europe. However, the number of undernourished people actually rose in Africa and the Near East and North Africa (Table 4.2). Among other things, Africa and Near East and North Africa have experienced continued civil unrest and war. No doubt, this has had an impact on social and political stability and consequent availability, access and utilization of food (Box 4.1).

As expected, undernourishment is closely associated with the level of devel-opment. In spite of the improvement experienced by the least developed countries undernourishment prevailed among more than a quarter of their population (28%). It was about double that of other developing countries (14%) (Table 4.3).

Table 4.2 World number of undernourished people by region, 1990–1992 and 2010–2012

Region	Number of people undernourished (millions)		
	1990–1992	2010–2012	Change 1990–1992 2010–2012
Africa	175.7	205.7	+30.0
Asia and Pacific	726.2	525.4	−200.8
Europe and Central Asia	9.9	7.2	−2.7
Latin America and Caribbean	66.1	38.3	−27.8
Near East and North Africa	16.5	33.9	+17.4
World	1,010.6	820.7	−189.9

Source FAO (2015). Computations made by the authors

Table 4.3 World proportion of undernourished people by development status, 1990–1992 and 2010–2012

Country development status	Proportion of population undernourished (%)		
	1990–1992	2010–2012	Change 1990–1992 2010–2012
Developed	<5.0	<5.0	...
Least developed	40.0	27.7	−12.3
Other developing	23.3	14.1	−9.3
World	18.6	11.8	−6.8

Source FAO (2015)

4.4   Survival, Disease and Other Threats

4.4.1   Epidemiological Triangle

Disease poses a risk to human life, health and survival. Epidemiologists have developed a helpful concept to look at the cause and propagation of disease (especially communicable diseases) and human survival. It consists of three elements: agent, host and environment (Friis and Sellers 1996). The agent must be present for the condition to develop. But to be effective the agent must find a susceptible host. Another element in the triangle is the physical, weather, social and economic environment that can either foster or hinder the success of the agent and the susceptibility of the host (Fig. 4.1). The following discussion uses and adds to this framework to review some of the factors that affect human survival.

4.4.2   Disease Reservoirs and Hosts

Humans are a recent success-story in survival by lessening the chance of becoming food for disease-causing micro-organisms and threats by macro parasitism of carnivores and predators including humans themselves. These hazards arise from the reservoirs of disease organisms in soil, water, and air, food sources, insects, other vertebrates including humans (Friis and Sellers 1996; Lancaster 1990).

Fig. 4.1 The epidemiological triangle

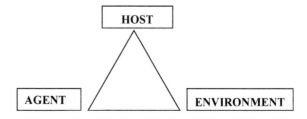

4.4.3   Agents

The threats may be agents of disease such as metals, chemical compounds, poisons and naturally occurring radiation. Soil contact exposes humans to microorganisms such as fungi, tetanus and anthrax. Water use places humans at the risk of cholera, schistosomiasis, and microorganisms that cause dysentery. Animal and other food sources also place humans at risk of botulism, Salmonella and E. coli infections. Some vertebrates are also reservoirs of microorganisms that may cause disease in humans, such as tuberculosis (bovine), rabies, plague, typhoid and brucellosis. Insects can be hosts to malaria, dengue, yellow fever and encephalitis. Humans themselves may be hosts to diseases that can be passed only from human to human such as the common cold, flu, measles, herpes, polio, hepatitis and smallpox (Friis and Sellers 1996; Lancaster 1990). Nevertheless, Diamond (1999) points out that some of these diseases may have originated in domestic or other animals and have become human diseases by mutation. Measles, tuberculosis and smallpox have close equivalents in cattle. Flu may have originated with pigs and ducks. Malaria may have come from birds. And more recently, HIV/AIDS might have been a mutation of viruses that infect monkeys.

4.4.4   Endowments and Modifiers

In terms of survival, humans have some genetic endowments that may be beneficial or not. Humans may inherit protection against some diseases. But they may be also born with congenital defects that affect their ability to survive. In-breeding in small, isolated populations contributes to this problem. Humans benefit from some acquired endowments, such as acquired immunity that protects them against viral and other disease agents. As noted, the adequacy of nutrition also greatly influences the body's resistance to disease agents.

4.4.5   Climate

The climate of a given area may encourage the survival of agents of disease or discourage them. For instance, malaria relies on favourable climatic conditions for the breeding of mosquitoes. Some types of bacteria and viruses also require favourable weather, thus the seasonality of some disease outbreaks.

4.4.6 Stressors

Family and social violence such as war may lead to traumatic experiences that result in death or disability of a temporary or permanent nature. Emotional shocks such as the loss of a family member may also affect the immune system and ability to thrive. Famines also interfere with both physical and intellectual functioning, and may lead to death. Natural disasters such as earthquakes, volcanic activity, storms and fires also result in death and/or disability.

4.4.7 Technologies

Technologies developed by humans modify and enhance their chances of survival. Tools have enlarged, among other things, the range of food sources and their exploitation. Nonetheless, tools have also been a source of injury. The domestication of plants and animals and their improved breeding has provided the basis for agriculture and more reliable and productive sources of food. However, domesticated animals have also been a source of health threats through zoonoses (diseases affecting humans from vertebrate hosts). The control and use of fire has allowed humans to cook food. It has provided heat during cold periods, and offered protection from predators, but it has also been a source of trauma and destruction of shelters. Improved shelter has shielded humans from the vagaries of weather. Clothing made from both animal and vegetable materials have protected humans from unfavourable weather. More adequate hygiene practices and sanitation have improved public health and contributed to survival. Medical technologies have also made a contribution to survival (McNeill 1998; Diamond 1999).

4.4.8 Human Wander and Travel

Technologies developed by humans led to improved transport, such as the use of the wheel and animal traction, the building of boats to transport people and goods, and for fishing. Improved production and specialization offered an opportunity for mutually beneficial trade. This increased human interaction also led to the spread of disease over greater distances.

4.4.9 Immunity, Fadeout, Perpetuation and Population Densities

Many disease agents provoke a reaction in the host that results in either death or the acquisition of immunity against the disease. In small, susceptible populations, many will not survive but those who do tend to be immune to the disease. This means that the agent will disappear (fadeout), or if a host is found that is not affected by the disease, such as animals and/or human carriers, it will wait for the next generation of people born without immunity to strike again. The shorter the period of the human contagious stage of a disease the larger the population required for the perpetuation of the disease in a given population. For instance, it is estimated that measles requires about 300,000 people to perpetuate itself in a given population (Lancaster 1990). Thus, some diseases have appeared and faded out because:

- they were not able to find an equilibrium point where they were able to keep the host alive long enough for the contamination of other individuals, or
- they killed all susceptible hosts and therefore ran out of a survival mechanism, or
- the contagious period was relatively short and scanty population density did not allow the agent to find enough susceptible hosts to survive (so just faded out).

4.5 Precarious Early Survival

4.5.1 Lack of Current Knowledge

It is difficult to assess the chances of survival in pre-historic times or even in early civilizations. It is also hazardous to guess what the major causes of death in those times were. Most evidence points to relatively short lives in pre-historic times and even during earlier civilizations.

4.5.2 Apparent Early Short Lives

According to Lancaster (1990) crude death rates of over 40 per thousand people were common in earlier times. Crude death rates over 45 per thousand usually result in declines in population, as fertility above 40 births per thousand is difficult to sustain. Life expectancy might have been as low as 25 years in pre-historic times. It might have improved to about 30 in classical Greece and early Roman times, and increased to about 35 in late Roman times (Table 4.4). Although some improvements might have been achieved, life expectancy is thought to have continued to be short with averages below 40 years of age during the Middle Ages.

Table 4.4 Crude death rates and life expectancy in early times

Era	CDR	Le
Pre-historic	56–40	18–25
Egyptian civilization	46	22
Greek and early Roman	40–33	25–30
Late Roman	39	35

Note (CDR) is the crude death rate or the number of deaths per thousand people. (Le) is the life expectancy or the average number of years people are expected to live at birth
Source Lancaster (1990)

4.5.3 Microbes, War and Trade

Infectious diseases were major cause of death. Some intestinal infections were endemic from contact with disease reservoirs in soil, water, food and other human beings. Some zoonoses were also major causes of disease and death. In tropical Africa and Asia, malaria is thought to have been a major cause of death. It spread to the Mediterranean area and also to Northern Europe as a summer disease. European colonization took it to the Americas. Some urban centres were large enough to perpetuate reservoirs of some infectious diseases, and poor hygienic conditions ensured negative natural increases in large cities. There was a continuing flow of people from rural areas to urban centres to replace those lost by disease. Tuberculosis seems to have been an important disease. Poor nutrition, hygiene and crowded housing have been associated with this major killer. Smallpox was another infectious disease that raged to epidemic proportions during classical times and the Middle Ages, to cause substantial mortality and even reductions in population. Like many other infectious diseases, it was taken to the Americas during European colonisation and might be one of the reasons for the decline in the population of indigenous people (McNeill 1998; Lancaster 1990).

War and trade also spread infectious diseases. Wars affect loss of life through various mechanisms:

- substantial armies brought a large number of disease carriers into contact with susceptible individuals
- crowded living conditions favoured the transmission of disease that often assumed epidemic proportions
- poor sanitation and hygienic conditions were also ideal for dysenteries and other intestinal conditions
- wars brought with them heavy destruction of human life not only of soldiers but also from the deliberate killing of civilian masses
- armies relied on the provision of food from occupied areas depriving the locals of their stores of food
- this was often made worse by the flight of rural populations that resulted in famines and made people more susceptible to communicable diseases (McNeill 1998; Lancaster 1990).

The caravan trade routes from China to Eastern Europe are thought to have been the pathway for the Black Death (bubonic plague). The plague reduced the population of China by about half and had a similar impact in the Middle East and Europe during the Middle Ages. Trading vessels were a major vehicle for the migration of the black rat that carries the fleas that transmit the plague bacillus. In some geographical areas, such as the Americas, the fleas found new hosts in local rodent populations (McNeill 1998).

4.6   Features of Mortality Decline

4.6.1   Improved Nutrition, Quarantine, Inoculation and Sanitation

Improved nutrition, at least in some parts of Europe, led to greater productivity and greater resistance to disease. Changes in the understanding of the causes of disease, and disease prevention methods and management also reduced epidemics. Until the 17th century, health status was thought to involve the equilibrium of the four humours of the body (black bile, blood, yellow bile and phlegm) corresponding to natural elements (earth, air, fire and water). A disequilibrium of the humours would cause illness (dyscrasia). Therapies usually consisted of purges, emetics to cause vomiting or loosing of sputum, bloodletting and sweating (Wingate 1972). This approach to disease was hardly helpful and might have even resulted in harm to those who were subjected to it.

The understanding that many diseases were caused by microorganisms spreading between people led to preventive measures, such as the quarantine of those affected to prevent the spread of the disease. The inoculation of people with low dosages of smallpox to prevent the disease seems to have been practiced in India and Asia as early as the 11th century. It became more widely practiced in Europe and the Americas in 19th century, with a reduction in mortality (McNeill 1998). The more scientific approach to infectious diseases of Pasteur, Koch, and others, led to the development and use of vaccines for the prevention of many infectious diseases. Improved knowledge about microorganisms and the spread of disease fostered the implementation of sanitary systems in urban centres that also diminished the transmission of disease from human and other wastes and improved the quality of the water supply (Lancaster 1990). These public health measures, added to the improved nutrition, substantially reduced of the burden of infectious disease and mortality in Europe and other areas of the world.

4.6.2 Effective Medicine

The influence of Galen—the Prince of Doctors—who lived in the 2nd century, and his theories on the cause of disease, was very pervasive and made medicine of doubtful benefit until changes took place in the understanding of the aetiology of disease (Wingate 1972).

The acceptance of the infection of humans by microorganisms had a major impact not just on the use of public health measures but also on the treatment of disease. The introduction of antiseptic methods in 1800s was a major step forward in the reduction of septic deaths in surgery and child birth. Isolation of people suffering from infectious diseases also had an impact on the spread of disease. Chemotherapy made some progress in 1800s with the use of quinine to treat malaria. Some analgesics were developed for the treatment of pain, such as aspirin that is now recognised as a drug with a wider impact than originally thought. Some antiseptic and anaesthetic drugs came into use at this time. Improved knowledge of anatomy and the management of haemorrhage helped the practice of surgery, child birth, and the treatment of trauma (Lancaster 1990).

4.7 Mortality Transition

4.7.1 Early Improvements in Survival

The impact on mortality and the chances of survival of the improvements in nutrition, the introduction of public health measures and less harmful medical practices, became noticeable in the 19th century. Statistical data is available for a number of European countries and Australia to show the trend towards lower crude death rates (Table 4.5).

Table 4.5 Crude death rates in selected countries, 1841–1850 to 1946–1950

Country	CDR					
	1841–1850	1861–1870	1881–1890	1901–1910	1921–1930	1946–1950
England and Wales	22.4	22.5	19.1	15.4	12.1	12.3
France	23.3	23.7	22.1	19.4	17.0	14.8
Netherlands	26.2	25.1	21.0	15.2	10.2	9.6
Spain	–	30.8	31.8	25.1	19.1	13.0
Sweden	20.6	20.2	17.0	14.9	12.1	10.4
Australia	–	16.6	15.3	11.2	9.4	9.9
Japan	–	–	–	–	20.7	13.6

Note (CDR) is crude death rate or the average annual number of deaths per thousand people. (–) Not available
Source Lancaster (1990)

Table 4.6 Death rates of children under five years of age in Sweden and England and Wales, 1851–1860 to 1921–1930

Years	Deaths per thousand children 0–4 years of age			
	Sweden		England and Wales	
	Males	Females	Males	Females
1851–1860	65	56	72	63
1871–1880	56	49	68	58
1891–1900	40	34	63	53
1911–1920	24	20	38	31
1921–1930	18	14	25	20
Change 1851–1860 1921–1930	−47	−42	−47	−43

Source Lancaster (1990)

In general, crude death rates show substantial declines after the 1861–1870 decade from above to below 20 deaths per thousand people. The fall in such countries as Spain and France occurred some decades later. Australia achieved rates below 20 deaths per thousand people by 1861–1870 possibly due to its younger population (Table 4.5). However, life expectancy data for later decades shows that survival in Australia was close to that observed in the Northern European countries and was better than that of England and Wales (Lancaster 1990).

Sweden and England and Wales were able to halve the mortality rate of children under 5 years of age during the second half of the 19th century (Table 4.6). This improved survival was observed prior to the fertility transition that gained root in European countries in the 20th century to complete their demographic transition.

4.7.2 Limited Early Diffusion of Survival Practices

It took considerable time for populations outside some European countries, and their offshoots such as Australia, New Zealand, Canada and the United Sates, to follow their success in improving chances of survival. Among them, India and to a lesser extent Sri Lanka had crude mortality rates two or three times higher than those of Australia, New Zealand, Canada and the United States in the period 1900–1930. In the Americas, Mexico had similar experience to that of Sri Lanka. Jamaica fared somewhat better but had crude death rates about twice as high as those of Australia in 1930 (Table 4.7). These examples of the disparity of mortality rates portrays inequalities in the starting point and pace of the mortality transition throughout the world.

Table 4.7 Mortality rates in selected populations, 1900–1930

Countries	CDR			
	1900	1910	1920	1930
Australia	12	11	10	9
New Zealand	9	10	10	9
Canada	16	13	13	11
United States	17	15	13	11
India	43[a]	44[a]	41[a]	34[a]
Sri Lanka	[b]	31[b]	30[b]	25[b]
Jamaica	22	23	26	17
Mexico	33	33	25	27

Note (CDR) is the crude death rate or the number of deaths per thousand people
[a]The figures for India are averages for 1891–1901, 1901–1911, 1911–1921 and 1921–1930
[b]The figures for Sri Lanka are averages for 1911–1915, 1916–1920, 1921–1925 and 1926–1930
Sources Mitchell (1993) Canada, Jamaica and Mexico; Meegama (1986) Sri Lanka; Das Gupta (1971) India; ABS (1988) Australia; CDC (undated) United States; SNZ (undated) New Zealand

4.7.3 Accelerating Pace of the Mortality Transition

In spite of time lags among countries, the decline in mortality that started in the 19th century continued in the 20th and now the 21st century. The average number of deaths per head of population in the world fell by more than half in the second half of the 20th century from about 19 deaths per thousand people in 1950–1955 to 8 per thousand in 2010–2015 (UN 2017).

In the period 1950–2015, the drop in the crude mortality rate was most pronounced in Africa and Asia that initially had the highest rates. However, it was also pronounced in Latin America and the Caribbean. The continuing decline in mortality in Europe is less apparent because of the ageing of the population. This is also a factor in Northern America and Oceania (Table 4.8).

The disparity in mortality rates, consequent survival, and number of years that people are expected to live in individual regions reflect differences in the stage of the mortality transition of different populations. By 2010–2015, populations in Northern America, Oceania and Europe had survival rates and consequent longevity much greater than those in Africa and Asia. The population of Latin America and the Caribbean had a smaller gap to bridge. However, the gains in longevity in Asia, Latin America and Caribbean and Africa that started their mortality transition later were much greater in the period 1950–2015. This meant a reduction in the gap in

Table 4.8 World mortality by region, 1950–2015

Years	CDR						
	Africa	Asia	Europe	Latin America	Northern America	Oceania	World
1950–1955	27	23	11	16	10	12	19
1970–1975	19	12	10	10	9	9	12
1990–1995	14	8	11	7	9	7	10
2010–2015	9	7	11	6	8	7	8
Change 1950–1955 2010–2015	−18	−16	–	−10	−2	−5	−11

Note (CDR) is the crude death rate or the number of deaths per thousand people. Latin America includes the Caribbean
Source UN (2017)

life expectancy between Northern America and Africa from 31 years in 1950–1955 to 19 in 2010–2015. The shrinking of the gap between Northern America and Asia was even greater from 27 to 7 years during the same period. On average, the world's life expectancy increased by 24 years in that period (Table 4.9).

As implied in the regional analysis, in spite of the gains made in survival and longevity, inequality continued to prevail between countries at different stages of development. But the gap between more and least developed countries declined by 13 years in the period 1950–1955 to 2010–2015. The gap between the more developed and other less developed countries, where most people live, narrowed even more by 14 years (Table 1.12).

Table 4.9 World life expectancy by region, 1950–2015

Years	Le						
	Africa	Asia	Europe	Latin America	Northern America	Oceania	World
1950–1955	38	42	64	51	69	62	47
1970–1975	47	57	71	61	72	67	58
1990–1995	52	65	73	68	76	73	65
2010–2015	60	72	77	75	79	78	71
Change 1950–1955 2010–2015	22	30	13	24	10	16	24

Note (Le) is the average number of years that people are expected to live at birth. Latin America includes the Caribbean
Source UN (2017)

4.7.4 Natural Increase and Stages of the Demographic Transition

The interaction between the starting time of the earlier mortality and the later fertility transitions that make up the demographic transition, led to changes in the natural increase rate (i.e. difference between birth and death rates) with consequent impact on the rate of population growth excluding migration.

Although on average, all countries in different stages of development have experienced a substantial fall in mortality, the additions to population have declined in more developed countries to a phase of demographic transition when birth and death rates are close to each other resulting in few additions to the population from natural increase by 2010–2015. The earlier decline in mortality and later fall in fertility in the least developed countries created its momentum and the rate of natural increase that had dropped by 1980–1985 was still higher in 2010–2015 than in 1950–1955. The dynamics of an earlier decline in fertility and sharper fall in mortality resulted in a much lower natural increase and the rate of additions to the population in other less developed countries during the same period (Fig. 4.2). The impact of the demographic transition on population growth is more pronounced when the natural increase for Europe is analysed. While in 1950–1955 natural increase was 10.3 per thousand people, it declined to a negative rate of 0.3 in 2010–2015 (Fig. 4.3).

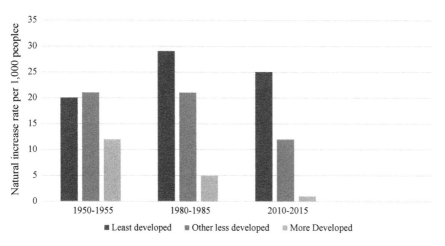

Fig. 4.2 Natural increase rate by stage of development 1950–1955, 1980–1985 and 2010–2015
Source UN (2017). Computations made by the authors

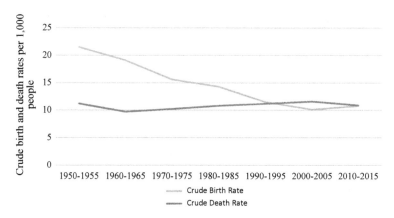

Fig. 4.3 Death and birth rates for Europe 1950–1955 to 2010–2015
Source UN (2017)

Box 4.2 Changes in causes of death: the epidemiological and demographic transitions

The Epidemiology Transition concept was put forward by Omran (1971). His basic premise is that changes occur in the pattern of mortality from infectious and non-infectious diseases. He described the transition in three major stages:

- *Age of pestilence and famine* when high mortality rates result in low life expectancy at birth to check population growth.
- *Age of receding pandemics* when life expectancy rises and population growth takes off.
- *Age of degenerative and made-made diseases* has longer life expectancy at birth with a stable population and growth dependent on fertility.

This implies a change in the proportion of deaths from different causes. Omran envisaged three models of the Epidemiological Transition.

One is the *Classical Model* of European countries that, through public health measures and medical management reduced mortality and degenerative/life style diseases displaced infectious diseases as the major causes of death. This is accompanied by a decline in population growth.

The second is the *Accelerated Epidemiological Transition* model that follows a similar path to the classical model but the time taken is much shorter as in the case of Japan. This model is also associated with a decline in fertility and control of population growth.

The third model is the *Delayed Epidemiological Transition* where social modernisation is delayed and public health and medical practices are eventually introduced but continued high fertility leads to large population growth.

One issue is how to distinguish between changes in mortality patterns because of the change in fertility and related age distribution and those changes due to improvements in the management of infectious and other diseases. Mortality follows an asymmetrical U-shaped age curve. In some cases, the riskier period of life is the first week after birth. Early childhood continues to be risky as the immune system fights disease agents and builds up immunity. From then on, mortality improves until it starts to rise again during adolescence. Thus, childhood is a period when humans are most venerable to infectious diseases while immunity is being developed by exposure. Many infectious diseases have become illnesses of childhood. Other important causes of death such as cardiovascular diseases and cancer tend to be the result of exposures and behaviours over periods of time, and are, in the main, diseases of adults. In addition, females are susceptible during their reproductive period to the risks of pregnancy and child birth.

4.7.5   Epidemiological Transition

Changes in knowledge and the application of public health and improved medical practices were factors in the steep fall in mortality. Associated changes in causes of death have been attributed to an Epidemiological Transition (Box 4.2). This is expressed in the proportion of deaths caused by infectious and non-communicable diseases. The analysis of age-specific mortality rates for Australia, a more developed country, and Peninsular Malaysia, at a different stage of development, provides two examples of the change in the relative importance of infectious and non-communicable diseases to the fall in mortality in these countries.

The method of analysis for each country is somewhat different because of the nature of the data available, but both display the effects of the Epidemiological Transition. The age-standardised analysis of mortality rates in Australia shows a substantial fall in overall mortality for both males and females from 1921 to 1991. A considerable contribution was the decline in infectious and respiratory diseases that made up about 9% of all causes in males in 1991 in comparison with 24% in 1921, with a comparable fall in the case of females. During the same period, there was an increase in mortality rates among males from cancer and circulatory diseases. This was not the case among females with a fall in the mortality rates from these causes. Nevertheless, the proportion of cancer and circulatory diseases rose substantially from 31 to 70% in the case of males and 36–73% in the case of females during the period (Table 4.10).

Although data for Peninsular Malaysia is less specific, the analysis of age-specific death rates in the period 1982–1990 reveals a fall in the aggregate mortality rates for all causes. However, it also shows a substantial decline in mortality rates from infectious diseases and a rise in death rates from cancer and heart attacks (Table 4.11).

Table 4.10 Australian age-standardised mortality rates by cause of death, 1921–1991

Causes of death	1921	1941	1961	1971	1981	1991
	Mortality rates per 100,000 people age-standardised 1991 Australian population					
Males						
Infectious/paras. and respiratory	417	242	125	134	103	84
Cancer and circulatory	544	814	956	985	807	618
Perinatal	54	43	20	17	7	5
Injury and poisoning	117	104	104	105	81	65
Other	601	374	333	120	111	113
All males	1,733	1,577	1,538	1,361	1,109	885
Females						
Infectious/paras. and respiratory	318	173	54	49	36	38
Cancer and circulatory	504	686	653	647	483	390
Perinatal	40	33	15	13	5	4
Injury and poisoning	34	40	42	46	30	25
Other	498	293	111	93	79	80
All females	1,394	1,255	875	848	633	537

Source AIHW (2002). Computations made by the authors

Table 4.11 Peninsular Malaysia changes in age-specific causes of death, 1982–1990

Causes of death	Change in age-specific mortality rates 1982–1990 (%)						
	Less than 1	1–14	15–29	30–44	45–69	60–64	65 and more
Infectious diseases and fever	−65.1	−60.3	−46.1	−46.1	−57.7	−59.4	
Cancer	−14.9	+20.0	+2.7	+17.3	+29.3	+28.9	
Heart attacks	+62.5	−23.6	−1.2	+18.2	+23.6	+37.5	
Injury and poisoning	−1.4	−27.1	−10.3	−0.4	−0.4	−11.4	
Other	−25.8	−22.0	−8.2	−7.8	−15.1	−31.6	
Old age (65 years and more)							−2.7
All causes	−36.3	−37.4	−14.9	−8.8	−11.3	−17.7	−2.7

Source Suleiman and Jegathesan (undated)

Box 4.3 Potential years of life lost and the burden of disease
One measure of the potential for survival and longevity is the *Potential Years of Life Lost* (PYLL). This concept involves the choice of a given age as the standard life expected. Then, the number of years of life lost due to mortality before the standard age is assessed. The standard might be life expectancy at birth in years of the population as a whole, that of a country with a long life

expectancy such as Japan, or what is the conventional working age of 15–65. There are a number of methods that can be used. One often adopted is

$$PYLL = \{[(d_i(S - x_i)]/\Sigma p_i\}$$

PYLL   Potential Years of Life Lost
S   standard age of potential survival in years
d_i number of deaths from population in age group (p_i)
x_i age of death (usually the mid-point of the age group (p_i)
Σp_i sum of population in age groups (p_i) below the standard age

The following table gives an example of the estimation of PYLL to 60 years of age given a number of deaths for each age group from birth to and including 59 years of age.

Age (years)	Age mid-point x_i	Years to age 60 $(S-x_i)$	No. deaths d_i	Years lost to 60 $d_i\,(S-x_i)$
0	0.5	59.5	1,309	7,7885.5
1–4	2	58	259	15,022
5–9	7.5	52.5	163	8,557.5
10–14	12.5	47.5	180	8,550
15–19	17.5	42.5	615	26,137.5
20–24	22.5	37.5	895	33,562.5
25–29	27.5	32.5	1,014	32,955
30–34	32.5	27.5	1,233	33,907.5
35–39	37.5	22.5	1,538	34,605
40–44	42.5	17.5	2,054	35,945
45–49	47.5	12.5	2,715	33,937.5
50–54	52.5	7.5	3,984	29,880
55–59	57.5	2.5	5,124	12,810
PYLL under 60 years of age				383,755
Population 0–60 years of age				16,039, 000
PYLL under 60 years of age per 1,000 people				23.9

Estimates can also be made for the contribution of each or some known causes if the number of deaths for that cause is known by age, and their proportion of the total PYLL.

The concept gives the same value to each death. However, the relative weight is determined by the number of years to the standard age selected. Thus, a death at a younger age has a weight of more years than a death at a later age. The concept does not also take into consideration that if a death is prevented from one cause, the surviving person can die from some other cause before the standard age is reached.

A derivation of the PYLL concept is the *Disability Adjusted Life Year* (DALY) (WHO 2013). This is concerned with the loss of health by a population taking into consideration years lost from disability from disease and other conditions in addition to the potential years of life lost through mortality.

$$DALY = YLL + YLD$$
$$YLL = N_{csat} * L_{sa}$$

N_{csat} number of deaths from cause by sex, age in year t
L_{sa} years of life lost by sex and age

$$YLD = I_{csat} * DW_{csa} * L_{csat}$$

I_{csat} number of incident cases for cause by sex and age
DW_{csa} disability weight of cause by age and sex
L_{csat} average duration by case in years for the cause by sex and age

This approach has been used to estimate the burden of disease from different causes in individual and groups of countries.

In accordance with the different models (or phases) of the epidemiological transition described by Omran (Box 4.2), the epidemiological transition has not progressed evenly among countries at different levels of development and progress tends to follow development expressed in terms of income per head of population. Years of life lost due to premature death is almost double when countries with high and low income levels are compared. Further, the higher the stage of development the lower the proportion of deaths from communicable diseases and the higher the proportion of non-communicable diseases (Table 4.12). This indicates a failure of human efforts to overcome communicable diseases in some less developed countries, and demonstrates the potential for future improvement in survival in countries where most people live in the world.

4.7.6 Survival and Healthy Lives

An important aspect to survival is the capacity to pursue both social and economic activities. A measure of this aspect is the healthy life expectancy at birth that measures the average number of years that people live in full health with the absence of disease or injury. On average, the number of years of healthy life are about 9 less than 71 years of life expectancy at birth. The gradient of health years of

Table 4.12 World years of life lost and causes of death by income level, 2012

	Country income level				
	Low	Lower middle	Upper middle	High	All
Years of life lost per 10,000 people	4.91	3.48	1.96	1.86	2.83
	Mortality cause as percentage of total years of life lost				
Cause of death					
Communicable and primary diseases	65.7	47.8	19.3	7.9	40.0
Non-communicable diseases	23.1	38.9	66.3	80.5	47.1
Injury	11.2	13.2	14.4	11.5	12.9
All causes	100.0	100.0	100.0	100.0	100.0

Note (Communicable and primary diseases) include infectious or contagious diseases, maternal causes, conditions arising from the perinatal period and nutritional deficiencies. (Years of life lost) is a measure of premature death based on a given standard of life expectancy at birth and the frequency of premature deaths and ages at which they occur (Box 4.3)
Source WHO (2015). Computations made by the authors

Table 4.13 World life expectancy and years of full health by country income level, 2013

Country income level	Years of life at birth	
	Le	Years of healthy life at birth
Low	62	53
Lower middle	66	57
Upper middle	74	66
High	79	70
World	71	62

Note (Le) is the average life expectancy at birth in years. (Years of healthy life at birth) is the average number of years of healthy life taking into account years in less than full health due to disease and injury
Source WHO (2015)

life follows closely the levels of income, with some gains in healthy life at the higher income levels (Table 4.13).

4.8 Survival, Health and Socio-economic Determinants

4.8.1 Survival and Development

The number of years of healthy life is one of the associations between longevity and development (Table 4.13). It has been shown that most of the gains in average life expectancy did not follow the order of development level. Least developed countries made substantial gains in life expectancy but not as much as other less developed countries, and the more developed countries made the least gains in life expectancy in the period from 1950–1955 to 2010–2015 (Table 1.12). In spite of the continuing gains in survival, the United Nations has assumed that substantial differences will prevail in the future (Table 1.17).

4.8.2 Survival and Income

In general terms, the association between the average income of countries and life expectancy has already been illustrated. Although, income per capita is important as it reflects capacity to access basic and other life needs, it does not fully explain differences in life expectancy. For instance, in early 2010s, the Philippines, with an income per capita (PPP $7,915) similar to that of Cuba (PPP $7,301), had a considerable lower life expectancy of 68 years compared with 79 in Cuba. At a higher income level, the United States with a larger income per capita (PPP $52,947) than Japan (PPP $36,927) had a substantial lower life expectancy (79 years) than Japan (84 years) (UNDP 2015).

The information available indicates that income tends to lose its relative power to explain additional years of life as it rises. There is evidence that there are other socioeconomic factors that are important determinants of health and longevity, such as literacy (Table 4.14). Further, poverty strongly correlates with health and survival because it influences the living and working conditions of poor people (WB 1993). A study of maternal and infant mortality in Malaysia indicated that income per se had little impact on health outcomes because of public health and other preventive services provided by transfers from the public sector (Hammer et al. 1995). This would suggest that income has a greater influence up to a given threshold. Social environment and support can also have an impact on health and survival. Poverty has been expressed as *capability deprivation* of a more fundamental nature than lowness of income which impact can be more variable (Sen 2000).

Table 4.14 World life expectancy, income and literacy by income level

Income level	Le (years)	GNI p.c. (PPP $)	Adult literacy (%)
Low	57	1,246	61
Middle	69	6,780	83
High	81	37,183	98
World	69	11,058	84
Low percentage of high	70	3	62

Note (Le) is the average life expectancy at birth in years in 2009. (GNI p.c.) is the gross national income per head of population in purchasing power parities for 2010. (Adult literacy) is the percentage of the literate population 15 years of age and over in 2005–2009
Source WB (2011). Computations made by the authors

4.8.3 Socio-economic Status, Survival and Health

A life-course approach to survival and health in Finland provided evidence that the socioeconomic environment in childhood had an influence on psychosocial characteristics of adults and their health behaviour and outcomes, and that socio-economic status (SES) depended to a great extent to SES origins. The study of life-course of poor parents, less education and lower paid jobs led to job and financial insecurity, more unemployment and work injury, poorer nutrition, and psychological distress in terms of hopelessness, hostile outlook, depression, males also exercised less, drank and smoked more (Lynch et al. 1997). According to Shaw et al. (1999: 211) ...*Whether we refer to mortality, morbidity, or self-reported health, and whichever indicator of socio-economic position we employ—income, class housing tenure, deprivation or education—we find that those who are worse off socio-economically have worse health.*

Box 4.4 Social determinants of health

The chances of survival, longevity and well-being are the result of a number of factors including genetic endowments, physical environment and the social environment. The latter influences individual responses and social and economic function with back up loops that determine access to education and health care as well as relative prosperity and well-being (Evans et al. 1994). The apparent association between country income per capita and life expectancy is a manifestation of the impact of socioeconomic inequalities on survival. However, a country income level per capita does not fully explain differences in survival and longevity among countries that abound in a confounding way, such in the case of United States with a substantially higher income per capita but a lower life expectancy than say Australia, New Zealand and Canada (UNDP 2015).

Furthermore, inequalities persist even within countries with average high income per capita reflecting socioeconomic inequalities among different groups in that society. A number of frameworks have been developed to examine the relationships between socioeconomic factors, health and survival. Evans et al. (1994) developed such a framework to examine some determinants of inequalities in health of populations. This approach was followed by the framework proposed in *Determinants of Health* by Wilkinson and Marmot (2003) published by the World Health Organization. They noted that recent new knowledge in human genetics helped to understand disease and the management of individual conditions, but posited that most general causes of disease that affect populations arise from the social environment. They proposed there were a number of social factors that influenced health outcomes.

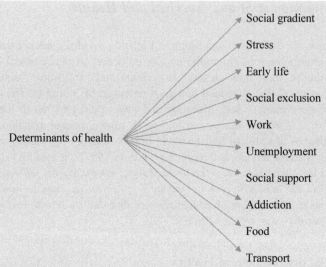

Social gradient is associated in an inverse relationship between social level and disease/premature mortality.

Stress at home, work or in a social context can affect health and result in premature death.

Early life environment affects early development and affect social functioning and work in adult life with an impact health.

Social exclusion with its associated characteristics of social discrimination, poverty, resentment causes poverty and has an impact on health and life expectancy.

Work differences may increase health risks and lack of control over work may lead to stress and health problems.

Unemployment can lead to stress, poor living conditions and risk of premature death.

Social support raises the level of emotional and practical resources that protect and promote health.

Addiction to alcohol, tobacco and drugs are associated with poor health outcomes and premature death.

Food supply at adequate levels promotes health while malnutrition leads to poor health. Excess and unbalanced diets have an impact on health and lead to premature death.

Transport can facilitate access to work and social interaction. However, it can also lead to lack of exercise, accidents and contribute to air pollution with deleterious effects on health.

Evidence was given for the impact of each of these factors on health and premature mortality.

> Although this framework was developed in the context of European societies with higher social development, it contains socioeconomic factors that affect survival and well-being in a more generic way.

Differences in health and survival have been observed in different countries when social determinants of health and survival were investigated (Box 4.4).

Differences in life expectancy and health according to social class in Belgium showed that people in lower social classes had lower life expectancies and an even greater number of years of disability (Table 4.15).

Similar differences in life expectancy were found in the United Kingdom for males in different social classes (Table 4.16). Among other examples, in Australia people in the quintile with relative greater socioeconomic disadvantage experienced about a third more premature mortality adjusted for disability than people in the quintile with the least relative disadvantage (Table 4.17). In the Australian context, indigenous people are particularly disadvantaged with lower birth weights, education and higher unemployment. This is associated with less balanced nutrition, tobacco and other substance use and their life expectancy is about 10 years behind the non-indigenous population (AIHW 2016).

Table 4.15 Differentials in life expectancy and unhealthy years in Belgium among social classes, 1990

Social class	Le	Unhealthy life expectancy during life time (years)
Life expectancy of high class	76.7	12.6
Difference between high and		
Middle	−2.0	+3.2
Low	−4.5	+8.0

Note (Le) is the average life expectancy at birth in years. (Unhealthy life expectancy during life time) is the average number of years of less than full health due to disease and injury
Source Van Oyen et al. (1994). Computations made by the authors

Table 4.16 Differentials in life expectancy of males in the United Kingdom among social classes, 1977–1981 and 1987–1991

Social class	Life expectancy at 15 years of age and differences (years)	
	1977–1981	1987–1991
Life expectancy classes I and II	58.8	60.5
Differences between I and II classes and		
III Non-manual	−1.9	−0.7
III Manual	−2.2	−2.4
IV and V	−3.7	−4.7

Note (Le) is the average life expectancy at 15 years of age
Source Shaw et al. (1999)

Table 4.17 Burden of disease and premature mortality by relative socio-economic disadvantage in Australia, 2011

Socioeconomic disadvantage quintile	DALY (000s)	DALY excess (%)
First	1,067	33.5
Second	1,020	28.2
Third	922	21.3
Fourth	800	13.3
Fifth	708	0.0
All	4,494	

Note (DALY) is the number of years of life lost and disability (Box 4.3). (DALY excess) is the percentage excess for the socioeconomic quintile if the age-specific rates were the same as those for the highest socioeconomic quintile. Each socio-economic quintile has the same number of people in the population. The socio-economic status is in accordance with the Index of Relative Socio-economic Disadvantage (IRSD) developed by the Australian Bureau of Statistics. People in each quintile are in IRSD order. The fifth quintile has the lowest and the first quintile the highest relative disadvantage
Source AIHW (2016)

This consistent inequality in health and premature mortality demonstrates the importance of social status and disadvantage to the capacity to survive and having a healthy life, with implications for social and economic functioning and wellbeing.

4.9 Survival and Longevity: Success and Dilemma

Humans have been a recent success story in survival in the planet's history. Poor nutrition, changing climatic conditions, disease, natural disasters and threats from other sources made human survival precarious. For thousands of years, human life expectancy was less than 30 years. High fertility rates of 40 births per thousand people were accompanied by similar death rates. Nutrition and reservoirs of infectious diseases had a major influence on human survival. Population size might increase or fall depending on circumstances.

About, 11,000 years ago, the advent of agriculture with the domestication of plants and animals made food production more abundant and reliable. This changed the nature of human settlement and provided an opportunity for specialisation and trade. However, these events also increased the chances of the propagation of infectious diseases that led to periods of population expansion and contraction due to epidemics, wars and famines. Larger population densities also favoured the perpetuation of many disease agents in humans. These factors constrained survival and population growth. This oscillation in population size was what Malthus saw as the natural law that balanced population size with the food available.

In the 18th century, major changes took place in both food production and the understanding of the sources and propagation of disease. These developments led to the implementation of public health measures that improved significantly the chances of survival in both urban and rural areas. Improvements in medical practice made it more effective. These advancements gave rise to a substantial decline in mortality in countries that applied the new public health measures and which benefited from improved nutrition and living conditions e.g. Europe, North America, Australia and New Zealand. This mortality transition gave rise to significant population growth from natural increase in these regions. At a later stage, greater child survival was associated with declines in fertility that led to a reduction in natural increase and eventually brought population growth to lower levels—the *demographic transition*.

The mortality transition spread to less developed countries—where most people live—in the 20th century, but falls in fertility lagged. The result was the doubling of the world's population in the hundred years from 1850 to 1950. A rise in fertility in more developed countries after the Second World War fuelled population growth further, and created its own momentum. The continuing rise in survival in most less developed countries was eventually followed by a decline in fertility in most of them. However, the momentum of a large number of people of reproductive age kept population growth at a high level and the world population almost rose three fold in the 65-year since 1950 to about 7.3 billion in 2015.

Survival was sustained by food production that expanded at a faster rate than population. It was also supported by other improvements in living conditions and the production of goods and services per head of population. Nevertheless, inequalities continue to prevail in terms survival and health conditions in countries at different stages of development and among socioeconomic groups within countries. Socio-economic disadvantage is a major factor affecting unequal levels of health and premature mortality in populations. It continues to pose major challenges to the improvement of the human condition.

Another important dilemma is the hefty addition to the world's population with longer lives. The growth in food production has had a major impact on the land use and the environment. The United Nations (2001) estimated that about a third of the world's forests have been converted to farm and other use, and that in the previous 150 years, about a third of the build-up of carbon dioxide in the atmosphere is attributed to deforestation. More intensive land use has led to soil erosion and salinization. Agricultural and population growth has placed strains on existing fresh water supplies. Growing urbanisation has further stressed the capacity of water and sanitation systems that harmed public health. The growth in the burning of fossil fuels for industrial, transport and domestic purposes has led to growth in emissions of carbon and sulphur dioxide with harmful impact on soil, animal and human health. The inevitable future growth in population will add to further crowding in areas with already high population densities. These and the catch up process implicit in the industrialisation of countries in less developed countries adds to the threats to anthropogenic emissions and wastes and pose risks to human survival.

References

Australian Bureau of Statistics (ABS). (1988). *Yearbook Australia 1988*. Canberra.
Australian Institute of Health and Welfare (AIHW). (2002). *Australia's health 2002*. Canberra.
Australian Institute of Health and Welfare (AIHW). (2016). *Australia's health 2016*. Canberra.
Brown, L. R. (1970). *Seeds of change*. New York: Praeger Publishers.
Center for Diseases Control and Prevention (CDC). (Undated). *Leading causes of death 1900–1998*. Retrieved September 19, 2016 from www.cdc.gov/nchs/data/dws/lead1900-98.pdf.
Das Gupta, P. (1971). Estimation of demographic measures for India 1881–1961 based on census age distribution. *Population Studies, 25*(3), 395–414.
Dawkins, R. (2006). *The selfish gene*. Oxford: Oxford University Press.
Diamond, J. (1999). *Guns, germs, and steel*. New York: W. W. Norton & Co.
Evans, R. G., Barer, M. L., & Marmor, R. (Eds.). (1994). *Why are some people healthy and other not? The determinants of health of populations*. Hawthorn NY: Walter de Gruyter Inc.
Food and Agriculture Organization (FAO). (2015). *The state of food insecurity in the world 2015*. Rome.
Friis, R. H., & Sellers, T. A. (1996). *Epidemiology for public health practice*. Gaithersburg: Aspen Publications.
Hammer, J. S., Nabi, I., & Cercone, J. A. (1995). Distributional effects of social sector expenditures in Malaysia, 1974–89. In D. van de Walle & K. Nead (Eds.), *Public spending and the poor—Theory and evidence*. Baltimore MD: Johns Hopkins University Press.
Herskind, A. M., McGue, M., Holm, N. V., Sorensen, T. I., Harvald, B., & Vaupel, J. W. (1996). The heritability of human longevity: A population-based study of 2872 Danish twin pairs born 1870–1900. *Human Genetics, 97*(3), 319–323.
Hjelmborg, J. V. B., Iachine, I., Skytthe, A., Vaupel, J. W., McGue, M., Koskenvuo, M., et al. (2006). Genetic influence on human lifespan and longevity. *Human Genetics, 119*, 312–321.
Lancaster, H. O. (1990). *Expectations of life*. New York: Springer.
Lynch, J. W., Kaplan, G. A., & Salomen, J. T. (1997). Why do poor people behave poorly? Variation in adult health behaviours and psychosocial characteristics by stages of the socioeconomic lifecourse. *Social Science and Medicine, 44*(6), 809–819.
Malthus, T. R. ([1798] 1980). *An essay on the principle of population*. Harmondsworth: Penguin Books.
McNeill, W. H. (1998). *Plagues and peoples*. New York: Anchor Books.
Meegama, S. A. (1986). *The mortality transition in Sri Lanka. In determinants of mortality change and differentials in developing countries: the five countries project*. New York: United Nations.
Mitchell, B. R. (1993). *International historical statistics—The Americas 1750–1988* (2nd ed.). New York: Stockton Press.
Omran, A. R. (1971). The epidemiological transition: A theory of the epidemiology of population change. *The Milbank Memorial Fund Quarterly, 49*(4), 509–538.
Sen, A. (1981). *Poverty and famines—An essay on entitlement and deprivation*. Oxford: Clarendon Press.
Sen, A. (2000). *Development as freedom*. New York: Anchor Books.
Shaw, M., Dorling, D., & Smith, D. (1999). Poverty, social exclusion, and minorities. In M. Marmot & R. G. Wilkinson (Eds.), *Social determinants of health*. Oxford: Oxford University Press.

Statistics New Zealand (SNZ). (undated). *Infoshare*. Retrieved September 23, 2016 from www.stats.govt.nz/infoshare.

Suleiman, A. B. & Jegathesan, M. (undated). *Health in Malaysia: Achievements and challenges*. Kuala Lumpur: Ministry of Health.

United Nations (UN). (2001). *Population, environment and development—The concise report*. New York.

United Nations (UN). (2017). *World population prospects—The 2017 revision—Volume I: Comprehensive tables*. New York: POopulation Division.

United Nations Development Programme (UNDP). (2015). *Human development report 2015*. New York.

Van Oyen, H., Rowlands, M. & Tafforeau, J. (1994). Regional inequities in health expectancy in Belgium. In C. Mathers, J. McCallum, & J.-M. Robine. (Eds.), *Advances in health expectancies*. Canberra: Australian Institute of Health and Welfare.

Wilkinson, R., & Marmot, M. (2003). *Social determinants of health—The solid facts* (2nd ed.). Copenhagen: World Health Organization.

Wingate, P. (1972). *The Penguin medical encyclopedia*. Harmondsworth: Penguin Books.

World Bank (WB). (1993). *World development report 1993*. New York.

World Bank (WB). (2011). *World development report 2012*. Washington DC.

World Health Organization (WHO). (2013). *WHO methods and data sources for global burden of disease estimates 2000–2011*. Geneva.

World Health Organization (WHO). (2015). *World health statistics 2015*. Geneva.

Chapter 5
Migration: Changing Flows and Views

5.1 Factors Affecting Migration

5.1.1 Out-of-Africa or Regional Origins

Migration has been a feature of human behaviour since pre-historic times. Evidence points to the origins of modern humans in Africa followed by their spread to other regions of the world. Regardless of whether the Out-of-Africa or Regional evolutionary theories are correct, it is apparent that Homo sapiens have spread from a point or points of origin to different parts of the planet (Chap. 1). Evidence indicates that humans moved during pre-historic times from Asia to Australia, the Americas and the Pacific Islands, and between Asia and Europe. However, it is likely that, as at present, most migration took place within regional boundaries. Migration was initially facilitated by the existence of land connections such as between Africa, Asia and Europe and North America and between Asia and Australia, but the invention of watercraft led to overseas flows. Improvements in the range and means of transport have made migration ever easier today.

5.1.2 Push and Pull Factors

Reasons for migration have been traditionally attributed to

- *push and*
- *pull factors*
  (Boswell and Crisp 2004).
  Push factors are those that reflect the physical, social and economic environment at the source. A major reason for migration is the availability of sources of food and other living resources. Accordingly, the *carrying capacity* concept might

© Springer International Publishing AG, part of Springer Nature 2018   117
Jo. M. Martins et al., *Global Population in Transition*,
https://doi.org/10.1007/978-3-319-77362-9_5

be used to explain why people move from one area to another. As the number of people rises or the sources of food are reduced, either because of environmental decay or exhaustion of existing resources, people may be forced to find new sources of food in other areas (Lewis 1963; Myrdal 1968).

Slash-and-burn agriculture in tropical climates has been a reason for people to move. As the soil becomes less fertile people move to another area that they can clear, burn and use the soil while it remains fertile (Brady 1996). This could lead to cyclical or circular migration and eventual return to the original area (Lawrence et al. 2010). Changes in climate that may make an area more or less accommodating to humans and sources of food, as happened during the Ice Ages, may also have a push or a pull effect (Piguet 2008).

Famines caused by wars, droughts and other natural disasters may also push people out of one area to another. Forceful migration may also take place when people are made to leave by marauding or occupying bands or tribes. Religious, political and ethnic discrimination and/or prosecution may also push people into migration. There may also be forced migration involving slavery, expulsion of minorities and transport of prisoners (Lewis 1963).

Pull factors are usually associated with incentives posed by the destination and tend to have an economic overtone. New fertile lands that can provide an improved source of food pull people to them. Industrialisation in the form of plantation-type of agriculture might offer higher incomes to unskilled people in low productivity farming in other countries, such as in the case of migrations to Fiji, Ceylon and Malaysia. The same applies to the setting up of mines (Myint 1967). Better climate, trade and better possibilities of employment and income have also been incentives for migration. Government incentives for migration from over populated to less populated areas are another stimulus to migration, as in the case of the encouragement of migration from Java to Sumatra and from more densely populated areas of the Philippines to Mindanao and in Sri Lanka to the Dry Zone (Myrdal 1968). However, the pull of work opportunities is a major factor and migrant workers constitute most of the migrant stock in recent times (ILO 2015).

5.1.3 Surplus Labour and Migration

One economic explanation of migration involves the concept of surplus labour and dual economies consisting of a traditional and a modern (industrial) sector. The proposition is that as population grows, the traditional sector becomes less efficient because the amount of land is fixed, and the output:worker ratio declines to a point where there is a surplus of labour. Traditionally, however, under-employed people will tend to continue to work on the land, and the larger number shares the available production. This constitutes the concept of *disguised-unemployment*.[1] It results in a

---

[1] The concept of "*disguised-unemployment*" also applies to the traditional service sector.

real difference in productivity between the traditional and the modern sector and incomes per capita in the traditional sector tend to be lower. The difference provides an incentive for people to move from rural-agricultural areas to urban-industrialised areas to secure higher per capita incomes (Ray 1998). This notion could be extended to differences in productivity and incomes in more and less developing countries, and incentives for international migration.

5.1.4 Labour Shortages

Industrial growth can lead to labour shortages and raise the price of labour in individual countries. Employers can use reservoirs of labour in less affluent countries to address their problems. By encouraging labour migration, employers can reduce the pressure on the price of labour and expand industrial production (Hirschman 2002; UN 2013a). In the past, the bulk of demand was for less skilled labour. The setting up of manufacturing in developing countries has shifted the demand for more skilled labour in developed countries (UN 2002, 2013a). The migration of skilled labour is not new: the migration of craftsmen, artists and other skilled people in short supply was common in the past.

5.1.5 Migrant Networks

The economic theories of migration have been criticised because they do not fully explain why people migrate (Hirschman 2002) in spite of the uncertainty of employment and the eventual equalization of labour prices in rural and urban areas (Ray 1998). A proposition is that because of a variety of factors, such as the push/pull and economic factors mentioned, some individuals take the leadership in migrating either on their own or family initiative. They then become the conduits for others to follow. Once started, family reunion and other factors maintain the flow of migrants from the point of origin to the destination. Migrants at the point of destination provide information and support to newcomers during their establishment period and also in times of need. These networks tend to link people at the point of origin and destination (Lewis 1963; Hirschman 2002; Boswell and Crisp 2004; UN 2013a). The new economics of migration have linked the concept of migrant networks with the economic interests of families. The suggestion is that families invest in migration of members of the family, as part of a diversification of risk, to ensure their future economic survival. The remittances of migrants are a return on this investment (Osaki 2003).

5.2 Social and Economic Effects

5.2.1 Forced Migration, Slavery, Transportation, Indenture and Trafficking

It is important to distinguish between forced and voluntary migration. Forced migration as a result of occupation of lands, slavery or forced transportation may benefit those who are left or came to the area of origin because they take over the resources of those who are forced to leave. However, it is unlikely to benefit those who are forcibly transported as slaves or prisoners. Nevertheless, forced migrants may provide labour to the benefit of people at the point of destination. This has been the case with slaves throughout history. The transport of slaves from Africa to the Americas from 16th to the 19th centuries is an example of large scale forced migration (Schroeder et al. 2009). Transported prisoners was another form of forced migration to the British colonies in North America and then to Australia after the United States independence (Braithwaite 1999). Those left behind may suffer from the loss of economic and physical protection provided by those who leave, but those who leave may eventually improve their lot in their new environment after their servitude is over. Forced migration may also have a structural demographic impact in the case of slaves and prisoners, as they tend to be male and young. They leave behind females and older males and lead to an inverse imbalance at the point of destination.

Indentured servitude was another form of migration to British North American colonies that involved servitude for a period of time in exchange for transport, shelter and subsistence during a contracted period (Tomlins 2001). Indentured workers became a substitute for slave labour in sugar and other plantations in Fiji, Sri Lanka, Malaya, after the abolition of slavery and led to the establishment of large ethnic minorities in those countries.

Refugees from pogroms, invasions and civil unrest also pose important social and economic questions. The impact of refugees on their hosts can be mixed. Much depends on local attitudes towards those who arrive, economic conditions prevailing and the numbers involved (Ditton 2012). Large numbers of refugees will require housing and other social amenities that may not be easily supplied, even under favourable economic conditions. These can lead to public and individual health problems and social tensions between hosts and refugees. In times of favourable economic conditions, refugees may provide a welcome additional source of labour, and not be seen as an economic problem to the hosts. They may also add to cultural diversity. However, in less favourable economic times refugees may add to the number of unemployed, and be seen as competing for the jobs available. Further, they can also be users of established welfare systems at the perceived cost of the local population, and cause resentment among the hosts (UN 1999). At the source, families often get broken up and physical and economic support weakened.

Legal restrictions imposed by receiving countries can lead to people smuggling and trafficking (UN 1999, 2002). Intended migrants may not reach their point of destination and may be left stranded elsewhere. Illegal migration and employment of illegal migrants in the reluctant host countries arises from the continuing demand for unskilled and cheap labour and legal restrictions that limit its access to these labour markets. It is apparent that the illegal status of these migrants increases their vulnerability (UN 1999), and they may be forced to accept lower pay, work in sweatshops or even lead them into prostitution (Boswell and Crisp 2004; Belanger 2014).

5.2.2 Worker Migration

Labour surplus and shortages have resulted in push-pull factors influencing migration from sending to receiving areas. In the past, worker migration was often of lesser skilled young males, who might have been followed by their families. These migrant flows can have a beneficial economic effect in both sending and receiving areas when it accommodates flows of workers from areas of low to higher productivity, as they will diminish disguised unemployment at the point of origin and might address labour shortages at the point of destination. They can also lead to migrant remittances to the point of origin that will improve the economic security of those left behind. However, it has been observed that the poorest people either do not migrate or migrate within small distances. This is attributed to a *poverty constraint* that prevents the poorest people from gaining access to sufficient funds involved in the move (Boswell and Crisp 2004). Thus, those in greatest need may be those less likely to benefit from migration. Migration presents risk and cost issues to potential migrants. In the absence of full knowledge, individuals who are risk-averse would likely to be more reluctant to migrate and individuals who have scarcer skills likely to gain most from migration in a higher paying country/area and would be more likely to migrate (Ray 1998). In more recent years, there have been some changes in the composition of worker migration, with a general demand for skilled workers in more developed countries, the destination of most migrant workers, but also an increase in the proportion of domestic female workers (UN 1999; OECD-UNDESA 2013; ILO 2015).

5.2.3 Brain Drain

Skilled people are in short supply in both more and less developed countries. The migration of skilled people to more developed ones, where the market price for their skill is higher has two aspects that might only be partly offset by any remittances that they might make to the point of origin. The first loss is the investment made by society in the human capital embodied in the person that migrates. The second is the withdrawal of scarce human capital from the production process, which may hinder productivity and development (Boswell and Crisp 2004). The migration of nurses and doctors from less to more developed countries is an example of this brain drain. However, similar effects are felt to the advantage of the receiving areas by students who have their education financed by families in the area of origin who do not return with their embodied human capital to their place of origin (Hirschman 2002). In recent years, the emigration rate of highly-skilled workers from developing countries was greater than the average; and in some small developing countries the number of highly skilled workers living in other countries can be larger than their number in the country of origin (OECD-UNDESA 2013).

5.2.4 Migrant Remittances

An aspect of migration that can have a positive effect at the point of origin is the remittances by migrants (UN 1999; Cooray 2012). These remittances to families can make a contribution to housing, nutrition, education of dependent children and support of the elderly. The remittances are often from developed to developing countries that suffer from exchange rates disadvantages. Thus, small amounts remitted can have an inflated value in the developing countries and may also make a significant impact on the balance of payments of developing countries (Boswell and Crisp 2004). Returning migrants may also bring with them savings that can be used for investments that increase the productivity of the land or improve the living conditions of families (UN 2013a).

5.2.5 Cultural Barriers

A major issue faced by both migrant and hosts are often differences in language, religion, eating habits and other cultural features such as family formation and relationships. Receiving countries have adopted different and at times changing stances regarding the integration of migrants. *Multiculturalism* allows migrants to keep their cultural traits and *assimilation* involves the civic integration of migrants into the main stream culture (UN 2013a). In any case, defensive mechanisms may institute barriers that discriminate against migrants leading to their lowered access to certain types of employment, inability to use their own language and restriction or even prohibition of religious practices. These practices lower the social and economic functioning of migrants and also prevent hosts from taking full advantage of the potential that migrants have to offer. They may cause social stress and mutual resentment (UN 1999). Cultural barriers can lead to the segregation of those affected from the mainstream and the creation of social enclaves where those discriminated against find support and a more comfortable environment. They may result in *China Towns* or *Little Saigons*. These can provide a safety valve for the expression of some cultural traits under controlled conditions. They also provide opportunities for host societies to share some of the benefits of migrant cultural traits without feeling threatened. However, they may not be a satisfactory solution to continuing cleavages in host societies.

5.2.6 Population Ageing and Migration

Declines in fertility in Europe below replacement level have led to population ageing. This has led to a perceived need for immigration to address imbalances in the age distribution and secure additions to people of working age. It is accepted that immigration may slow down the ageing process. However, bias in the age of migrants towards adulthood could be a long-term constraint, unless population growth takes place (Alho 2008).

5.3 Changing Views and Policies on International Migration

5.3.1 Government Policies on Immigration

Changing economic conditions in the 37-year period 1976–2013 led to shifts in policies about the benefits of immigration by receiving countries. In the early 1970s, buoyant economic conditions in Europe, United States, Canada and Australia made immigrants a welcome addition to the labour force. As economic conditions changed and unemployment increased during the late 1970s and 1980s, immigration to more developed countries was viewed as less beneficial, and in some cases, was seen as an unwelcome addition to the number of people unemployed. It was also felt that it gave rise to social stress, as immigrants were seen as competitors for the available jobs and as dependents on national welfare systems of the host country. Accordingly, the proportion of more developed countries that felt that levels of immigration should be maintained declined from 79% in 1976 to 38% in 1996, while the intention to lower immigration rose from 18 to 60% during the same period. As economic recovery took place in late 1990s and early 2000s the proportion that intended to raise immigration rose to 8% in 2005 in contrast with only 2% in 1996. Recovery from the Global Financial Crisis, and possibly concerns over population ageing in Europe, raised the proportion of more developed countries who wished to raise immigration further to 24% in 2013. Policies in less and least developed countries were possibly affected by other factors such as civil unrest and even wars. Accordingly, the proportion of both less and least developed countries wishing to lower their levels of immigration rose substantially between 1976 and 1996 and declined since then to 2013, especially among least developed countries (Table 5.1).

Table 5.1 Government policies on immigration by stage of development, 1976–2013

Immigration policies by stage of development	Years				
	1976	1986	1996	2005	2013
	Percentage of all countries				
Raise					
More developed	3	0	2	8	24
Less developed	9	5	5	5	7
Least developed	5	2	2	2	2
World	*7*	*4*	*4*	*6*	*11*
Maintain/no intervention					
More developed	79	62	38	79	63
Less developed	88	80	61	70	77
Least developed	93	90	71	78	90
World	*86*	*76*	*55*	*72*	*73*
Lower					
More developed	18	38	60	13	12
Less developed	3	15	34	25	16
Least developed	2	8	27	20	8
World	*7*	*20*	*40*	*22*	*15*

Note The total number of countries in the survey was 150, 164, 193, 194 and 196 respectively in 1976, 1986, 1996 and 2005 and 195 in 2013
Source UN (2013a)

5.3.2 Government Policies on Emigration

Shifts in government policies on emigration have been lesser than those on immigration.

The reasons for changes might arise from perceptions that emigration reflects either unfavourable economic conditions that should be rectified or social conditions pushing people into emigration. In some cases, there might also be a belief that emigration involves the loss of skilled people who are necessary for the country's economic and social development (UN 1999, 2013a).

The major policy changes in more developed countries took place in the 1990s when there was an increase in the proportion to lower the level of emigration from 12% in 1986 to 25% in 1996. This proportion fell to 16% in 2013 that is similar to the level in 1976 (15%). Another shift was the proportion of less and least developed countries that decided to encourage emigration from about 3% and 2% respectively in 1996 to 14% and 17% in 2013 (Table 5.2). The timing of the policy shifts was different in the more and the less developed countries. The major shift in the more developed countries took place in the late 1980s and 1990s, while the shift in the less developed countries occurred earlier in 1980s and then latter in 2000s. It is difficult to document the reasons for the early shift in policy related to emigration in less developed countries. However, the late 1970s and early 1980s saw a major

Table 5.2 Government policies on emigration by stage of development, 1976–2013

Emigration policies by stage of development	Years				
	1976	1986	1996	2005	2013
	Percentage of all countries				
Raise					
More developed	3	6	2	0	0
Less developed	4	5	3	8	14
Least developed	0	0	2	8	17
World	*4*	*5*	*3*	*6*	*10*
Maintain/no intervention					
More developed	82	82	73	83	84
Less developed	84	71	74	68	58
Least developed	93	81	80	74	67
World	*83*	*73*	*74*	*72*	*64*
Lower					
More developed	15	12	25	17	16
Less developed	12	25	23	25	29
Least developed	7	19	18	18	17
World	*13*	*22*	*23*	*23*	*26*

Note The total number of countries in the survey was 150, 164, 193, 194 and 196 respectively in 1976, 1986, 1996 and 2005 and 195 in 2013
Source UN (2013a)

upsurge in the number of refugees from developing countries arising from unstable social conditions (UN 2002). There was also a rise in the concern with the conditions of emigrants at the point of destination (UN 1999). Improved economic conditions seem to have influenced the change in more developed countries from 1996 to 2013 (Table 5.2).

5.4   Taxonomy and Information

5.4.1   Definitions and Taxonomy

The assessment of the extent and nature of migration is made difficult by the lack of a worldwide consensus on definitions of who is a migrant. A number of concepts are used in defining migrants. Sometimes differences in nationality are used, in others changes in country of permanent residence might be the criteria. However,

- *citizenship*
- *place of birth*
- *previous residence*
- *length of stay in a country*
- *purpose of the stay*

all might have a bearing on the definition of what constitutes a migrant. A problem is the lack of consistency in the application of set criteria (UN 2002).

The United Nations has proposed that a long-term migrant be defined as *a person who moves to a country other than his or her usual residence for a period of at least a year and short-term migrant as a person who moves for at least three months but less than a year* (UN 2002). Further, the United Nations has used four different classifications of migrants

- *labour*
- *family*
- *refugees and asylum seekers*
- *undocumented*

However, these classifications can be used differently in varying countries. This makes the measurement of the different components of migrant flows a hazardous task. Therefore, the measurement of migrant flows and stocks has to rely on estimates of varying quality (UN 2002).

5.4.2 Sources of Data

A varied number of sources are used in the classification and assessment of migrant stocks and flows. These sources vary from country to country depending on administrative arrangements. These may include:

- *registers of population and foreigners*
- *administrative sources concerned with residence and work permits, visas and exit clearances*
- *information collected at borders and points of entry/exit concerned with international travel*
- *population census, household and other surveys of the population* (UN 2002)

All these sources have strengths and problems. Although the number of deportations may give some idea of the minimum dimensions of illegal migrants, it is obvious that illegal migrants are difficult to enumerate. Illegal migrants are also likely to avoid being identified by census and household surveys because of their legal status. Some countries have reasonable mechanisms to count inflows but are less concerned with outflows leading to the possibility of great overestimation of net flows or addition to the stock of migrants (UN 2002). Accordingly, in addition to problems with definitions there are also problems with the sources of data on which estimates of migrant flows and stocks rely. Nevertheless, most countries make an effort to estimate such flows and rely on census, surveys and registers to estimate the stocks of migrants.

5.5 Stocks and Flows

5.5.1 Where Are the Immigrants?

The United Nations has estimated that there were 244 million immigrants in the world in 2015. This was the equivalent of 3% of the world's population at that time. The stock of immigrants rose by 89.5 million people in the 25-year period 1990–2015. This represented an average annual growth rate of 1.8% during the period that was higher than the average growth rate of the world population. The largest stocks of immigrants were in Europe (31%) and Asia (31%) followed by Northern America (22%). The largest rates of growth were in Northern America (2.7% p.a.) and Oceania (2.2% p.a.) (Table 5.3). It is relevant that a large proportion of immigrants in Europe was partly due to the dismemberment of the Soviet Union. Previously to this event, people moving inside the Soviet Union were not classified as immigrants, but once their republics of origin became separate countries they were newly classified as such (UN 2002). However, it is evident that the pace of immigration has grown substantially in Europe (UN 2016). Some of the changes in Africa and Asia from 1990 to 2000 reflected a greater degree of stability in the two regions during this period that allowed the return of refugees to their country of origin (UN 2002) (Table 5.4).

The pulling effect of the higher price for labour, social and economic security resulted in the more developed countries hosting about 59% of the world's migrants[2] in 2015 (Table 5.5). While migrants represented only 2% of the population in less developed countries, they made up 10% of the population of more developed countries. The share of the world's stock of migrants in less developed countries was reduced from 47% in 1990 to 41% in 2015 (Table 5.5), with compensating increases in the proportion hosted by the more developed countries during that period. Financial crisis in some developing countries in late 1990s, improved economic conditions in more developed countries and also security issues in the country of origin of some migrants were some of the reasons for the changes.

A review of the net flow of migrants since 1950 shows some changes in the origin and destination of migrants. While Africa and Latin America and the Caribbean were net senders of migrants from 1950 to 2010 and Northern America and Oceania were net receivers, Europe that was a net sender in the decade 1950–1960 became a net receiver in the decade 1970–1980, as socioeconomic conditions improved in Europe and fertility declined, and Asia that was a net receiver in the two decades from 1950 to 1970, partly due to inflows to the Middle East oil countries, became a net sender in the following decades to 2010, in spite of the continuing net inflow of migrant workers to high-income oil countries (Table 5.4).

The destination of most migrants to the more developed countries in Europe, Northern America and Oceania led to migrants becoming a larger and increasing proportion of the population in 2015 in Oceania (21%), Northern America (15%)

---

[2]The term migrant is used as proxy for immigrant.

Table 5.3 Distribution of the world immigrant population by region, 1990–2015

Region	Immigrants (Millions)				Percentage of total			
	1990	2000	2010	2015	1990	2000	2010	2015
Africa	15.6	14.8	17.1	20.6	10.1	8.6	7.7	8.5
Asia	49.9	49.3	67.8	75.1	32.4	28.5	30.7	30.8
Europe	49.0	56.3	69.2	76.1	31.8	32.6	31.4	31.2
Lat. Am. and Car.	7.1	6.6	8.1	9.2	4.6	3.8	3.7	3.8
Northern America	27.8	40.4	51.2	54.5	18.0	23.4	23.2	22.4
Oceania	4.7	5.4	7.3	8.1	3.0	3.1	3.3	3.3
World stock	154.2	172.7	220.7	243.7	100.0	100.0	100.0	100.0

Note Figures may not add due to rounding
Sources UN (2013b, 2016). Computations made by the authors

Table 5.4 World net migrant flows by region and stage of development, 1950–1960 to 2000–2010

Region and stage of development	Average net number of migrants per year (thousands)					
	1950–1960	1960–1970	1970–1980	1980–1990	1990–2000	2000–2010
Africa	−101	−185	−487	−501	−443	−388
Asia	116	12	−319	−294	−1,334	−1,780
Europe	−427	41	414	525	960	1,866
Lat. America and Car.	−80	−318	−439	−708	−707	−1,155
Northern America	403	324	792	880	1,438	1,282
Oceania	89	126	39	98	87	175
More developed	29	601	1,307	1,475	2,548	3,455
Less developed	−29	−601	−1,307	−1,475	−2,548	−3,455

Source UN (2013c)

Table 5.5 Distribution of the world immigrant population by stage of development, 1990–2015

Stage of development	Immigrants (Millions)				Percentage of total			
	1990	2000	2010	2015	1990	2000	2010	2015
More developed	82.3	101.4	129.7	143.5	53.4	58.7	58.8	58.9
Less developed	71.9	71.3	91.0	100.2	46.6	41.3	41.2	41.1
World stock	154.2	172.7	220.7	243.7	100.0	100.0	100.0	100.0

Note Figures may not add due to rounding. The figures for 2015 are a guess-estimate based on available information
Sources UN (2013b, 2016). Computations made by the authors

and Europe (10%) than in counties in Africa, Asia and Latin America and the Caribbean where migrants made up 2% of the population (Table 5.6). The United States and Canada in Northern America and Australia and New Zealand in Oceania are countries that have growing populations fuelled by immigration that at times adds more people than natural increase (e.g. Australia).

The implicit preferred destination of most migrants meant that their proportion of the population in more developed countries rose from 7% in 1990 to 12% in 2015, while it fell slightly at less than 2% in less developed countries during the same period (Table 5.7).

An analysis of the stock of migrants in 2013, according to their region of origin and destination, shows that most migration tends to take place within each regional boundary. The exceptions being Northern America and Latin America and the Caribbean that have each other as their major destination. The flows indicate that Northern America was the largest net gainer of population from migration followed by Europe and Oceania, while Latin America and the Caribbean and Asia and Africa lost population due to the emigration of their people (Table 5.8).

Further examination of the origin and destination of the stock of migrants in 2013 outside their region of origin identifies migration corridors from one region to another. The importance of Northern America as a major destination as indicated before is apparent. It is also clear that Northern America and Oceania were relatively small sources of interregional migration, while Asia and Latin America and the Caribbean were the largest regions of origin of migrants to other regions, followed by Europe and Africa (Table 5.9).

The major destination from Africa was Europe (56%), followed by Asia (28%) and Northern America (13%). Europe (48%) and Northern America (41%) were the

Table 5.6 Immigrants as a proportion of the population by region, 1990–2015

Region	Immigrants as percentage of population			
	1990	2000	2010	2015
Africa	2.5	2.1	1.9	1.7
Asia	1.6	1.4	1.5	1.7
Europe	6.8	7.9	9.5	10.3
Lat. America and Car.	1.6	1.2	1.3	1.4
Northern America	9.8	12.7	14.2	15.2
Oceania	16.2	16.1	16.8	20.6
World average	2.9	2.9	3.1	3.3

Sources UN (2012, 2016). Computations made by the authors

Table 5.7 Immigrants as a proportion of the population by stage of development, 1990–2015

Stage of development	Immigrants as percentage of population			
	1990	2000	2010	2015
More developed	7.2	8.7	10.3	12.0
Less developed	1.8	1.5	1.5	1.5
World average	2.9	2.9	3.1	3.3

Note The figures for 2015 are a guess-estimate based on the information available

Sources UN (2012, 2016). Computations made by the authors

Table 5.8 Origin and destination of the stock of immigrants by region, 2013

Destination	Origin (millions)								Net gain/loss
	Africa	Asia	Europe	LAC	NA	Oceania	Uncertain	World	
Africa	*15.3*	1.1	0.8	0.0	0.1	0.0	1.4	18.6	−12.3
Asia	4.4	*54.0*	7.6	0.7	0.6	0.1	*3.6*	70.8	−21.8
Europe	8.7	18.7	*37.9*	4.5	1.0	0.3	1.5	72.4	+13.9
LAC	0.0	0.3	1.2	5.4	*1.3*	0.0	0.2	8.5	−28.2
NA	2.0	15.7	7.9	*25.9*	1.2	0.3	0.0	53.1	+48.8
Oceania	0.5	2.9	3.1	0.1	0.2	*1.1*	0.1	7.9	+6.1
World	30.9	92.6	58.5	36.7	4.3	1.8	6.7	231.5	

Note LAC Latin America and Caribbean, *NA* Northern America. Uncertain are the number of immigrants whose origin is not known. The net gain/loss column is the difference between the number received and sent. Figures may not add due to rounding
Source UN (2013b). Computations made by the authors

Table 5.9 Origin and destination of interregional migration by region, 2013

Destination	Origin of interregional migrant stock					
	Africa	Asia	Europe	LAC	NA	Oceania
Immigrants (millions)	15.6	38.7	20.6	31.2	3.2	0.7
	Percentage					
Africa		2.8	3.9	0.0	3.1	0.0
Asia	28.2		36.9	2.2	18.8	14.3
Europe	55.8	48.3		14.4	31.3	42.9
LAC	0.0	0.8	5.8		40.6	0.0
NA	12.8	40.6	38.3	83.0		42.9
Oceania	3.2	7.5	15.0	0.3	6.3	
World	100.0	100.0	100.0	100.0	100.0	100.0

Note LAC Latin America and Caribbean, *NA* Northern America. Figures may not add due to rounding
Source Table 5.8. Computations made by the authors

major destinations for migrants from Asia, with Oceania (8%) as a smaller player. Migrants from Europe had Northern America (38%) and Asia (37%), with Oceania (15%) in a lesser role, as major destinations. The major destination for migrants from Northern America were Latin America and the Caribbean (41%) followed by Europe (31%) and Asia to a lesser extent (19%). The major destination of migrants from Latin America and the Caribbean was Northern America (83%), with Europe attracting a lower proportion (14%). Migration from Oceania was mostly to two regions namely Europe and Northern America (each 43% of the total) (Table 5.9).

5.5.2 Largest Migrant Hosts

The migrant corridors apparent in the analysis of 2013 data of origin and destination of migrants gives some indication of the largest hosts of the world's migrant stock. Accordingly, the United States was the largest host country with 19% of the world migrant population in 2015. Other traditional receiving countries such as Canada (3%) and Australia (3%) also had significant but lower proportions of the total migrant population. However, some European countries that in the past were senders of people became large hosts in more recent decades, such as Germany (5%), the United Kingdom (4%), Spain (2%) and Italy (2%). As stated earlier, the dismemberment of the Soviet Union led to Russia (5%), the Ukraine (2%) and Kazakhstan (1%) being large hosts to migrants from previous Soviet republics in 2015. Saudi Arabia (4%) and the United Arab Emirates (3%), two major oil producing countries, also had large migrant worker populations. India (2%) and Pakistan (2%) have been hosts to refugees from neighbour countries due to social disruption and wars. South Africa (1%) is another country that became a large host to people from neighbour countries also going through economic and social unrest (Table 5.10).

The attraction of the United States as a destination for migrants is obvious from the analysis of the stock of migrants from Mexico, China and India. The large number of migrants from within the old Soviet Union in Russia, Ukraine and Kazakhstan is also apparent. Similarly, the partition of British India that eventually became Pakistan, India and Bangladesh is no doubt relevant to the number of migrants in these countries. The increasing importance of work offered in the United Arab Emirates to migrants from India is also clear. The same applies to Germany to migrants from Poland. The possible push from unrest in Afghanistan, Palestine and Myanmar respectively to Iran, Jordan and Thailand is also reflected in the number of migrants in the countries of destination (Table 5.11).

Countries with the highest proportion of migrants in their populations in 2015 (Table 5.12) could be classified into five major groups

- *Middle East oil countries that have recruited both skilled and unskilled labour*
- *Middle East countries with refugees from social and civil war unrest*
- *Traditional receiving countries with active migration programs*
- *Other countries with labour shortages*
- *Those that arose from the dismemberment of the Soviet Union*

Table 5.10 Fifteen countries with largest immigrant populations, 2015

Country	Migrants	
	People (millions)	Percentage world total
United States of America	46.6	19.1
Germany	12	4.9
Russian Federation	11.6	4.8
Saudi Arabia	10.2	4.2
United Kingdom	8.5	3.5
United Arab Emirates	8.1	3.3
Canada	7.8	3.2
Australia	6.8	2.8
Spain	5.9	2.4
Italy	5.8	2.4
India	5.2	2.1
Ukraine	4.8	2
Pakistan	3.6	1.5
Kazakhstan	3.5	1.4
South Africa	3.1	1.3
Other	100.1	41.1
World	243.6	100.0

Note Figures may not add up due to rounding
Source UN (2016). Computations made by the authors

Table 5.11 Fifteen countries/territories with single largest number of migrants from a single country of origin, 2000 and 2015

Country		Migrants (millions)	
Origin	Destination	2000	2015
Mexico	United States	9	12
China	United States	1	2
India	United States	1	2
India	United Arab Emirates	1	3
Poland	Germany	1	2
Russia	Ukraine	4	3
Russia	Kazakhstan	2	2
Ukraine	Russia	4	3
Kazakhstan	Russia	3	3
Bangladesh	India	4	3
India	Pakistan	2	2
China	Hong Kong	2	2
Afghanistan	Iran	2	2
Palestine	Jordan	1	2
Myanmar	Thailand	1	2

Source UN (2016)

Table 5.12 Fifteen countries with largest proportion of immigrants, 2015

Country	Migrants as a percentage of country total population	
	2000	2015
United Arab Emirates	80	88
Qatar	61	75
Kuwait	58	74
Bahrain	36	51
Singapore	34	45
Jordan	40	41
Oman	28	41
Lebanon	21	34
Saudi Arabia	25	32
Switzerland	22	29
Australia	23	28
Israel	31	25
New Zealand	18	23
Canada	18	22
Kazakhstan	19	20

Note The table includes countries with one million people or more
Source UN (2016)

Israel with 25% of its population made up of migrants is a special case. It was created after World War II as a home of a particular cultural group, and has been a receiving country since then. The United Arab Emirates (88%), Qatar (75%), Kuwait (74%), Bahrain (51%), Oman (41%) and Saudi Arabia (32%) are oil producing countries that recruit both skilled and unskilled workers. These six countries have attracted in addition to migrants from neighbour countries such as Egypt, Yemen and Jordanians/Palestinians, a large number of Indians, Pakistanis, Bangladeshis, Filipinos and Sri Lankans (Kapiszewski 2006). Jordan (41%) and Lebanon (34%) have been hosts to refugees from Middle East unrest. Australia (28%), New Zealand (23%) and Canada (22%) have active immigration programs. Singapore (45%) and Switzerland (29%) are countries with small populations and low fertility and substantial economic growth that found themselves short of labour. Kazakhstan (20%) is a country that arose from the disbarment of the Soviet Union and has a substantial proportion of people who originated from other former Soviet republics.

5.5.3   Characteristics of Migrant Stocks and Flows

Data on international migration tends to rely on the assessment of existing stocks of migrants. However, while stocks are a measure at a point in time flows take place over a period of time. This has an implication for the estimation of actual flows to and from over time, as the stock at a given point in time is obviously the result of net migration over time. Thus, the assessment of actual flows is quite precarious and tends to be underestimated when the assessment relies on the destination and origin of the stock of migrants at a point in time. Both Canada and Australia with active immigration programs and relevant statistics give examples of the underestimation of actual flows. It was estimated that Canada's net migration over the 5-year period of 1996–2001 added 841,000 people to that country's population. However, this net figure glossed over that actual flows amounted to 1,593,000 people made up of immigrants (1,217,000) and emigrants (376,000) (SC 2005). Similarly, estimated net overseas migration added 124,000 people to the Australian population in the year 2004–05. Nevertheless, this figure was the result of considerably higher flows of permanent and long-term arrivals (431,000) and departures (307,000) (ABS 2008).

5.6   Age and Sex of Migrants

The median age of international migrant population was 39 years in 2015 (UN 2016). The median age is affected by a number of considerations such as the proportion of children, usually associated with refugees, work migration that tends to involve a lower proportion of children and older people, as well as the proportion of migrants that return to the country of origin in older ages (UN 2012).

Accordingly, the proportion of younger people under 20 years of age in 2010 was substantially higher in less developed countries (23%) where the proportion of refugees was higher than in more developed ones (10%). This was also the case in Africa (28%) and lower in worker-pulling countries in Northern America (10%), Europe (11%) and Oceania (11%). In a complementary manner, the proportion of migrants of working age (20–64 years) was much higher in countries in Northern America (79%), Europe (75%) and Oceania (71%) than in Africa (67%), Asia (68%) and Latin America and the Caribbean (65%). Usually, aged people do not migrate for work purposes. However, those of working age who migrate will tend to age over time and add to the stock of aged people in the country of destination, unless they return to the country of origin after retirement. In some cases, programs concerned with migrant family reunion may also add to the number of aged migrants. Oceania with the largest proportion of migrants in its population among the regions (Table 5.6), also had the largest proportion of aged people in its stock of migrants (18%) compared with the world average of 12% and even larger than the average of 13% in more developed countries. In contrast, only 4% of the migrate stock in Africa was aged 65 years and over. Accordingly, migrants in the worker-pulling regions of Europe, Northern America and Oceania had considerably higher median ages of respectively 42, 42 and 46 years than Africa (30 years), Asia (35 years) and Latin America and the Caribbean (37 years) (Table 5.13).

In general terms, the proportion of migrants in younger ages below 25 years tends to be lower than the proportion of people of this age in the total population, and the proportion of migrants in ages 25 and over tends to be higher than the proportion in the total population (UN 2012).

Table 5.13 Age distribution of the stock of immigrants by region and stage of development, 2010

Region/stage of development	Percentage age distribution of migrants (years of age)			Median age (years)
	0–19	20–64	65 and over	
Africa	28.3	67.4	4.3	30
Asia	21.3	68.4	10.3	35
Europe	10.8	75.3	13.9	42
Latin America and Caribbean	22.5	64.9	12.6	37
Northern America	9.7	78.5	11.8	42
Oceania	11.3	71	17.7	46
World average	15.6	72.9	11.6	39
More developed	10.4	76.4	13.1	42
Less developed	23.2	67.6	9.2	34

Note Figures may not add up due to rounding
Source UN (2012)

Table 5.14 Proportion of females in the stock of immigrants, 2000 and 2015

Region	Percentage females	
	2000	2015
Africa	47	46
Asia	46	42
Europe	52	52
Latin America and Caribbean	50	50
Northern America	50	51
Oceania	51	51
World average	49	48

Source UN (2016)

On average, the proportion of females in the stock of migrants was 48% in 2015. As in the case of age, a number of factors affect the proportion of females in migrant stocks that varies substantially from region to region. These factors include the purpose of migration, that in the past has been biased towards males of working age, demand for skilled and unskilled labour, opportunities for family reunion, as well as the longer life expectancy of females. Worker-pulling countries in Europe, Northern America and Oceania had a higher proportion of female migrants than males, while Africa and Asia had higher proportions of males, and Latin America and the Caribbean had about an equal proportion of males and female migrants (Table 5.14).

5.7   Migrant Workers

5.7.1   Population of Working Age and Migrants

It has been estimated that migrant workers constituted 70% of the stock of 232 million immigrants in 2013. In this context, the term *migrant worker* applies to migrants who are 15 years of age and over and who are either employed or actively seeking employment, regardless of the original reason for migration. It excludes refugees, students, trainees, retirees or dependents. *Migrant domestic workers* are a subset of migrant workers in an employment relationship concerned with cooking, cleaning, gardening, and other house duties (ILO 2015).

The work motive of much migration (Sect. 5.2.2) has led to migrants constituting a larger proportion of people 15 years and over of age (4%) than their proportion in the total population (3%) in 2013. Similarly, migrants made up a larger proportion of workers (4%) than their proportion of people 15 years of age and over. This implies a greater participation of migrants in the labour force than the rest of the population. Migrants were even a larger proportion of domestic workers (17%) (Table 5.15).

Table 5.15 World population and migrant workers, 2013

Population	People (millions)		Migrants
	World	Migrants	Percentage of world
Population	7,152	232	3.2
Population 15 years of age and over	5,271	207	3.9
Workers (15 years of age and over)	3,390	150	4.4
Domestic workers (15 years of age and over)	67.1	11.5	17.1

Sources UN (2013c), ILO (2015). Computations made by the authors

5.7.2 Sex of Population of Working Age and Migrant Workers

The examination of the sex of the population 15 years of age and over, workers and domestic workers in 2013, reveals a gendered association of males with work in general and females with domestic work. However, there are some differences between the migrant and non-migrant populations. Accordingly, there was a higher proportion of males (52%) than females in the migrant stock while there were slightly more females in the non-migrant population (50%). The implicit greater male participation in the labour force was reflected in both the migrant and non-migrant populations with males being respectively 60% and 56% of workers. The specialisation of females in domestic work was also obvious. Females constituted about 80% of all domestic workers, with a smaller proportion of migrant (73%) than non-migrant (82%) females, as male domestic workers formed a minority but a larger proportion of migrant than non-migrant domestic workers (Table 5.16).

Table 5.16 World population of working age, workers and domestic workers by sex, 2013

Sex	Percentage		
	Migrants	Non-migrants	All
Population 15 years of age and over			
Males	51.9	49.9	49.9
Females	48.1	50.1	50.1
Persons	100.0	100.0	100.0
Workers			
Males	55.7	60.2	60
Females	44.3	39.8	40
Persons	100.0	100.0	100.0
Domestic workers			
Males	26.6	18.5	19.9
Females	73.4	81.5	80.1
Persons	100.0	100.0	100.0

Source ILO (2015)

5.7.3   Migrant Workers and Labour Force Participation

As might be expected from work-driven migration, the participation of migrants in the labour force was substantially higher (73%) than that of non-migrants (64%). Nevertheless, this difference was almost entirely due to the much larger participation rate of migrant females (67%) than that of non-migrant females (51%) as the difference between males was small (78 and 77%) (Table 5.17).

5.7.4   Economic Activity and Migrant Workers

Most migrants were employed in the service sector (71%) of the economies of their host countries in 2013, with lower proportions in industry (18%) and agriculture (11%) (Table 5.18). This distribution places a greater emphasis on services than the worldwide distribution of employment in services that is only 56% and lower employment in agriculture that is 25% on average in the world, but it is similar to employment in industry that stands at 19% of the world's labour force (ILO 2016).

Table 5.17 World labour force participation rates of migrant and non-migrant populations by sex, 2013

Population of working age	Percentage labour force participation rate		
	Males	Females	All
Non-migrant	77.2	50.8	63.9
Migrant	78.0	67.0	72.7
World average	77.2	51.4	64.3

Note The labour force participation rate is usually measured as the proportion of the population of working age that is either employed or actively seeking employment. Often the working age is set at 15–64 years of age. However, countries may vary the cut-off points, definitions and get different results. An effort has been made by ILO to overcome these inconsistencies but the results may not be precise or entirely consistent
Source ILO (2015)

Table 5.18 World migrant workers by economic sector and sex, 2013

Economic activity sector	Percentage		
	Males	Females	Persons
Agriculture	11.2	11.1	11.1
Industry	19.8	15.3	17.8
Services	69.1	73.7	71.1
All	100.0	100.0	100.0

Note Figures may not add up due to rounding
Source ILO (2015)

The sex distribution confirms the greater specialisation of females in services (74%) than males (69%). This was due to the greater employment of females in domestic work, while males and females had about the same proportion of employment in agriculture (Table 5.18).

5.7.5 Migrant Workers and Income of Host Countries

The attraction of employment and higher incomes lead migrant workers to countries with high incomes. The distribution of the stock of migrant workers in 2013 shows that about three quarters of them were in high income countries, less than one quarter in middle income countries and only 2% in low income countries. The higher the income, the higher the number of domestic workers too (Table 5.19).

Similarly, there was an association between the level of income of the host country and the proportion of migrant workers in the labour force. The proportion of migrant workers was about 16% of all workers in high income countries but less than 2% in low and middle income countries. Migrant domestic workers also constituted a larger proportion of all domestic workers, especially in high income countries where they outnumbered (66% of all) non-migrant domestic workers. However, the hierarchy of the distribution is less even, as the proportion of migrant domestic workers was higher in low than lower-middle income countries and even lower in upper-middle income countries (Table 5.19).

Table 5.19 World migrant workers by stage of development of host countries, 2013

Stage of development	Percentage of stock of migrant workers		Migrant workers as percentage of workers	
	All workers	Domestic workers	All workers	Domestic workers
Low income	2.4	4.2	1.4	10.5
Lower-middle income	11.3	6.2	1.5	4.4
Upper-middle income	11.7	10.3	1.4	3.7
High income	74.7	79.2	16.3	65.8
World	100.0	100.0	4.4	17.1

Note Figures may not add up due to rounding
Source ILO (2015)

5.7.6   Labour Force Participation of Migrant Workers in Host Countries

On average, the labour force participation rate tends to be lower in high income than other countries. Some of this is related to the varying participation rate of females in the labour force. Accordingly, the labour force participation rate of lower-middle income countries in 2013 was affected by the low participation rate of females in India, while the higher participation rate in upper-middle income countries was influenced by the higher participation rate of females in China (ILO 2015). With the exception of migrant workers in low income countries, the labour force participation of migrant workers (73%) was higher than non-migrant workers (64%). While the participation rate tends to lower as the country income rises, the participation rate of migrant workers tends to rise with the income of the host country (Table 5.20). The low rate of migrant workers in low income countries might be partly due to the larger proportion of dependents that tends to be higher in less developed countries (Table 5.13).

5.7.7   Regional Distribution of Migrant Workers

The importance of migrant workers in the labour force was substantial in regions that have experienced labour force shortages in Europe (e.g. Germany) and the Arab States (e.g. United Arab Emirates and Saudi Arabia), countries with active migration programs in Northern America (e.g. Canada and United States) and South-Eastern Asia and the Pacific (e.g. Australia and New Zealand). It was also in these countries where migrant workers comprised a large proportion of the all workers in 2013. The continuing presence of migrant workers in Eastern Europe and Central and Western Asia in countries arising from the dismemberment of the Soviet Union was also apparent (Table 5.21).

The labour force participation rate of migrant workers was highest in countries where they constituted a large proportion of the labour force. The participation rate of migrant workers in 2013 was relatively low (below the average of 73%) in Africa and Latin America and the Caribbean where they made up a low proportion of the labour force (Table 5.21).

Table 5.20 Labour force participation rate of migrant worker by stage of development of host country, 2013

Stage of development	Labour force participation rate (%)		
	Migrant	Non-migrant	All
Low income	59.4	77.8	77.5
Lower-middle income	69.7	59.6	59.7
Upper-middle income	70.7	68.6	68.7
High income	74.1	58.8	60.8
World average	72.7	63.9	64.3

Source ILO (2015)

Table 5.21 World migrant worker distribution and labour force participation by region, 2013

Region	Migrant worker stock percentage distribution	Migrant worker percentage all workers	Migrant workers labour force participation percentage
Northern Africa	0.5	1.1	52.3
Sub-Saharan Africa	5.3	2.2	63.1
Latin America and Caribbean	2.9	1.5	65.0
Northern America	24.7	20.2	73.7
Northern, Southern and Western Europe	23.8	16.4	72.9
Eastern Europe	9.2	9.2	73.9
Central and Western Asia	4.7	10.0	72.3
Arab States	11.7	35.6	76.0
Eastern Asia	3.6	0.6	75.2
South-Eastern Asia and Pacific	7.8	3.5	76.5
Southern Asia	5.8	1.3	71.0
World	100.0	4.4	72.6

Source ILO (2015)

5.8 Refugees

The number of refugees tends to fluctuate due to the uneven flare up of civil unrest, pogroms and wars (Sect. 5.2.1). The numbers also depend on the pace of re-settlement in the country of origin, as situations change, or in some host country. Refugees are a small proportion of displaced people most of whom are within their national borders (UNHCR 2016).

In 2015, there were 15.5 million people who had refugee status. The number was about the same as in 2000 but lower than in 1990 (18.5 million), when wars and civil unrest in Asia and Africa led to a larger number of refugees. More than half of the refugee population (54%) was in Asia in 2015, about a third (31%) in Africa and a lower proportion in Europe (12%). Major changes took place in Africa where the refugee population decreased between 1990 and 2010 to increase substantially by 2015. Major fluctuations have also taken place in Europe where the dismemberment of Yugoslavia led to pogroms, civil unrest and wars and had increased the number of refugees by the year 2000 (Table 5.22).

The analysis of the origin and host region of refugees in 2015 shows that most refugees were hosted in their region of origin, namely Asia and Africa. The major inter regional movements were to Europe that received most refugees who left Africa and Asia and to a lesser extent to Northern America (Table 5.23).

Ten countries hosted more than half (60%) of the refugees in the world, with Turkey (16%) and Pakistan (10%) hosting more than a quarter. All of these countries are either in Asia close to the Middle East and Afghanistan or in Africa (Table 5.24). These are areas where conflict and fighting have prevailed for a number of decades.

It is apparent that population size and economic circumstances of host countries places different degrees of burden on their capacity to host refugees (Table 5.25). The host countries of Chad, Djibouti, South Sudan and Mauritania have relatively poor resources to cope with the inflow of refugees, while Lebanon and Jordan with

Table 5.22 World refugees by host region, 1990–2015

Region	Refugees (millions)				Percentage of world total			
	1990	2000	2010	2015	1990	2000	2010	2015
Africa	5.4	3.6	2.4	4.8	29.2	23.1	15.5	31.0
Asia	9.9	8.8	10.5	8.4	53.5	56.4	67.7	54.2
Europe	1.3	2.5	1.6	1.8	7.0	16.0	10.3	11.6
Lat. Am. and C.	1.2	…	0.4	0.1	6.5	…	2.6	0.6
Nth. America	0.6	0.6	0.4	0.4	3.2	3.8	2.6	2.6
Oceania	0.1	0.1	…	…	0.5	0.6	…	…
World	18.5	15.6	15.5	15.5	100.0	100.0	100.0	100.0

Note (…) means less than 100,000 or 0.0%
Source UN (2012), UNHCR (2016). Computations made by the authors

Table 5.23 World refugees by region of origin and host, 2015

Region	Refugees (millions)		Origin-host difference
	Origin	Host	(millions)
Africa	5.3	4.8	0.5
Asia	9.3	8.4	0.9
Europe	0.5	1.8	−1.3
Latin America and Caribbean	0.2	0.1	0.1
Northern America	…	0.4	−0.4
Oceania	…	…	…
Uncertain	0.2	n.a.	0.2
World	15.2	15.2	

Note (…) means less than 100,000 and (n.a.) not applicable. Figures may not add due to rounding
Source UNHCR (2016). Computations made by the authors

Table 5.24 Ten countries with largest refugee populations, 2015

Country	Refugees	
	People (millions)	Percentage world total
Turkey	2.541	16.4
Pakistan	1.561	10.1
Lebanon	1.07	6.9
Iran	0.979	6.3
Ethiopia	0.736	4.8
Jordan	0.664	4.3
Kenya	0.533	3.4
Uganda	0.477	3.1
Democratic Republic of Congo	0.383	2.5
Chad	0.37	2.4
Other	6.169	39.8
World	15.483	100.0

Note Figures may not add up due to rounding
Source UNHCR (2016). Computations made by the authors

Table 5.25 Ten countries with the highest number of refugees per head of population, 2015

Country	Refugees per 1,000 people	Population millions	GDP p.c. PPP$ (2011)
Lebanon	183	5.85	16,623
Jordan	87	9.16	11,407
Nauru	50	0.01	n.a.
Turkey	32	78.27	18,660
Chad	26	14.01	2,022
Djibouti	22	0.93	2,903
South Sudan	21	11.88	1,965
Mauritania	19	4.18	2,945
Sweden	17	9.76	43,741
Malta	17	0.43	28,828

Note (GDP p.c. PPP$ 2011) is the average gross domestic product per head of population in purchasing power parities of 2011. (Population) is as at 2015 and the same applies to refugees. (n.a.) means not available
Sources UN (2017), UNDP (2015), UNHCR (2016)

average middle incomes hosted a large number of refugees in relation to their population that would make difficult to meet demands on housing and other infrastructure. The pressures on Nauru—a small island with a small population—with a large number of refugees per head of population must also be substantial.

5.9 Migrant Remittances

There has been an increasing interest in migrant remittances and their effect on households at the point of origin. In a survey of the literature Osaki (2003) noted a number of factors that might influence remittances:

- *Migrant income*
- *Education*
- *Family status*
- *Duration of migration*
- *Family assets*
- *Migrant gender*

Research findings indicate that the level of migrant income and education are positively related to migrant remittances. Migrant with higher education and skill tend to have better income earning opportunities and therefore can better afford to remit. Migrants with dependent wives and children are likely to remit more because of the needs of their dependent families. The larger the number of dependent children the greater the likelihood of remittances and the greater their size. The initial establishment costs of newly arrived migrants lead to a lag in the capacity of migrants to remit, and there is a trend for remittances to increase after this initial period. Migrant remittances are also more likely to take place when the family left behind is asset-poor. Further, there is a tendency for migrant females, although earning less, to remit more frequently than males. Although remittances can, in some cases, be used to invest in the productive capacity of the households at the point of origin, there are indications that they tend to be used mostly for the consumption needs of the households and the education of children (Osaki 2003).

The volume of migrant remittances grew considerably to reach about US $582,000 million in 2015. It represented US$2,387 per head of the migrant population. The remittances have risen substantially well above the rise in the number of migrants, even taking into account purchasing power changes (Table 5.26).

Most of the inflows of migrant remittances were to middle income countries (71%) in 2014 (Table 5.27). These included China, India, Mexico, Philippines,

Table 5.26 World inflow of migrant remittances, 1990–2015

Year	Remittances US$ millions	Migrant stock million people	Remittances per migrant
1990	64,034	154.2	415.27
2000	126,750	172.7	733.93
2010	460,527	220.7	2,086.67
2015	581,640	243.7	2,386.70
Average growth percentage per year	8.8	1.8	7.0

Note Migrant remittances are in US dollars (millions) at current prices
Sources WB (2016), Table 5.3

Table 5.27 World inflow of migrant remittances by stage of development, 2010 and 2014

Countries by stage of development	Percentage of total remittances	
	2010	2014
Low	2.0	2.4
Middle	71.5	71.1
High	26.5	26.5
World	100.0	100.0

Source WB (2015). Computations made by the authors

Nigeria and Egypt as large receivers of remittances (Table 5.28). Low income countries received only a small proportion of remittances (2%). However, high income countries received a considerable proportion of remittances (27%) in 2014. France, Spain and Belgium were large receivers of migrant remittances in the same year. Migration within the European Union has led to some countries to have both large inflows as well as outflows as in the case of Germany, France, Belgium and the United Kingdom (Tables 5.28 and 5.29).

The analysis of the remittance flows reveals the importance of diasporas to family support even in high income countries. This seems to apply among others to Russia (Table 5.29) that had substantial outflows as well as inflows to and from former Soviet Union republics.

The United Sates, with the largest number of migrants (Table 5.10), was also the major origin of migrant remittances. Some European countries with labour shortages created by low fertility but growing economic activity such as Germany and Switzerland also were major sources of migrant remittances. Considerable migrant remittances originated in the oil producing countries in the Middle East with relatively large numbers of migrant workers such as Saudi Arabia, United Arab Emirates, Kuwait, Qatar and Oman. The special cases of Israel and Russia as sources of migrant remittances are also noteworthy (Tables 5.28 and 5.29).

Table 5.28 Migrant remittances to countries with largest inflows, 2014

Country	Remittances US$ millions		
	Inflows	Outflows	Net inflow
India	70,389	6,222	64,167
China	62,332	4,155	58,177
Philippines	27,273	183	27,090
France	25,195	13,835	11,360
Mexico	24,462	1,002	23,460
Nigeria	20,829	58	20,771
Egypt	19,570	351	19,219
Bangladesh	14,983	33	14,950
Vietnam	12,000	…	12,000
Belgium	11,450	4,497	6,953
Spain	10,750	363	10,387

Source WB (2016). Computations made by the authors

Table 5.29 Migrant remittances from countries with largest outflows, 2014

Country	Remittances US$ millions		
	Outflows	Inflows	Net outflows
United States	56,311	6,908	49,403
Saudi Arabia	36,924	273	36,651
Russia	32,640	7,777	24,863
Switzerland	24,693	2,349	22,344
Germany	20,836	17,629	3,207
United Arab Emirates	19,280	...	19,280
Kuwait	18,129	4	18,125
Luxembourg	12,700	1,784	10,916
United Kingdom	11,569	4,932	6,637
Qatar	11,230	499	10,731
Israel	11,514	859	10,295
Oman	10,301	39	10,262

Source WB (2016). Computations made by the authors

The importance of migrant remittances in relation to a country resources can be very substantial, especially in countries with relatively small economies. Migrant remittances can represent as much as the equivalent of about a quarter of the Gross Domestic Product, as in the case of Tajikistan, Kyrgyz, Nepal, Tonga, Moldova and

Table 5.30 Highest migrant remittances inflow as a proportion of GDP, 2014

Country/Territory	Received remittances
	percentage of GDP
Tajikistan	36.6
Kyrgyz	30.3
Nepal	29.2
Tonga	27.1
Moldova	26.2
Liberia	24.6
Bermuda	23.1
Haiti	17.4
Gambia	21.2
Colombia	20.2
Samoa	17.6
Honduras	17.4
Lesotho	17.9
Armenia	17.4
West Bank/Gaza	17.1
El Salvador	16.8
Jamaica	16.3
Lebanon	16.2
Kosovo	16.1

Source WB (2016)

Liberia in 2014, but also make considerable contributions in other countries (Table 5.30).

5.10 Internal Migration and Urbanization

Although internal migration is more frequent than international migration, it is nevertheless more difficult to define and measure. The measurement becomes easier the larger the distances involved. Some countries rely on censuses of population to assess the degree of internal migration, while others conduct specific surveys or keep population registers that make the measurement of population movements easier. All of these sources of information can provide a sense of the dimensions involved but all suffer from a lack of consistent definitions, and often accuracy is dependent on purposeful administration. Factors influencing internal migration are similar to the push-pull factors involved in international migration:

- *existence of dual economies with substantial differences in productivity and incomes*
- *relative surplus and shortages of labour*
- *opportunities for divisions of labour and specialisation*
- *civil unrest and unfavourable treatment of minorities*

However, internal migration usually entails smaller costs and domestic income differentials tend to be lower. People seeking higher education and or training in skilled occupations may also move for that purpose. In addition, there has been large domestic migration from over-populated rural areas to others where land is available, such as the migration of people from Java to Sumatra in Indonesia. Nevertheless, a major phenomenon has been the migration from rural to urban areas because of the perceived employment opportunities. Urbanization has been an expression of industrialization. It was a feature of the Industrial Revolution in Europe and North America and it has become a common feature of developing countries as they industrialize. This is the subject of the next chapter (Chap. 6).

5.11 Change and Growth

Differences in social and economic conditions at the point of origin and destination are the main drivers of migration. Risks and costs of migration are also important variables. The risks involve uncertainty, in the absence of knowledge about the future and the place of destination, and costs are not only economic but also entail the loss of social networks and support. Consequently, migration tends to flow to domestic areas or countries where either social or economic conditions, or both, appear to be an improvement, and to be more frequent to places with lower social and economic costs. Thus, most migration tends to take place within national borders, and to nearby countries within the same region. Nevertheless, international migration within and across regions has grown substantially partly because of the increasing globalisation of the world economy, but also possibly because of the growth of migrant networks that diminishes uncertainty and risks and the lowering of travel costs. Migration has also been encouraged by economic growth in higher income countries that led to higher demand for labour than that available domestically.

A number of changes have taken place in migration patterns since World War II.

- Europe that had been a major war theatre in 1940s experienced economic recovery in the 1960s that was associated with a decline in fertility and ageing of its population; that led to a change from being a net sender of migrants, mostly to traditionally migrant receiving countries, to a net receiver of migrants, mostly from Africa and Asia.
- Traditional migrant receiving counties such as the United States, Canada, Australia and New Zealand that were net receivers of European migrants had to place more emphasis on migrants from Asia.
- The rising incomes of some Middle East oil producing countries, with relatively small populations, led to a demand for both skilled and unskilled workers, including female domestic workers, from Asia but also from Africa.

Thus, both the origin and destination of migrant flows went through changes but growth in net flows between countries and regions has also taken place, including flows within Europe and Asia. The analysis of the growing flow of migrant remittances shows both the value of migrants in labour markets in some countries but also the more intricate relationships of diasporas with countries of origin across the regions of the world.

Population growth almost tripled between 1950 and 2015 but migration rose at a faster rate. However, as the average annual rate of the world population growth declined in more recent decades that of the migrant stock has remained high resulting in the international migrant stock continuing to rise as a proportion of the world's population.

In line with the basic stimulus for migration, most migration has taken place from less to more developed higher income countries. Possibly because of costs in emigration much of worker migration has taken place between middle and high income countries, as poor people have difficulty in meeting the cost of migration. The plight of refugees has been somewhat different as they seek shelter usually in neighbouring low or middle income countries. Population ageing in more developing countries will continue to encourage migration to these countries to reduce the impact of larger dependency rates, as the proportion of people of working age falls. This issue might also become a matter of concern in some middle-income countries that are experiencing falls in fertility to below replacement levels. Nevertheless, differences in the levels of income between countries should continue to stimulate migration from lower to higher income countries.

References

Alho, J. M. (2008). Migration, fertility and aging in stable populations. *Demography, 45*(3), 641–650.

Australian Bureau of Statistics (ABS). (2008). *Migration—Australia, 2006-07.* Canberra.

Bellanger, D. (2014). Labor migration and trafficking among Vietnamese migrants in Asia. *Annals, AAPSS, 653*, 87–106.

Boswell, C., & Crisp, J. (2004). *Poverty, international migration and asylum.* Helsinki: UNU World Institute for Development Economics Research.

Brady, N. C. (1996). Alternatives to slash-and-burn: A global imperative. *Agriculture, Ecosystems & Environment, 58*, 3–11.

Braithwaite, J. (1999). *Crime in a convict republic.* History of Crime, Policing and Punishment Conference. Canberra: Australian National University.

Cooray, A. V. (2012). The impact of migrant remittances on economic growth: Evidence from South Asia. *Review of International Economics, 20*(5), 985–998.

Ditton, M. J. (2012). *Health rights and health problems of migrants living in the Thai-Burma border region.* Lampender: Edwin Mellen Press.

Hirschman, C. (2002). *Population and society: Historical trends and future prospects.* Retrieved April 19, 2004, from http://faculty.washington.edu/charles/Population%20and%20Society%20rev%20Aug%202002.pdf.

International Labour Organization (ILO) (2015). *ILO global estimates on migrant workers.* Geneva.

International Labour Organization (ILO) (2016). *Employment—ILO estimates and projections.* Geneva: ILOSTAT. Retrieved December 28, 2016, from www.ilo.org/ilostat/faces/oracle/webcenter/portalapp/.

Kapiszewski, A. (2006). *Arab versus Asian migrant workers in the GCC countries.* Beirut: United Nations Secretariat.

Lawrence, D., Radel, C., Tully, K., Schmook, B., & Schneider, L. (2010). Untangling a decline in tropical forest resilience: Constraints on the sustainability of shifting cultivation across the globe. *Biotropica, 42*(1), 21–30.

Lewis, W. A. (1963). *Theory of economic growth.* London: Unwin University Books.

Myint, H. (1967). *The economics of the developing countries.* London: Hutchinson University Library.

Myrdal, G. (1968). *Asian drama—An inquiry into the poverty of nations.* Harmondsworth: Penguin Books.

Organisation for Economic Co-operation and Development and United Nations (OECD-UNDESA) (2013). *World migration in figures.* Paris.

Osaki, K. (2003). Migrant remittances in Thailand: Economic necessity or social norm? *Journal of Population Research, 20*(2), 203–222.

Piguet, E. (2008). *Climate change and forced migration.* Geneva: United Nations High Commissioner for Refugees.

Ray, D. (1998). *Development economics.* Princeton, NJ: Princeton University Press.

Schroeder, H., O'Connell, T. C., Evans, J. A., Shuler, K. A., & Hedges, R. E. M. (2009). Trans-Atlantic slavery: Isotopic evidence of forced migration to Barbados. *American Journal of Physical Anthropology, 139*, 547–557.

Statistics Canada (SC). (2005). *Population growth components (1851–2001 censuses).* Retrieved December 23, 2016, from www.statcan.gc.ca/tables-tableaux/sum-som/l01/cst01/demo03-eng.hmt.

Tomlins, C. (2001). Reconsidering indentured servitude: European migration and the early American labor force, 1600–1775. *Labor History, 42*(1), 5–43.

United Nations (UN). (1999). *Report of the Technical Symposium on International Migration and Development of the Administrative Committee on Coordination (ACC) Task Force on Basic*

Social Services for All. New York: Economic Social Council. Retrieved April 19, 2014, from www.un.org/documents/ecosoc/cn9/1999/ecn91999-3.hmt.

United Nations (UN) (2002). *International migration report 2002*. New York.

United Nations (UN) (2012). *International migration report 2011*. New York.

United Nations (UN) (2013a). *World population policies 2013*. New York.

United Nations (UN) (2013b). *International migration report 2013*. New York.

United Nations (UN) (2013c). *World population prospects—The 2012 revision—Volume I: Comprehensive tables*. New York.

United Nations (UN) (2016). *International migration report 2015—Highlights*. New York.

United Nations (UN) (2017). *World population prospects—The 2017 revision—Volume I: Comprehensive tables*. New York.

United Nations Development Programme (UNDP). (2015). *Human development report 2015*. New York.

United Nations High Commissioner for Refugees (UNHCR). (2016). *Global trends forced displacement in 2015*. Geneva.

World Bank (WB). (2015). Migration and remittances—Recent developments and outlook. Washington DC.

World Bank (WB). (2016). Migration and remittances data. Washington DC. Retrieved December 30, 2016, from www.worldbank.org/en/topic/migrationremittancesdiasporaiissues/brif/migration-remittances-data.

Chapter 6
Urbanization: A Way of Living

> *It is thus that through the greater part of Europe the commerce and manufacture of cities, instead of being the effect, have been the cause and occasion of the improvement and cultivation of the country.*
>
> Adam Smith (1776)

6.1 Population Growth and Concentration

The exceptional population growth of the last century was accompanied by the concentration of people in large urban centres nurtured by internal migration from rural to urban areas. For the first time in recorded history, most people now live in urban areas (Fig. 6.1).

The higher rates of population growth in urban areas above the world average, and the lower than average rates in rural areas reflect a hefty rate of migration from rural to urban areas. Other than the expansion of cities by annexation of surrounding territories (and their residents), the only plausible explanation for this is rural migration to urban areas because there are negative rates of population growth of rural areas in more developed countries during the six decades from 1950 to 2011 (Table 6.1).

6.2 Cities and Urban Settlement

The definition of what constitutes a city or an urban area vary from country to country. The estimates of urban populations by the United Nations reflect a wide range of definitions concerned with the size of the population in a given settlement and its density, proportion of people employed in agriculture and other industries, and infrastructure characteristics (UN 2014b). Cities have been part of human history and have been often associated with

© Springer International Publishing AG, part of Springer Nature 2018   151
Jo. M. Martins et al., *Global Population in Transition*,
https://doi.org/10.1007/978-3-319-77362-9_6

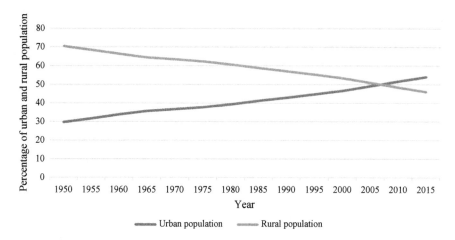

Fig. 6.1 World population: proportion of people living in urban and rural areas 1950–2015
Note The 2015 data are preliminary estimates
Source UN (2014a)

Table 6.1 World population growth of urban and rural areas, 1950–1970 and 1970–2011

Stage of development	Population average annual rate of growth (%)	
	1950–1970	1970–2011
World	1.89	1.55
Urban	2.98	2.41
Rural	1.36	0.87
More developed	1.8	0.51
Urban	2.09	0.89
Rural	−0.48	−0.48
Less developed	2.23	1.85
Urban	4.04	3.33
Rural	1.74	1.03

Source UN (2012)

- *places of social gathering and cultural events*
- *exchange of goods and services*
- *technological change.*

Two major technological changes boosted the establishment and growth of urban settlements:

- *agricultural revolution*
- *industrial revolution*

The first urban settlements might have been associated with social meeting places of cultural or religious nature, but some 10,000 ago, the agricultural revolution led to higher densities of people in given locations due to the more sedentary mode of food production. It also gave rise to attachment to more fixed property, in terms of developed tracts of land and domesticated animals. This led to differences in ownership and inequality, as well as the potential for conflict over property. In some cases, large scale irrigation meant more work to build and maintain it than what one family and neighbours could do. This needed social organisation to undertake the work involved, and control of common water sources and use. The production of surplus food from higher agricultural productivity made possible specialisation in crafts by some people, who exchanged their crafts for the surplus food from agriculture. In turn, some of these more sophisticated products could be used to enhance agricultural production, and the living of those working in agriculture. This is what Adam Smith (1970 [1776]) saw as the complementary nature of the products of agriculture and those of the cities and the mutual benefit to them. He also identified these complementary functions as the basis on which divisions of labour could take place that led to greater efficiency in manufacturing. In the exchange of commodities, barter is awkward as it requires the meeting of people who wish to exchange one specific product for another specific one, to mutual advantage. The need for a more flexible way of exchange became apparent and hence the use of money and credit as means of exchange. This facilitated the establishment of market places where both agricultural and manufactured products could be exchange more easily. With time, urban settlements evolved to perform a number of functions

- *Cultural* sometimes with religious traits
- *Industrial* for the production of manufactures
- *Mercantile* for the exchange of agricultural products and manufactures
- *Service* such as credit and education
- *Administrative and political* for social organisation and the preservation of order

The industrial revolution of the 19th century increased the interdependence of different factors of production, its scale and the employment of a greater number of people in a given location. It meant larger conglomerations of people at greater risk from industrial and human wastes and the transmission of infectious diseases. However, substantial scientific progress took place about that time that led to improved public health measures, such as better sanitation and the prevention and more successful management of infectious diseases, that reduced the burden of the higher health risks in urban areas in countries undergoing industrialisation at that time (Chap. 4: Sects. 4.6 and 4.7).

6.3 Perspectives on Urbanization

A number of views have been put forward in relation to urbanization and urban growth. In their review of a number of perspectives, Balchin et al. (2000) mention:

- The *central place theory* that is concerned with the distribution of goods and services from urban centres to the surrounding areas. This involves hierarchical networks of urban centres of different sizes and at different distances depending on their function and capacity to handle the distribution of varied commodities.
- The *urban base theory* that involves the demand for goods and services the urban centre exports to pay for the imports it needs. It is also concerned with urban employment and the multiplier effect of the production of basic commodities that generate additional employment and the effect on urban employment when the demand for one of its basic commodities declines.
- *Keynesian notions* have been used to explain the growth of urban centres, whereby urban areas growth is dependent on the absorption of savings from elsewhere so that their investments are greater than their savings.
- The *dependency theory* is another variation of the role of urban centres that exploit their surrounding areas. Urban centres siphon surplus from other areas and use them to further their own growth at the expense of rural areas.
- The *modernization theory* sees urban centres as generative of economic growth that through the tickle down effect benefits people in rural areas as well.
- The *urban primacy notion* postulates that some cities, as major ports or administrative centres, tend to assume a primal role and promote their superiority in both internal and external trade.

These views are similar to those put forward by Kasarda and Crenshaw (1991) in an earlier review of theories of urbanization:

- *modernisation/ecology*
- *dependency/world-systems*
- *distributive coalitions/urban bias*

All these notions have been criticised because they fail to fully explain the complexity of the factors that are part of the urbanization process. Their empirical application has often not been found to be useful predicators. For instance, a study by Kasarda and Janowitz (1974) found, in a survey of urban and rural populations in England (excluding London), that increasing in size and density of population did not lessen kinship and friendship bonds. People living in areas of larger and denser populations had more social ties than those living in rural areas. Further, they participated more in community affairs. The research found that the length of residence rather than population size and density to be the major factor in community interest. However, the sample excluded London which may have influenced the results because of London's more heterogeneous population and migrant population.

Some propositions pertain to the minimum or optimal size of urban centres. It has been postulated that some urban centres are too small to take advantage of economies of scale. As urban centres grow the costs of providing transport and public utilities tend to fall. However, after they reach given thresholds, costs start to rise because of diseconomies of scale. Thus, urban costs are assumed to follow a U-shaped curve. But different services have different cost turning points.

For example, different types of manufacturing use technologies with different scales of efficient production. The same applies to services and public utilities such as urban transport, power generation and water supplies. Therefore, there is no uniformity in the scale of production of the aggregate and the minimum and optimal scales vary for different industries and services; and the aggregate turning points are difficult to determine. It has been suggested that the minimum efficient size of urban centres might be in the range of 100,000–500,000 people and that the optimal size about 500,000 people (Balchin et al. 2000). However, there is no agreement on this or other sizes.

Further, different perspectives on urbanization have led to perceptions that urban centres can play either a *generative* or *parasitic* role in economic growth and development (Balchin et al. 2000). The first sees urban centres as the producers of surplus that can be shared with surrounding non-urban areas, as posited by Adam Smith, while the second perceives urban centres as absorbers of surplus created outside them.

Unlike Adam Smith, Marx and Engels (1951) in the 1800s saw the division of labour in urban areas and related production as the basis of exploitation of one class by another. Tonnies (2002) perceived large cleavages between rural and urban communities: *gemeinschaft* (communal bind) and *gesellschaft* (associational bind). The people in the rural village were seen as having personal relationships and interests based on kinship and their neighbours that led to a sense of community with a shared purpose. In contrast, human relationships in cities were seen as impersonal and individualistic based on economic and political interests derived from the industrial means of production and related services. While the first had a cohesive effect on society the other led to alienation of people living in cities.

Another pessimistic view was held by Simmel (2000). He observed that the rural rhythm of life was more even, slow and habitual with a different impact on human psyche than the more crowded and rapid mode of the metropolis. The divisions of labour and market exchange of products also led to alienation between the individuals involved in the production and the product itself and between the producers and the users. The dominance of the money economy and anonymity of interests among producers and users and an absence of personal relationships reinforced individualism and lack of social cohesion. Simmel saw living in large cities as a way of liberating the individual from the close relationships prevailing in smaller settlements. However, life became more precise and more mechanistic because of the demands of the more complex interdependence arising from divisions of labour. He saw this as a trade-off in the attainment of livelihood between dependence on nature and on other people. The gain in individual independence came at a cost of the need for protection from the increasing pressures. This led to the development of defensive mechanisms that reduced sensitivity and fostered more impersonal relationships.

Another perspective on the impact of the division of labour was held by Durkheim (Schoultz 1972; Ozden and Enwere 2012). He argued that the divisions of labour in the urban setting imposed social interdependence that led to *organic solidarity* in the complex social milieu of more individualistic behaviour by people with different roles and experiences.

Weber (1958) discussed the structure of a city in the context of its size but also of its construct. Thus, Weber conceived a city with a number of features

- *fortification*
- *market*
- *court of law of its own*
- *associated administrative structure with a degree of autonomy*

The city economic life depended on non-agricultural production and commerce. The latter was concerned not only with its own production but also the marketing of produce of people nearby. He saw an evolution from traditional and communal relationships to impersonal and bureaucratic ones in the urban setting (Schoultz 1972). This appears to portray what Weber might have perceived as ideal cities in Europe in the middle ages and 16th century, before the Industrial Revolution.

Park (1936) was concerned with human ecology and the application of what has been suggested to be quasi-Darwinian approaches to human relationships in what he called the *web of life*. Thus, he used the term *symbiosis* to denote social relationships that were natural rather than cultural. These relationships were regulated by competition. However, human beings, unlike other living organisms, tended to control these natural drives by developing *institutional* or *moral order*. Park saw that human ecology consisted of social order that regulated natural drives on three levels:

- *economic*
- *political*
- *moral*

For Park (1925), cities were not only the result of their physical, institutional and administrative features. They were also an organism with attitudes and sentiments, customs and traditions. In line with his human ecological perspective, the city reflected and it was influenced by its economic, political and moral dimensions. Urban life varied depending on:

- *physical organisation*
- *occupations from the divisions of labour*
- *culture*

These interact with each other to give the city its own character. The city was seen as a group of areas. The diversity of people tended to lead to segregation and isolation, with residential areas of people with similar characteristics and interests of cultural, racial or vocational nature. The city was thought to provide for change from more traditional family relationships, culture and status to associations based on occupation and related interests. The divisions of labour that dominated city life made the individual dependent on others with different occupations, as part of the overall industrial set up. This steered people to make associations not based on custom or emotion but on rational common interests. The process of competition inherent in the industrial process and change and instability led people to *continuous readjustment*. The departure from more traditional ties and the continuous process of readjustment to changed circumstances influenced the social context that fostered non-compliant behaviour such as crime and vice. This led to further segregation based on *moral regions* rather than on occupational or other economic interests. Thus, people with less common or acceptable traits came together to form segregated communities where different *moral codes* prevailed. These people might not necessarily be *abnormal* or *criminal* but had tastes and more central interests, for example in the arts.

Wirth (1938) further elaborated Simmel's perceptions of urban life. He posited that urbanism was a way of life characterised by

- *large sized and permanent settlement*
- *large population density*
- *a high degree of heterogeneity*

The large number of people with different characteristics living close together influenced the social framework that in turn changed them. This was marked by a great degree of

- *individualism*
- *anonymity*
- *superficiality in relationships*

The large number of people with varying characteristics and backgrounds resulted in individualism and mostly anonymous and non-intimate relationships. The large density entailed diverse interests and occupations. Closeness led to obvious contrasts and potential conflict. Heterogeneity carried with it flexibility in social structures and mobility and also diffidence and instability in relationships and loose socialisation. Money became the linking medium between people rather than personal relationships, and the satisfaction of mass rather than individual requirements became the norm.

In his *Right to a City*, Lefebvre also emphasised a more holistic concept of a city, beyond its physical expression. He proposed that urban space was made up of three interlaced elements:

- *perceived space*
- *conceived space*
- *lived space*

Perceived space relates to sensory impressions from apparent features. Conceived space consists of mental conceptual ideas about what that space represented. Lived space is the conjunction of physical and mental aspects of space and living experiences in a social context. He argued that urban planning and administration tended to reflect the interests of a few rather than the living aspects of most and emphasised the perceived or conceived rather than the living space. He also advocated that the urban space should mirror dweller's ideas about their own activities and uses of their urban space, and that urban dwellers be given access to the urban centre rather than being dispersed in ghettos (Purcell 2002).

Another perspective is concerned with globalisation and urban transformation. Sassen (1991) examined economic changes that have taken place and the rise of global cities: New York, London and Tokyo. She identified two major economic trends that had an impact on urban settlements and led to the transformation of some into global cities

- *spatial dispersion of industrial production*
- *concentration of industrial and commercial command*

The dispersion of industrial production from major urban centres in more developed countries to take advantage of lower labour costs in less developed countries, resulted in the loss of manufacturing activity and employment in many urban areas in developed countries, but fostered the growth to urban settlements in less developed ones. The greater concentration of ownership and management of the more dispersed industrial and commercial activity created demand for support services for the larger global organisations. In this process, cities such as New York, London and Tokyo changed from large industrial to considerable service and command centres. These global cities became:

- *command centres in the organisation of the world economy*
- *key location for finance and specialised firms*
- *sites for the creation and production of innovative products*
- *markets for financial products, such as derivatives and wealth funds*

Sassen (2005) postulated that the concentration of command functions in a complex global context resulted in the outsourcing of tasks to specialised firms in accounting, legal, public relations, programming, telecommunications and other services. The concentration of these services in the global city made it an *information centre*. The global nature of these activities led to inter-city networks and transactions. A feature of the traditional urban centre was the symbiotic relationship with its surrounding area and the nation state. However, the global dispersion of industrial production and marketing of products by these international organisations effected a disconnect between the organisations in global cities and their immediate regions and countries. It also diminished the regulatory power of national governments and led to the use of the global city as *organizational commodity* by global corporations. The loss of better paid manufacturing jobs by global city dwellers were often traded for low paid service work. This increased income inequality in global cities between those in high paid occupations and the lowly paid service workers. Sassen also saw immigration as a major feature of the global economy with an impact on urban settlement and increased the number of shanty dwellers in the global city.

These various perspectives on urbanization lead to perceptions that people in urban areas have a different way of life than those in rural areas. The growth of urbanization fostered by rural to urban migration raises questions of the risks involved in moving from rural areas with a more traditional, habitual, closer and secure social environment to a risky and uncertain urban one. Some of these have already been discussed (Chap. 5: Sects. 5.1 and 5.10).

6.4 Urban Population Growth

6.4.1 Degree and Pace of Urbanization

The substantial rate of growth of the number of people living in urban settlements has reflected the pace of industrialisation, first in more developed and then in less developed countries. The global urban population grew from 746 million people in 1950 to an estimated 3,957 million in 2015. The average rate of annual growth of 2.6% was well above that of the whole population of the world and led to urban dwelling becoming the most common mode of habitation (Table 6.2 and Fig. 6.1). The spread of industrialisation from more to less developed countries is expressed in the proportion of urban population in more and less developed countries. In 1950 about 60% of the urban population were in more developed countries but by 2015 about 75% of the much larger urban population lived in less developed countries and only 25% in more developed ones (Table 6.2).

Table 6.2 World urban population by stage of development and region, 1950–2015

Stage of development/region	1950	1970	1990	2010	2015	Average annual growth rate 1950–2015 percentage
World urban population (millions)	746	1,350	2,285	3,571	3,957	2.6
	Percentage of total urban population					
More developed	59.5	49.8	36.4	26.8	24.9	1.2
Other less developed	38.5	47.2	58.9	66.4	67.6	3.4
Least developed	2.0	2.9	4.7	6.8	7.5	4.6
Africa	4.3	6.1	8.6	11.1	11.9	4.1
Asia	32.8	37.4	45.3	52.2	53.4	3.3
Europe	37.9	30.7	22.1	15.1	13.8	1.0
Latin America & Caribbean	9.3	12.2	13.7	13.1	12.7	3.0
Northern America	14.7	12.6	9.3	7.8	7.5	1.5
Oceania	1.1	1.0	0.8	0.7	0.7	1.9

Note Figures may not add up due to rounding. The 2015 data are preliminary estimates
Source UN (2014c). Computations made by the authors

Table 6.3 World proportion of population in urban settlements by stage of development and region, 1950–2015

Stage of development/ region	1950	1970	1990	2010	2015	Difference 1950–2015
	Percentage of total population					
World	29.6	36.6	42.9	51.6	54.0	24.4
More developed	54.6	66.7	72.4	77.1	78.3	23.7
Other less developed	19.0	26.9	36.8	49.1	52.2	33.2
Least developed	7.5	12.8	21.1	28.6	31.4	23.9
Africa	14.0	22.6	31.3	38.3	40.4	26.4
Asia	17.5	23.7	32.3	44.8	48.2	30.7
Europe	51.5	63.0	70.0	72.7	73.6	22.1
Latin America & Caribbean	41.3	57.1	70.5	78.4	79.8	38.5
Northern America	63.9	73.8	75.4	80.8	81.6	17.7
Oceania	62.4	71.3	70.7	70.7	70.8	8.4

Note Figures may not add up due to rounding. The 2015 data are preliminary estimates
Source UN (2014b). Computations made by the authors

The rate of growth of urbanization in countries at varying stages of development shows that the lower the level of urbanization the higher the rate of urban growth. As Davis and Golden (1954) pointed out, as the level of urbanization becomes greater, the rate of urban growth declines. Thus, the least developed countries with the lowest level of urbanization of 8% in 1950 had the highest average annual rate of urban growth of 4.6% in the period 1950–2015 to reach the still lowest level of 31% in 2015, while the more developed countries with the highest level of urbanization of 55% in 1950 experienced the lowest average annual rate of urban growth of 1.2% to attain still the highest rate of urbanization of 78% in 2015. The other less developed countries with an intermediate level of urbanization in 1950 (19%) also had an in-between rate of urban growth (3.4%) that raised their level or urbanization to 52% in 2015 (Tables 6.2 and 6.3).

Consequently, more developed countries, reflecting their higher level of industrialisation, continued to have the top level of urbanization compared to less developed countries in 2015. In the period 1950–2015, countries in Latin America and the Caribbean experienced the largest proportional growth in urbanization. Most of this proportional growth took place in the period 1950–1990, with lower growth in 1990–2015. The second largest proportional increase in regional urbanization was in Asia, at a steadier pace from 18% in 1950 to 48% in 2015 (Table 6.3). The relative low level of urbanization in Asia was influenced by the low levels of urbanization in more populous countries such as India (33%), Bangladesh (34%) and Pakistan (39%) in 2015 (UN 2014b).

Table 6.4 World urban population by settlement size, 1970–2011

Population size	Urban population distribution			Average annual rate of growth		
	1970	1990	2011	1990–1970	2011–1990	2011–1970
	Percentage					
Less than 500,000	61.6	58.4	50.9	2.4	1.6	1.9
500,000 to 1 million	9.5	9.0	10.0	2.4	2.7	2.6
1 million to 5 million	18.0	20.0	21.4	3.1	2.5	2.8
5 million to 10 million	8.1	6.2	7.8	1.3	3.3	2.3
10 million or more	2.9	6.4	9.9	6.6	4.3	5.4
All urban population	100.0	100.0	100.0	2.6	2.2	2.4

Note Figures may not add up due to rounding
Source UN (2012). Computations made by the authors

6.4.2   Urbanization Level

In 2011, about one half (51%) of the world's urban population lived in settlements of less than half million people. This represented a lower growth rate than that of urban centres of half a million or more in the period 1970–2011. The growing dominance of megacities of 10 million or more people is a major feature of the pattern of urban growth. Their average annual rate of growth was 5.4% compared with an average of 2.4% for all urban settlements in that period. Accordingly, megacity population that made up only 3% of the world's urban population in 1970 constituted 10% of that total in 2011. In general, the rate of urban growth was larger in the two decades 1970–1990 (2.6%) than in the following 21-year period of 1990–2011 (2.2%), but the rate of growth of urban settlements of 10 million or more (4.3%) continued to be higher than average (2.2%) and the same applied to urban settlements of 5–10 million (3.3%). In the period under review, the trend was for larger urban conglomerations and a smaller proportion in settlements of less than one million people (Table 6.4).

6.4.3   Growth of Megacities

The trend for larger urban centres has risen from the growth of individual urban centres and from the conurbation of more than one urban centre into larger metropolitan areas such New York/Newark in the United States and Osaka/Kobe in Japan.

In 1950 there were only two urban settlements with 10 million or more people: New York/Newark and Tokyo. This number increased to 29 urban conglomerations by 2015. The initial emergence of Tokyo/Yokohama as the major urban settlement in the world after New York/Newark was followed by others in Latin America such as Sao Paulo and Mexico City, Mumbai, Osaka/Kobe and Kolkata in Asia, and Los Angeles/Long Beach in Northern America by 1990. The number then rose substantially in Asia with industrialisation in China, and in other Asian, African and European countries (Table 6.5).

In accordance with the urban supremacy notion, most of these cities are seaports engaged in national and international trade and transport. They also have major airports for the transport of people and freight. These megacities include Tokyo/Yokohama and Osaka/Kobe in Japan, New York/Newark and Los Angeles/Long Beach in the United States, Shanghai and Guangzhou/Shenzhen in China, Sao Paulo/Santos and Rio de Janeiro in Brazil, Mumbai and Kolkata in India and Lagos in Nigeria. Other inland cities such as Delhi in India, Beijing in China, Moscow in Russia, Cairo in Egypt and Mexico City are major administrative centres that became major markets and transport hubs, in accordance with the central place theory of urbanization. In addition, their large scale enabled the establishment of major education and health service organisations which attract people seeking higher education or specialist health services.

These megacities reflect organic urban growth into conurbations that attract people for a number of reasons, mostly because of employment opportunities in the wide range of specialist functions and services in markets serving large populations. Like other large urban settlements, they pose challenges in gaps between their rapid growth fuelled by migration and available urban infrastructure. The scale of industrial, commercial and human wastes can lead to major environmental hazards and require infrastructure and organisation for waste management and sanitation. The large number of people and industrial/commercial production place pressure on water sources and supplies that require major administrative capacity and infrastructure. Large urban centres depend on the production of energy and distribution. In addition to transport involved in trade and commerce nationally and internationally, urban transport is an important element in getting people, goods and services from varied points in these large conurbations. Power generation, industrial production and transport can be a major sources of air pollution with related health risks. Adequate housing for rapidly growing populations is a major issue and has resulted in slums growing in many of these large cities.

Although there is migration from one urban area to another and urban areas can expand their geographic limits by the annexation of surrounding territories, when urban areas are viewed as a whole, the demographic process that creates urban growth is migration from rural areas. This happens because rural fertility is sufficiently high to allow for migration, or local employment opportunities are lacking. However, the migration process largely selects young adults, which suggests that over time there are fewer people in rural areas capable of having children. Evidence suggests that this is already occurring because of the *ageing in place* of rural populations (WHO 2011; Hara 2015). A question is what will happen to urban growth when the fertility of rural areas no longer creates the people that are the source of rural to urban migration.

Table 6.5   World urban agglomerations of 10 million or more people, 1950–2015

Megacity	Country	Population millions				
		2015	2010	1990	1970	1950
Tokyo	Japan	38	37	33	23	11
Delhi	India	26	22			
Shanghai	China	24	20			
Sao Paulo	Brazil	21	20	15		
Mumbai	India	21	19	12		
Mexico City	Mexico	21	20	16		
Beijing	China	20	16			
Kinki M. A. (Osaka/Kobe)	Japan	20	19	18	15	
Cairo	Egypt	19	17			
New York/Newark	United States	19	18	16	16	12
Dhaka	Bangladesh	18	15			
Karachi	Pakistan	17	14			
Buenos Aires	Argentina	15	14	11		
Kolkata	India	15	14	11		
Istanbul	Turkey	14	13			
Chongqing	China	13	11			
Lagos	Nigeria	13	11			
Manila	Philippines	13	12			
Rio de Janeiro	Brazil	13	12			
Guangzhou, Guangdong	China	12				
Los Angeles/Long Beach/Sta. Ana	United States	12	12	11		
Moscow	Russia	12	11			
Kinshasa	D. R. Congo	12				
Tianjin	China	11				
Paris	France	11	10			
Shenzhen	China	11	10			
Jakarta	Indonesia	10				
London	United Kingdom	10				
Bangalore	India	10				
Population urban centres 10 million or more		469	369	143	55	24

Note Figures may not add up due to rounding
Source UN (2014d)

6.5   Urbanization: Economic Organisation and Income

6.5.1   Mode of Production: Agriculture, Industry and Services

Industrialisation and the earnings differentials of agricultural and industrial work
have often seen as major stimuli for rural to urban migration, and the growing
degree of urbanisation (Chap. 5: Sects. 5.1 and 5.10). In this context, it would be
expected that the level of urbanization would be negatively associated with the level
of agricultural production. The analysis of these two variables for countries in all
regions of the world confirms that the degree of urbanization is negatively associated with the proportion of gross domestic product (GDP) from agricultural
production, with a few exceptions. For instance, in 2009–2010, Ethiopia and
Cambodia with high proportions of GDP from agricultural production of 51% and
35% respectively had low levels of urbanization, 17% and 20% respectively.
Towards the other end of the range, the Netherlands and Japan with low proportions
of GDP from agricultural production, 2 and 1% respectively, had high degrees of
urbanization, 87% and 91% respectively (Fig. 6.2).

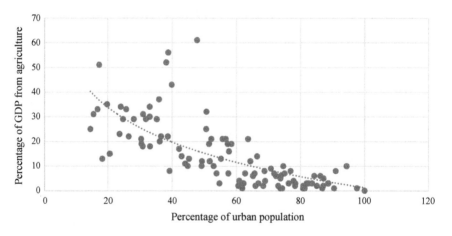

Fig. 6.2 Proportion of country urban population and gross domestic product from agriculture
2009–2010
Note The percentage of urban population in each country is for 2010 as estimated by the United
Nations. The percentage of gross domestic product (GDP) from agriculture is for 2009 as
estimated by the World Bank. A number of countries which GDP had a large proportion of
industrial production from oil and other mineral extraction such as Saudi Arabia, United Arab
Emirates, Nigeria and Norway were excluded from this analysis. Both are unweighted measures of
urbanization and production
Sources WB (2011), UN (2014c)

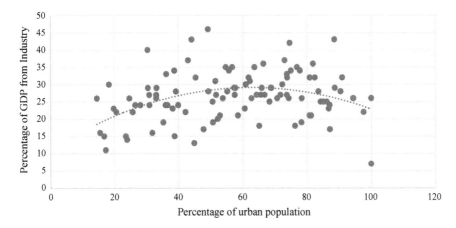

Fig. 6.3 Proportion of country urban population and gross domestic product from industry 2009–2010

Note The percentage of urban population in each country is for 2010 as estimated by the United Nations. The percentage of gross domestic product (GDP) from industry is for 2009 as estimated by the World Bank. A number of countries which GDP had a large proportion of industrial production from oil and other mineral extraction such as Saudi Arabia, United Arab Emirates, Nigeria and Norway were excluded from this analysis. Both are unweighted measures of urbanization and production

Sources WB (2011), UN (2014c)

The corollary to this trend would be that the degree of urbanization would be positively associated with a greater proportion of GDP from industrial production. The analysis of these two variables only partly validates this proposition. With some exceptions, again, as the proportion of GDP from industrial production rises the associated level of urbanization also increases to a point. However, the proportion of industrial production as a proportion of GDP falls after that point as urbanization continues to grow (Fig. 6.3). Accordingly, Kenya with a low proportion of GDP from industrial production (15%) also had a low level of urbanization (24%); China with a high proportion of GDP from industrial production (46%) had a medium level of urbanization (49%) but Australia with 89% of its population living in urban settlements showed a decline in the proportion of GDP from industrial production (29%) (Fig. 6.3).

The analysis of the association between the degree of urbanization of countries and the proportion of GDP from services points to the increasing role that services play as social and economic modernization takes place. This is in agreement with the proposition that large cities become large service and command centres of the global economy. For example, Vietnam (39%), South Africa (66%) and Belgium (78%) had increasing proportions of GDP from service production and associated rises in their level of urbanization of 30, 62 and 98% respectively (Fig. 6.4).

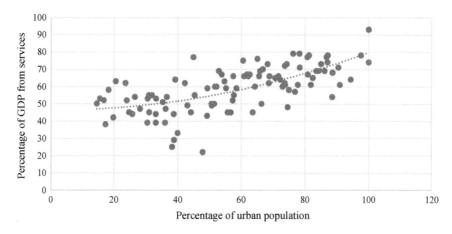

Fig. 6.4 Proportion of country urban population and gross domestic product from services 2009–2010
Note The percentage of urban population in each country is for 2010 is as estimated by the United Nations. The percentage of gross domestic product (GDP) from services is for 2009 as estimated by the World Bank. A number of countries which GDP had a large proportion of industrial production from oil and other mineral extraction such as Saudi Arabia, United Arab Emirates, Nigeria and Norway were excluded from this analysis. Both are unweighted measures of urbanization and production
Sources WB (2011), UN (2014c)

6.5.2   Urbanization: Economic Organization, Productivity and Income

The observed transformation of economic organisation with the degree of urbanization raises questions regarding socioeconomic aspects of its consequences. Quigley (2009) in his review of urbanization and development found evidence, mostly from more developed and from some developing countries, that urbanization was associated with greater productivity and improved earnings of people in urban settlements. This arose from a number of factors and the law of large numbers related to people, goods and services, and influenced productivity in production and marketing. In addition to internal economies of scale experienced in early stages of industrialisation, large urban settlements created external economies of scale from greater specialisation and productivity in intermediary inputs that could be shared by many final producers. The larger pool of labour and capital also resulted in a better fit between them that improved productivity. Large scale also allowed for the establishment of specialised service organisations to support other production units. The bigger stock of educated people in larger urban settlements provided stimulus for innovation in a learning and knowledgeable environment. Evidence was found for the localisation of economies from the synergistic effect of learning from others' experiences. Available evidence also pointed to a higher degree of productivity in urban than rural areas and in larger than smaller cities. However, these gains need to

Table 6.6 Urbanization and income per head of population by country income level, 2010

Country income level	Urban population percentage	GNI per capita ($ PPPs)	Proportion change from previous level	
			Urban percentage	Income per capita
High	79	37,183	1.360	3.754
Upper middle	59	9,904	1.546	2.676
Lower middle	38	3,701	1.322	2.970
Lowest	29	1,246		

Note Income per capita is expressed in gross national income per head of population in purchasing power parities international dollars in the year 2010, as estimated by the World Bank. The proportional change is the ratio of a given level to the previous level of urbanization and income per capita: High/Upper middle; Upper middle/Lower middle; and Lower middle/Lowest
Sources UN (2014c), WB (2011). Computations made by the authors

be considered in the context of higher and often rising land, housing and transport costs that go with higher earnings and tend to reduce the gains from higher productivity. Other concerns are the unpriced externalities of pollution from transport and power generation, congestion and risks from the greater crowding in the communication of disease and other enhanced risks from higher densities.

Data for countries of the degree of urbanization and income levels reflect the exponential increase in income as the degree of urbanization rises. Thus, countries with the lowest average degree of urbanization of 29% had the lowest average income of $1,246 per head of population, while countries with the highest degree of urbanization of 79% had an average income of $37,183 per head of population. This difference of 50% points in urbanization was associated with a difference of $35,937 in income per head of population. Although the level of urbanization rises less from upper middle to high income per capita level than the previous step, it has the highest proportional increase in income per capita (Table 6.6). This is in line with the notion that the degree of urbanization and productivity follows an asymmetric U-shaped curve (Quigley 2009). Urban centres have become central to the world's productive capacity and it is estimated that 70–80% of the world's gross domestic product is generated in urban settlements (UN 2012; UNH 2013).

6.5.3 Urbanization, Industrialisation and Income Inequality

Kuznets (1955) proposed that income inequality rose as societies move from an economy based on agriculture to one grounded on industry, and then fell after a given level of industrialization based on the experience of industrialisation in Europe and North America in the 1950s, when manufacturing was a dominant industrial mode. His premise was that a shift from agriculture to manufacturing tended to increase productivity and value added resulting in income growth. This resulted in higher income but more unequal incomes in industrialised urban

Table 6.7 Urbanization and income inequality by income level, 2014–2015

Country income level	2015 Urban population percentage	2014 Gini coefficient
Lowest	31	65
Low middle	40	32
Upper middle	64	23
High	80	N.A.

Note The proportions of urban population are preliminary estimates for 2015 made by the United Nations as percentages of the total population. The Gini coefficient is a conventional measure of the degree of income inequality presented as a percentage. The higher the coefficient the higher the inequality of income. Where 0 would indicate perfect equality with each unit having the same proportion of all income, and 100 would mean perfect inequality and that one unit would have all the income and all the others none
Sources UN (2014c), WB (2016a)

settlements, at first, than in rural areas. Consequently, industrialisation, urbanization and economic growth increased income inequality at early and middle stages of industrialization and urbanization. He proposed that as growth took hold and education and skill rose, inequality tended to fall after economic growth reached a certain point. Therefore, he expected that income inequality would have an inverted U-shaped pattern along the pathway of industrialisation and urbanization.

A review of the literature of evidence supporting Kuznets propositions showed varying results (e.g. Ganaie 2015). Some research found support for the inverted U-shaped pattern between income growth and inequality, others found it in some countries but not others, and yet others did not find support for the hypothesis. Data quality, models, methods of statistical analysis influence the assorted and at times contrary findings. Another issue is that some countries have followed different political, legal and fiscal ways of dealing with income inequality. Unfortunately, there is no comprehensive data base for countries in the world concerned with income inequality. The World Bank data base on an indicator of income inequality (the Gini coefficient) has large gaps that hinder a comprehensive analysis of this issue (WB 2016a). The estimates from the spread of income inequality shows a positive relationship between income per capita and urbanization (as per Table 6.6) but an inverse relationship between income and urbanization and income inequality (Table 6.7). However, this is an incomplete picture as the data set does not include an aggregate measure of income inequality for high income countries.[1] The World Bank aggregates from low and middle income countries would indicate a decrease rather than an increase in income inequality, as industrialisation and income grows rather than the inverted U-shaped pattern proposed by Kuznets.

Another possibility is a U-shaped pattern, if inequality increases with income per capita in high income countries. Data on income inequality from Organisation for

---

[1]It is curious that the Gini coefficients for high income countries such as the United States (US) are not included in the World Bank's data base, when the US Gini coefficient is available from the US Census Bureau and the OECD.

Economic Co-operation and Development (OECD) indicates that the unweighted average of the Gini coefficient of the more industrialised countries (excluding Russia) was 32% in 2014 (ranging from 24% in Iceland to 39% in the United States) (OECD undated). If this estimate was to prevail then the Gini coefficient of high income countries would be higher than the coefficient in upper middle countries (23%) and result in a U-shaped pattern of income inequality among countries in relation to their level of industrialisation and associated urbanization. Nevertheless, the wide range in both OECD and other middle income countries points to possible fiscal interventions that affect household disposable income, rather than just the effects of industrialisation and urbanization. This is reflected in the relatively low Gini coefficients in Denmark (25%), Norway (25%), Finland (26%), Sweden (28%), Netherlands (28%) and the higher coefficients in the United States (39%), United Kingdom (36%), Spain (35%) and Portugal (34%).

Box 6.1 Urbanization, industrialization and household consumer inequality: China and India

China and India make up more than one third of the world's population. Both are developing countries but at different stages of development, industrialisation and urbanization (Table 6.12). As the two largest developing societies, they offer examples of differences in the stages of moving from agricultural to industrial production and from rural to urban settlements. They also provide illustrations of disparities in household consumption between rural and urban populations and the degree of inequality in them.

Both countries carried out surveys of household consumption in urban and rural areas in 2005 that have been the subject of analysis to assess differences in household allocations to different commodities in urban and rural areas; as well as propensities to consume diverse commodities as the levels of household expenditure rise (Martins et al. 2017). The analysis of these data indicated that household consumption expenditures were higher in China than India, as expected from the higher incomes per head of population in China. It also showed that following the same income pattern household consumption was higher in urban than rural areas in both countries. Further, in accordance with Engel's Law the proportion of household expenditures on food declined as income rose, between and within countries.

An extension of this analysis here confirms the substantial differences in the levels of household expenditure between urban and rural households. In addition, it revealed greater inequality in household consumer expenditure in urban areas with almost twice the level of household expenditure than those in rural areas in both countries (Table 6.13).

Yet another perspective and pathway is that associated with economic level, urbanization, agriculture, industry and services production. As countries move from agricultural to manufacturing production income grows. As further growth takes place services tend to replace industrial production as the major contributor to gross domestic product. While manufacturing tends to take place in a framework of higher but more level incomes, services are known for their variability of income from highly paid jobs in such activities as finance to lowly paid ones in food services and cleaning. Consequently, the growth of large urban centres with a concentration of work in services and high average incomes can also lead to large income inequalities. The United Sates experience offers illustrations of this pattern (Noss 2014). Cities with high levels of service activity such as New York City, Washington DC, Atlanta City, New Orleans and Miami have a considerably greater degree of income inequality than other urban centres in the United States. This is in line with the trend for economic growth and income inequality in more developed countries that has been documented and discussed by Picketty (2014).

6.6 Gender and the City

A major feature of the perceived rural and urban dichotomy is the differences in the types of production, their configuration and impact on social characteristics and organisation. It is understood that there are earning differentials and a wider range of occupations and paid work in urban settlements. Do the characteristics of urban settlements and their social and economic organisation have an influence on the *production* and *reproduction and caring* roles played by males and females in society? Among others, the following have been suggested as urbanization aspects of relevance (UNH 2013):

- *demographic characteristics*
- *divisions of labour*
- *human capital*

It is posited that urban settlements give females greater access to paid work, services and impose a lower degree of constraints from social norms concerning the perceived higher position of males in the family and society (Tacoli and Satterthwaite 2013). A demographic expression of these opportunities is that fertility tends to be lower in urban than rural areas. Lower fertility has been associated with the level of education of females and access to contraception, as well as female participation in the formal labour force offered by urban social and economic environments. The higher fertility of females migrating from rural to urban areas has been found to converge with lower fertility in urban areas. However, females who are poor in urban settlements have higher fertility than the urban average. This is attributed to lower education and lower access to contraception services. Varying cultural practices of the gendered roles of males and females have influenced the migration of males and females to urban areas. Accordingly, greater migration by males to urban centres has been the pattern in the past, especially in sub-Sahara Africa. Nevertheless, females tend to outnumber males in urban centres in older ages, as they have a longer life expectancy than males. Female migration to urban centres has risen in more recent years in Latin America and the Caribbean, Asia and even sub-Sahara Africa (WB 2016b; UNH 2013). An example of the *feminisation* of the urban setting is that in the Netherlands where there were more males aged 20–24 years than females of the same age in 2014. Yet, females of that age out-numbered males in the major urban centres of Amsterdam, Hague, Rotterdam and Utrecht, as high as 138 females per 100 males in Utrecht (CBS 2015).

Employment opportunities in the formal sector influences the relationships between male and females and the relative independence of females, and conse-quently their participation in the household's decision making. It has been postu-lated, perceptions of the females' contribution to the family held by both males and females depend on whether the work carried out by females has a monetary expression. Thus, female work related to reproduction, caring and even shared work with males in agriculture without payment is considered to be a normal female contribution. The contribution from paid work outside the family is seen as a different contribution that gives females more power in the family's decision making. This is more likely to take place in urban than rural areas and gives females in urban areas a greater degree of sharing in family decision making than their counterparts in rural areas (Bradshaw 2013).

Participation in paid work by females gives them greater independence but does not usually lead to sharing housework and caring for children with males. Thus, females in urban settlements are concerned both with the *production function*, usually associated with males, but also with the burden of their traditional *repro-duction and caring function*. This could also mean that daughters may be asked to share this responsibility for caring, at the cost of the time that they dedicate to education, especially in poor urban households (Tacoli and Satterthwaite 2013).

Access to education in urban areas impacts females' contribution to human capital and on their skill and opportunities for advancement. The continuing gap between males and females' level of education, as well as cultural perceptions of what might be female work tends to discriminate participation by females in some occupations deemed to be male work and to push females into service type occu-pations. Although males might often have longer work experience in some occu-pations, partly because of their production rather than reproduction functions, females tend to be paid less than males for similar type of work (WB 2016b; UNH 2013; Tacoli and Satterthwaite 2013). In spite of the enhancement of the position of females related to paid work in the urban environment, the perceptions of traditional male and female roles tend to be pervasive in the types of work offered to females and their rates of pay.

The evidence of the importance of education, work in the formal sector and access to health/reproduction services to females in urban settlements coincides with findings that urban settlements are perceived having a beneficial impact on female lives. A survey of perceptions in Bangalore, Johannesburg, Kampala, Kingston and Rio de Janeiro showed that the three most important features of urban settlements to female welfare were: access to education, meaningful work and health care (UNH 2013).

The impact of urbanization on male and female relationships and their respective positions in society might be partly the result of education, evolving social values and understanding of females' contribution to society as well as urbanization per se. Nevertheless, the urban environment may continue to enhance the context in which the transition of the perceptions of the females' contributions to society, from mostly a *reproduction* to a better recognised *production* contribution.

6.7   Urbanization: Banlieue and Slums

The growth of urban settlements stimulated by industrialisation, fuelled by rural to urban flows (added by international migration) has led to urban spread in developed and developing countries. It has been suggested that there are two major ways of explaining suburbanisation in more developed countries, such as in the United Sates (Follain and Malpezzi 1981):

- *Accessibility model*
- *Blight flight model*

The first proposes that economic growth is the reason for urbanization. As income rises the demand for larger and better houses increases. The fixed nature of the amount of land in urban centres and lower land costs in the periphery leads people who can afford the higher transport costs to move to the suburbs. The second relies on the understanding that as urban growth takes place, urban centres become more crowded, noisy and less attractive to live in, and infrastructure tends to lag behind population growth with consequent urban decay. Again, those who can afford move to the suburbs leaving low-income people behind in poor living conditions.

The move of middle-income people from city centres has been described in the United States as the *flight to the suburbs*. And in the 1950s and 1960s, as black people migrated from the Southern agricultural states to urban settlements in the Northern industrial states, it became sometimes labelled as the *white flight to the suburbs*. Questions related to urban segregation along racial lines have been the subject of much analysis. Although most findings support the racial segregation proposition, some have found that the segregation is more related to relative incomes rather than along racial lines (e.g. Bradford and Kelejian 1973).

Examples of the suburbanisation in the United Sates abound such as New York City and Newark, New Jersey, Greenwich, Connecticut. Canada also offers examples such as Toronto and Scarborough, and Montreal and Laval. In France, an example is the *banlieue* of Paris in Versailles, and in the United Kingdom the original Greenwich in London. They have provided residential space for growing cities, as alternatives to the crowded and more expensive land in the city centres. They have been associated with the growing use of motor vehicles as a means of transport and the building of substantial highways and extended suburban rail networks.

Another feature of urbanization has been the concentration of disadvantaged and often poor people in given urban areas. The English term *slum* was first associated with *a room of low repute* or *low, unfrequented parts of town* in London (UNH 2003). In Latin America, the *favelas* of Rio de Janeiro have a similar derogative connotation, and in some countries *barrios* also have that association. The *kampungs* of Jakarta are an Asian expression of highly dense, inadequate housing, poorly serviced and low-income urban concentrations.

Slums are not new but they have grown as urbanization has swollen fed by migration to the cities. In a developing country context, Todaro (1969) proposed that the apparent income differential between rural and urban areas could lead to false expectations and different realities. Because of the *expected differential*, the rate of migration could be higher than the growth rate of employment in the urban setting. The *expected differential* might be higher than the *real differential* in income between rural and urban, due to the probability of being unemployed on arrival at the urban settlement. Some migrants, at least for a time, would tend to be unemployed, or in the informal sector, and provide a flow of migrants to crowded urban slums. Todaro's proposition has been criticised on the basis that real workers tend to be risk averse and rational. Consequently, only those with a likelihood of getting a job in the urban formal sector are likely to migrate (Duranton 2009).

The UN-Habitat has defined a *slum household* as one that has lack of one or more of the following characteristics (UNH 2016):

- *improved water supply*
- *improved sanitation facilities*
- *sufficient living area*
- *adequate structural and durability features*
- *security of tenure*

United Nations estimates for 2001 point to the ubiquitous positive association between stage of development and degree of urbanization: the higher the rate of development the greater the proportion of urban population. However, these estimates also reveal a negative association between the proportion of people in urban settlements and the latter's proportion of people living in slums: the lower the level of development and urbanization the higher the proportion of urban population living in slum conditions. Although in 2001 more developed countries had a higher proportion of people living in urban areas (76%) than less developed ones (41%), they had a much lower proportion of 6% of their urban population living in slums compared with 43% in less developed countries (Table 6.8). This meant most slum dwellers lived in less developed countries at that time.

The proportion of people living in slums in urban areas in developing countries fell from 43% in 2001 to 36% in 2005, and further declined to 30% in 2014 (Table 6.9). However, the absolute number climbed further due to the larger number of people living in urban areas (Tables 6.2 and 6.3). The less industrialised Sub-Sahara Africa (56%) and Southern Asia (31%) continued to have a large proportion of their urban population living in slums, while Northern Africa (12%)

Table 6.8 World urban population and proportion living in slums, 2001

Stage of development	Urban population millions	Urban population percentage of total population	Slum population percentage of urban population
World	2,923	47.7	31.6
Developed	902	75.5	6
Developing	2,022	40.9	43
Least developed	179	26.2	78.2

Note Developing includes both least and other less developed countries
Source UNH (2003)

Table 6.9 Slum dwellers in developing countries as a proportion of urban population by region and sub-region, 2005–2014

Region	Percentage of urban population living in slums			Difference 2005–2014
	2005	2010	2014	
Developing regions	35.6	32.6	29.7	−5.9
Northern Africa	13.4	13.3	11.9	−1.5
Sub-Sahara Africa	63.0	61.7	55.9	−7.1
Latin America and the Caribbean	25.5	23.5	21.1	−4.4
Eastern Asia	33.0	28.2	26.2	−6.8
Southern Asia	40.0	35.0	31.3	−8.7
South-eastern Asia	34.2	31.0	28.4	−5.8
Western Asia	25.8	24.6	24.9	−0.9
Oceania	24.1	24.1	24.1	...

Note Oceania excludes the more developed countries of Australia and New Zealand
Source UNH (2016). Computations made by the authors

had the lowest proportion. Developing countries in Latin America and the Caribbean (21%), Oceania (24%), Western Asia (25%), Eastern (26%) and South-eastern Asia (28%) had lower but substantial proportions of their urban population living in slum conditions (Table 6.9).

India's growing urbanization provides an example of the gravitation of migrants with low skills and incomes to inadequate housing in city slums. It has been estimated that in 2005–2006 53% of Delhi's urban population were slum dwellers, 52% in Hyderabad, 47% in Mumbai, 39% in Chennai, 34% in Indore, 31% in Kolkata and Meenut, and 29% in Nagpur (Bhagat 2014).

6.8   Urbanization and the Environment

Urban settlements have become the major sources of economic production, employment and the setting in which most people live, and make a disproportional contribution to economic production in relation to their population (UNH 2016). The association of high population density of urban centres and production entails more intensive activity and demand for improved management of living conditions and of industrial interdependences, wastes and emissions. The absence or lagging of adequate investment in infrastructure and services lead to public health concerns, environmental contamination, as well as traffic congestion, poor working conditions and higher economic costs.

Power generation and reliance on motor vehicle transport for both commercial and private use have been features of industrialisation and urbanization with an impact on the environment. In 2006, estimates of electricity consumption per head of population pointed to the growing demand for power with the degree of urbanization. High income countries used almost six times (5.9) as much electrical power per head of population as middle income countries at a lower level of industrialisation, and they in turn consumed five times (5.3) as much as low income countries. Over the 16-years 1990–2006, electricity consumption per head of population of the world's growing population grew by 30%. The higher industrial growth rate of middle income countries (WB 2010) was reflected in their higher rate of electricity consumption per head of population during that period (58%) compared with high (28%) and low (19%) income countries with smaller growth rates (Table 6.10).

Growth in power generation and transport contributed to higher rates of carbon dioxide emissions adding to the level of air pollution in urban centres. Following the same pattern as electricity consumption, carbon dioxide emissions were four times higher in high income than middle income countries in 2005, and middle income five times higher than low income countries. The share of carbon dioxide

Table 6.10 Urbanization and electricity production per head of population by income level, 2005, 2006, and change 1990–2006

Country income level	2005 Percentage urban population	Electricity consumption per capita (kW h)		
		2006		Percentage change 1990–2006
		Use	Change on previous level	
World	49	2,750		30
High income	78	9,675	5.9	28
Middle income	45	1,647	5.3	58
Low income	26	311		19

Sources UN (2014c), WB (2010). Computations made by the authors

Table 6.11 Urbanization and carbon dioxide emissions by income level, 1990–2005

Country income level	2005 Percentage urban population	Carbon dioxide emissions per capita metric tons			Percentage share of the world emissions
		1990	2005	Percentage change 1990–2005	
World	49	4.0	4.2	5.0	100
High income	78	11.8	12.7	7.6	50
Middle income	45	2.6	3.0	15.3	48
Low income	26	0.7	0.6	−14.7	3

Note Figures may not add up due to rounding
Sources UN (2014c), WB (2010). Computations made by the authors

emissions was almost evenly shared between high (50%) and middle (48%) income countries. During the 15-year period 1990–2005, emissions of carbon dioxide per capita rose by 5%, with higher growth of 15% in middle income countries and an actual decrease of 15% in low income countries (Table 6.11). Thus, the world carbon dioxide emissions grew both in absolute but also per head of population meaning a growing rate of emissions and atmospheric pollution. In addition to carbon dioxide, emissions of methane and nitrous dioxide added to air pollution. Further, sulphate particles in the atmosphere from industrial sources have led to acid rain that affect soil, vegetation and buildings (WB 2010).

As well as these environmental threats, others related to waste management, housing and sanitation pose constraints to the attainment of potential gains from urbanization. For many years, Smokey Mountain in Manila, Philippines, stood as great visual expression of the lack of investment in urban services and pollution control, opportunities for gainful employment and access to adequate housing in a large urban centre. It resulted in a leaking mountain of waste that emitted methane

Table 6.12 China and India population, urbanization, income and production 2004–2005

Country	2005 Population millions	2005 Urban population percentage	2004 GNI p. c. PPP $	2004 GDP percentage		
				Agriculture	Industry	Services
China	1,321.6	42.5	5,530	15	51	35
India	1,144.1	29.2	3,100	22	26	52

Note The population for 2005 and proportion in urban settlements is as estimated by the United Nations. The gross national income per head of population are expressed in purchasing power parities international dollars for 2004. The proportion of gross domestic product from the value added by agriculture, industry and services are estimates by the World Bank for 2004
Source UN (2014a, 2017), WB (2005)

Table 6.13 Inequality in household consumer expenditures and rural and urban inequality in China and India 2005

Country	Urban household consumer expenditure rural = 1.000	Inequality Gini coefficient percentage	
		Rural households	Urban households
China	2.2	15.8	22.8
India	1.8	17.9	22.2

Note The index of inequality is the Gini coefficient estimated by the authors for household consumer expenditures within rural and urban areas in 2005
Source Martins et al. (2017). Computations made by the authors

and contaminated the soil, atmosphere, and nearby streams. It was an example of slum squatting that provided inadequate and unsafe shelter and poor income from garbage scavenging for some 40,000 poor people who lived on it. This same environment affected their health and offered few opportunities for their children (Abad 1991; Auer 1990).

6.9 Urban Agenda

In the 21st Century, most people live in urban settlements, for the first time. Urban centres have become the hubs generating economic growth. Paris with 16% of France's population accounts for 27% of its GDP, Metro Manila has 12% of the population of the Philippines but generates 47% of that country's GDP, and Kinshasa with 13% of the population of the Democratic Republic of the Congo produces 85% of its GDP (UNH 2016). Economic growth and urbanization have been linked with technological revolutions in the production of food and other goods and services, and continue to impact the pace and nature of economic and social transformation. Technological changes have supported the almost three-fold increase in the world's population since the 1950s and urban settlements have absorbed much of this growth, with rising income per head of population, in spite of the large population growth. These are some of the features that Adam Smith saw as being beneficial to both the city and the country.

The urbanization dilemma is similar and linked to that of economic growth: how to attain it and benefit from it and at the same time manage the social and environmental pressures that it poses. There is no previous experience to the pace and scale of the changes that are taking place to guide people along helpful pathways to acceptable outcomes. Nevertheless, past and current experiences of more developed countries, further along the industrialization and urbanization path, point to examples of favourable as well as harmful practices. A major concern is the impact of rapid urban and industrial growth without or lagging investment in infrastructure and provision of urban services that result in social and economic imbalances and threats to environmental conditions (Florida 2015).

Urban settlements offer opportunities for greater diversity and the symbiotic outcome of the interaction of people with different interests and skills that can lead to innovation and allow experimentation in a larger risk pool. Urban heterogeneity has provided a social environment in which gendered perspectives about the roles and positions of males and females in the family, work and society have changed. It has given females enhanced opportunities for engagement in paid work, greater independence and sharing in family decision making, but has not eliminated gendered inequalities. The diversity of occupations and growing uncoupling of economic activity that has led to increasing service functions have been associated with larger income inequalities in urban centres and contrasts that can result in social stress. The increasing scale of urban settlements and the growing number of megacities of 10 million or more people pose issues related to the management of growing and more complex economic and social interdependencies and the responsibilities of various levels of public administration. Similarly, the economic, technological, and other drivers of social change exemplified by urban settlements continuously replace existing ways of life with new forms of social relations (Berman 1982).

This is compounded by the global dispersion of economic activity and the evolution of some urban centres as *global cities* such as New York, London, and Tokyo. They have become global command centres of large international corporations and led to the establishment of large specialised service firms with a global reach. Thus, global cities have a lower interest and relationship with their surrounding hinterland and local and national government than other urban centres because of their international interest and focus.

The growing trend towards urbanization in developing countries where most people live could provide a way of accommodating the substantial projected increment in population in following decades. Technological changes could improve power generation and transport emissions that are one of the plights of urbanization, as well as housing conditions. They might also facilitate the coordination of services that are required in the larger urban environment. Nevertheless, purposeful investments in infrastructure, urban facilities and services, access to adequate housing, gainful and meaningful employment and improvements in human capital are obvious essential items on an agenda for urban living.

References

Abad, R. G. (1991). Squatting and scavenging in Smokey Mountain. *Philippine Studies, 39,* 263–286.

Auer, C. (1990). Health status of children living in a squatter area in Manila, Philippines, with particular emphasis on intestinal parasitoses. *South East Asian Journal of Tropical Medicine and Public Health, 21*(2), 289–300.

Berman, M. (1982). *All that is solid melts into the air.* New York: Penguin.

Bhagat, R. M. (2014). *Urban migration trends, challenges and opportunities in India*. World Migration Report 2015. Geneva: International Organization for Migration.

Balchin, P. N., Isaac, D., & Chen, J. (2000). *Urban economics: A global perspective*. Houndsville: Palgrave.

Bradford, D. F., & Kelejian, H. H. (1973). An econometric model of the flight to the suburbs. *Journal of Political Economy, 81*(3), 566–589.

Bradshaw, S. (2013). Women's decision-making in rural and urban households in Nicaragua: The influence of income and ideology. *Environment & Urbanization, 25*(1), 81–94.

Central Bureau voor de Statistiek (CBS). (2015). *Many women prefer urban environment*. Retrieved March 24, 2017, from www.cbs.nl.

Davis, K., & Golden, H. H. (1954). Urbanization and the development of pre-industrial areas. *Economic Development and Cultural Change, 3*(1), 6–24.

Duranton, G. (2009). Are cities engines of growth and prosperity for developing countries? In M. Spence, P. C. Annez, & R. M. Buckley (Eds.), *Urbanization and growth* (pp. 67–113). Washington DC: World Bank.

Florida, R. (2015). *The urban housing crunch costs the U. S. economy about $1.6 trillion a year*. Retrieved December 7, 2017, from www.city.lab.com.

Follain, J. R., & Malpezzi, S. (1981). The flight to the suburbs: insights gained from an analysis of central-city vs suburban housing costs. *Journal of Urban Economics, 9*, 381–398.

Ganaie, A. A. (2015). Kuznets inverted U hypothesis of income inequality: looking inside the available economic literature. *Journal of Poverty, Investment and Development, 9*, 138–148.

Hara, T. (2015). *A shrinking society—Post demographic transition in Japan*. Tokyo: Springer.

Kasarda, J. D., & Janowitz, M. (1974). Community attachment in mass society. *American Sociological Review, 39*(3), 328–339.

Kasarda, J. D., & Crenshaw, E. M. (1991). Third world urbanization: Dimensions, theories, and determinants. *Annual Review of Sociology, 17*, 467–501.

Kuznets, S. (1955). Economic growth and income inequality. *American Economic Review, 45*(1), 1–28.

Martins, J. M., Yusuf, F., Brooks, G., & Swanson, D. A. (2017). Demographics and market segmentation: China and India. In D. A. Swanson (Ed.), *The Frontiers of applied demography*. Springer International Publishing.

Marx, K., & Engels, F. (1951). *Selected works* (Vol. I & II). Moscow: Foreign Languages Publishing House.

Noss, A. (2014). *Household income: 2013*. United States Census Bureau: American Community Survey Briefs.

Organisation for Economic Co-operation and Development (OECD). (Undated). *OECD Income Distribution Database*. Retrieved March 22, 2017, from www.oecd.org.

Ozden, K., & Enwere, C. (2012). Urbanization and its political challenges in developing countries. *Eurasian Journal of Business and Economics, 5*(10), 99–120.

Park, R. E. (1925). The city: Suggestions for the investigation of human behaviour in the urban environment. In R. E. Park, E. W. Burgess, & R. D. McKenzie (Eds.), *The city* (pp. 1–46). Chicago: University of Chicago Press.

Park, R. E. (1936). Human ecology. *American Journal of Sociology, 42*(1), 1–15.

Picketty, T. (2014). *Capital in the twenty-first century* (A. Goldhammer Trans.). Cambridge MA: Belknap Press of Harvard University Press.

Purcell, M. (2002). Excavating Lefebvre: The right to the city and its urban politics of the inhabitants. *GeoJournal, 58*, 99–108.

Quigley, J. M. (2009). Urbanization, agglomeration, and economic development. In M. Spence, P. C. Annez, & R. M. Buckley (Eds.), *Urbanization and growth* (pp. 115–128). Washington DC: World Bank.

Sassen, S. (1991). *The global city—New York, London and Tokyo*. Princeton, NJ: Princeton University Press.

Sassen, S. (2005). The global city: Introducing the concept. *Brown Journal of World Affairs, 11*(2), 27–43.

Schoultz, L. (1972). Urbanization and political change in Latin America. *Midwest Journal of Political Science, 16*(3): 367–387).

Simmel, G. (2000). The metropolis and mental life. In G. Bridge & S. Watson (Eds.), *The Blackwell city reader* (pp. 11–19). Oxford & Malden, MA: Wiley-Blackwell. Retrieved March 12, 2017, from www.blackwellpublisshing.com/content/BPL_Images/Content_store/sample_chapter/0631225137/Bridge.pdf.

Smith, A. (1970 [1776]). *The wealth of nations*. Harmondsworth: Pelican Books.

Tacoli, C., & Satterthwaite, D. (2013). Gender and urban change. *Environment & Urbanization, 25*(1), 3–8.

Todaro, M. P. (1969). A model of labour migration and urban unemployment in less developed countries. *American Economic Review, 59*(1), 138–148.

Tonnies, F. (2002). *Community and society—Gemeinschaft und gesellschaft* (C. P. Loomis Trans.). Mineola, NY: Dover Publications.

United Nations (UN). (2012). *World urban prospects: The 2011 revision—Highlights*. New York.

United Nations (UN). (2014a). *World urbanization prospects: The 2014 revision*. New York. *File 2: Percentage of population at mid-year residing in urban areas by major area, region and country, 1950–2050*. Retrieved March 5, 2017, from www.esa.un.org/unpd/wup/index.hmt.

United Nations (UN). (2014b). *World urbanization prospects: The 2014 revision – Highlights*. New York.

United Nations (UN). (2014c). *World urbanization prospects: The 2014 revision*. New York. *File 3: Urban population at mid-year by major area, region and country, 1950–2050*. Retrieved March 5, 2017, from www.esa.un.org/unpd/wup/index.hmt.

United Nations (UN). (2014d). *World urbanization prospects: The 2014 revision*. New York. *File 11a: The largest 30 urban agglomerations ranked by population size at each point in time, 1950–2030*. Retrieved March 5, 2017, from www.esa.un.org/unpd/wup/index.hmt.

United Nations (UN). (2017). *World population prospects, The 2017 revision*. Volume I: Comprehensive tables. New York.

United Nations Human Settlements Programme (UNH). (2003). *Slums of the World: The face of urban poverty in the new millennium*. Nairobi.

United Nations Human Settlements Programme (UNH). (2013). *State of women in cities 2012–2013—Gender and the prosperity of cities*. Nairobi.

United Nations Human Settlements Programme (UNH). (2016). *Urbanization and development—Emerging futures*. Nairobi.

Weber, M. (1958). *The city* (D. Martindale & G. Neuwirth Trans. and Ed.). Glencoe, IL: The Free Press.

Wirth, L. (1938). Urbanism as a way of life. *American Journal of Sociology, 44*(1), 1–24.

World Bank (WB). (2005). *World development report 2006*. Washington DC.

World Bank (WB). (2010). *World development report 2010*. Washington DC.

World Bank (WB). (2011). *World development report 2012*. Washington DC.

World Bank (WB). (2016a). *Gini index*. Retrieved March 5, 2017, www.data.worldbank.org.

World Bank (WB). (2016b). *Global monitoring report 2015/2016—Development goals in an era of demographic change*. Washington DC.

World Health Organization (WHO). (2011). *Global health ageing*. Geneva.

Chapter 7
Ageing Transformation

7.1 Ageing Drivers

7.1.1 Stable and Unstable Age Populations

Euler's stable population model elaborated by Dublin and Lotka (Swanson et al. 2016; Yusuf et al. 2014) indicates that populations when subjected to constant fertility, mortality and migration rates will tend to converge to the same age distribution in the long-run. However, empirical evidence shows that these components of population-change vary over time and from country to country (UN 2017a, b). Accordingly, both the absolute and relative age distributions of countries have also varied over time, even though they may share some similar traits. The reality is one of unstable age distributions rather than the stable population model, as useful as that model has been in the analysis of population characteristics.

7.1.2 Surges and Wanes

Although there is some evidence the world population might have fallen at times, the trend in recent centuries has been for continuing population growth, in spite of some hiccups (Table 1.1). This growth has relied on fertility rates well above replacement level and their momentum, which ensured that, on average, a large proportion of the population was made up of children and young adults (Tables 3.3 and 3.5). The Baby Boom in more developed countries of the late 1940s and 1950s led to an upsurge in the world's fertility that waned in late 1960s and 1970s (Tables 1.10 and 3.3). This has been accompanied by steep falls in fertility rates of less developed countries in more recent decades—even in Africa that has kept an average fertility rate well above replacement level (Table 3.3). This decline in

© Springer International Publishing AG, part of Springer Nature 2018   181
Jo. M. Martins et al., *Global Population in Transition*,
https://doi.org/10.1007/978-3-319-77362-9_7

fertility has been accompanied by falls in mortality that has added to longevity in both more and less developed countries (Tables 1.12 and 4.9).

According to the United Nations (UN 2005a), the world is experiencing an *unprecedented transformation* with a transition from high fertility and mortality to low fertility and mortality. Three phases have been proposed in this transition. The first involves a decline in mortality and a rise in the proportion of younger people and children. In the second stage, fertility falls and the proportion of children declines while the proportion of young and older adults increases, with an increment in the segment of working age. This is followed by the third phase of the transition when long runs of both low fertility and mortality reduces the proportion of both children and adults of working age and leads to a rising proportion of old-age people.

The experience of recent decades indicates that rises and falls in fertility have been the major drivers to changes in age distribution of the world's population, while the continuing downward trend in mortality has played a complementary role in the ageing transformation.

An analysis of changes in birth and death rates of the world from 1950–1955 to 2010–2015 shows the relative importance of fertility and mortality to the changes that have taken place in population growth and age distribution during that period (Table 7.1). The fertility effect was substantially higher than the mortality effect. The outcome was a reduction in the average annual population growth rate from 1.8% in 1950–1955 to 1.2% in 2010–2015, and an inevitable reduction in the proportion of children in the world's population and longer longevity that associated with ageing of earlier cohorts led to rising median age of the population and a greater proportion of old-age people. The migration effect also played a role in changes in age distribution at local, country and regional levels, both at the point of origin and destination, as migrant population tends to be different from the average age distribution with a lower proportion of children and old-age people, but its impact was lower than that of either fertility or mortality (UN 2005a).

Table 7.1 World natural increase rates, 1950–1955 and 2010–2015

Rates	Average births and deaths per hundred people		
	1950–1955	2010–2015	Difference 1950–1955 2010–2015
Crude birth rate	3.69	1.96	−1.73
Crude death rate	1.91	0.77	−1.14
Natural increase	1.75	1.19	−0.56

Note The crude birth rate in this case is the number of births during the period per hundred people. The crude death rate is the number of deaths during the period per hundred people. Natural increase is the difference between the crude birth and death rates during the period. In this case, natural increase is the average percentage growth rate of the population during the period
Source UN (2017a). Computations made by the authors

7.2 Transformation and Ageing

The fertility surge of the 1950s and 1960s and its momentum led to a reduction in the world's average median age from 24 years in 1950 to 22 in 1970, as fertility lost its momentum in the 1980s the median age rose to 24 years in 1990 and continued to increase to reach 30 years in 2015. Nevertheless, even taking into account migration, these median ages gloss over different experiences in more and less developed countries at different stages of transition. It is other less developed countries—including the two most populous countries of China and India—that tend to set the world's median age, while more and least developed countries tend to be at the two extremes of the distribution. Accordingly, the median age of least developed countries, that on average did not experience a decline in fertility until the late 1970s, fell slightly from 19 years in 1950 to 18 in 1990. As the fertility momentum faded, the median age rose to 20 years in 2015. In 2015, these countries were on average only slightly older in 2015 than they were in 1950. However, other less developed countries, at an early stage of their transition, experienced a substantial drop in their median age from 22 years in 1950 to 19 in 1970. As the fall in fertility took hold in these countries, the median age rose to 22 years in 1990 and continued to increase to 29 in 2015: an increase of 10 years in the period 1970–2015. More developed countries with substantial fertility declines from the levels of the Baby Boom of the late 1940s to 1960s to the 1970s were the countries where the median age rose most from 29 years in 1950 to 41 in 2015: an increment of 13 years in that period (Table 7.2).

The various stages of the ageing transformation in different countries is apparent from trends in regional median ages. Thus, Africa followed closely the pattern of

Table 7.2 Median age of world's population by stage of development and region, 1950–2015

Stage of development/ region	Median age (years)						Change 1950–2015 (years)
	1950	1970	1990	2000	2010	2015	
World	23.6	21.5	24	26.3	28.5	29.6	+6.0
Least developed	19.4	17.9	17.5	18.2	19	19.6	+0.2
Other less developed	21.7	19.0	22.3	25.1	27.9	29.3	+7.6
More developed	28.5	30.6	34.4	37.3	39.9	41.1	+12.6
Africa	19.3	17.8	17.6	18.4	19.1	19.4	+0.1
Asia	22.1	19.5	23.0	26.0	28.9	30.3	+8.2
Europe	28.9	31.7	34.6	37.7	40.4	41.6	+12.7
Lat. America and Car.	19.9	18.6	21.7	24.2	27.4	29.2	+9.3
Northern America	30.0	28.2	32.8	35.4	37.2	37.9	+7.9
Oceania	27.9	24.8	28.6	30.9	32.2	32.8	+5.0

Source UN (2017b). Computations made by the authors

the least developed countries, Asia and Latin America and the Caribbean kept similar paths as the other less developed countries, while Europe's course followed that of the more developed countries. Northern America and especially Oceania where the Baby Boom was more substantial experienced a fall in their median ages between 1950 and 1970, from 30 to 28 years in the case of North America, and from 28 years to 25 in Oceania. But as the fertility momentum waned their median ages rose respectively to 38 and 33 years in 2015 (Table 7.2). It is relevant that the rate of migration was higher in Oceania than Northern America; and that population growth from migration in Northern America and Oceania played a greater moderating role in their ageing process than in Europe.

An analysis of the intensity of the rise in fertility above replacement level in a large number of more developed countries in Europe and Northern America indicates that the higher the boom in fertility the lower the bust, such as in the United States, Australia and New Zealand, and that countries that had a low rise in fertility during the boom years were those with greatest busts, such as Portugal, Spain, Italy and Hungary, with consequent impact on ageing of their populations (Reher 2015).

7.3 Transformation Path and Clustering

7.3.1 Transformation Phases and Ageing

Examination of the age distribution patterns indicates that different fertility and mortality experiences have led to clustering of countries at different transitional stages in groups with diverse age distributions in 2015 (Table 7.3).

7.3.2 High Fertility and High Mortality: Child Populations

The first group with high fertility (TFR about 6–7) and low life expectancy (about 50–60 years) started its mortality transition but the fertility transition was not pronounced by 2015. This resulted in a high proportion of children (about 45–50%) and a very low proportion of old-age people 65 years and over of age (about 2.5–3.0%). People of working age constituted about 50% of the population, as in the case of Chad, Mali and Somalia (Table 7.3).

Table 7.3 Age distribution, fertility and life expectancy of selected countries, 2015

Country	Age distribution (%)			2010–2015	
	0–14	15–64	65 and over	TFR	Le
Chad	47.6	50.0	2.5	6.3	51.7
Mali	47.9	49.5	2.5	6.4	56.2
Somalia	46.7	50.6	2.7	6.6	54.9
Egypt	33.1	61.8	5.1	3.4	70.8
Pakistan	35.0	60.5	4.5	3.7	65.9
Philippines	32.2	63.2	4.6	3.1	68.5
India	28.7	65.7	5.6	2.4	67.6
South Africa	29.3	65.6	5.1	2.6	59.5
Venezuela	28.2	65.5	6.3	2.4	73.9
China	17.7	72.6	9.7	1.6	75.7
Australia	18.8	66.2	15	1.9	82.3
New Zealand	20.0	65.4	14.6	2.0	81.3
United States	19.2	66.1	14.6	1.9	78.9
Germany	13.1	65.8	21.1	1.4	80.4
Italy	13.7	63.9	22.4	1.4	82.3
Japan	13.0	61.0	26.0	1.4	83.3
World	26.1	65.6	8.3	2.5	70.8

Note (*TFR*) Total fertility rate or the average number of children born to a female during her reproductive period; (*Le*) Life expectancy or the average number of years a person is expected to live at birth
Source UN (2017a). Computations made by the authors

7.3.3 Lowering Fertility and Mortality: Child and Young Adult Populations

In this second group, the fertility transition started (TFR about 3–4) and life expectancy (about 60–70 years) improved further. The proportion of children continued to be high (about a third of the population) and the proportion of people 65 years of age and over increased somewhat but it was still low (about 4–5%). The proportion of those of working age rose (about 60–65%) as the proportion of young adults grew, for example Egypt, Pakistan and the Philippines (Table 7.3).

7.3.4 Converging Fertility and Mortality: Young Adult Populations

A third group of countries continued their mortality and fertility transitions, as fertility and mortality declined, the proportion of children remained high (about 25–30%) and the proportion of old-age people continued to be low, but the proportion of the population of working continued to rise, as illustrated by the experiences of India, South Africa and Venezuela. The low life expectancy of South Africa in 2010–2015 was the outcome of the HIV/AIDS epidemic that has affected the downward trend in mortality in that country in more recent years (Table 7.3).

China stood out with fertility well below replacement level (TFR 1.6), improved mortality and almost three quarters (73%) of the population of working age (Table 7.3).

7.3.5   Low Fertility and Low Mortality: Replacement of Young Through Immigration

Another group was made up of countries that continued to have relatively high levels of immigration. Immigrants tend to be young adults and their children who bias the population distribution towards the young, as long as population growth takes place, in spite of low fertility at or below replacement level (TFR about 1.5–2.1) and high life expectancies (about 79–82 years). Their population under 15 years of age was about a fifth of the total (about 18–20%) and the proportion of old-age people rose (about 14–16%) as the echo of the earlier fertility boom started to be felt, but the population of working age remained high at two thirds (about 63–66%). This group included Australia, New Zealand and the United States (Table 7.3).

7.3.6   Low Fertility and Mortality: Older Populations

The last group experienced fertility rates well below replacement level (TFR about 1.2–1.5) for a considerable time, while their life expectancy continued to rise (about 78–83 years). Their proportion of children shrunk to less than 15% while the population 65 years of age and over rose to more than a fifth of the total population (about 20–26%). This meant that the proportion of working age was reduced (about 60–66%). This group included Germany, Italy and Japan (Table 7.3). These are countries that are experiencing what could be called post-transition stages with a higher number of deaths than births and potentially shrinking populations as in the case of Japan (Chap. 3: Sect. 3.4.4).

7.4   Pace of Change

Implicit in this analysis is that the rates of growth of different age groups have varied as the age distribution of the world's population changes. This has happened in aggregate and also across countries at different stages of development and regions. At the global level, where migration cancels itself out, the decline in fertility has meant that the child population (0–14 years) grew at a lower average annual rate (1.23% p.a.) than the average for the whole population (1.64% p.a.) in the 65-year period of 1950–2015. The population of working age (15–64 years) rose at a faster rate (1.76% p.a.) than the average. However, old-age people (65 years and over) grew at the fastest rate (2.40% p.a.), considerably above the average (Table 7.4). This has substantial implications to changes in child and old age dependency (Table 3.5) with socioeconomic consequences.

As it is now the established pattern, the rates of growth of the three age groups varied substantially among countries at different stages of development and regions. The common trend was the rate of growth of old-age people (65 years and over) above the whole population average. It was greatest in least and other less developed countries that started their transition later and it was lowest in more developed countries that began their transition earlier. In all three stages of development, the population of working age grew faster than average. However, in least and more developed countries the rate of growth was only slightly above average and it was in other less developed countries, including China and India, where the rate of growth of 15–64 years old grew substantially above average. The child population (0–14 years) actually declined in more developed countries, due to the decrease in Europe, and its rate of growth in both least and other less developed countries was below average for all age groups reflecting the fall in fertility over the 65-year period. In Africa, with the highest population growth rate of all regions, the rate of

Table 7.4 Growth of population age groups by stage of development and region, 1950–2015

Stage of development/region	Age (years)			
	0–14	15–64	65 and over	All
	Average annual rate of growth 1950–2015 (%)			
World	1.23	1.76	2.4	1.64
Least developed	2.41	2.47	2.56	2.44
Other less developed	1.33	2.08	2.75	1.88
More developed	−0.12	0.69	1.93	0.66
Africa	2.53	2.55	2.64	2.54
Asia	1.16	1.97	2.73	1.76
Europe	−0.33	0.48	1.68	0.46
Lat. America and Car.	1.33	2.3	3.2	2.03
Northern America	0.56	1.15	2.03	1.11
Oceania	1.39	1.8	2.49	1.75

Source UN (2017a). Computations made by the authors

growth of people aged less than 65 years was about the same as that of the whole population, but the rate of growth of old-age people (65 years and over) was faster than the average. In all other regions, the rate of growth of old-age people was also above average, especially in the case of Latin America and the Caribbean (Table 7.4). These differences have implications for the degree of dependence on people of working age and are harbingers of future conditions.

7.5 Ageing: Socio-economic Dynamics

The antecedents of population ageing are the effects of changes in the components of population-change, which primarily involve fertility, with a secondary effect due to mortality and a tertiary effect from migration. As stated in previous chapters dealing with these aspects of population dynamics, changes have been associated with social factors and stimulus with feedback loops. The mortality and fertility transitions have had different starting points that have led to diverse impacts on countries and regions of the world at various phases of their transitions, with transitional impact on the socio-economic fabric of societies at country and regional levels, and countries at different stages of development.

The transitional population ageing phases have physiological, social and economic dimensions. They are expressed in terms of varying capacity for physical and social activity, and also in different degrees of labour force participation and social dependency. These are manifested in changing wants for social, health and income support. The interaction of these elements affects outcomes in the manner of living arrangements, wellbeing and consumer behaviour (Fig. 7.1).

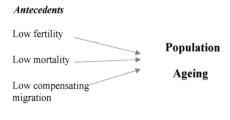

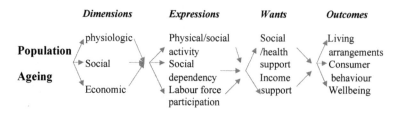

Fig. 7.1 Population ageing: antecedents, dimensions, expressions, wants and outcomes

7.6 Physical and Socio-economic Activity

7.6.1 Ageing: Physical and Social Activity

Different phases of the life cycle are associated with varying levels of physical activity. Surveys of physical activity in many countries indicate that the level of activity tends to fall as people age. This could be attributed to the tendency to reduced physical and mental effort or to biological factors associated with ageing, or both. However, it is apparent that the very economy in movement can have an impact on the capacity for physical exercise and maintenance of both physical and social functioning (Mechling and Netz 2009).

The proportion of people with disability is an issue of substantial relevance to physical and social activity, participation in the labour force and related income generation. This also has an obvious impact on social dependency and household consumption patterns.

The proportion of people with one or more disabilities in a population tends to increase with age and to grow more rapidly at older ages. Australia's experience is an example where in 2015 the proportion of people with profound or severe activity limitation rose from 3% at the age of 35–44 years to 9% at 65–69. Then, it accelerated to 29% at the age of 80–84 and reached 63% at 90 years of age and over. The Australian data indicates that there was an improvement in disability rates at all age groups in recent years, but that the pattern of accelerating disability with age remained similar (Fig. 7.2). This general pattern has been identified in population surveys in many other countries. For instance, an examination of the prevalence of disability among workers in some European countries confirmed substantial rises in disability among employees in older ages, as reflected in the growing number of sick-days leave as age rose in Germany (Scheil-Adlung 2013). In addition to physical limitations mental capacity also tends to diminish with age. For example, in 2014, serious difficulty in concentrating, remembering, or making decisions were found to increase from about 4% of the United States population aged 18–64 years to 6% at 65–74 years of age and 19% at 85 years and over (USDHHS 2016).

Another reinforcing factor is the changing nature of the demands for physical energy at work and the more passive nature of leisure activities. This has led to a more sedentary life style and behaviour associated with age. Recent experience in England was that on average about 30–40% of adults (16 years of age and over) spent 6 hours or more in sedentary activity per day. This increased during the weekend days. After a decline in the proportion from 16–24 years of age (about 45%) to 35–44 (about 25%), the proportion rose substantially at 55–64 years of age (about 35%) and continued to increase to reach about 60–65% at 85 years of age and over (Fig. 7.3). An earlier survey in the United Kingdom, showed that amount of free time was associated with age and followed an asymmetric U-curve. It declined from 16–24 years of age to reach its lowest level at 25–44 years of age as participation in the labour force rose. Then, free time started to increase to reach its highest level at

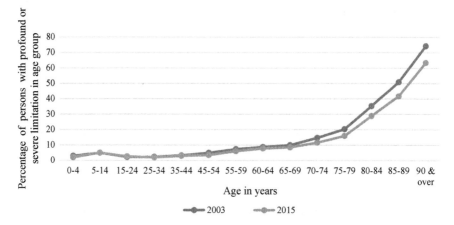

Fig. 7.2 Proportion of people with profound or severe core activity limitation in Australia by age 2003 and 2015
Source ABS (2016)

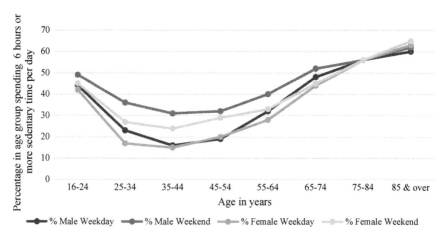

Fig. 7.3 Sedentary behaviour time of 6 h or more per day of adults by age and sex, England 2012
Source Townsend et al. (2015)

65 years of age and over, as time spent in paid work declined to an average of only a few minutes per day. However, the time spent on social life that declined from 25–44 to 45–64 years of age remained low, while the time spent on sedentary leisure activities such as watching television, listening to radio and music rose substantially (Lader et al. 2006).

A study of how old-age people in the United States spent their time found that participation in the labour force was a key factor in time use. People aged 55–59 years onwards spent less time in paid work and more time at leisure than did adults under the age of 55. They spent more time sleeping and doing house work.

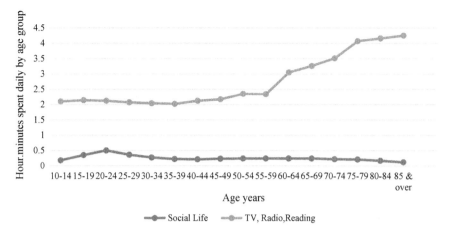

Fig. 7.4 Average time spent per day on social life and television watching and reading Japan 1996
Source SBJ (1997)

The time in socialising activities remained low from the age of 55–69 to 70 years and over. Social activity time remained about the same for those in employment but it declined for those not in employment. While, the amount of time watching television rose for both the employed and non-employed (Krantz-Kent and Stewart 2007).

The trade-off between social life and sedentary leisure time spent watching television and reading is apparent from Japanese experience. The amount of time spent on social life declined with age after reaching a peak at 20–24 years of age while the time watching television and reading rose substantially after the age of 55–59 to reach its highest level at 85 and more years of age (Fig. 7.4).

These examples of the association between age and physical and social activity have been drawn from more developed countries with more readily available and systematic surveillance of their population. However, studies carried out in developing countries such as Sri Lanka, Malaysia and Chile have shown similar patterns (Katulanda et al. 2013; Lian et al. 2016; Celis-Morales et al. 2016) that affect socioeconomic dependency.

7.6.2   Ageing and Labour Force Participation

The varying degrees of capacity during the life cycle for physical and other activity are major determinants in labour force participation. However, concerns with health of children and old-age people, the importance of education and training of younger people that determine the quality of future human capital, child bearing by females and also cultural attitudes regarding the role of females all have a bearing on participation of the population in the labour force. In turn, participation in the

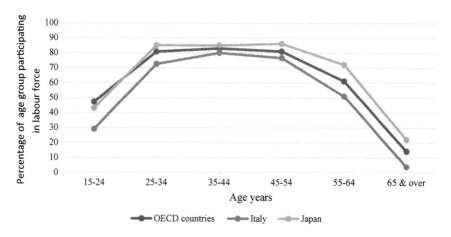

Fig. 7.5 Labour force participation rates of OECD countries, Italy and Japan by age 2015
Note OECD is the Organisation for Economic Co-operation and Development. Its membership is made up of about 35 countries which have reached a high degree of industrialisation
Source OECD (2017)

labour force is a major factor in population productivity and capacity to enhance the living standards of not only those employed but also for opportunities for investments in human capital, in terms of the health and education of children, and the provision of adequate living standards for old-age people.

As expected, labour force participation tends to follow a hump-shaped curve. It is lower at young ages when some people are gaining further education and training and not in the labour force. Then, participation rises to reach a peak at 35–54 years of age. It declines at 54–64 years of age either due to disability or lack of employment opportunities and early retirement, and it is reduced further at 65 years of age and over (Fig. 7.5). This has implications for population productivity, as countries at different stages of their mortality and fertility transitions have varying proportions of children and old-age people, and therefore diverse proportions of people of working age (Tables 7.3 and 7.4) to produce goods and services for all.

7.6.3 Ageing and Income Generation

Participation in the labour force is the major source of income for employed people and their dependents. It is also an opportunity for social engagement, self-expression and satisfaction. It can also have some negative effects such as stress and conflict between work and family time. Income from employment tends to vary with age. It starts usually low at 15–24 years of age and climbs to reach its highest level at about 45–54 years of age. It then declines to lower levels at 55–54 and 65 years of age and over (e.g. Fig. 7.6). This hump-shaped curve relationship

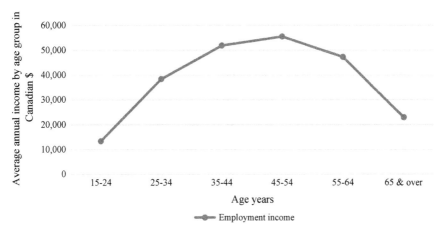

Fig. 7.6 Average annual employment income by age Canada 2010
Source SC (2017)

between age and income generation, with a fall in income at older ages, prevails both in developed and developing countries (Martins et al. 2012). It has been suggested that this variation with age is partly due to the interaction of the levels of education and experience of people of different ages (e.g. Rupert et al. 1996). It is posited that new cohorts tend to have a higher level of education that enhance their earning capacity. This implies that older cohorts will have a lower level of education in cross-sectional analysis of earnings. However, people also gain experience that favour their earning capacity. Nevertheless, at a point in time both past education and experience become less relevant and earning capacity declines.

The age-pattern of income generation means that populations with either a higher proportion of young or old-age people will tend to have a lower average income base for both consumption and support of dependent children and old-age people, other things being equal. This is of relevance to opportunities for income redistribution to support old-age people and investments in future human capital in the form of the education and training of today's children.

7.6.4 Labour Force Bonuses and Deficits

Given the age patterns of both labour force participation and income generation from employment, an important dynamic in the ageing transformation is the opportunity for increases in productivity offered by rises in the proportion of people of working age, at different stages of the transformation. However, the same dynamic can also lead to deficits in the proportion of working age and potential losses in population productivity. The latter is one of the issues faced by some countries with ageing populations and smaller number of people flowing into the

Table 7.5 World population of working age by stage of development and region, 1950–2015

Stage of development/region	Working age people as percentage of total population		Percentage difference
	1950	2015	1950–2015
World	60.7	65.6	4.9
Least developed	55.6	56.3	0.7
Other less developed	59.1	67.2	8.1
More developed	64.9	66.0	1.1
Africa	55.4	55.5	0.1
Asia	59.6	67.9	8.3
Europe	65.7	66.6	0.9
Lat. America and Car.	56.2	66.8	10.6
Northern America	64.8	66.3	1.5
Oceania	62.8	64.5	1.7

Note Working age is 15–64 years of age
Source UN (2017a). Computations made by the authors

labour force. Some European countries have made efforts to meet these deficits through immigration (Chap. 5: Sects. 5.5 and 5.6).

A review of changes in age distribution between 1950 and 2015 reveals that the proportion of people of working age (15–64 years) increased by 5%. The high dependency ratios of least and more developed countries have meant that the proportion of people of working age increased only slightly, even though it was considerably higher in more than least developed countries. A demographic bonus has been experienced by the other less developed countries where the proportion of people of working age surged from 59 to 67% during the period. It was in Latin America and the Caribbean and Asia where the gains were largest with only relatively small benefit in Europe, Northern America and Oceania (Table 7.5) that relied on the momentum of their fertility boom and later immigration to enhance the proportion of people in the labour force (Chap. 5: Sects. 5.5 and 5.6).

Thus, some countries at a middle phase of the ageing transformation experience a demographic bonus, in terms of a high proportion of people of working age due to past higher fertility that resulted in larger flows of young adults into working age, without great effect on the proportion of old-age dependent people. Other countries face a deficit of people of working age from lower flows of young adults into working age, because of long-term low fertility and increasing losses from people leaving the labour force as they reach old age (Box 7.1).

Box 7.1 Ageing and working age

Ageing dynamics arising from surges and wanes in fertility lead to increasing rates of child (0–14 years of age) dependency on the working age population (15–64 years) during the surge in fertility. As fertility falls, child dependency rates decline with a bonus in terms of a larger proportion of people of working age from flows due to past higher fertility. When fertility keeps on falling and its momentum fades away, the proportion of people of working age declines and old age (65 years and over) dependency rates rise leading to deficits in the labour force to maintain an increasing proportion of old-age people. The experiences of Korea and Germany provide examples of countries that benefit from demographic bonuses or face deficits.

In 1950–1955, Korea had a total fertility rate (TFR) of 5.7 children per female well above replacement level of 2.1. This gradually declined to about replacement level (TFR 2.23) in 1980–1985. Fertility continued to fall to considerably below replacement level and was 1.23 children per female in 2010–2015. One outcome was a drop in the child dependency rate on the population of working age from 78% in 1950 to 19% in 2015. The total dependency rate of children and old age people fell from 83 to 37%, as the increment in the old age dependency rate from 5% in 1950 to 18% in 2015 did not match the fall in child dependency. This resulted in the increase in the proportion of people of working age from 55% in 1950 to 73% in 2015 (Fig. 7.7). However, if fertility trends persist the demographic bonuses could turn into eventual deficits in working-age people to sustain an increasing proportion of old-age people, as those of working age reach old age.

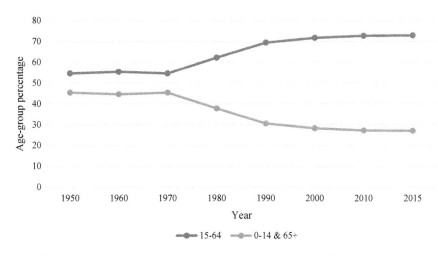

Fig. 7.7 Republic of Korea age distribution and working age 1950–2015
Source UN (2017a). Computations made by the authors

The pattern of falling proportions of people of working age and rising proportions of old-age people is being experienced by a number of countries including Germany. Fertility in Germany rose from about replacement level of 2.13 children per female in 1950–1955 to above replacement level of 2.47 in 1960–1965. It dropped to below replacement level of 1.71 in 1970–75, and continued to fall to 1.43 in 2010–2015. This meant that fertility in Germany declined to below replacement level in 1970–1975 well before Korea in 1990–1995. Like Korea, Germany gained from a reduction in the child dependency rate since 1980, in spite of rise in old age dependency since 2000. During the period 1970–2000 the total dependency on people of working age dropped from 59 to 47%, as child dependency fell more than any changes in old age dependency. During this 30-year period Germany benefitted from a demographic bonus in terms of an increase in the proportion of people of working age from 63% in 1970 to 68% in 2000. However, the bonus started to fade as the old age dependency rate became larger than the child dependency and total dependency rose from 47% in 2000 to 52% in 2015; while the proportion of people of working age was reduced to 66% in 2015 (Fig. 7.8), in spite of immigration of people of working age.

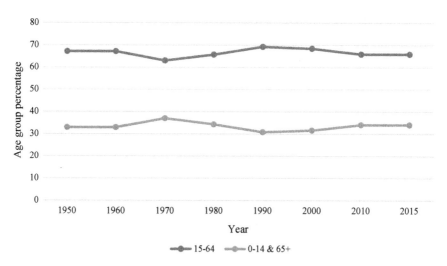

Fig. 7.8 Germany age distribution and working age 1950–2015
Source UN (2017a). Computations made by the authors

7.6.5   Dependency Transition

The ageing transformation dynamics have led to substantial changes in social dependency during the 65 years from 1950 to 2015. However, these changes have not affected countries in the same way. The convention is that children (0–14 years of age) and old-age people (65 years and over) are considered dependent on the people of working age (15–64 years). In fact, there is an increasing proportion of people over the age of 14 years who are studying and undergoing other training who might be dependent on others for their living. On the other end of the range, there are people who continue to work after the age of 64 years and are not dependent on others for their living. Nevertheless, the convention provides useful indicators of dependency trends on people who are in the labour force. Usually, they are the people who produce the goods and services on which the population relies for their living and are those who provide most of the taxation base for transfers of social benefits for those who are dependent on them (Swanson 2008).

The analysis of the age distribution of the world's population reveals that on average the dependency ratio in 2015 was lower (53%) than that in 1950 (65%). In other words, there was an increase in the proportion of people of working age to support children and old-age people. The falls in dependency were mostly in other less developed countries, where most people live, from 69 to 49%. Although dependency also fell in both least and more developed countries these falls were relatively small. This meant the maintenance of relatively high dependency ratios of 80 and 78% in least developed countries respectively in 1950 and 2015 and of lower dependency ratios in more developed counties of 54 and 52% in the same years. The patterns of dependency levels in Africa followed closely those in least developed countries, while those in Asia and Latin America and Caribbean those of other less developed countries. The dependency ratios of Europe, Northern America and Oceania were about those of the more developed countries (Table 7.6). As would be expected, these trends are similar to those observed in changes in age distribution.

7.6.6   Child Dependency

The overall dependency ratios are the sum of child and old-age dependency ratios and show considerable diverse trends. The world's child dependency ratio dropped from 56% in 1950 to 40% in 2015. This decline was most pronounced in more (42–25%) and other less developed countries (63–39%) where fertility fell most during the period 1950–2015. The decline was relatively small from 74 to 71% in least developed countries where high fertility and its momentum continued to be felt for some time. Again, regional patterns followed those of least developed countries in Africa, other less developed countries in Asia and Latin America and the Caribbean, and more developed countries and those in Europe, Northern America and Oceania (Table 7.6).

Table 7.6 World dependency ratios by stage of development and region, 1950–2015

Stage of development/region	Child dependency ratio (%)		Old-age dependency ratio (%)		Dependency ratio (%)	
	1950	2015	1950	2015	1950	2015
World	56	40	8	13	65	53
Least developed	74	71	6	6	80	78
Other less developed	63	39	7	10	69	49
More developed	42	25	12	27	54	52
Africa	75	74	6	6	80	80
Asia	61	36	7	11	68	47
Europe	40	24	12	26	52	50
Lat. America and Car.	72	38	6	11	78	50
Northern America	42	28	13	22	54	51
Oceania	48	37	12	18	59	55

Note Child dependency ratio is the ratio of the number of children 0–14 years of age to the population of working age 15–64 years, as a percentage. Old-age dependency ratio is the ratio of old people 65 years of age and over to the population of working age, as a percentage. The Dependency ratio is the ratio of the sum of the child and old-age populations to the population of working age, as a percentage. Figures may not add up because of rounding
Source UN (2017a). Computations made by the authors

7.6.7 Old-Age Dependency

The trend in old-age dependency runs in the opposite direction to that of child dependency. Globally, it rose from 8% in 1950 to 13% in 2015. This was partly due to the ageing of people born during the fertility boom of the late 1940s and 1950s and also to longer longevity from falls in mortality. The major changes took place in more developed countries where old-age dependency more than doubled from 12% in 1950 to 27% in 2015. It remained at 6% in least developed countries and rose from 7 to 10% in other less developed countries over the same period. The regional patterns are similar but in reverse to those observed in child dependency (Table 7.6).

7.7 Ageing and Intergenerational Dependency

7.7.1 Increasing Wants

Population ageing results in larger proportions of people with disability that is usually associated with greater prevalence of disease and need for health care. This is in addition to support needed by a greater proportion with other disability. These greater needs for support are in inverse relationship to the falling income generation of old-age people and need for income support to maintain adequate standards of living. It has been suggested that in countries such as Korea, ageing after years of low fertility, with smaller families and a greater degree of individualism, the traditional caring of aged people by the family has declined (Lee and Kim undated). This more recent experience in some developing countries was preceded by that of more developed countries that started their ageing transformation earlier and led to other forms of intergenerational support, with social transfers from a declining proportion of younger people in the labour force to old-age people.

7.7.2   Ageing and Demand for Health Care and Social Services

The rising prevalence of disability as people age (Fig. 7.2) leads to a higher demand for hospital and other health care. For instance, in 2014–15, the rate of use of hospital services in the Australia was almost four times higher at 65 years of age and over than it was at 15–64 (Fig. 7.9). Similar patterns of use prevail in other developed countries such as the United States (DeFrances et al. 2008) and have also been found to apply to developing countries such as Malaysia (IPH 2015). Similarly, the demand for home support services also rises with age (e.g. Legare et al. 2015).

This results in a larger proportion of health care expenditure being spent in the provision of health care for old-age people. Accordingly, in the Netherlands people aged 65 years and over made up about 16% of the total population in 2011 but health services used by them constituted about 64% of the total health care expenditure. The pattern of health expenditure by age was that for people up to the

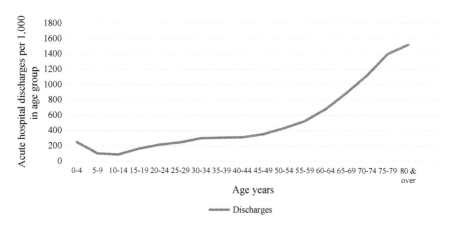

Fig. 7.9 Discharges rates from acute hospitals by age Australia 2014–15
Source AIHW (2016), ABS (2017). Computations made by the authors

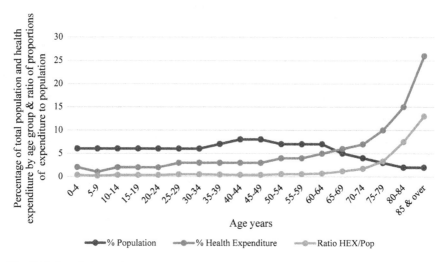

Fig. 7.10 Population and expenditure on health care Netherlands 2011
Sources OECD (2015a), SN (2014). Computations made by the authors

age of 64 years their proportion of total expenditure was below their proportion of
the total population. Once the age of 65 and over was reached the related proportion
of health services expenditure rose to reach about 13 times their proportion of the
population at the age of 85 years and over (Fig. 7.10).

A major implication of this pattern is that countries with ageing and older
populations require higher proportions of their gross domestic product to meet
higher demands for health services (Fig. 7.11).

7.7.3 Ageing and Income Support

The decline in earning capacity of people of old age is both an individual and social
issue. Lower family size, geographical distances and greater independence (Lee and
Kim undated), among others, have loosen the dependence of old-age people on
younger family members, especially in more developed countries. This can lead to
poverty among old-age people in the absence of social mechanisms to maintain an
adequate level of living standards. The ageing of populations and increasing
longevity place a higher proportion of the population at risk and demand social
transfers to fund the supply of health and supporting services, as well as income to
provide for food, shelter and other basic needs. This usually means transfers from
those in the labour force to those of old age in varying forms, such as old-age
pensions, subsidised or free health services and other social support that old-age
people need but cannot afford from their individual or household earnings. Many of
the more developed countries have set up institutional mechanisms for such

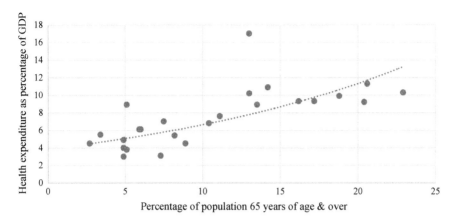

Fig. 7.11 Proportion of population 65 years of age and over and health expenditure as proportion of gross domestic product sundry developed and developing countries
Note The percentage of people 65 years of age and over are as at 2010, as per United Nations (UN) estimates. The percentages of health expenditure as a proportion of gross domestic product are for 2012, as per World Health Organisation (WHO) estimates. The countries in the graph are: Botswana, Egypt, Kenya, Morocco, Republic of South Africa and Tunisia in Africa; China, India, Indonesia, Japan, Korea, Malaysia, Sri Lanka, Thailand in Asia; Germany, Italy, Portugal, Spain and United Kingdom in Europe; Canada and the United States in Northern America; Argentina and Mexico in Latin America and the Caribbean; Australia and New Zealand in Oceania
Sources UN (2017a, b), WHO (2015). Computations made by the authors

transfers and other less developed countries are in the process of facing this challenge, as their demographic bonuses come to an end. It is estimated that on average public social spending is the equivalent of about 21% of gross domestic product (GDP) in countries of the Organisation for Economic Co-operation and Development (OECD). It varied from as high as 32% in France with an older population to less than 10% in Mexico with a much younger population. It accounted for only 2% in India and Indonesia at earlier stages of their ageing transformation. Pensions and health services expenditure made up about two thirds of public social spending (OECD 2016).

Most of the expenditure on old-age pensions come from public transfers through either taxation or some other social mechanism, or both. In 2011, public expenditure on old-age pensions represented 7.9% of GDP in OECD countries while privately funded pensions were 1.6% of GDP, for a total of 9.4% of GDP. Concerns with the fiscal burden of higher proportion of old-age people and a lower proportion of people of working age have led some OECD countries to raise the age at which people can access pension benefits and also to lower the value of the pensions. These and other measures are aimed at keeping public expenditures on pensions to about 11–12% by 2050 (OECD 2015b).

The importance of public transfers for income support of aged people is portrayed in the sources of income of households in Australia according to the age of the household reference person in 2009–10. The weekly average income at 55–64

Table 7.7 Household weekly income by age of the household reference person Australia, 2009–10

Household reference person age (years)	Salaries and wages	Personal business	Other personal	Government pensions and allowances	Household average weekly income $
	Percentage of all sources				
15–24	72.6	2.7	10.4	14.2	1,476
25–34	82.3	4.2	2.4	10.9	1,855
35–44	75.9	7.4	2.9	13.8	2,001
45–54	80.6	4.7	4.6	10.1	2,150
55–64	57.9	6.1	13.4	22.6	1,685
65 and over	12.1	1.6	19.0	67.2	838
All ages	61.3	4.7	8.3	25.3	1,688

Note Figures may not add due to rounding. The household average weekly income is in Australian dollars ($)
Source ABS (2011)

declined to 78% of that at the peak at 45–54 years of age. It fell further at 65 years of age and over to 50% of the average of those at 55–54. This represented 39% of that at 45–54. However, this much lower income at the age of 65 years and over relied on a 67% contribution by government pensions and allowances. Without that transfer it would have been only 13% of the average income at 45–54 years of age (Table 7.7). It could be pointed out that there were about twice as many people in households in which the reference person was aged 45–54 years than those in which the reference person was 65 years and more of age (ABS 2011). Nevertheless, after taking into account the number of people in the household, and net of respective government pensions and allowances, the difference was still more than fourfold. And the level of income of older people without government pensions and allowances would place them at great risk of poverty.

7.7.4 Intergenerational Transfers: Productivity and Distributional Issues

The ageing transforming trends that lead to higher proportions of old-age people and lower proportions of people of working age raise the importance of institutional frameworks that will effect the necessary transfers from one generation to another. It also points to the lower proportion of people who will be the source of the production needed to sustain living standards of a population with a greater degree of dependency. Thus, in addition to the distribution issue there is also a productivity issue. The first will be dependent on willingness and acceptance of social distribution that impinge on the taxation base provided by those with higher earnings above essential needs. The second will have to rely both on increasing productivity of those at work but also on the distribution of productivity gains. Past trends show that productivity gains have been an essential feature of human activity and that they are likely to continue, in spite of environmental threats (Chap. 1: Sect. 1.7). This presents different fiscal burdens in countries at varying stages of the ageing transformation. They are being felt more immediately in more developed countries with potentially shrinking and ageing populations, but they will also affect some developing countries as their proportion of people in working age declines and their proportion of old-age people becomes larger, as in the case of Korea.

7.8 Ageing, Wellbeing and Other Outcomes

7.8.1 Changing Living Arrangements

A feature of the life cycle is the change in living arrangements usually involving family formation and intergeneration relationships. However, cultural and socioeconomic factors also have a bearing on living arrangements, as well as the level of disability and related dependence.

It has been postulated that the living arrangements of old-age people have changed in the United Sates over time as the result of development and related socioeconomic changes. Accordingly, in a society with an emphasis on agricultural production, that may have consisted of two generations working together, about 70% of old-age people lived in cohabitation with children or in-laws and only about 11% lived either alone or only with spouse in 1850. This could be attributed to younger generations not leaving their parents' household rather than parents moving in with children in old age. As industrial development took place, work became more oriented to individual wages and salaries, relative incomes rose and gave more individual independence, children left home to form their own families and parents remained on their own. The pace of change increased in the second half of the 20th century. The proportion of old-age people living with their children that had fallen to 37% in 1950 dropped further to 15% in 1990, while those living alone or with spouse rose to about 70% by 1990. The proportion of old-age people living in institutions that was only 0.7% in 1850 rose to 6.8% in 1990 (Ruggles 2001). If this trend prevails in other countries, it is expected that old-age people in countries at varied stages of development will have different living arrangements.

7.8.2 Old-Age Living Arrangements and Development

The examination of the living arrangements of people 60 years of age and over indicates that the pattern varies with countries' stage of development (UN 2005b).

Table 7.8 World living arrangements of old-age people by stage of development and region

Countries stage of development/region	Percentage of all living arrangement				
	Alone	Couple only	With children/ grandchildren	With others	All modes
World	14	25	56	5	100
More developed	25	43	27	5	100
Less developed	7	13	75	5	100
Africa	8	9	74	8	100
Asia	7	16	74	4	100
Europe	26	43	26	4	100
Latin America and Caribbean	9	16	62	14	100
Northern America	26	47	19	8	100

Note The data is for people 60 years of age and over in period 1990–2000. No data for Oceania was available on a consistent basis for that period
Source UN (2005b)

Thus, in more developed countries the proportion of people 60 years of age and over living alone or as a couple only was 68% while 27% lived with children or grandchildren, during the period under review (1990–2000). The reverse applied in less developed countries, about 75% lived with children or grandchildren and 20% as a couple only or alone. The regional pattern followed closely the stage of development. Old-age people in Africa and Asia lived mostly with their children or grandchildren (74%) and 17 and 23% alone or couple only respectively. Those in Europe and Northern America living alone or couple only represented 69 and 73% respectively, while those in Latin America and the Caribbean were 25% (Table 7.8).

A number of factors was found to be associated with living independently and with family:

- *Gross domestic product (GDP) per capita*
- *Education*
- *Life expectancy at birth*
- *Kinship availability*
- *Percentage of urban population*

Correlation analysis indicated that old-age people were more likely to live independently either alone or as a couple only as GDP per capita, education, life expectancy and the proportion in urban areas rose but lower when kinship availability increased, while living with family was the inverse (Table 7.9). However, the importance of the rate of urbanisation tends to be lower once the analysis was controlled for other variables. Usually GDP per capita and education tend to be closely associated. The same applies to life expectancy and fertility that affects the number of younger people used in the kinship availability index in the analysis at country level. This points to GDP per capita as a major significant factor

Table 7.9 Factors associated with living independently or with family of old-age people, Pearson correlation coefficients

Indicator	Pearson correlation coefficients	
	Living with family	Living independently
Gross domestic product per capita	−0.81	0.81
Education	−0.71	0.69
Life expectancy	−0.59	0.57
Kinship availability	0.84	−0.83
Urban population	−0.62	0.6

Note The Gross domestic product per capita is for 1995. Education is the average number of years of education of people aged 25 years and over in1995. Life expectancy is the average number of years people were expected to live at birth in 1990–1995. Urban population is the percentage of people living in urban areas in 1995. Kinship availability is the ratio of people aged 20–55 to those aged 60 years and over. Old-age people are those aged 60 years of age and over in 1995. Living independently means living alone or couple only. Living with family means with children, grandchildren or any other family
Source UN (2005b)

influencing living arrangements of people 60 years of age and over in countries at different stages of development and regions. Regional characteristics also seem to be important, especially in the case of European countries. Nevertheless, the global trend is towards increasing old-age independent living (UN 2005b).

7.8.3 Old-Age Living Arrangements of Males and Females

It has been observed that the living arrangements of old-age males and females tend to vary. A particular feature is the larger proportion of old-age females living alone than males in all regions of the world and their lower proportions in couples only (Table 7.10). The usual trend is for females in marriage to be younger than males and to have a longer life expectancy than males. Thus, in countries in Europe and Northern America where old-age people tend to live independently (Table 7.8) the females' longer life expectancy leads to them surviving their spouse and live alone more frequently. This also tends for a larger proportion of males than females living as couples only. While in other regions, of predominantly less developed countries, the majority of old-age people live with children and others, the proportion in independent living is relatively small and leads to a lower but still a larger proportion of surviving females to live alone (Tables 7.10 and 7.11).

The continuing improvements in life expectancy of males and females and economic security have led to greater proportions of both males and females living as couples only, but also to a continuing difference in the proportion of males and females living alone and as couples, as illustrated by United States data for 2012. Independent living rose for both males (94%) and females (84%), but mostly the longer life expectancy of females continued to lead to a larger proportion

Table 7.10 Living arrangements of old-age people by region, circa 1990–2000

Region	Percentage of all living arrangements							
	Alone		Couple only		With others		All	
	Male	Female	Male	Female	Male	Female	Male	Female
Africa	6.1	9.9	10.6	6.2	83.3	83.8	100	100
Asia	2.8	7.9	14.9	8.8	82.3	83.4	100	100
Europe	14.7	34.7	54.6	29.5	30.8	35.8	100	100
Lat. Am. and Car.	7.8	8.7	14.8	10.6	77.3	80.8	100	100
Northern America	14.9	34.5	60.1	39.7	25.0	25.8	100	100

Note Figures may not add up due to rounding. Data for Northern America is only for the United States and does not include Canada. The data are for people 60 years of age and over in period 1990–2000. No data for Oceania were available on a consistent basis for that period
Source UN (2005b). Computations made by the authors

Table 7.11 Living arrangements of old-age people United States, 2012

Living arrangements	Percentage distribution of living arrangements by age (years of age)					
	65–74		75 and over		65 and over	
	Males	Females	Males	Females	Males	Females
Alone	22	46	19	36	17	27
Couples only	70	33	74	46	77	57
	92	79	93	82	94	84
Other	8	21	7	18	6	15
All modes	100	100	100	100	100	100

Note Figures may not add up due to rounding. Other includes living with children and other relatives as well as other arrangements
Source USCB (2013)

of males than females living as couples, while a larger proportion of females than males living alone or in other living arrangement (Table 7.11).

7.8.4 Some Intraregional and Within Country Differences

It has been shown that living arrangements of old-age people vary from one region to another and with stage of development. European patterns reflected the more developed stage of these countries. However, regional aggregates can gloss over differences among them. A study of living arrangements of old-age people in France, Germany, Russia and Bulgaria indicated that the trend was for independent living arrangements of living alone or couple only. However, lower income per capita and life expectancies were associated with a lower proportion of old-age

Table 7.12 Living arrangements of old-age people France, Germany, Russia and Bulgaria

Living arrangements	Percentage of all living arrangements			
	France	Germany	Russia	Bulgaria
Alone	38	35	39	21
Couples only	53	56	32	46
	91	91	71	67
Other	9	9	29	33
All modes	100	100	100	100
Life expectancy at 60 years				
Females	*26*	*25*	*19*	*20*
Males	*21*	*20*	*14*	*16*
GDP p.c. PPP $	*26,820*	*26,428*	*8,490*	*6,366*

Note The data is from the Generations and Gender Surveys of some European countries, and population of 60–79 years of age in this case. The information is circa 2007. GDP p.c. PPP$ is gross domestic product per head of population in purchasing power parities in 2007
Source de Jong Gierveld et al. (2012)

Table 7.13 Living arrangements of old-age people China, 2012

Living arrangements	Percentage of all living arrangements		
	Rural	Urban	All
Alone	12	12	12
Couple only	35	39	37
	47	51	49
Other	53	49	51
All modes	100	100	100

Note Other includes living with children, other relatives and other modes. Old-age people are those 60 years of age and over
Source Ren and Treiman (2014)

people in independent living in Russia and Bulgaria than in France and Germany (Table 7.12). It has also been suggested that different housing markets and affordability may play a role in differences in independent living arrangements and co-residence (de Jong Gierveld et al. 2012).

These deviations are as relevant in Europe as they are in Asia and other regions. An example of differences within countries of the living arrangements of old-age people is offered by the analysis of these modes of living in rural and urban areas of China in 2012. The rise of independent living follows the higher income of households in urban areas (Martins et al. 2017) to reach 51% in urban in comparison with 47% in rural areas (Table 7.13).

Nevertheless, the observed trend is for a growing proportion of old-age people to live independently rather than in co-residence, as their economic conditions and physical and mental functioning allows.

7.8.5   Disability and Institutionalisation

The degree of physical and mental functioning tends to decrease with age and accelerate in late 70s (Fig. 7.2). This increases the level of dependency and need for support in activities of daily living and leads to an increasing number of old-age people to become residents of nursing homes and other institutions in more developed countries, and to a substantial lesser extent in less developed countries where old-age people tend to rely more extensively on family for support. Accordingly, observed levels of institutionalisation of old-age people are considerably higher in more than less developed countries. For instance, the average level of institutionalisation of people 60 years of age and over in Japan (3.8%) was considerably higher than that in the Philippines (0.1%), and in Switzerland (6.7%) than Bulgaria (0.4%). Regardless of the stage of development, institutionalisation of old-age people accelerated between age 65–69 and 75 years and over (Table 7.14). As would be expected, females with a longer life expectancy tend to have higher levels of institutionalisation. For example, in Europe on average 3.4% of old-age females lived in institutions compared with 1.9% of males (UN 2005b).

Table 7.14   Old-age people in institutions by region and selected countries, circa 1990–2000

Region/country	Percentage of age group in institutions (years of age)				
	60–64	65–69	70–74	75 and over	All 60 and over
Africa					
Cape Verde	0.2	0.1	0.3	0.1	0.2
Zimbabwe	1	1	1.3	5.5	1.5
Asia					
Japan	1.2	1.5	2.2	8.8	3.8
Philippines	0.1	0.1	0.1	0.2	0.1
Europe					
Bulgaria	0.2	0.2	0.3	0.7	0.4
Switzerland	1.6	2	3.5	15	6.7
Latin America and Caribbean					
Mexico	0.3	0.3	0.4	0.8	0.4
Uruguay	2.6	2.6	2.9	5	3.3
Northern America					
Canada	1.5	2.1	3.6	16.2	6.4
United States	0.8	1.2	2.1	10.4	4.1
Oceania					
New Zealand	3.6	3.9	4.7	15.7	7.5

Note The data is for the period 1990–2000
Source UN (2005b)

Concerns with the impact of institutionalisation on the quality of life old-age people and costs involved have led some more developed countries to increase their level of support of old-age people activities of daily living and other care at home and reduce their levels of institutionalisation, as in the case of Australia, Denmark and Sweden (UN 2005b).

7.8.6 Formal Care and Female Informal Care

The provision of informal care, usually by a spouse or female relative, has been a mechanism to enhance independent living of old-age people with disability, but this can interfere with female participation in the labour force. An alternative is for the provision of formal long-term home support services that have been found to diminish the move of old-age people to shared or nursing home accommodation. It has also been found that increasing government expenditure on formal care increases the likelihood of female participation in the labour force in the European setting facing labour force deficits in their populations (Viitanen 2007).

7.8.7 Ageing and Long-Term Care Fiscal Implications

The increasing trend towards greater longevity, but also longer lives without major disability, the provision of home-based care and day-care centres to support old-age people, and the substantial projected increase in the number and proportion of old-age people in the European context has considerable implications to future fiscal demands. Estimates of public expenditure on long-term care, including community-based as well as residential care, show substantial growth in public expenditures for this purpose, however, they remain well below those on medical and hospital care. Expenditure projections for Germany were from 1.2% in 2000 to 3.3% in 2050, Spain 0.7–1.6%, Italy 1.0–2.4 % and United Kingdom from 1.4 to 2.9% (Comas-Herrera et al. 2006). As important as they are these levels of public expenditure will continue to be well below those involved in health care and pensions and allowances of old-age people.

7.8.8 Ageing and Changing Consumer Priorities

Lower participation in the labour force, diminished earnings, declining physical activity and increasing disability leads to changes in priorities in household consumption and expenditures in old age (Martins et al. 2012). Accordingly, there is a propensity to give priority in the household budgets of old-age people to items with a home orientation, such as housing and food consumed at home. Increasing

Table 7.15 Household consumer propensities in old age United States, Japan and Malaysia

Household expenditure type	Old-age consumer propensity index		
	United States	Japan	Malaysia
Home orientation	1.034	1.133	1.138
Increasing disability	1.908	1.395	1.694
Work related	0.823	0.851	0.823
Time use	0.69	0.823	0.783
Capacity for some pursuits	0.807	0.786	0.849

Note The data is from household expenditure surveys in the United States (2011), Japan (2005) and Malaysia (2009–10). The Old-age consumer propensity index = $(g_i/\sum g_i)/(g_x/\sum g_x)$, where g_i is expenditure of households headed by old-age people 65 years of age and over (60 years and over in Japan) on a given item and g_x is the average expenditure of all households on the same item. *Home orientation* items include food, housing and related items such domestic fuel and power. *Increasing disability* items are mainly health services. *Work related* items include transport, clothing and footwear. *Time use* items consist of expenditures on recreation and culture (including reading materials and hotel accommodation). *Capacity for some pursuits* items include alcoholic beverages, tobacco hotel and food away from home where that was available separately (also pocket money in the case of Japan)
Sources USBLS (2013a), SBJ (2006), DOS (2011). Computations made by the authors

disability and illness are given the highest priority. However, low or no participation in the labour force means less need for transport, change to wearing more informal clothing, and lower related household expenditure. The more sedentary nature of leisure time leads to lower expenditures on recreational activities. This also applies to alcohol and tobacco use, as old age tends to have an impact on capacity to use them. The analysis of the propensity of old-age people to give priority to items with a home orientation and health care in the United States and Japan are an illustration of this priority. However, a similar propensity is observed in less developed countries as illustrated in the case of Malaysia. A trade-off is the lower priority given to expenditures on transport, clothing and footwear, tobacco and alcohol beverages use, and recreation (Table 7.15).

7.8.9 Wellbeing and Life Satisfaction

It has been documented that old-age people have lower incomes and levels of consumption, they experience greater disability than younger people, but they are also more likely to have more personal time as their participation in the labour force declines and lower levels of responsibility for children, even if they live with them. The longer longevity also seems to be associated with the later onset of profound disability leading to longer healthy lives in old age. This still leaves the question on how old-age people see the value of their extended life expectancy in terms of their own perceptions of wellbeing. It has been suggested that wellbeing involves three major concepts:

- *Life evaluations* that consist of individual evaluation of life as whole or some aspects of it.
- *Experiential or affect considerations* that consist of the feelings experienced by individuals, at a given point in time, these could be of a positive or negative in nature, such as happiness and contentment or sadness, anger and anxiety.
- *Putative self-realisation functioning elements* of sense of purpose, engagement, resilience and competence in terms of capabilities but also potential realisation.

It has been proposed that each one of these concepts capture different aspects of wellbeing, but that there is greater correlation between life evaluation measures and experiential ones than with those of self-realisation functioning. Another pathway is the relationship between these measures and other variables that could be perceived as determinants of wellbeing such as income, social contact and life expectancy (OECD 2013).

It has been found that income effects are lower on *happiness* than *life satisfaction* but that they do not differ greatly. Also, life evaluations can change with policies that affect wellbeing and vary more among countries than experiential (emotional) considerations (Helliwell et al. 2015).

Two major hypotheses have been put forward regarding levels of perceived wellbeing in old age. One is that perceived wellbeing during the life cycle takes a U-shaped curve with higher perceptions of wellbeing early in adult life dropping to its lowest level in middle age and then rising among old-aged people. Another is that perceived wellbeing is highest in young adulthood, it then falls to middle age and flattens out during older age (Morgan et al. 2015).

United Kingdom population surveys (2012–2015) indicate that the life evaluative measure of *worthwhile life* tends to follow the U-shaped curve, in accordance with the first hypothesis. However, it drops after 70–74 years of age to reach its lowest point at 90 years of age and over. The measures of *life satisfaction* and *happiness* also follow a similar pattern but do not reach the same heights or as great dips in old age as *worthwhile life*. The experiential negative feeling of *anxiety* rises in a dome shaped curve from young adults to 50–54 years of age, it then drops and flattens out in older ages (Fig. 7.12).

The analysis of data from the General Social Surveys of the United States (1972–2006) involving levels of *happiness* and of data from Eurobarometers (1976–2002) measuring *life satisfaction* in European countries found that both followed a U-shaped curve, in accordance with the first hypothesis. The findings applied both to males and females. The same research was extended to a large number of developing countries. The results were mixed and the U-shaped pattern

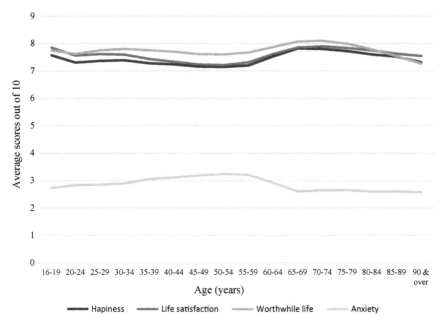

Fig. 7.12 Average personal wellbeing by age United Kingdom 2012–2015
Note The data is from the United Kingdom annual population surveys for 2012–2015. The sampled population are adults 16 years of age and over. Individuals were asked *Overall, how satisfied are you with your life nowadays? Overall, to what extent do you feel the things you do in your life are worthwhile? Overall, how happy did you feel yesterday? Overall, how anxious did you feel yesterday?* The scoring was 0 *not at all* and 10 *completely*
Source ONS (2016)

was found in some but not other developing countries (Blanchflower and Oswald 2007). This points to the possibility that either stages of development and or cultural traits may be relevant to perceived wellbeing in old age.

Loneliness is another dimension of wellbeing that has been the subject of evaluative research. One study in countries in Eastern and Western Europe (France, Germany, Russia, Bulgaria and Georgia) indicated that the transfers downwards from parents to children and upwards from children to parents had an impact on the level of loneliness of old-age people. It was hypothesised that according to exchange theory, giving has a cost and that too much giving leads to higher costs. According to equity theory, receiving more support than giving may result in guilt and distress, and giving more than receiving support may lead a sense of being exploited. Thus, a balance in giving and receiving may enhance wellbeing. However, altruism theory perspectives posit that giving is its own reward and not a cost. The study found that old-age people living as couples only felt the lowest levels of loneliness while those living on their own were the loneliest. Living with children provided a degree of protection against loneliness but not as much as living as a couple with a partner. Downward transfers from parents to children were most common but upward transfers from children to parents were more common late in the life of parents. In accordance with the altruism theory, old-age people providing downward support were least lonely while those receiving upward support from their children were the loneliest (de Jong Gierveld et al. 2012).

A major study based among other sources on the Gallup World Poll data, for 156 countries, 2005–2014, concerned with happiness, positive and negative emotions and explaining determinants (Helliwell et al. 2015) revealed that the level of happiness was positively correlated to:

- *GDP per capita (purchasing power parities)*
- *Social support (having someone to count on)*
- *Healthy years of life (expected years of life at birth without disability)*
- *Freedom to make choices (with what to do in life)*
- *Generosity (donations to charity)*

and negatively with:

- *Perceptions of corruption (in government or business)*

The major explanatory factors were social support, GDP per capita and healthy years of life. It also found that, on average, the level of happiness in the world for males and females tended to be highest early in adult life and to decline to ages in the 50s and to plateau in older ages. Experiential emotions such as enjoyment, laughter and interest tended to fall with age, while the feeling of restfulness followed a U-shaped curve pattern with age. Negative experiential factors had a lower impact on happiness levels and tended to follow a hump-shaped pattern of rising from young adult age to middle age and then falling such as in the case of anger, stress and worry (males). They tended to rise with age in the case of depression, sadness and pain. The earlier indication that the average does not fit all countries at different levels of development is apparent from the analysis of levels of life evaluation. The level of life evaluation followed a U-shape curve with age in countries in Northern America, Australia and New Zealand, Latin America and the Caribbean, South East Asia, South Asia and East Asia, while counties in Western Europe, Middle East, and Sub-Sahara Africa followed the world average pattern of decline and plateau in older ages. Countries in Eastern Europe and Central Asia showed a steep decline from young adult age that continued in older ages (Helliwell et al. 2015). Thus, the world average pattern of wellbeing masks substantial differences in the level of perceived wellbeing of old-age people in countries at varying stages of development and different cultures.

7.9 Presumptive Futures

The world is going through an ageing transformation that poses questions for which there is no previous guiding experience. Therefore, the experience of those countries that are leading the transformation because of their earlier decades of fertility below replacement level such as Japan provide learning opportunities. However, their experiences do not have the dimensions of those that will be faced by the ageing transformations of China and India, which together make up more than one third of the world's population. The ageing of the world population in following decades is inevitable because of the momentum of the rise in fertility in the 1950s and early 1960s and consequent fall in the 1970s and following years (Table 3.3). What is less certain is the extent of the transformation depending on the trend of falling fertility.

The United Nations (2017a) world population projections indicate a rise in the proportion of old-age people (65 years of age and over) from 8% in 2015 to almost double to 16% in 2050. This average is highly influenced by the projected substantial rise in the proportion of old-age people in other less developed countries, where most people live, from 7% in 2015 to 17% in 2050. This is supported by the projected increase from a higher base of 18% in 2015 to 27% in more developed countries. The projected proportion of old-age people more than doubles in Asia and Latin America and the Caribbean, but also rises in all other regions (Table 7.16).

Table 7.16 World population projections and proportion of old-age people and dependency by stage of development and region, 2015 and 2050

Country stage of development/region	Population (millions)		Percentage population 65 years and over		Dependency ratio percentage	
	2015	2050	2015	2050	2015	2050
World	7,383	9,772	8.3	15.8	53	59
More developed	1,253	1,298	17.6	26.6	52	73
Other less developed	5,173	6,557	6.9	16.4	49	59
Least developed	957	1,917	3.5	6.6	78	57
Africa	1,194	2,528	3.5	6.0	80	61
Asia	4,420	5,257	7.6	17.8	47	56
Europe	741	716	17.6	27.8	50	75
Lat. America and Carib.	632	780	7.6	19.4	50	57
Northern America	356	435	14.8	22.5	51	65
Oceania	40	57	11.8	18.2	55	62

Note The population is per the United Nations estimates for 2015 and the medium variant projection for 2050. Old-age people are those 65 years of age and over. The dependency ratio is the percentage of the sum of people 0–14 and 65 years and over by the population 15–65 years of age. Figures may not add up due to rounding
Source UN (2017a). Computations made by the authors

This large increment in the projected proportion of old-age people is only partly compensated by a decline in the proportion of dependent children (0–14 years of age), as average fertility is assumed to continue to decline on average. Accordingly, the dependency ratio of children and old-age people on people of working age (15–64 years of age) is projected to increase in the world from 53% in 2015 to 59% in 2050. This projected rise in the average dependency ratio will be most felt in more developed countries and to increase from 52% in 2015 to 73% in 2050, while the ratio is projected to fall from 78 to 57% in the least developed countries, due to their continuing drop in fertility. The dependency ratio in other less developed countries is also projected to rise close to the world average from 49 to 59%, during the 35-year period. Europe is projected to be in the forefront of the increment in the dependency ratio from 50 to 75% during this period. Smaller increases are projected in the countries of the other regions with the exception of Africa where the ratio is projected to fall (Table 7.16).

Within the regional averages and various stages of development there are large differences in the degree of the ageing transformation projected for individual countries. The examples of China and India, two developing, and of Germany and Japan, two more developed countries, that have had different starting points in their ageing transformation offer a sketch of diverse experiences. China and India with different fertility rates and starting points in their decline in fertility show two contrasting projected futures. China, that had a demographic bonus from its earlier decline in fertility, is projected to almost double its dependency ratio from 38% in 2015 to 67% in 2050. Over the same period, India's dependency ratio is projected to fall slightly from 52 to 48%. Japan, where the decline in fertility started early, is projected to reach a dependency ratio of 96% in 2050 from an already high ratio of 64% in 2015. Germany with an upsurge in fertility above replacement level in the 1960s and a later starting point in its fertility dip below replacement level is also projected to experience an increase in its dependency ratio from 52 to 77% over those years, but with a delayed effect. These changes would mean that while India is projected to have a demographic bonus during the period 2015–2050, Germany and Japan would be facing a demographic deficit in terms of increasingly high dependency ratios, and China that has had a demographic bonus in past decades would have to face a considerable rise in its dependency ratio. Thus, India and China would exchange their relative positions, over the 2015–2050 period, and be in similar circumstances as Germany and Japan in 2015. But Japan and Germany would be breaking new ground that they and other countries have not experienced before (Table 7.17).

These projections indicate that countries at varying stages of development will be at diverse stages of their ageing transformation set in place by their own past and current fertility experiences. Those in the lead of the transformation process will offer learning opportunities about impact and a range of possible responses. One such response is that of Japan with a low rate of immigration to add to the low flow of people into working age, that has increased the labour force participation rate of old-age people 65–69 years of age (SBJ 2017). Another has been that of Sweden that narrowed the gap between the level of labour force participation of males and

Table 7.17 Population projections and proportion of old-age people and dependency in China, India, Germany and Japan, 2015 and 2050

Country	Population (millions)		Percentage population 65 years and over		Total dependency ratio (%)	
	2015	2050	2015	2050	2015	2050
China	1,397	1,364	9	26	38	67
India	1,309	1,659	6	13	52	48
Germany	82	79	21	31	52	77
Japan	128	109	26	36	64	96

Note The population is per the United Nations estimates for 2015 and the medium variant projection for 2050. Old-age people are those 65 years of age and over. The dependency ratio is the percentage of the sum of people 0–14 and 65 years and over by the population 15–65 years of age. Figures may not add up due to rounding
Source UN (2017a). Computations made by the authors

females. Yet another has been Germany's improvements in the productivity of its labour force (USBLS 2013b). These examples deal with the possibility of enhancing productive capacity of ageing countries but do not ensure intergenerational transfers required to maintain adequate standards of living of those who require health care and other social support, beyond their capacity or that of their immediate family. Pension and formal social support schemes are in place in many more developed countries. The same applies to health care. However, they will require increasing fiscal support. Some developing countries with a growing number and proportion of old-age people have relied on family co-residence for the support of old-age people, or have tolerated lower living standards for old-age people. In the absence of formal intergenerational transfer institutions, as families become smaller and extended families become less common, they will face a major challenge in the provision of adequate support for old-age people. These challenges may be exacerbated if the argument that human longevity has virtually no limit is correct (Oeppen and Vaupel 2002) and the argument that there is a limit is wrong (Olshanky et al. 1990).

Another dimension facing all is the quality of life of the larger proportion and number of old-age people living longer lives. The preference for independent living has been accompanied by lower physical and social activity and more sedentary use of leisure time. This in turn tends to have an impact on health and social interaction that has been found to be associated with personal wellbeing in old age. Extended participation in the labour force would provide a degree of activity and social interaction. However, the increasing sedentary nature of work itself raises what it is a more general problem of less physical activity. Accordingly, the enhancement of wellbeing of the growing proportion and number of old-age people involves not only intergenerational transfers linked to income, social support and health care but also opportunities for an active physical and engaged social life. It also implies social and cultural changes to reduce sedentary work and leisure time.

References

Australian Bureau of Statistics (ABS). (2011). *Household expenditure survey Australia 2009–10: Summary of results*. Canberra.

Australian Bureau of Statistics (ABS). (2016*). Disability, ageing and carers, Australia: Summary of findings, 2015*. Canberra.

Australian Bureau of Statistics (ABS). (2017). *Australia estimated resident population by age and sex 2014*. ABS.Stat. Retrieved February 6, 2017, from www.abs.gov.au.

Australian Institute of Health and Welfare (AIHW). (2016). *Admitted patient care 2014–15: Australian hospital statistics*. Canberra.

Blanchflower, D. G., & Oswald, A. J. (2007). Is well-being U-shaped over the life cycle? *IZA Discussion Papers*, No. 3075.

Celis-Morales, C., Salas, C., Alduhishy, A., Sanzana, R., Martinez, M. A., Leiva, A., et al. (2016). Socio-demographic patterns of physical activity and sedentary behaviour in Chile: Results from the national health survey 2009–2010. *Journal of Public Health, 38*(2), 98–105.

Comas-Herrera, A., Wittenberg, R., Costa-Font, J., Gori, C., di Maio, A., Patxot, C., et al. (2006). Future long-term care expenditure in Germany, Spain, Italy and the United Kingdom. *Ageing & Society, 26*, 285–302. Retrieved February 19, 2017, from www.cambridge.org/core.

DeFrances, C. J., Lucas, C. A., Buie, V. C., & Golosinskiy, A. (2008). *2006 National hospital discharge survey*. National Health Statistics Reports, No. 5.

de Jong Gierveld, J., Dykstra, P. A., & Schenk, N. (2012). Living arrangements, intergenerational support types and older adult loneliness in Eastern and Western Europe. *Demographic Research, 27*(7), 167–200. Retrieved February 23, 2017, from www.demograhic-research.org/Volumes/Vol27/7/; https://doi.org/10.4054/demres.2012.27.7.

Department of Statistics Malaysia (DOS). (2011). *Report on household expenditure survey 2009/10*. Putrajaya.

Helliwell, J., Layard, R., & Sachs, J. (Eds.). (2015). *World happiness report 2015*. New York: Sustainable Development Solutions Network.

Institute for Public Health & Institute for Health Systems Research (IPH). (2015). *National health & morbidity survey, 2015. Healthcare demand*, Vol. III. Kuala Lumpur: Ministry of Health Malaysia.

Katulanda, P., Jayawardena, R., Ranasinghe, P., Rezvi Sheriff, M. H., & Matthews, D. R. (2013). Physical activity patterns and correlates among adults from a developing country: Sri Lanka diabetes and cardiovascular study. *Public Health and Nutrition, 16*(9), 1684–1692.

Krantz-Kent, R., & Stewart, J. (2007). How older Americans spend their time? *Monthly Labor Review*, May 2007: 8–26.

Lader, D., Short, S., & Gershuny, J. (2006). *The time use survey, 2005*. London: Office of National Statistics.

Lee, S.-L., & Kim, D.-S. (undated). *Korean population at 22 glances*. Statistics Korea.

Legare, J., Decarie, Y., Deslandes, K., & Carriere, Y. (2015). Canada's oldest old: A population group which is fast growing, poorly apprehended and at risk from lack of appropriate services. *Population Change and Lifecourse Strategic Knowledge Cluster Discussion Paper Series, 3*(1), article 9.

Lian, T. C., Bonn, G., Han, Y. S., Choo, Y. C., & Piau, W. C. (2016). Physical activity and its correlates among adults in Malaysia: A cross-sectional descriptive study. *PLoS ONE, 11*(6), e1057730. Retrieved January 27, 2017, from https://doi.org/10.1371/journal.

Martins, J. M., Yusuf, F., & Swanson, D. A. (2012). *Consumer demographics and behaviour*. Dordrecht: Springer.

Martins, J. M., Yusuf, F., Brooks, G., & Swanson, D. A. (2017). Demographics and market segmentation: China and India. In D. A. Swanson (Ed.), *The frontiers of applied demography*. Switzerland: Springer.

Mechling, H., & Netz, Y. (2009). Aging and inactivity—Capitalizing on the protective effect of the planned physical activity in old age. *European Review of Aging and Physical Activity, 6*(89). https://doi.org/10.1007/s11556-009-052-y.

Morgan, J., Robinson, O., & Thompson, T. (2015). Happiness and age in European adults: The moderating role of gross domestic product per capita. *Psychology and Aging, 30*(3), 544–551.

Oeppen, J., & Vaupel, J. (2002). Broken limits to life expectancy. *Science, 296,* 1029–1031.

Office for National Statistics (ONS). (2016). *Measuring national well-being: At what age is personal well-being the highest? United Kingdom 2012–2015.* Annual Population Survey.

Olshansky, S. J., Carnes, B. A., & Cassel, C. (1990). In search of Methuselah: Estimating the upper limits of human longevity. *Science, 250,* 634–640.

Organisation for Economic Co-operation and Development (OECD). (2013). *OECD guidelines on measuring subjective well-being.* Paris.

Organisation for Economic Co-operation and Development (OECD). (2015a). *Health at a glance 2015.* Paris.

Organisation for Economic Co-operation and Development (OECD). (2015b). *Pensions at a glance 2015.* Paris.

Organisation for Economic Co-operation and Development (OECD). (2016). *Society at a glance 2016.* Paris.

Organisation for Economic Co-operation and Development (OECD). (2017). *OECDStat. Labour force statistics, LBS by age and sex, labour force participation rates.* Paris. Retrieved January 26, 2017, from www.stats.oecd.org.

Reher, D. S. (2015). Baby booms, busts, and population ageing in developed countries. *Population Studies, 69*(S1), S57–S68.

Ren, Q., & Treiman, D. J. (2014). *Living arrangements of the elderly in China and consequences for their emotional well-being.* PSC Research Reports, 2014, Report 14-184.

Ruggles, S. (2001). Living arrangements and well-being of older persons in the past. *Population Bulletin of the United Nations, Special Issue, 42–43,* 111–161.

Rupert, P., Schweitzer, M. E., Severance-Lossin, E., & Turner, E. (1996). Earnings, education and experience. *Federal Reserve Bank of Cleveland Economic Review, 32*(4), 2–12.

Scheil-Adlung, X. (2013). *Older workers: How does ill health affect work and income?* Geneva: International Labour Organization.

Statistics Bureau of Japan (SBJ). (1997). *Survey of time use and leisure activities—Summary of results 1996.* Tokyo: Ministry of Internal Affairs.

Statistics Bureau of Japan (SBJ). (2006). *Family income and expenditure survey 2005.* Tokyo: Ministry of Internal Affairs.

Statistics Bureau of Japan (SBJ). (2017). *Labour force and labour force participation rate by age group. Historical data.* Ministry of Internal Affairs: Tokyo.

Statistics Canada (SC). (2017). *Income and earnings statistics 2010, age groups. National household survey 2011.* Ottawa. Retrieved January 29, 2017, from http://www12.statcan.gc.ca.

Statistics Netherlands (SN). (2014). *Dutch census 2011.* The Hague/Heerlen.

Swanson, D. A. (2008). Population ageing and the measurement of dependency: The case of Germany. *Applied Demography, 21,* 8–10.

Swanson, D. A., Tedrow, L., & Baker, J. (2016). Exploring stable population concepts from the perspective of cohort change ratios: Estimating the time stability and intrinsic *r* from initial information and components of change. In R. Schoen (Ed.), *Dynamic demographic analysis* (pp. 227–258). Dordrecht: Springer B. V. Press.

Townsend, N., Wickramasinghe, K., Williams, J., Bhatnagar, P., & Rayner, M. (2015). *Physical activity statistics 2015.* London: British Heart Foundation.

United Nations (UN). (2005a). *The diversity of changing population age structures in the world.* Mexico City: United Nations Secretariat.

United Nations (UN). (2005b). *Living arrangements of older persons around the world.* New York.

United Nations (UN). (2017a). *World population prospects—The 2017 revision—Volume I: Comprehensive tables.* New York.

United Nations (UN). (2017b). *World population prospects—The 2017 revision—Volume II: Demographic profiles*. New York.

United States Bureau of Labor Statistics (USBLS). (2013a). *Consumer expenditure in 2011*. BLS Reports, 2013, 1042.

United States Bureau of Labor Statistics (USBLS). (2013b). International labor comparisons. *Spotlight on Statistics*. May, 2013.

United States Department of Health and Human Services (USDHHS). (2016). *Health, United States, 2015*. Hyattsville MD.

United States Census Bureau (USCB). (2013). *America's families and living arrangements: 2012*. Washington DC.

Viitanen, T. K. (2007). *Informal and formal care in Europe*. IZA Discussion Paper Series, 2007, No. 2648.

World Health Organization (WHO). (2015). *World health statistics 2015*. Geneva.

Yusuf, F., Martins, J. M., & Swanson, D. A. (2014). *Methods of demographic analysis*. Dordrecht: Springer.

Chapter 8
Gender Dilemma: Difference and Equality

> History is likely to judge the progress in the 21st century by one
> major yardstick: is there a growing equality of opportunity
> between people and among nations?... The most persistent of
> these [issues] has been gender disparity, despite a relentless
> struggle to equalize opportunities between women and men.
> The unfinished agenda for change is considerable.
>
> United Nations Development Programme (1995)

8.1 Sex Differences

The survival of the human species is dependent on the different but complementary sex characteristics of males and females. It relies on the genetic difference of the x and y chromosomes that distinguish females with an xx pair and males with a xy pair ((Chap. 3: : Sects. 3.1.2 and 3.1.3). This difference is characterised by complementary reproductive organs and associated hormonal similarities and differences in surges and balance. Female and male gonads develop early in pregnancy. Genital differentiation takes place in the first two months of pregnancy. The generation of testosterone leads to the formation of male other sexual organs, while other female sex organs are developed without the influence of androgens. Brain sexual differentiation takes place later in the second half of pregnancy, as a result of the impact of sex hormones on the development of brain cells in their development masculine and feminine features are accentuate and the opposite are de-accentuate. This stimulus is reactivated again after birth and during puberty. Fluctuations in the maternal hormone levels during gestation can also influence masculine and feminine accentuations of the foetus and later on in the life of the offspring. It is posited that the effect of testosterone on male brain development and its absence in that of the female brain is a major factor in sexual differentiation in cognition and some aspects of behaviour (Savic et al. 2010).

The cumulative effect of hormonal surges and levels leads to differences in the physical appearance of males and females. Although some females may be taller than males, on average males are taller than females. The same applies to physical strength due to differences in muscular mass and fat tissue, with females having more adipose tissue and males' greater muscularity. Males and females also have different hair distribution and breast tissue, the latter related to female's feeding of offspring in early childhood. Bone mineral mass is also greater in males than females adding greater weight to males. Body proportions and shape also tend to differ with males having broader shoulders and narrowed hips, and females with a larger pelvis to cope with the passage of offspring. These differences, some of which may be present before, tend to become more accentuated during and after puberty that begins earlier in females and ends later in males. Some of these distinctions diminish and become less accentuated later in life (Wells 2007).

Other differentiations pertain to the process of reproduction. While it is the male chromosomes with an x or a y that determines the sex of the foetus added to the female x, it is the female that carries the foetus and influences it by her own hormonal balance during gestation, nourishing through the placenta, and breast-feeding of the offspring after birth (Savic et al. 2010). This imposes a greater burden on the female and her physical capacity, especially if frequently pregnant or when her nutritional status is less than adequate. This affects not only the mother but also the quality of the offspring (Wells 2007).

There are also sex dissimilarities related to cognitive abilities, language and physical capacity. For instance, males have greater capacity to deal with mental spatial rotation and motor performance such as throwing distance and speed and females have greater ability in vocabulary and speech production (Voyer et al. 1995; Hyde 2005).

Birth rates of 105 males to 100 females are the norm with males being more vulnerable during pregnancy and childhood (Kramer 2000). Males have a higher infant mortality and lower life expectancy than females, while females carry the burden of maternal mortality (UNDP 2014).

8.2 Gender Identity and Behaviour

8.2.1 Sex Differences and Gender Stereotypes

Sex differences in adults are apparent. Female are more involved with child carrying and early caring of offspring and males with physical strength and related capacity for heavy work has led to the association of females with *reproduction and caring* functions and of males with *production* functions. And personality characterisations that males are *independent, assertive, rational, competitive and focused on individual objectives* and females are *understanding, caring, responsible, considerate, sensitive, intuitive and focused on communal objectives* (Palan 2001).

8.2.2 Sex Typing, Gender Identity and Behaviour

While physical differentiation of the sexes is less apparent in childhood, children evolve ideas about appropriate male and female *preferences, skills, personality attributes, behaviours concepts of self* and about how males and females are supposed to behave in what is understood as *sex typing* (Benn 1983). Sex typing can evolve into gender or *...meanings ascribed to male and female social categories within a culture. When people incorporate these cultural meanings into their own psyches, then gender becomes part of their identities.* (Wood and Eagly 2015: 461). Gender identity theory is concerned with how biological, cognitive and social factors work together and result in individual differences in physical attributes and behaviour, such as male size and physical strength and female child bearing and nursing, that are translated into social categories with cultural nuances of what males and females are and how they behave (Wood and Eagly 2015). A number of theories have been offered to explain this process.

Psychoanalytical theory was an early explanation that involved children's observation of the genital differences in males and females and their identification with the parent of their same sex. This clear cut and simple account has been followed by others that include greater social content in sex typing and gender identity.

Social learning theory ...shifts the unit of study from global traits inferred from behavioural signs to the individual's cognitive activities and behaviour patterns, studies in relation to the specific conditions that evoke, maintain, and modify them and which they, in turn, change (Mischel 1973: 265). In this perspective, sex typing by the child takes place by observation and learning of what self labelling is appropriate in the social context that rewards and punish modelling along gender stereotypes of behaviours that are socially more acceptable. Thus, gender identity evolves and the stereotyped behaviour is adopted in accordance with social norms (Mischel 1970).

Cognitive-developmental theory provides an alternative perspective where the children are central to their own sex typing. Children in their cognitive development observe differences in males and females in terms of biological sex differences and associated behaviour and label themselves accordingly. Their need for cognitive consistency stimulates children to adopt *attitudes, activities* and *choice of peers* congruent with their own sex typing and perceived roles as males and females (Kohlberg 1966).

Gender schema theory is based on the understanding that *...schema is a cognitive structure, a network of associations that organizes and guides an individual perception... what is perceived is a product of the interaction between the incoming information and the perceiver's preexisting schema* (Benn 1981: 355). In this context, children *...learn to encode and to organize information in terms of an evolving gender schema* (Benn 1983: 603). Accordingly, children develop a sense of their own gender stereotypes and regulate and evaluate the adequacy of their personal *attributes, attitudes, preferences,* and *behaviour* in the context of the gender schema that becomes the *prescriptive standard* or *guide* (Benn 1981, 1983).

Biosocial constructionist theory is concerned with biological and social factors that ...*shape the meanings that individuals and societies ascribe to men and women* (Eagly and Wood 2013: 350). Physical features related to male physical size and strength and female child bearing and caring lead to some tasks to be more effectively done by one of the sexes in the context of their ecological and socioeconomic circumstances. This is an expression of biological features inter-action with social environment to lead to the division of labour between males and females. Social psychological processes evolve the division of labour into *gender role beliefs* that such roles are *natural* and prompt males and females to accept these roles and self-regulate their behaviour accordingly (Eagly and Wood 2013).

8.2.3   Stereotype Threat, Group Bias and Context

The use of gendered stereotyping can lead to attitudes and behaviours that can have a deleterious impact on performance of both males and females. When a certain stereotype is given the performance of either sex is likely to be affected regardless of their capability when the gender stereotype is absent (Pennington et al. 2016). This may affect male performance in caring and female in assertiveness. Another issue is group bias arising from individuals striving for positive social identification with their sex and consequent biased evaluation of the better performance and adequacy of their own sex. Psychological gender differences can be changed given the context in which they are expressed. For instance, sex characteristic aggressive behaviour in males and caring in females can change depending on the context in which males and females find themselves (Hyde 2005).

8.2.4   Gender Similarity Hypothesis

A meta-analysis of psychological gender differences undertaken by Hyde (2005) indicated that males and females are more alike than they are different. Differences were examined in terms of cognitive abilities, verbal and non-verbal communica-tion, social or personality variables, aggression and leadership, psychological well-being such as self esteem, and motor behaviour such as throwing. The major differences were found in motor performance by males associated with muscle mass and bone size after puberty. Another difference was in sexuality with males being more active than females and also more casual in their attitudes towards sexual relationships, but with similar satisfaction. Yet another moderate difference was found in aggression, with physical aggression being greater in males, with lesser difference in verbal aggression. Relatively small differences were found in cognitive abilities, leadership and self-esteem.

8.3 Son Preference

Sex differences between males and females can be translated into gendered perceptions of the place and value of each in the family and society at large. Thus, in traditional *patriarchal* households the male is the head of the family with authority over the female and any children. In this value system, the male assumes the role of provider and protector and the female has a subordinate role of reproduction and housekeeping. An extension of this is a *patrilineal* kinship system that involves the pooling of the family resources, with the product of the work of the male offspring being of benefit to the parents, but that of the female offspring accruing to the family of the male whom she mates. In multigenerational cohabitation along these lines, the family also benefits from the support of the male child in old age but not of the female child (UNFPA 2012). These practices are often associated with the male offspring inheriting the land or the business from his father, while the female offspring may be given a dowry, particular household or personal goods or inheritance (Das Gupta et al. 2003). Thus, male offspring can be seen as a benefit to the family and female offspring as a cost.

These beliefs and practices can mould family-shared attitudes and behaviours that favour male over female offspring and result in selection of male offspring. This active male preference is observable in a variety of countries with different social and cultural characteristics but is absent in others. Accordingly, the male preference takes varying forms depending on local features. In South Asia, females are seen as *costly* as parents may need to provide a dowry or wedding expenses while it is the family of her mate that will benefit. Female offspring also carry the family honour and to diminish the risk of loss they are married early. In turn, they may be subjected to pressure or even physical violence to produce a male offspring. In China and other Asian countries, males are the joint product of males and females but their social identity is inherited from their fathers (Das Gupta et al. 2003).

The discriminatory selection of male offspring can be exercised at different stages in the reproduction process

- *before pregnancy*
- *during pregnancy*
- *at birth*
- *after birth during early childhood*

Contraception can be used as a device to either avoid conception after the desired birth of male offspring has occurred or by not using it and continue attempts at producing male offspring. In the latter alternative, the female offspring could end up with more siblings, and depending of household resources she could suffer from lower nutritional intake and other developmental shortfalls (WB 2011). Selection during pregnancy can be exercised by abortion after diagnostic assessment of the sex of the foetus. The use of ultrasound technology has increased opportunities for sex selection and appears to have resulted in the rise of male selection in some countries. Infanticide at the time of birth can be part of the selection process, but it is difficult to distinguish from stillbirth. Neglect of female offspring is a way of exercising selection in early childhood and results in the premature mortality of daughters (Das Gupta et al. 2003).

The result of these selection mechanisms is reflected in

- *sex ratio at conception*
- *sex ratio at birth*
- *child sex ratio*

The various methods of sex selection have resulted in sex ratios at birth (SRB) well above average in a large number of countries in Asia and Southern Europe. SRBs in China (116) and India (111), with about one third of world's population, are considerably higher showing a substantial degree of male preference and effective means of sex selection. The same applies to Vietnam (111) and Pakistan (109) that also have high SRB levels. Armenia, Azerbaijan and Georgia, with smaller populations, also have substantially high SRBs ranging from 110 to 114. To a lesser degree, Albania and Montenegro in Southern Europe exercise male preference selection in births (SRBs of 108 and 107 respectively). Hong Kong (107), Singapore (107) and the Republic of Korea (107) show similar male preferences as per their SRBs (Table 8.1).

Estimates from modelling of excess under 5 years of age mortality, above that it would be expected, indicate considerable signs of neglect of female children in a

Table 8.1 Sex ratio at birth in selected countries, 2015

Country/territory	Sex ratio at birth
East and Southeast Asia	
China	116
Hong Kong	107
Republic of Korea	107
Singapore	107
Vietnam	111
South Asia	
India	111
Pakistan	109
West Asia	
Armenia	113
Azerbaijan	114
Georgia	110
Southern Europe	
Albania	108
Montenegro	107

Note The sex ratio at birth is the ratio of male births per 100 female births. The average ratio is 105–106

Source UNDP (2016)

Table 8.2 Excess of female child mortality in selected countries, 2005–2010

Country	Mortality ratio under 5 years of age (per 100)		Excess female deaths under 5 years of age (000 s per year)
	Observed (UN estimates)	Expected (life expectancy)	
Afghanistan	98	110	14.2
Bangladesh	103	120	13.8
China	71	122	99.5
India	88	119	261.8
Nepal	94	120	4
Pakistan	105	119	23.2
Total			418.1

Note Mortality sex ratios are the ratios of male mortality rates under 5 years of age to female rates. Observed ratios are from World Population Prospects 2010. Expected ratios are the life expectancy estimates by regressing life expectancies against mortality sex ratios in the rest of the world. Excess female deaths are the annual difference between the numbers of observed and expected deaths per year
Source UNFPA (2012)

number of countries in Asia. It has been estimated by the UNFPA[1] that there was an excess of female mortality less than five years of age in six countries in Asia amounting to 418,000 per year in the period 2005–2010. Most of it in India (63%) followed by China (24%) (Table 8.2).

The sex gap between males and females aged 0–19 years of age in 2010 for a number of countries in Asia and Southern Europe was estimated to be about 7.6%. The gap ranged from 0.7% of the female population in Pakistan to 14.2% in China. The second most populated country, India had an estimated gap of 5.6% (Table 8.3). The UNFPA (2012) estimated that there were 117 million *missing females* or 8% of the female population in 2010 in the selected countries, and consequently a *male surplus* in the *marriage market* in these countries. This gap is likely to continue for years to come.

8.4   Difference and Equality

8.4.1   Dimensions and Context

Male preference and selection in some cultures raise wider raging questions on differences and equality between males and females in society. It has been suggested that these could be examined in terms of variables related to

---

[1]UNFPA is the United Nations Fund for Population Activities.

Table 8.3 Sex gap in selected countries in females aged 0–19 years of age, 2010

Country/territory	Sex gap population 0–19 years of age	
	Thousands	(%)
East and Southeast Asia		
China	23,687	14.2
Hong Kong	27	4.4
Republic of Korea	260	4.8
Singapore	11	1.9
Vietnam	245	1.7
South Asia		
Afghanistan	502	5.7
Bangladesh	354	1.2
India	13,197	5.6
Nepal	114	1.7
Pakistan	281	0.7
West Asia		
Armenia	31	7.4
Azerbaijan	104	7.8
Georgia	19	3.8
Southern Europe		
Albania	15	3.1
Montenegro	2	2.7
Total	38,850	7.6

Note The estimates of missing females aged 0–19 years of age rely on United Nations' estimates in World Population Prospects 2010. The estimation of the gap assumes that the male to female mortality pattern is a function of only mortality levels and is not affected by local factors. Excess male mortality as observed among adults is taken as a reference. These estimates also do not take into consideration any corrections in the gap due to international migration. The percentage gap is in terms of the estimated female population of that age in 2010
Source UNFPA (2012)

- *capabilities*
- *agency*
- *economic opportunities*

in the context of

- *households*
- *formal and informal institutions*
- *economic framework*

that affect social and economic transformation and human development (Sen 2000).

8.4.2 Capabilities

The observed greater female mortality during childhood in some countries runs contrary to the usually higher mortality rates of males in the first day, week and year of life and greater vulnerability that affects lower expectancy of life of males that might be of a genetic nature, to some extent (Kramer 2000). Nevertheless, the quality of offspring is affected by the health of the mother. The frequency of pregnancy affects female resources involved in reproduction and lactation. The substantial decline in fertility in recent decades (Table 1.10) that reduced demands on female reproductive resources has contributed to the fall in the world's average infant mortality from 142 infant deaths per thousand live births in 1950–1955 to 35 per thousand in 2010–2015 (UN 2017).

Risks involved during the pregnancy and birth can result in maternal mortality, still-birth or other harm to mother and offspring. Consequently, the availability of health services related to the support of females during pregnancy, delivery and the postnatal period can make a major difference to female wellbeing and to the quality of offspring. Substantial progress has been made in reducing maternal mortality from a world average of 385 maternal deaths per hundred thousand live births in 1990 to 216 and 2015. However, the disparity between developed (12/100,000) and developing (239/100,000) countries in 2015 was still about 20 fold (Table 8.4). As would be expected, the gap was even wider between countries and was estimated to range from 3/100,000 in such countries as Finland and Greece to 856 in Chad and 1,360 in Sierra Leone. The extreme case of Sierra Leone makes it clear that informal and formal institutions failed to deal with the interrelated factors that affect

Table 8.4 World maternal mortality by stage of development and region, 1990 and 2015

Country stage of development/region	Maternal mortality ratio		
	1990	2015	Difference 2015–1990
Developed	23	12	−11
Developing	430	239	−191
World	385	216	−169
Northern Africa	171	70	−101
Sub-Sahara Africa	987	546	−441
Eastern Asia	95	27	−68
Southern Asia	538	176	−362
South-eastern Asia	320	110	−210
Western Asia	160	91	−69
Caucasus and Central Asia	69	33	−36
Latin America and Caribbean	135	67	−68
Oceania[a]	391	187	−204

Note Maternal mortality ratio is the number of maternal deaths per 100,000 live births per year. The regional ratios exclude countries in Europe, Northern America and [a]Australia and [a]New Zealand

Source WHO (2015). Computations made by the authors

female health and ability to survive and give birth to healthy children. About 2015, females in Sierra Leone received an average of only 2 years of education, child malnutrition was 38%, and only 60% of births had skilful attendance at delivery. And in addition to the extreme maternal mortality, child mortality under five years of age was 120 per thousand live births (WHO 2016; UNDP 2016). These inter related features point to lags in the organisation of adequate services to protect mothers and their children that affect the whole family, in spite of Malaysia and Sri Lanka providing examples of how developing countries can reduce maternal mortality at a relative low cost (Pathmanathan et al. 2003). In addition to the important female loss, maternal mortality has an impact on the development of any previous offspring, as it reduces household resources to care for and educate children born prior to the death of the mother (Martins 2003).

The adequacy of female nutrition affects female health and ability to develop both her physical and cognitive capabilities. The supply of safe water and sanitation also impact on female and male health and development. Their inadequacy represents an additional burden on female adults and children as they carry responsibility for housekeeping, following traditional gender roles.

Education of males and females is a major enhancer of their capabilities that influences their wellbeing, health, economic activity and contributions to society. Adult literacy rates have improved in recent decades from a world average of 76% in 1992 to 84% in 2015 (UNDP 1995, 2016). Nevertheless, females continue to lag in literacy in comparison to males in lower income countries, especially those in Sub-Sahara Africa and Southern Asia (Table 8.5). Access to education facilities and

Table 8.5 World literacy sex parity of youth and adults by income level and region, circa 2015

Country income level/region	Sex parity literacy index	
	Youth (15–24 years of age)	Adult (15 years of age and over)
Low	0.85	0.74
Lower middle	0.93	0.83
Upper middle	1	0.95
High	...	...
World	0.96	0.91
Caucuses and Central Asia	1	1
Eastern and South-eastern Asia	1	0.96
Europe and Northern America	...	...
Latin America and Caribbean	1	0.99
Northern Africa and Western Asia	0.96	0.86
Pacific	...	...
Southern Asia	0.91	0.76
Sub-Sahara Africa	0.86	0.76

Note The sex parity index is the difference between male and female literacy. A value below one indicates a difference in favour of males. Parity is considered to be between 0.97 and 1.03. (...) means no known difference
Source UNESCO (2016)

informal institutional attitudes that favour male over female education are important constraints that persist more often in countries at a lower stage of development. On average, females are close to parity in enrolments in primary and lower secondary education but lag in upper secondary education. It is males that are below parity, in the world average, as far as tertiary education is concerned. Females' enrolments are below those of males at all levels of education in low income countries, and also in upper secondary and tertiary education enrolments in lower middle income countries in Sub-Sahara Africa, Northern Africa and Western Asia (Table 8.6). The relative disadvantage of females in literacy and primary and secondary education has a feedback loop on fertility and infant mortality, as rising female education is associated with lower fertility and infant mortality. It is also important in female employment opportunities and consequent ability to negotiate their position in the household and society (Bradshaw 2013).

The gendered characterisation of males and females is reflected in the type of education of children and young people. Accordingly, in a study of over 100 countries few females were enrolled in vocational secondary education (WB 2011). A similar review of the field of study at tertiary level shows a clear gender bias. Males were predominant in fields of study in agriculture, engineering and construction and science and females in education, health and welfare (Table 8.7).

Table 8.6 World education enrolment sex parity in primary, secondary and tertiary education by income level and region, circa 2015

Country income level/region	Sex parity education enrolment index			
	Primary	Lower secondary	Upper secondary	Tertiary
Low	0.93	0.86	0.74	0.53
Lower middle	1.02	1.02	0.93	0.97
Upper middle	0.97	1.00	1.06	1.16
High	1.00	0.99	1.01	1.25
World	0.99	0.99	0.98	1.11
Caucuses and Central Asia	0.99	0.99	0.98	1.04
Eastern and South-eastern Asia	0.99	1.01	1.01	1.11
Europe and Northern America	1.00	0.99	1.01	1.28
Latin America and Caribbean	0.98	1.03	1.13	1.29
Northern Africa and Western Asia	0.95	0.93	0.96	0.99
Pacific	0.97	0.95	0.94	1.39
Southern Asia	1.06	1.04	0.94	0.93
Sub-Sahara Africa	0.93	0.88	0.82	0.70

Note The Sex parity education enrolment index is the difference between male and female enrolment in primary, lower and upper level secondary, and tertiary education. A value below one indicates a difference in favour of males. Parity is considered to be between 0.97 and 1.03
Source UNESCO (2016)

Table 8.7 Tertiary education field of study of males and females in selected countries, circa 2010

Field of study	Predominance of males or females taking the field of study (%)		
	Male	Female	Neutral
Agriculture	74	3	22
Engineering, manufacturing and construction	100	…	…
Science	68	13	20
Services	59	21	21
Education	6	84	10
Health and welfare	4	82	13
Arts and humanities	6	55	39
Social sciences, business and law	16	23	61

Note The study included between 87 and 97 countries, depending on information available. Percentages may not add due to rounding
Source WB (2011)

These differences have implications for employment opportunities in occupations with different rates of earnings, usually in the favour of males.

8.4.3 Agency

In the gender context, agency could be expressed, among other things, in

- *choices in family formation and reproduction*
- *control over family assets and allocation of household expenditure*
- *allocation of family tasks and time use*
- *community and political involvement*

The strength of agency in these areas influences male and female roles, their relative power in the household and society, but the actions that they take independently mould and change social informal and formal institutions that have feedback loops that may add to social flexibility or constraints in choices made.

Institutionalised perceptions and attitudes can lead to verbal or even physical coercion, in some societies, that may inhibit female's (and at times also male's) choices in family formation and composition, as in the case of son preference. Nevertheless, an important factor that has an influence on family formation and composition is knowledge and access to contraception. It facilitates choices regarding the timing of first child, spacing between pregnancies and family size. All have a bearing on females' health, time use, and opportunities for employment and work outside the house. Much progress has been made in female access to contraception worldwide that is reflected in the reduced fertility rates worldwide (Table 3.3). The lower than average contraceptive use in Africa, some areas in Asia and Oceania (Table 8.8) are associated with higher fertility rates (UN 2017) and

Table 8.8 World contraception prevalence by region, 2015

Region	Contraceptive prevalence (%)		Unmet need for family planning (%)
	Any method	Modern methods	
Northern Africa	53	48	15
Sub-Sahara Africa	28	24	24
Eastern Asia	82	62	5
Central Asia	57	52	14
Southern Asia	59	50	14
South-eastern Asia	64	57	12
Western Asia	58	40	14
Europe	69	59	10
Latin America and Caribbean	73	67	11
Northern America	75	69	7
Australia and New Zealand	69	66	10
Melanesia, Micronesia, Polynesia	39	31	25
World	64	57	12

Note Contraceptive prevalence is expressed as a percentage of married females or in-union aged 15-49 years of age who use contraception
Source UN (2015)

maternal mortality (WHO 2015). It has been postulated that lack of knowledge, opposition by partners and fear of its effects are often more significant barriers to use than access to contraception (WB 2011).

Equality in household decision making regarding family assets and allocation of household expenditures is influenced by both formal and informal institutionalised social rules and norms. The laws of inheritance of family assets vary considerably from equal sharing of inheritances by both sexes to complete inequality in favour of males. The degree of inequality follows not only the stage of development but also patrilineal norms in some countries that favour males (Table 8.9). Unequal access to assets tends to weaken female bargaining power in household decision making. As mentioned earlier (Chap. 6: Sect. 6.6), informal social norms are influenced by education and whether the female contribution is seen as an extension of house-keeping or from paid work outside the house. The degree of female agency and exercise of preferences have an impact on household allocations that favour investments in education of children and their nutrition, as well as household supplies to the benefit of females and of the whole family (WB 2011). The importance of these female priorities and agency increases as household income and resources decline in all countries, at difference stages of development.

Male and female gendered roles result in differences in time spent in unpaid and paid work. This affects male and female free time to pursue personal interests and

Table 8.9 Daughters and widows inheritance by region, circa 2010

Region	Inheritance share		
	Equal	Unequal	Customary
Daughters/Widows	Percentage of countries		
Daughters			
Middle East and Northern Africa	–	100	–
South Asia	50	50	–
Sub-Sahara Africa	59	34	7
East Asia and Pacific	75	25	–
OECD countries, Latin America and Caribbean, Europe, Central Asia	100	–	–
Widows			
Middle East and Northern Africa	–	100	–
South Asia	50	50	–
Sub-Sahara Africa	44	46	10
East Asia and Pacific	75	25	–
OECD countries, Latin America and Caribbean, Europe, Central Asia	100	–	–

Note OECD countries are those that reached an advanced level of economic development and met criteria to join the Organisation for Economic Co-operation and Development
Source WB (2011)

also what is perceived to be the importance of male and female contributions to the household and their related bargaining power in decision making. On average, females tend to spend more hours at work per day than males in developing and developed countries. In both cases, males spend, on average, more time in paid work and females more time in unpaid work. The gap in average hours worked per day between females and males narrows from developing (0.93 hours) to developed (0.33 hours) countries, mostly from the lower average paid working hours of males in developed (3.96 hours) compared to those in developing (4.98 hours), but also from an increase in male hours in unpaid work from 1.20 to 2.16 hours, as female number of hours of unpaid work remains about the same in both developing and developing countries, 4.30 and 4.20 hours respectively (Table 8.10). Thus, development is associated with increasing female engagement in paid work and males rising commitment to unpaid work, the latter often associated with housework and caring of children. However, it does not lead to equality in time spent in either paid or unpaid work by the two sexes.

Equality in the formation of social capital and agency exercised by males and females is yet another dimension of human development that affects the influence that males and females exert on society and their relative impact on both informal and formal social and political institutions and resulting social norms and rules.

An illustration of male and female agency in their participation in the political process is the proportions who join a political party. The degree of membership of political parties varies considerably from region to region being highest in South

Table 8.10 Average hours of work of employed and unemployed people by sex, circa 2015

Country stage of development paid/unpaid work	Average hours work per day		Difference female-male
	Male	Female	
Developing			
Paid work	4.98	2.79	−2.17
Unpaid work	1.20	4.30	+3.10
All developing	6.16	7.09	+0.93
Developed			
Paid work	3.96	2.25	−1.71
Unpaid work	2.16	4.20	+2.04
All developed	6.12	6.45	+0.33

Note The average number of hours of work per day relate to 28 developing and 37 developed countries
Source ILO (2016). Computations made by the authors

Table 8.11 Male and female membership of political parties, circa 2005–2007

Region and level of development	Membership of a political party (%)		
	Males	Females	Difference female-male
Middle East and North Africa	5	2	−3
Latin America and Caribbean	5	2	−3
OECD countries	10	7	−3
East Asia and Pacific	11	7	−4
Europe and Central Asia	11	5	−6
Sub-Sahara Africa	17	10	−7
South Asia	26	7	−19

Note OECD countries are those that reached an advanced level of economic development and met criteria to join the Organisation for Economic Co-operation and Development
Source WB (2011). Computations made by the authors

Asia and Sub-Sahara Africa. Females' proportion tends to be in the same direction as that of males but it is considerably lower (Table 8.11).

The substantial inequality of females in political party membership is reflected in the shares of parliament seats held by females. Their share is on average less than a third of parliament seats. With the lowest proportion in the Arab States (16%) and South Asia (17%) and highest in Latin America and the Caribbean (28%), the latter is at par with that in the more developed countries of the OECD[2] (28%) (Table 8.12). This substantial inequality hinders female agency in promoting issues that they have an interest in and their contribution to formal institutions that determine and shape the legal apparatus of societies, as well as government

---

[2]OECD is the Organisation for Economic Cooperation and Development, which members have reached an advanced level of economic development.

Table 8.12 Male and female seats in parliament, 2015

Region and level of development	Share of seats in parliament (%)		
	Males	Females	Ratio male/female
Arab States	84	16	5.3
East Asia and Pacific	80	20	4.0
Europe and Central Asia	81	19	4.3
Latin America and Caribbean	72	28	2.6
South Asia	83	17	4.9
Sub-Sahara Africa	77	23	3.3
OECD countries	72	28	2.6

Note OECD countries are those that reached an advanced level of economic development and met criteria to join the Organisation for Economic Co-operation and Development
Source UNDP (2016). Computations made by the authors

economic priorities and allocation of resources for human development, including their own.

8.4.4 *Economic Opportunities*

The agricultural and industrial revolutions and more recent technological developments have changed the economic apparatus and possibilities for both male and female development (Chap. 1: Sects. 1.4–1.6). Mechanisation and the use of power tools has reduced the importance of male physical strength in production and created greater opportunities for female participation in agriculture and industry. Progress in narrowing the gap between male and female education is another factor that has raised human capital and opportunities for lesser sex segregation at work. Lower rates of fertility reduced the demand on females' time dedicated to the reproduction and caring function and increased opportunities for female work in production outside the house. These trends have been associated with urbanisation that has had an impact on social organisation and relationships between males and females (Chap. 6: Sect. 6.6). Nevertheless, formal barriers have persisted. A survey of legal gender differences found that the greater the legal inequality of females, the lower the female employment to population ratio, the female/male earnings ratio, the proportion of firms with a female top manager, and what was interpreted as a feed back loop to female lower secondary education (WB 2015). In addition to formal rules, social perceptions of the roles of males and females continue to constrain female participation in the labour force, the type work that they perform and their rate of pay.

The gap in labour force participation of females has narrowed somewhat in recent decades because of the decline in male's participation in the aftermath of the Global Financial Crisis. In 1995, the male (80%) to female (52%) difference in the

Table 8.13 World labour force participation rate by sex, 1995 and 2015

Sex	Labour force participation rate (%)		
	1995	2015	Difference 1995-2015
Females	52	50	−2
Males	80	76	−4
Difference female-male	−28	−26	

Note Labour force participation rate is the proportion of the population of working age, usually 15–64 years of age, who are working or actively procuring employment
Source ILO (2016). Computations made by the authors

labour force participation rate was 28%. The gap was reduced slightly to 26% in 2015, when the male rate (76%) fell more than the female's (50%) from that in 1995 (Table 8.13).

   These differences in the formal sector of the economy have prevailed over time with female participation rates around 50%, on average. The difference in female participation in the labour force compared with that of males was substantial at 26% in 2009 (Table 8.14). The differences ranged from 16% in East Asia and the Pacific region to 49% in the Middle East and Northern Africa. The gap was also high at 47% in South Asia. On average, in all regions females' participation rates have been lower than males'. These comparisons do not include high income countries with an average gap of 18% (Table 8.14). A review of this gap in the twenty largest economies (G20) shows that substantial gaps continued in 2012, as high as 58% in Saudi Arabia, 52% India and 44% in Turkey. Mid-range gaps of 22 and 23% were found in Brazil and Korea, and 21% in Japan and Italy. Lower gaps of 8% were estimated for Canada, 9% in France, and 11 and 12% in the United States and the United Kingdom respectively, and 14% in China (Table 8.17).

Table 8.14 World labour force participation rate by region and sex, 1980 and 2009

Region	Labour force participation rate (%)			
	Males		Females	
	1980	2009	1980	2009
East Asia and Pacific	86	80	67	64
Europe and Central Asia	77	69	58	51
Sub-Sahara Africa	83	81	57	61
Latin America and Caribbean	81	80	36	52
South Asia	86	82	33	35
Middle East and Northern Africa	76	75	21	26
High income countries	75	70	45	52
World	82	78	50	52

Note Labour force participation rate is the proportion of the population of working age, usually 15–64 years of age, who are working or actively procuring employment
Source WB (2011)

Table 8.15 Average hours of work of employed people by sex, circa 2015

Country stage of development paid/unpaid work	Average hours work per day		Difference female-male
	Male	Female	
Developing			
Paid work	6.36	5.09	−1.27
Unpaid work	1.31	4.11	+2.80
All developing	7.67	9.20	+1.53
Developed			
Paid work	5.42	4.39	−1.03
Unpaid work	1.54	3.30	+1.76
All developed	6.96	7.69	+0.73

Note The average number of hours of work per day relate to 23 developing and 23 developed countries
Source ILO (2016). Computations made by the authors

Table 8.16 Employment distribution by economic sector and sex, circa 2012

Economic sector	Percentage distribution		
	Females	Males	Difference female-male
Communication services	31	16	+15
Retail, hotels and restaurants	21	17	+4
Manufacturing	13	12	+1
Finance & business	4	4	–
Electricity, gas and water	0.5	1	−0.5
Mining	0.5	2	−1.5
Transport and telecommunications	2	7	−5
Agriculture and other primary	27	29	−2
Construction	1	11	−10
All sectors	100	100	

Note Percentages may not add up due to rounding
Source WB (2011)

Employment in paid work enhances the bargaining position of females in the household as well household resources. Institutionalised informal social norms have meant that females continue to carry out most of the unpaid work of employed people in their reproduction and caring function in the household in both developing and developed countries. On average, employed males spend about 55% of the hours in paid work by both sexes in the household in developing and developed countries, while females spend 76 and 68% of the hours spent by households in unpaid work in developing and developed countries respectively. The net result is that females spend more hours of work per day than males (Table 8.15).

Table 8.17 Labour force participation, incidence of part-time employment and gender pay gap in twenty industrialised countries by sex

Country	Labour force participation rate (%)		Incidence of part-time employment (%)		Gender pay gap (%)
	Males	Females	Males	Females	
Argentina	81	56	14	39	na
Australia	83	70	13	38	16
Brazil	83	61	10	25	na
Canada	82	74	12	27	19
China	84	70	na	na	8
France	75	67	6	22	14
Germany	82	72	9	38	17
India	79	27	na	na	na
Indonesia	85	53	na	na	17
Italy	75	54	8	32	11
Japan	84	63	10	35	27
Korea	78	55	7	15	38
Mexico	83	48	14	29	na
Russia	78	68	3	5	na
Saudi Arabia	79	21	7	13	na
South Africa	62	48	5	12	na
Spain	81	69	6	23	11
Turkey	76	32	7	24	na
United Kingdom	83	71	12	39	18
United States	79	68	9	18	18

Note Labour force participation rate is the proportion of males and females either employed or actively seeking employment aged 15–64 years (2012 or latest available year). Incidence of part-time employment is the proportion of males and females that work less than 35 h per week aged 15 years or more (2012 or latest available year). Gender pay gap is the percentage difference in pay between males and females aged 15 years or more (2011 or latest year available. China's data are for six major cities only. (na) means no data available
Source OECD (2014)

The noted dominance of male and female in different fields of study (Table 8.7) is reflected in the sector of the economy in which males and females are predominant, and their type of occupation and consequent rates of earnings.

The distribution of female employment by economic sector points to a predominance in services (Table 8.16). It has been estimated 50% of employed people in 2015 have service types of occupations, but the proportions were 62% for females and 43% for males (ILO 2016).

Sex segregation in the economic sector of employment as well as type of occupation is associated with substantial gaps in earnings. Accordingly, employed males tend to earn more than females. The gap can be as high as 38% in Korea and

27% in Japan but are usually at least as 10% in the twenty largest economies for which there are data available. Some of this gap arises from the greater proportion of females that work part-time. It can be as high as 39% in the United Kingdom and Argentina and 38% in Australia and Germany (Table 8.17). This could represent lack of opportunity for full-time employment or a matter of convenience arising from the larger proportion spend by females in the reproduction and caring functions, along traditional roles of males and females in society.

The gendered pay gap has been the subject of study by the International Labour Office (ILO), among others. The gap is reduced when *explained* differences in education, experience, economic activity, location, work intensity and occupation are considered. However, *unexplained gaps* continued to persist when the explaining factors are taken into consideration (ILO 2015). This could be due to lack of formal regulations regarding equal pay for equal work (WB 2015) or informal norms related to perceived roles of males and females and their reward, regardless of the level of development.

8.5 Gendered Inequalities in Transition

Differences in genetic material of males and females result in different physical features such as sex organs and brain, as well as different hormonal levels that accentuate these dissimilarities and capacities, especially after puberty. Another major difference is the female closer association with the reproductive process that involves females carrying and feeding of the offspring and the risks involved. These and other sex characteristics lead to sex typing and gender identification in childhood and stereotype attitudes as to what males and females are and how they should behave. Indeed, along with socio-economic status, sex is one of the cornerstones of social stratification in virtually every society and culture (Geist and Meyers 2016; Massey 2007). Gendered social norms tend to associate males' physical strength with the production of resources for self and family and females with reproduction and caring for the family. This differentiation has often evolved into patriarchal and patrilineal social order that gives the male authority in decision making and male succession in unequal terms with females. Much progress has taken place in fostering female capabilities in terms of health and education, as well female agency to promote their standing in the household and society. Technological advancements and changes in socioeconomic organisation have taken place that diminish reasons for sex specialisation and provide consequent opportunities for equality between the sexes. Yet, although socioeconomic development has reduced inequalities between males and females, inequalities persist in adequate access to maternal and child health services, enrolment and completion of schooling, knowledge and access to contraception and related choice in reproduction, inheritance and ownership of family assets, choice in task allocation and time use, exercise of political power, opportunities and support for labour force participation, burden of family work, and gaps in equal pay for equal work (Bonita 1998; Mills 2003; Ridgeway 2011).

Nevertheless, the large variation among countries shows the substantial potential for greater equality. This is another example of the transitional nature of human society.

References

Benn, S. L. (1981). Gender schema theory: A cognitive account of sex typing. *Psychological Review, 88*(4), 354–364.

Benn, S. L. (1983). Gender schema theory and its implications for child development: Raising gender-aschematic children in a gender-schematic society. *Signs, 8*(4), 598–616.

Bonita, R. (1998). *Women, ageing and health: Achieving health across the life span.* Geneva: Global Commission on Women's Health. World Health Organization.

Bradshaw, S. (2013). Women's decision-making in rural and urban households in Nicaragua: The influence of income and ideology. *Environment & Urbanization, 25*(1), 81–94.

Das Gupta, M., Zhenghua, J., Bohua, L., Zhenming, X., Chung, W., & Hwa-Ok, B. (2003). Why is son preference so persistent in east and south Asia? A cross-country study of China, India and the Republic of Korea. *Journal of Development Studies, 40*(2), 153–187.

Eagly, H. A., Wood, W. (2013). The nature-nurture debates: 25 years of challenges in understanding the psychology of gender. *Perspectives on Psychological Science, 8*(3), 340–347.

Geist, C. & Meyers, K. (2016). Gender stratification. *Oxford Bibliographies.* https://doi.org/10. 1093/obo/9780199756384-0138. Retrieved December 20, 2017, from http://www. oxfordbibliographies.com/view/documents/obo-9780199756384/obo-9780199756384-0138. xml.

Hyde, J. S. (2005). The gender similarities hypothesis. *American Psychologist, 60*(6), 581–592.

International Labour Office (ILO). (2015). *Global wage report 2014/15—Wages and income inequality.* Geneva.

International Labour Office (ILO). (2016). *Women at work—Trends 2016.* Geneva.

Kohlberg, A. (1966). A cognitive-development analysis of children sex-role concepts and attitudes. In E. E. Maccoby (Ed.), *The development of sex differences.* Stanford: Stanford University Press.

Kramer, S. (2000). The fragile male. *British Medical Journal, 371*(7276), 1609–1612.

Martins, J. M. (2003). Maternal health: costs, values and benefits. *Proceedings of Global Forum for Health Research.* Geneva.

Massey, D. (2007). *Categorically unequal: The American social stratification system.* New York: Russell Sage Foundation.

Mills, M. (2003). Gender and inequality in the global labor force. *Annual Review of Anthropology, 32,* 41–62.

Mischel, W. (1970). Sex-typing and socialization. In P. H. Mussen (Ed.), *Carmichael's manual of child psychology.* New York: John Wiley & Son.

Mischel, W. (1973). Towards a cognitive social learning reconceptualization of personality. *Psychological Review, 80*(4): 252–283.

Organisation for Economic Co-operation and Development, International Labour Office, International Monetary Fund & World Bank Group (OECD). (2014). *Achieving stronger growth by promoting a more gender-balanced economy.* Report prepared for the G20 labour and employment ministerial meeting, Melbourne, Australia, 10–11 September 2014.

Palan, K. M. (2001). Gender identity in consumer behaviour research. *Academy of Marketing Science Review, 10,* 1–28.

Pathmanathan, I., Liljestrand, J., Martins, J. M., Rajapaksa, L. C., Lissner, C., de Silva, A., et al. (2003). *Investing in maternal health—Learning from Malaysia and Sri Lanka.* Washington DC: World Bank.

Pennington, C. R., Heim, D., Levy, A. R. & Larkin, D. T. (2016). Twenty years of stereotype threat research: A review of psychological mediators. *PLoS One, 11*(1): e0146487. Retrieved April 25, 2017, from https://doi.org/10.1371/journal.pone.

Ridgeway, C. (2011). *Framed by gender: How gender inequality persists in the modern world.* Oxford: Oxford University Press.

Savic, I., Garcia-Falgueras, A., & Swaab, D. F. (2010). Sexual differentiation of the human brain in relation to gender identity and sexual orientation. *Progress in Brain Research, 186,* 41–62.

Sen, A. (2000). *Development as freedom.* New York: Anchor Books.

United Nations (UN). (2015). *Trends in contraceptive use worldwide 2015.* New York.

United Nations (UN). (2017). *World population prospects—The 2017 revision.* New York.

United Nations Development Programme. (1995). *Human development report 1995.* New York.

United Nations Development Programme. (2014). *Human development report 2014.* New York.

United Nations Development Programme. (2016). *Human development report 2016.* New York.

United Nations Educational, Scientific and Cultural Organization. (UNESCO). (2016). *Gender review—Creating sustainable futures for all.* Paris.

United Nations Fund for Population Activities (UNFPA). (2012). *Sex imbalances at birth: Current trends, consequences and policy implications.* Bangkok.

Voyer, D., Voyer, S., & Bryden, M. P. (1995). Magnitude of sex differences in spatial abilities: A meta-analysis and consideration of critical variables. *Psychological Bulletin, 117*(2), 250–270.

Wells, J. C. K. (2007). Sexual dimorphism of body composition. *Best Practice & Research Clinical Endocrinology & Metabolism, 21*(3), 415–430.

Wood, W., & Eagly, A. H. (2015). Two traditions of research on gender identity. *Sex Roles, 73,* 461–473.

World Bank (WB). (2011). *World development report 2012.* Washington DC.

World Bank (WB). (2015). *Women, business and the law 2016.* Washington DC.

World Health Organization (WHO). (2015). *Trends in maternal mortality 1990 to 2015.* Geneva.

World Health Organization (WHO). (2016). *World health statistics 2016.* Geneva.

Chapter 9
Deviance: Social Change and Control

> When deviant behaviour occurs in a society—behaviour which
> flouts its basic values and norms—one element in its coming
> into being is a breakdown in social controls, those mechanisms
> which ordinarily operate to maintain valued forms of
> behaviour.
>
> Howard S. Becker (1955)

9.1 Deviant and Criminal Behaviour

Deviant behaviour can be described as a departure from social customs, values, norms and rules in various social contexts. Social constraints on individual behaviour continuously evolved in given cultural and economic settings as the result of individuals' interactions with their social environment. One type of behaviour or sign may be accepted in a group or a society at a given time and found to be socially unacceptable at others. The so called *father* of sociology, Durkheim described responses to deviance *…If I attempt to violate the rules of law they react against me so as to forestall my action, if there is still time. Alternatively, they annul it or make my action conform to the norm if it is already accomplished but capable of being reversed; or they cause me to pay the penalty for it if it is irreparable… if in my mode of dress I pay no heed to what is customary in my country and in my social class, the laughter I provoke, the social distance at which I am kept, produce, although in a more mitigated form, the same results as any real penalty* (Durkheim 1982: 51).

This perspective differentiates two major types of deviance: the breaking of formal laws/criminal behaviour and departure from adopted social customs and or beliefs held either by groups or by society at large. Accordingly, criminal behaviour is deviant but not all deviant behaviour is criminal. Both are of substantial import to those who behave in a deviant manner and those who are exposed or in some other more direct way affected by deviant behaviour. Among other things, Durkheim saw social integration and regulation as a basis of the social bond that promotes adherence to social values, norms and rules. However, he proposed that inequities

© Springer International Publishing AG, part of Springer Nature 2018   243
Jo. M. Martins et al., *Global Population in Transition*,
https://doi.org/10.1007/978-3-319-77362-9_9

in the division of labour and social inequality could lead to a breakdown in the social bond and *anomie* or a state of disassociation between goals and social means to achieve them, and lack of norms to resolve the conflict: ... *Since the lower classes are not, or no longer are, satisfied with the role that has fallen to them by custom and law, they aspire to functions that are prohibited to them and seek to dispossess those who exercise them* (Durkheim 1984: 310).

Others have followed Durkheim's association of deviance with social disadvantage and the labour market. For instance, Rusche proposed *...that most crimes are committed by members of those strata who are burdened by strong social pressures and who are relatively disadvantaged in satisfying their needs when compared with other classes... Unemployed masses, who tend to commit crimes of desperation because of hunger and deprivation, will only be stopped from doing it through cruel penalties...* (Rusche and Dinwiddie 1978: 3–4).

9.2 Social Ideals, Means and Anomie

The concept of *anomie* was used by Merton in his discussion of deviance ...*It is only when a system of cultural values extols, virtually above all else, certain common symbols of success for the population at large while its social structure rigorously restricts or completely eliminates access to approved modes of acquiring these symbols for a considerable part of the same population, that antisocial behaviour ensues on a considerable scale.* (Merton 1938: 680) ...*Whatever the sentiment...concerning the ethical desirability of coordinating the means-and-goals phases of the social structure...lack of such coordination leads to anomie.* (Merton 1938: 682). In his *strain theory of deviance*, Merton proposed that there are two elements that influence deviant behaviour

- *social/cultural goals, purposes and interests that act as an* **aspirational reference**
- *social regulation and control* **modes of achieving these interests**

Merton offered a matrix with five alternatives of social adjustment to these two elements

Social adaptation	Cultural goals	Institutionalised means
Conformity	+	+
Innovation	+	−
Ritualism	−	+
Retreatism	−	−
Rebellion	±	±

Two extreme adaptations are apparent. The one adopted by most people is *conformity* and the acceptance of both the goals and the institutionalised means of achieving them that leads to social stability. The other extreme, and least adopted, is *retreatism* that rejects both the goals and means thus placing people who adopt this stance at the margin of society. Another adaption involves the acceptance of social goals but conflict with the institutionalised means of achievement leading to *innovation* and/or possible use of illegitimate means of achieving aspired goals. Yet another adaptation relates to the conflict by conformity with and *ritualism* with social norms and rules but frustration with, and rejection of, cultural goals. *Rebellion occurs when emancipation from the reigning standards, due to frustration or marginalist perspectives, leads to the attempt to introduce a "new social order"* (Merton 1938: 678).

Different types of adaptations to social pressures and circumstances are seen as being influenced by personality and the cultural environment. Deviance is implicit in the adoption and use of socially unacceptable means. In addition to personality and the cultural environment, social and economic stratification may also make a difference to individuals' access to socially acceptable means of achieving socially promoted goals and lead to the use of socially unacceptable ones. This theory falls short of explaining what causes deviance. Merton accepted that his framework does not fully explain what social structural features predispose individuals to one rather than another adaptive behaviour, the frequency or variations in one type rather than other of conformity or rejection of acceptable social norms and rules, or the consequences of the adoption or rejection of them (Merton 1938).

9.3 Psychosocial Development

9.3.1 Moral Development

One conventional psychological perspective sees deviance as a lack of socialisation, when the ego or social identity is expressed in behaviour in conflict with that socially acceptable. A *psychological development* approach has been postulated by Kohlberg (1981). He envisaged that people went through a number of stages in their *moral development* at three levels

Pre-conventional (3–7 years of age)	
Stage 1	*Obedience and punishment*
	Behaviour is in a socially accepted way that avoids punishment
Stage 2	*Self-interest*
	Behaviour is in a socially accepted way because of the benefit/reward arising from it
Conventional (8–13 years of age)	
Stage 3	*Conformity and interpersonal accord*
	Behaviour is in compliance with social norms and seeking of others' approval

(continued)

(continued)

Stage 4	Authority and social order
	Behaviour is in agreement with and support of social order and perspectives
Post-conventional (adulthood)	
Stage 5	Social contract
	Behaviour acceptable to society is part of the bonding with society and of social values agreed to
Stage 6	Universal principles
	Behaviour reflects generally accepted norms beyond individual benefit

These stages were seen as sequential and built on each other in the context of social interaction. Thus, deviance could be seen as a breakdown in moral development.

9.3.2 Social Cognitive Development and Biological Determinism

In social cognitive theory, a number of sociostructural factors influence human behaviour and deviance by implication. Economic conditions, socioeconomic status, educational and family structures affect behaviour largely through their impact on people's aspirations, sense of efficacy, personal standards, affective states, and other self-regulatory influences, rather than directly...*in these agentic transactions, people are producers as well as products of social systems* (Bandura 2001: 15). In this context, the promotion of determinative ancestral programming and universalised traits as an appropriate explanation of the shaping of human behaviour has been questioned. It is posited that biological factors may offer potentials and constraints rather than determining psychosocial behaviour, in view of the concurrent existing cultures of an aggressive, pacific, egalitarian, or autocratic nature (Bandura 2001).

9.3.3 Social Learning and Modelling

In his discourse on *social learning theory*, Bandura (1973) postulated that people learn from

- *observation*
- *modelling*

of behaviour. Observational learning of others' behaviour involves the study of the performance not only of the action itself but also verbal and facial expressions, body language as well as aspects in response behaviour. From their observation, people gain an understanding of what is accepted and rewarded and what is not accepted and punished. They also learn about context in which the performance and response takes place. Modelling is another learning mechanism in which people model their own behaviour from their observations. However, as people have different types of capabilities and interests, their modelling of observed behaviour tends to lead to individual expressions and even innovation that might result in responses that are different from those inferred from the observation of others' behaviour. Behaviour regulatory mechanisms include stimulus, cognitive and reinforcement control. The latter has a facilitating function and involves *external* and *self-reinforcement* ...*Responses that cause unrewarding or punishing effects tend to be discarded, whereas those that produce rewarding outcomes are retained and strengthened* (Bandura 1973: 20) ...*people similarly set themselves certain performance standards and respond to their own behaviour in self-satisfied or self-critical ways in accordance with their self-imposed demands* (Bandura 1973: 28).

Another proposition of relevance to deviance is that people who strive to maintain certain modes of behaviour tend to associate with others who have similar interests and standards of behaviour that involve social acceptance, mutual support and favourable self-evaluation of their behaviour. The social learning perspective posits that behaviour tends to influence the environment that sequentially has a regulatory function on the response behaviour. Thus, individual behaviour is influenced but it also has an impact on the social environment. In this context... *detrimental reciprocal systems are often unknowingly created and mutually sustained when particular social practices evoke deviant behaviour, which, due to its aversive properties, creates the very conditions likely to perpetuate it.* (Bandura 1973: 41)

9.4 Social Control and Differentiation

9.4.1 Social Differentiation

A *social differentiation theory* proposed by Sutherland, in line with the social learning approach to deviance, posits that

- *deviant (criminal) behaviour is learned; it is neither accidental or caused by genetic or biological processes;*
- *deviant (criminal) behaviour is learned in social interaction and passed from one person to another;*
- *people who pursue deviant behaviour associate differentially with others who condone deviant (criminal) activities;*
- *people engage in deviant (criminal) behaviour because they have an excess of definitions favourable to the breaking of social norms and laws over definitions unfavourable to the violation of these norms and laws.*

The adoption of deviant (criminal) behaviour includes learning the direction of motives, drives, rationalisation and attitudes involved and simple or complicated modes of deviance. These propositions do not infer that deviant behaviour is the result of the intensity of exposure to deviant behaviour but rather to the balance pattern or ratio of exposure to both deviant and non-deviant behaviour. Sutherland acknowledges the shortfall in the explanation of motivation and other affective and cognitive factors that may lead to social differentiation and deviance. (Sutherland et al. 1995)

9.4.2   Social Labelling

Sociologists have examined the labelling of people as deviant and some aspects of its implications. Among them, Howard Becker postulated that deviance is the result of society and groups making social behaviour rules, the breach of which are tantamount to deviance. When these rules are not met by some people, they are labelled *outsiders*. In this context, Becker proposes that deviance is not so much in the nature of act but is the result of the application of the rules and the punishment of the *offender*. Thus, the deviant is the person who has been labelled and deviant behaviour is whatever people so label. Further, he points out that because not all who act in what is considered deviance from social norms are identified as deviants, this presents challenges in the examination of common personality, other traits and social circumstances that are associated with or cause deviance. Inequality in the labelling of individuals can also lead to social inequities, because being labelled as a deviant has important social consequences to the individual. Becker proposes that labelling has an impact on an individual's self-image and consequent social identity and status that affect the individual's participation in society (Becker 1995).

Lemert differentiated between primary and secondary deviance. He proposed that primary deviance arose from departures from a variety of social/cultural norms that may not cause social response and can be rationalised and accepted as part of the individual's role in society. Secondary deviance is a response to sanctions imposed by others on primary deviance (Lemert 1995). Accordingly, these responses may result in labelling of the individual as a deviant and consequent consistent deviant behaviour, as postulated by Bandura (Sect. 9.3.3).

9.4.3   Neutralization of Social Control

Sykes and Matza (1957) postulated that deviant behaviour is associated with a value system that is the inversion of the values held by society. Their focus was on juvenal delinquency. They accepted evidence that some deviants may feel and express guilt, shame, admiration and respect for those who follow social rules and laws. However, they noted that the normative system of society is characterised by *flexibility* on what rules apply under varying situations. This can result in justification of deviance by rationalisation of either the act or motive. Sykes and Matza identified a number of *techniques of neutralization* used by deviants to reduce the effectiveness of social control

- *denial of responsibility*
- *denial of injury*
- *denial of the victim*
- *condemnation of the condemners*
- *appeal to higher loyalties.*

9.4.4 Social Bonding and Control

Another perspective is that some people find deviance interesting, attractive and even rewarding. A question is then why most people do not deviate in a consistent manner. Hirschi (1995) proposed that there are a number of factors that influence conformity with social norms

- *attachment*
- *commitment*
- *involvement*
- *beliefs.*

Attachment to others involves the adoption of social norms/rules and deviance from these creates conflict with the expectations of others. However, if some people are not sensitive to the expectations of others then they do not feel obliged to follow social norms/rules and feel free to deviate from them. *Commitment* to social norms/ rules brings with it perceived gains in terms of material things, a status in society and potential prospects. This stimulates conformity and commitment to conventional lines of behaviour. *Involvement* in conventional activities provides a diversion from deviant behaviour. Parents' domination and work activities tend to reinforce integration with conventional behaviour. However, during adolescence people may find themselves in a situation where parental domination and personal interests may influence the adoption of a set of values that can lead to problems with social integration and deviance. *Beliefs* also play a role in conformity with socially acceptable values and norms or deviance from them. In the social control approach, it is assumed that people can either adopt the prevailing social or group value system or another that flouts it. The first leads to conformity and the latter to deviance. Unlike the neutralization approach where deviant behaviour is rationalised, in social control theory there is no need to do so, as people who deviate may have no commitment to or belief in the values, norms and rules of society or group. Therefore, they perceive no obligation to conform with the prevailing value system and the behaviour that arises from it. Hirschi's sees not one factor but a conjunction of factors as the reasons for conformity or deviance ...*We have not suggested that delinquency is based on beliefs counter to conventional morality; we have not suggested that delinquents do not believe these acts are wrong. They may well believe that these acts are wrong, but the meaning and efficacy of such beliefs are contingent on other beliefs, and, indeed, on the strength of other ties to the conventional order* (Hirschi 1995: 77).

9.5   Crime and Punishment and Economics

Some forms of deviant behaviour assume substantial social importance and may be made illegal/criminal with formal material sanction and punishment. As with other forms of deviance, what is considered illegal in some societies might not be so in others, for example prostitution. In addition to psychological and sociological perspectives on deviance, and criminal behaviour in particular, crime and punishment have been the subject of economic study. Among others, Gary Becker (1974) suggested that criminal activities are important economic ventures that involve considerable public expenditure on police, criminal courts and related activities, corrective services such as prisons and other forms of punishment, as well as private expenditures on advice, guards and other forms of protection. He mentioned the findings of the United States Crime Commission on the direct costs from criminal activity related to expenditures on illegal consumption of goods and services, such as narcotics and prostitution, losses due to fraud, theft and vandalism, forgone income due to assault, homicide, and costs arising from other crimes against persons and property. It was estimated that these and the costs of policing and forms of public and private protection, legal processes, detention and other forms of punishment amounted then to about 4% of the national income of the United States. Becker pointed out that these estimates may be greatly understated, as they did not include public and private expenditures on such areas as the enforcement of much relevant legislation, the value that people attach to life and of the emotional harm done to victims of crime.

Becker's approach followed the economic analysis of choice with the assumption that ...*a person commits an offense if the expected utility to him exceeds the utility he could get by using his time and other resources at other activities. Some persons become "criminals", therefore, not because their basic motivation differs from that of other persons, but because their benefits and costs differ... criminal behavior becomes part of a much more general theory and does not require* ad hoc *concepts of differential association, anomie, and the like, nor does it assume perfect knowledge, lightning-fast calculation, or any of the other caricatures of economic theory* (Becker 1974: 9). He expressed the *supply of criminal offenses* as the function

$$O = O(p, f, u)$$

where O is the frequency of offenses during a given period, p is the probability of conviction per offense, f is the punishment per offense and u is a variable of influencing characteristics, such as income available to the person, education and law-abidingness values. He postulated that the greater the p and f the lower the frequency of offenses. Offenders may have risk preferences that may influence $p\,f$. Evidence cited indicated that the importance of p was greater than that of f. However, efforts involved in rising $p\,f$ had a social cost in law enforcement, other public and private protection activities, legal procedures, prison and other punishment activities such as probation and parole. Becker proposed that if the social goal was to deter crime then the value of apprehension p could be raised close to 1 and that of punishment f could be made to exceed the gain from the criminal offense. But an increase in $p\,f$ would raise the social cost involved in apprehension and punishment. The proposed social welfare function to be minimised was

$$L = L(D, C, bf, O)$$

where L is the social loss to be minimised, D is the damage done, C is the cost of combating offenses, b is the coefficient of different types of punishment f and O is the offense frequency. Becker accepted that the probability of conviction varies with age, sex, race and income. He also accepted that people may not undertake criminal activities even if criminal activity would result in higher income than what they usually earn because of ethical values that they hold (Becker 1992). Thus, some of the motivation and actual behaviour could be attributed to the variable u in Becker's function for the *supply of offenses*. However, this variable was given limited attention in much of Becker's analytical arguments.

9.6 Deviance: Rebellion and Social Change

Unlike criminal offenses that are the object of formal recording, other deviant behaviour in populations is difficult to measure because it is often of a transitional nature and subjected to informal sanctions that do not involve formal administrative processes. Nevertheless, cohabitation before, or as an alternative to, legal marriage offers an illustration of evolving social practices and acceptance of previously deviant behaviour in some societies. In some developed countries, cohabitation has changed from being socially a less accepted form of union than marriage to become more frequent in a rising proportion of unions, in Scandinavia, other European countries and the United States (Sweeney et al. 2015).

Australian data shows that legal marriage continues to be the major form of union. In 2011, 59% of people aged 15 years and over were either married or in cohabitation. Most were legally married (49%) and the proportion in cohabitation was 10% in 2011, a more than two-fold rise from a lower 4% in 1986 (AIFS 2017).

The analysis of the pattern by age indicates that cohabitation has been on the rise among females of all ages. It tends to be higher the lower the age. Accordingly, the proportion of females aged 15–19 years with a partner who were in cohabitation was 88% in 2011 compared with 78% in 1996. Similarly, 66% of partnered females aged 20–24 years in 2011 were in cohabitation in contrast with 46% in 1996. However, cohort analysis points to a declining cohabitation trend as the age of females rises. The cohort of females 15–19 years of age in 1996, with a partner, had a cohabitation rate of 78%. Fifteen years later in 2011, females at the age of 30–34 years, with a partner, had a cohabitation rate of only 22%. This declining trend also applies to other female cohorts aged 15–19 in 2001 and 2006 (Table 9.1). The pattern is similar in the case of males over the same period. One possible explanation is that most females who enter into a partnership when they are older tend to get legally married without previous cohabitation. Another possibility is that females who enter into cohabitation partnerships early in life eventually marry at an older age. This is supported by the findings that 77% of people who married in 2013 had been in cohabitation before marriage compared with 16% in 1973 (AIFS 2017).

The rising trend in cohabitation in some countries is reflected in the proportion of births to unmarried mothers, with a possible loss of stigma previously attached to birth outside marriage. In 2007, in fourteen more developed countries, more than half of births were to unmarried females in Iceland (66%), Sweden (55%), and Norway (54%). But the proportions were also high in France (50%), Denmark (46%), United Kingdom (44%), United States (40%), Netherlands (40%), Ireland (33%), Germany (30%), and Canada (30%). The proportions were lower but still

Table 9.1 Proportion of partnered females in cohabiting relationship Australia, 1996–2011	Age (years)	Percentage of partnered females in cohabited relationships			
		1996	2001	2006	2011
	15–19	77.7	82.1	85.9	87.7
	20–24	46.3	57.1	64.9	66.4
	25–29	22.3	30.2	37.3	38.9
	30–34	12.5	17.1	21.0	22.4
	35–39	8.8	11.9	15.2	16.6
	40–44	7.1	9.5	12.5	14.5
	45–49	5.7	8.1	10.5	12.7
	50–54	4.3	6.4	8.8	10.8
	55–59	2.7	4.5	6.5	8.5
	60–64	1.6	2.7	4.3	6.0
	65–69	1.2	1.7	2.7	4.2
	70–74	0.9	1.3	1.8	2.6
	75–79	0.9	1.1	1.5	1.8
	80–84	0.8	1.4	1.3	1.6
	85 and over	1.2	2.4	2.8	1.7

Source AIFS (2017)

Table 9.2 Proportion of births to unmarried females, several countries, 1980–2007

Country	Percentage of births to unmarried females		Percentage increase 1980–2007
	1980	2007	
Iceland	40	66	26
Sweden	40	55	15
Norway	15	54	39
France	11	50	39
Denmark	33	46	13
United Kingdom	12	44	32
United States	18	40	22
Netherlands	4	40	36
Ireland	5	33	28
Germany	12	30	18
Canada	13	30	17
Spain	4	28	24
Italy	4	21	17
Japan	1	2	1

Source Ventura (2009). Computations by the authors

high in Spain (28%) and Italy (21%). An exception was Japan with a proportion of only 2%. The rising trend was for increments in the proportion of unmarital births by as much as 39% points in the 27-year period 1980–2007 in Norway and France. The rise in the proportion of nonmarital births during the period was substantial in most cases especially in those where the proportion was relatively low in 1980 such as the Netherlands (4%), Ireland (5%), Italy (4%) and Spain (4%) (Table 9.2).

These illustrations point to rebellion by younger people to social norms. They gain acceptance and following among peer groups and eventually become the social norm rather deviant behaviour, at least in some societies.

9.7 Criminal Offenses

9.7.1 Types of Criminal Offenses

Criminal offenses recorded by police vary considerably by country. A review of criminal offenses recorded by police in ten European countries shows that major criminal offenses per head of population differed by more than seven fold between Sweden (5,181/100,000) and Poland (672/100,000). In all cases, offenses related to property were several-fold greater than those related to bodily harm (Table 9.3).

The differences are quite pronounced between countries with higher and lower income per head of population: in general, the countries with higher average

Table 9.3 Major criminal offenses recorded by police, several European countries, 2015

Country	Offenses per 100,000 people							GDP p.c. PPP$
	Intention. homicide	Assault Robbery and other	Sexual violence	Offenses against persons	Offenses against property	Other offenses	All	
Sweden	1	134	178	313	4,752	116	5,181	47,823
Poland	1	37	5	42	613	17	672	49,547
Germany	1	218	42	261	2,218	75	2,554	41,767
England and Wales	1	835	112	947	2,899	44	3,890	41,178
France	2	532	50	583	2,423	11	3,017	47,999
Netherlands	1	342	44	386	4,569	86	5,041	37,255
Italy	1	163	7	171	1,719	54	1,944	26,436
Spain	1	202	21	224	868	26	1,118	34,696
Croatia	1	50	14	65	675	67	807	26,856
Hungary	1	143	6	150	1,322	62	1,533	22,489
Ten-country average	1	334	44	379	2,086	46	2,511	

Note Offense is an act by a person for which a legal penalty can be imposed by law. Intentional homicide is the unlawful death purposely inflicted on a person by another person. Assault, robbery and other includes physical attack resulting in bodily harm, robbery, that is the forceful theft from a person, kidnapping that is the unlawful detention of person against the person's will. Sexual violence includes rape and other sexual assault. Offences against a person are the subtotal of the three previous types of offenses. Offenses against property include theft and burglary. Other offenses include drug related offenses. The rates for Italy relate only to sexual assault. The rates for England and Wales in the cases of intentional homicide and sexual violence relate 2014. The rates for homicide in the Netherlands are for 2013. GDP p.c. PPP$ is Gross Domestic Product (GDP) per capita at purchasing power parities in 2015 international dollars. These rates are indicative rather than comprehensive because of they reflect differences in national recording perspectives, in spite of Eurostat efforts. The GDP figures for England and Wales are those for the United Kingdom

Source Eurostat (2017a, 2017b), WB (2017). Computations made by the authors

income also have a greater number of offenses recorded by police per head of population. This is in contrast with Durkheim's and Rusche's propositions (Sect. 9.1). As Gary Becker noted, the assessment of the actual situation is hindered by ...*grave limitations in the quantity and quality of the data on offenses*... (Becker 1974: 45).

In addition to real differences from local circumstances, some may arise from what people consider worth reporting to police in different social and cultural contexts. For instance, in spite of the high rate of offenses recorded by police in Sweden, a household survey in that country indicated that in 2015 only 48% of offenses against property and 26% of offenses against a person were reported to the police (Bra 2016). The considerable variation in sexual offense rates also points to possible reluctance in reporting offenses of a sexual nature and the differing social stigma attached to them in different countries. For instance, in Sweden the rate of reported sexual violence offenses (178/100,000) is above that of assault (134/100,000), but the inverse is the norm in all other nine countries, especially in Italy that reported no rape cases and low rate of sexual assault (7/100,000) (Table 9.3). Yet another possible issue is the criteria used by police in different countries in the recording of offenses and their type.

Nevertheless, although there are substantial rate variations, there is a degree of consistency in the greater rate of offenses against property than against a person, also observed in other countries outside Europe such as the United States, Australia and Japan (Tables 9.4, 9.5 and 9.6).

The quality of data makes international comparisons of criminal behaviour difficult and may lead to flawed conclusions. Greater consistency may be found in intentional homicide because of its social importance that has been described as the worst of crimes which ...*ripple effect goes far beyond the initial loss of human life and can create a climate of fear and uncertainty. Intentional homicide also victimises the family and community of the victim*... (UNODC 2014: 9). The frequency of intentional homicide recorded varies considerably by region. The Americas with about 14% of the world's population accounted for 36% of intentional homicides in 2012. Similarly, Africa with 15% of the population reported 31% of the number of intentional homicides in all regions. These regional disparities between population and frequency of intentional homicides were reflected in the rate of 17 homicides per hundred thousand people in the Americas and 13/100,000 in Africa compared with 3/100,000 in Asia, Europe and the Oceania (Table 9.7).

Thirteen countries accounted for 65% of intentional homicide in the world in 2012. Among them, four countries in Latin America—Mexico, Brazil, Columbia and Venezuela—had rates above 20/100,000 compared with the world average of 7/100,000. Rates in Venezuela (55/100,000) and Columbia (32/100,000) were particularly high, but so were those in South Africa (32/100,000) and D. R. Congo (29/100,000) in Africa (Table 9.8). The rate of 9/100,000 in the Russian Federation was well above the average for European countries (3/100,000), but in line with higher homicide rates in Eastern Europe (UNODC 2014). Again, homicide rates were not closely associated with income per head of population (Table 9.8) and the same applied to poverty rates as estimated by the World Bank (WB 2017). This could

Table 9.4 Major crime offense rates by type United States, 2000–2015

Year	Crime rates per 100,000 people						
	Crime against a person				Crime against person	Crime against property	All major crime
	Murder and manslaughter	Assault	Robbery	Rape			
2000	5.5	324.0	145.0	32.0	506.5	3,618.3	4,124.8
2005	5.6	290.8	140.8	31.8	469.0	3,431.5	3,900.5
2010	4.8	252.8	119.3	27.7	404.6	2,945.9	3,350.5
2015	4.9	237.8	101.9	28.1	372.7	2,487.0	2,859.7
Change 2015 − 2000	−0.6	−86.2	−43.1	−3.9	−133.8	−1,131.3	−1,265.1

Note Murder and manslaughter includes nonnegligent homicide. Assault is the violent attack of a person by another. Robbery is the forceful taking of another's property by a person. Rape is the forced imposition of sexual intercourse by a person on another. Crimes against property include burglary, larceny-theft and motor vehicle theft. These figures give perspectives on relative weights and trends. They are not comprehensive and do not include all crimes such as drug related offenses that are relatively large in the United States context. Consequently, they may not be comparable with figures in other tables that may have a different scope
Source FBI (2017). Computations made by the authors

Table 9.5 Major crime offense rates by type Australia, 2010–2016

Offense type	Crime rates per 100,000 people		
	2010	2016	Difference 2016 − 2010
Murder	1.0	0.9	−0.1
Manslaughter	0.1	0.1	0.0
Attempted murder	0.9	0.8	−0.1
Homicide and related offences	2.1	1.9	−0.2
Assault	1,011.2	960.5	−50.7
Sexual assault	85.6	95.2	9.6
Robbery	66.4	38.8	−27.6
Other	4.9	4.5	−0.5
Offences against persons	1,170.3	1,102.8	−67.5
Offenses against property	3,359.6	3,231.1	−128.5
All major offenses	4,529.9	4,333.9	−196.1

Note Crime offenses are as reported to police by crime victims or other people. Offense is an act by a person for which a legal penalty can be imposed by law. Murder is the unlawful killing of another person with intent to kill or cause bodily harm. Manslaughter is the unlawful killing of another person without the intention to kill or under circumstances of diminished control. Attempted murder is the attempted unlawful killing of another person with intent to kill or cause bodily harm. Sexual assault is physical or intent contact of a sexual nature towards another person without consent, it includes rape and other sexual assault. Robbery is the use of force or threat to gain property from another person. Other includes burglary, fraud and deception, motor vehicle theft. The rates for assault are the average for states and territories of Australia excluding Victoria and Queensland. Rates may not add due to rounding
Sources ABS (2017a, 2017b). Computations made by the authors

Table 9.6 Major crime offense rates by type Japan, 2015

Offense type	Crimes per 100,000 people
Homicide	0.7
Assault and other violence	51.2
Rape	0.9
Robbery	1.9
Crimes against persons	54.8
Crimes against property	669.6
Other	140.1
All	864.6

Note Types of crime are not closely defined, but similar to those in Table 9.4
Source SBJ (2017a, b). Computations made by the authors

Table 9.7 Intentional homicide by region, 2012

Region	Homicide			Population percentage of total
	Number	Rate per 100,000 people	Percentage of total	
Americas	157,000	16.7	35.9	13.5
Africa	135,000	12.9	30.9	15.1
Asia	122,000	2.9	27.9	60.3
Europe	22,000	3.0	5.0	10.6
Oceania	1,100	3.0	0.3	0.5
All	437,100	6.3	100.0	100.0

Note Intentional homicide is the unlawful death purposely inflicted on a person by another person. Population is as at 2010
Source UNODC (2014), UN (2017). Computations made by the authors

lead to the conjecture that although poverty and low income could be contributing factors to intentional homicide, cultural and other social causes may account for the substantial differences in countries with similar incomes and poverty rates.

The highest average intentional homicide rate in the Americas in 2012 was associated with the largest proportion of firearm use as a homicide mechanism, while the inverse applied in Europe and Oceania. However, this association does not explain the substantial difference in rates in Africa and Asia where the proportion of the use of firearms and other mechanisms are about the same (Table 9.9). This reinforces the notion that the frequency of intentional homicide tends to arise from a number of causes including varying cultural and social characteristics, circumstances and responses to given stimuli. India with a recorded homicide rate close to that of the average for Asia offers an example of the importance of local social norms and responses to perceived departure from them: about a fourth of homicides have been attributed to offenses over dowries (Marwah 2014). An examination of a sample of homicides in South Africa with the homicide rate of

Table 9.8 Intentional homicide, largest frequency countries, 2012

Country	Homicides			Percentage of the world population	GDP p. c. PPP$
	Number	Rate per 100,000 people	Percentage of world total		
D. R. Congo	18,586	28.8	4.3	0.9	653
Ethiopia	11,048	12.6	2.5	1.3	1,231
Nigeria	33,817	21.3	7.7	2.3	5,339
South Africa	16,259	31.5	3.7	0.7	12,330
United States	14,827	4.8	3.4	4.4	50,520
Mexico	26,037	22.2	6.0	1.7	16,234
Brazil	50,108	25.5	11.5	2.8	15,118
Columbia	14,670	31.9	3.4	0.7	11,840
Venezuela	16,072	55.4	3.7	0.4	n.a.
China	13,410	1.0	3.1	19.5	11,146
India	43,355	3.5	9.9	17.7	4,828
Pakistan	13,846	8.1	3.2	2.5	4,367
Russian Federation	13,120	9.2	3.0	2.1	24,124
Total	285,155	7.2	65.2	57.0	

Note Intentional homicide is the unlawful death purposely inflicted on a person by another person. The figures for China relate to 2011. The population is as 2010. GDP p.c. PPP$ is Gross Domestic Product per head of population at purchasing power parities 2012 international dollars, or nearest year. (n.a.) Not available
Source UNODC (2014), UN (2017), WB (2017). Computations made by the authors

Table 9.9 Intentional homicide mechanism by region, 2012

Region	Homicide mechanism percentage			Homicide rate per 100,000 people
	Firearms	Sharp objects	Other	
Americas	66	17	17	16.3
Africa	28	30	42	12.6
Asia	28	25	47	2.9
Europe	13	33	54	3.0
Oceania	10	55	35	3.0
World	41	24	35	6.5

Note Intentional homicide is the unlawful death purposely inflicted on a person by another person
Source UNODC (2014)

32/100,000 well above the African average of 13/100,000 showed that homicide arose from misunderstandings or arguments in 52% of the cases. Most homicides took place on Saturdays and Sundays and later in the afternoon and early morning, and alcohol consumption was involved in most. The commission of some other criminal offense such as robbery was involved in another 20% of cases, and mob-action in 10% of cases (SAPS 2016).

9.7.2 Criminal Behaviour: Sex and Age

A distinguishing feature of deviance, in general, and criminal behaviour in particular is what has been called the invariability in sex and age over time and place. Accordingly, although females are known to engage in deviant behaviour such as in unions, and having children outside legal marriage, drunkenness, drug use, sleeping away from home without parent consent and driving motor vehicles without license, males tend to deviate more frequently from social norms and engage in illegal behaviour more often than females (e.g. Robbins and Martin 1993; Lanctot and Le Blanc 2002; Kaufman 2009; Gopal and Marimuthu 2014). A reason given is that the style of females tends to be different from that of males in responding to stimulus in given social contexts, and males in stressful and confrontational situations tend to use violence more than females (Kaufman 2009). Evidence from Australia, Canada and the United States crime statistics supports the common perception that males tend to be responsible for about two thirds to three quarters of recorded criminal offenses (Table 9.10).

It has been proposed, differences between male and female rates of criminal offenses could arise from a number of reasons (Steffensmeier 1996):

- *biological* endowments such as physical strength, and sexual and affective differences
- *gender norms*, moral development and social control differences
- that influence

Table 9.10 Sex of perpetrators of crime in Australia, Canada and United States, 2015

Country	Percentage		
	Male	Female	All
Australia (offenders)	77.8	22.0	100.0
Canada (violations)	76.3	23.7	100.0
United States (arrests)	73.1	26.9	100.0

Note Offenders are the number of people proceeded against and recorded by police for criminal offenses. Violations relate to the number of people who the police have proceeded against for criminal offenses. Arrests relate to the number of people arrested by police in relation to criminal offenses

Sources ABS (2017c), SC (2017a), FBI (2017). Computations made by the authors

- *motivation* differences in terms of taste for risk, shame, self-control, and perceived costs and rewards
- *opportunity* differences such as association with deviant people in settings that facilitate or promote criminal behaviour
- *context* of offence differences.

Physical prowess is supportive of criminal behaviour that involves violence. It favours males who are more likely to be involved in violent crimes than females. Where female sexual behaviour is involved such as in prostitution, males still tend to play a dominating role in control of female behaviour as pimps and standover men. Social control of males and females also tends to involve different expectations and closer supervision of females. This can lead to lower female risk-taking behaviour and deviance. Female socialisation also involves greater emphasis on the needs of others rather than that of males' socialisation. These factors have a bearing on female motivation in terms of perceived costs and rewards involved, as well as in embarrassment, shame and guilt. Constraints and sanctions on female behaviour to conform to female stereotypes tend to reduce their opportunities to associate with others in settings where deviant behaviour is not only accepted but also at times promoted. Further, these differences may lead to changes in the context of offenses. In cases of violence, female offenses tend to be more in a family context.

Among others, two major arguments can be considered when examining the invariability of crime rates between males and females. One is that males and females are substantially different in regard to their cognitive, emotional and behaviour characteristics arising from their biological and psychological endowments and experiences that result in differences in deviance between them. Another is that external constraints and opportunities experienced by males and females are different and lead to different deviant behaviour. A study of structural disadvantage using such indicators as family disruption, poverty, racial composition, unemployment and income inequality confirmed that the level of offenses by males far outweighed that of females. This was especially so in cases where violence was involved. The importance of structural disadvantage was larger the greater the seriousness of the offense, as in the case of homicide and robbery, than in the case of lesser offenses such as burglary and theft. The association of structural disadvantage with aggravated assault did not follow that related to other violent crimes against persons. It was also weaker in the case of homicide by females that was more prevalent in the killing of more immediate family and relatives. A finding of the analysis was that the high levels of criminal offenses by males were good predicators of high levels by females, as the variations in the level of offense were similar for males and females, and there were greater similarities than differences in the impact of structural disadvantage between male and female criminal behaviour. (Steffensmeier and Haynie 2000).

Evidence from recorded crimes, where the offender is known, indicates that crime rates surge in adolescence and reach a peak in early adulthood both for males and females, and then decline with age (e.g. Fig. 9.1; Tables 9.11, 9.12 and 9.13).

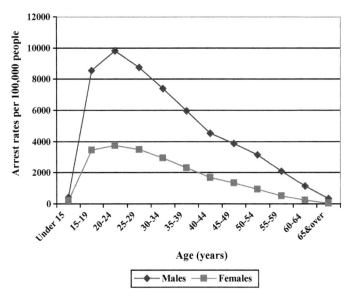

Fig. 9.1 Arrests of males and females by age United States 2015
Sources FBI (2017), USCB (2017). Computations made by the authors

Table 9.11 Arrest rates by age United States, 2015

Age (years)	Arrests per 100,000 people	Percentage of total	
		Arrests	Population
Under 15	323	2.4	19.0
15–19	5,143	13.1	6.6
20–24	6,876	18.8	7.1
25–29	6,160	16.6	7.0
30–34	5,189	13.5	6.7
35–39	4,140	10.1	6.3
40–44	3,107	7.5	6.3
45–49	2,601	6.5	6.5
50–54	2,033	5.5	6.9
55–59	1,285	3.4	6.8
60–64	687	1.6	5.9
65 and over	189	1.1	14.9
All	2,588	100.0	100.0

Note Percentages may not add because of rounding
Sources FBI (2017); USCB (2017). Computations made by the authors

Table 9.12 Arrest rates by age Japan, 2014

Age (years)	Arrests per 100,000 people	Percentage of total	
		Arrests	Population
Under 14	79	4.5	11.8
14–19	680	18.6	5.7
20–29	319	15.6	10.1
30–39	220	13.5	12.7
40–49	199	13.9	14.5
50–59	173	10.2	12.2
60 and over	149	23.7	33.0
All	207	100.0	100.0

Note Percentages may not add because of rounding
Sources SBJ (2016, 2017b)

Table 9.13 Persons accused of crime rates by age Canada, 2015

Age (years)	Persons accused per 100,000 people	Percentage of total	
		Persons accused	Population
3–11	161	0.6	9.7
12–17	4,952	11.8	6.6
18–34	6,154	50.9	23.1
35–54	3,033	30.2	27.7
55–89	637	6.6	28.9
Other ages (a)			4.0
All	2,905	100.0	100.0

Note (a) There are no recorded persons accused of crime below three or over 89 years of age.
Percentages may not add because of rounding
Sources SC (2017a, b)

This is what Hirschi and Gottfredson (1983) described as the robust relationship between age and crime across time, place and social condition.

In the United States context, Cohen (1955) observed that delinquency in young males arose from *status frustration*. Given the values and aspirations of society, some found themselves short of the social resources to realise them. The resulting feeling of failure led some to experience frustration and resulted in the weakening of their social bonds. Consequently, they abandoned generally accepted social norms/ rules and associated with others with similar experiences to form deviant subcultures, gaining status among them with the show of breaking social norms and intimidation. These were said to often start with breaking school discipline and troublesome behaviour that evolve into more serious deviance in later years.

Another view is that youth is a difficult period of life with the transition from childhood to adult life. The tensions experienced may emerge in the form of deviant behaviour. However, deviant behaviour may also arise from a spirit of adventure, experimentation and aggression. Matza (1961) pointed out that although most young people go through this risky period only a small proportion use deviant behaviour as their response to the transition, and many who do so only deviate occasionally.

Title and Grasmick (1997) examined the question of the *invariance of age and crime* put forward by Hirschi and Gottfredson (1983) and their theory, that crime is the result of the interaction between

- *low self-control* (assumed to be constant throughout life, after childhood)
- *criminal opportunity.*

Title and Grasmick found that although in most cases the frequency of crime followed the pattern of peaks in early age (under 25 years), there were some departures depending on the type of crime. For instance, tax cheating followed a hump-shaped curve rather than the usual inverted J-curve. Consequently, they concluded that age-crime is not invariant but highly generalised. In their study, they used a number of variables to capture dimensions of self control and opportunity. A substantial finding was that self-control varied with age following a U-shaped curve being high in young age, lowest in middle age and then surging in older ages. Although not statistical significant, they found substantial age differences in opportunity to commit different types of crimes. For instance, in the case of minor theft and use of force opportunities were larger in early ages that corresponded to the reported pattern of crime.

The United States experience that the age-peak for criminal behaviour varies for different types of crime is also found in other countries such as Australia where crimes recorded by the police such as robbery and theft peaked earlier in the late teens while homicide and violent assault peaked in the early twenties, the same applying to fraud and deception crimes (Table 9.14).

A review of crime and deviance during the life cycle by Sampson and Laub (1992) confirmed that age-specific crime rates peak early in life. It also examined perspectives concerning *continuities* and *discontinuities* in criminal behaviour during the life cycle, and the influence of life events on age related transitions in behaviour. They noted some previous assertions such as Hirschi and Gottfredson's notion of the invariant in age-crime rates over time, place and crime types; Farrington's contention that the shape of the age-crime curve reflected variations in the prevalence and that the incidence of crime did not change with age; and also Blumenstein and Cohen's argument that crime rates per individual are constant during individual's crime career. They suggested that there are two basic concepts in life-course analysis

- *trajectory* in the development of aspects of the life cycle
- *transitions* that reflect specific life events.

The trajectory consists of such aspects of life as schooling, work life, marriage, parenthood, self-esteem, and possible criminal behaviour, while transitions are major life events such leaving school, first employment and first marital union.

Table 9.14 Offenders of major crimes by age Australia, 2015

Age (years)	Offenders per 100,000 people				
	Homicide and related offenses	Acts intended cause injury	Robbery	Theft	Fraud/ Deception
10–14	0.2	203.0	19.2	354.6	13.4
15–19	4.4	656.8	*67.8*	*1,385.9*	124.4
20–24	*7.4*	*696.9*	32.6	695.0	*133.5*
25–29	5.4	607.1	23.1	455.0	111.4
30–34	5.2	566.1	21.0	390.0	103.8
35–39	5.0	537.4	15.8	345.7	89.5
40–44	3.9	457.5	8.8	266.2	73.6
45–49	4.7	326.3	5.0	185.1	50.4
50–54	1.7	197.0	2.9	117.4	28.9
55–59	1.3	102.4	0.9	74.1	16.0
60–64	1.8	66.3	0.2	53.2	11.0
65 and over	1.2	23.6	–	23.1	3.5

Source ABS (2017b, c). Computations made by the authors

Accordingly, transitions are embedded in the trajectory. They posited that the interaction between trajectories and transitions might lead to life changes. The life cycle approach was also said to be concerned with the

- *social meaning of age throughout the life cycle*
- *intergenerational transmission of social patterns*
- *effects of macro level events (such as wars) and structural location (e.g. class and gender).*

Cited evidence pointed to the importance of behaviour in childhood to deviant and criminal behaviour in adulthood. Aggressiveness in childhood was found to be linked with aggression and criminal behaviour later in life. Childhood misbehaviour was associated with drinking, marital violence and severe treatment of children. Child antisocial behaviour was also related later in life to educational achievement, adult employment, occupational status, employment stability and divorce. However, longitudinal studies indicated that most antisocial children do not turn out to be antisocial adults. And similarly, it was found that the majority of adult criminals had no history of previous criminal behaviour. This led to a reassessment of continuities in deviant behaviour during the life cycle and possible events that may strengthen social bonding and stability to reduce deviant behaviour.

A number of studies cited pointed to the significant impact of some life cycle events. It was found that although marriage may not reduce criminal behaviour, it led to lower antisocial behaviour in drinking and drug use. Episodes of unemployment were found to increase the rate of criminal behaviour, and moving from areas of higher to lower crime rates tended to lower crime reoffending experiences.

Sampson and Laub posited that it was the strength of the attachment in marriage rather than marriage itself that made the difference in reducing deviance. Similarly, it was the interest and involvement in the job rather than employment per se that made the difference in reducing deviance, in general, and criminal behaviour. Thus, the review indicates that the impact of transitional events is dependent to a great extent on the quality and strength of their nature. Further, it was contended that parent and social reactions to deviant behaviour had an impact on life changes that may lead to school failure, incarceration and social labelling that reduced employment opportunities and fed continuity of antisocial behaviour. Accordingly, transitory life cycle events may lead to discontinuity as well as continuity of deviance and criminal behaviour.

9.7.3 Victims of Crime

In view of the perception that criminal behaviour is more widespread than reported to the police, some countries have conducted household surveys to gain another perspective on the dimensions of criminal behaviour. These surveys are based on interviews of individual members of households and therefore exclude victims of homicide. Similar to the pattern in Sweden (Sect. 9.7.1), findings from a household survey in the United Sates indicated that only 35% of property crimes and 48% of violent crimes were reported to police in 2015. The proportion of rape and sexual assault reported to police was particularly low at 31% (Table 9.15).

The same survey showed that in 2015, females were more likely to be victims of violent crime than males in the United States (Truman and Morgan 2016), in

Table 9.15 Victimization rates by type of crime reported and not reported to police United States, 2015

Type of crime	Victimization rates per 1,000 people		
	Reported to police	Not reported to police	All
Rape/sexual assault	0.5	1.1	1.6
Robbery	1.3	0.8	2.1
Assault	6.8	7.6	14.4
Violent crime	8.6	9.5	18.1
Property crime	38.3	71.3	109.6
All	46.9	80.8	127.7

Note Victimization rates are the ratio of the number of victimizations experienced by the specific population by the number of people in that population multiplied by 1,000. The household survey on which these figures are based relates to persons 12 years of age and over. Violent crime excludes homicide. Property crime includes burglary, theft and motor vehicle theft

Source Truman and Morgan (2016). Computations made by the authors

Table 9.16 Proportion of male and female victims of major crimes by type Canada, 2014

Type of crime	Percentage		
	Males	Females	All
Sexual assault	12.6	87.4	100.0
Physical assault	55.3	44.7	100.0
Robbery	59.5	40.5	100.0
Violent crime	43.6	56.4	100.0
Theft of personal property	50.4	49.6	100.0

Note The household survey on which these figures are based relates to people 15 years of age and older. Violent crime excludes homicide
Source SC (2017c). Computation made by the authors

contrast with the greater proportion of males than female offenders (Fig. 9.1). This is in line with a similar Canadian household survey that found females constituted a larger proportion of victims of violent crime (56%) in 2014 and that half of the victims of theft of personal property (50%) were also females (Table 9.16). In England and Wales the proportion of male 16 year of age and over who were victims of crime was about the same as females (respectively 16 and 15%) (ONS 2016).

Crimes reported to the police in Australia showed that the sex of victims of crime varied across the type of crime, with females being predominantly the victims of sexual assault (85%) and males the victims of homicide (63%) and robbery (76%). Females made up more than half of the victims from kidnapping/abduction (58%) and males were the majority of victims from blackmail/extortion (67%) and assault (55%) (Table 9.17).

In general, it could be said that the predominance of males as offenders is not closely reflected in victimization, and excluding homicide, female victims of crime are as much likely to be victims of crime as males. However, there are differences depending on the type of crime.

Table 9.17 Victims of major crimes by sex Australia, 2010

Type of crime	Percentage		
	Males	Females	Persons
Homicide and related offenses	**62.7**	37.3	100.0
Assault	**55.2**	44.8	100.0
Sexual assault	14.8	**85.2**	100.0
Kidnapping/abduction	41.9	**58.1**	100.0
Robbery	**75.8**	24.2	100.0
Blackmail/extortion	**67.2**	32.8	100.0

Note The offenses are as recorded by the police and refer to crimes against a person/s
Source ABS (2011). Computations made by the authors

Table 9.18 Victims of violent crime by age United States, 2015

Age (years)	Victimization rates per 1,000 in age group	
	Violent crime	Serious violent crime
12–17	31.3	7.8
18–24	25.1	10.7
25–34	21.8	9.3
35–49	22.6	7.8
50–64	14.2	5.7
65 and over	5.2	1.5
All	18.6	6.8

Note Victimization rates are the ratio of the number of victimizations experienced by the specific population by the number of people in that population multiplied by 1,000. The household survey on which these figures are based relates to persons 12 years of age and over. Violent crime includes rape or sexual assault, robbery, aggravated and simple assault, it excludes homicide. Violent crime includes rape or sexual assault, robbery, aggravated assault, it excludes homicide
Source Truman and Morgan (2016)

Table 9.19 Proportion of adult population victims of crime England and Wales, 2016

Age (years)	Percentage of victims in age group		
	Males	Females	All
16–24	21.8	21.0	21.4
25–34	19.7	19.4	19.6
35–44	16.2	17.4	16.8
45–54	18.0	15.0	16.5
55–64	12.3	13.2	12.8
65–74	8.8	8.7	8.8
75 and over	5.2	5.8	5.5
All	15.6	14.9	15.2

Note The figures relate to adults 16 years of age and over interviewed in a household survey of England and Wales for the year ending March 2016. The figures exclude victims of homicide
Source ONS (2016)

Victimization rates based on household surveys tend to show peaks in adolescence, with later surges in the case of serious violence (Tables 9.18 and 9.19).

As shown, most crimes are not reported to police. Therefore, victimization rates from police records suffer from underreporting of violent crimes and crimes against property. An advantage of the victimization rates for Australia based on crimes reported to the police is that they include homicide. Australian victimization rates show peaks in the 15–24 age bracket. Sexual assault and robbery being more predominant in 15–19 years of age and assault at 20–24 years of age, when victims from homicide also start to become larger (Table 9.20).

Table 9.20 Victims of crime by age and major type Australia, 2015

Age (years)	Victims per 100,000 in age group					
	Homicide	Assault	Sexual assault	Robbery	Kidnapping/ abduction	Blackmail/ extortion
0–9		154	99	…	2	…
10–14		764	314	23	4	1
15–19	1	1,704	352	91	5	4
20–24		1,956	130	80	5	5
25–34	3	1,763	77	54	4	3
35–44		1,469	56	32	2	3
45–54	2	966	36	23	1	2
55–64		469	16	15	…	1
65 and over	1	186	7	8	…	1
All	2	971	90	31	2	2

Note Crimes are as recorded by the police. Assault is the average for four of the six states of Australia and the two territories. Homicide rates are for 0–19, 20–34, 35–54 and 55 years of age and over. (…) Denotes less that 0.5/100,000
Sources ABS (2016a, 2017b). Computations made by the authors

The available evidence points to an overlap in the ages of offenders and victims, with a propensity for them to peak in late adolescence and early adulthood. However, age-peaks for different types of crime persist. These no doubt reflect a mixture of what Cohen called status frustration, Hirschi and Gottfredson's self-control and opportunity that may influence continuities and discontinuities in criminal behaviour during the life cycle, as posited by Sampson and Laub, and the low opportunity cost of crime in late adolescence and early adulthood implied by Gary Becker.

9.7.4 Crime and Imprisonment

As suggested by Gary Becker (1974), there are alternatives available to society when it imposes sanctions on people who commit crimes. Some may be mild ones such as cautioning. Gary Becker suggested that one sanction that could hurt the offender materially is a fine. He suggested that it was cheap in comparison to the cost to society of imprisonment. Nevertheless, imprisonment is a punishment often used for major and violent crimes. The frequency of imprisonment varies considerably from country to country. For instance, Sweden with a high rate of reported criminal offenses (Table 9.3) has a low rate of imprisonment (Table 9.21). Although rates of imprisonment vary, usually more than 90% of those in prison are males (Tables 9.21, 9.22 and 9.23).

Table 9.21 Prison population in selected European countries, 2013

Country	Prisoners per 1,000 people	Male prisoners percentage
Poland	2.1	96.6
Hungary	1.8	92.3
Romania	1.7	95.3
Czech	1.6	94.2
United Kingdom	1.4	95.3
Spain	1.4	92.4
Portugal	1.4	94.0
Greece	1.2	94.7
Belgium	1.1	96.1
Italy	1.1	95.7
France	1.0	96.8
Germany	0.8	94.3
Netherlands	0.8	94.3
Switzerland	0.8	94.8
Sweden	0.6	94.2
Average 15-countries	1.2	95.3

Sources Eurostat (2017a, b). Computations made by the authors

Table 9.22 Prison population of the United States, 2005–2015

Year	Prisoners per 1,000 people	Male prisoners Percentage
2005	5.2	93.0
2010	5.2	93.0
2015	4.8	92.7

Note The prisoner population refers to prisoners under federal and state authority regardless where they are held, including private and contract institutions. The prison population includes people who are in prison for causes that may not have been included in Table 9.4, such as crimes related to drugs
Sources Carson and Anderson (2016), USCB (2012, 2017). Computations made by the authors

Table 9.23 Prison population in Australia, 2006–2016

Year	Prisoners per 1,000 people	Male prisoners Percentage
2006	1.7	92.9
2011	1.7	93.0
2016	2.1	92.0

Note The prisoner population refers to prisoners under federal and state authority regardless of where they are held
Source ABS (2016b). Computations made by the authors

Among fifteen countries in Europe (excluding Russia) in 2013, rates of imprisonment ranged from 2.1 prisoners per thousand people in Poland to 0.6 in Sweden with an average of 1.2/1,000 for all 15 countries (Table 9.21). Attitudes towards punishment and alternative options used tend to influence the rate and length of imprisonment. As a stock, the prison population at a given point in time reflects past flows of prisoners in and out of prison, and their length of stay.

In the United Sates the prison population declined in from 5.2 prisoners per thousand people in 2005 to 4.8 in 2015 (Table 9.22). However, it continued to be about four times higher than the average for the large fifteen European countries mentioned (Table 9.21). On average, European countries tend to have older populations than the United States. Part of the difference in imprisonment rates may be due to the dissimilar proportions of people in adolescence and young adulthood at risk of criminal behaviour. Therefore, a comparison with Australia with a similar age distribution to may be more relevant.

Australia experienced a substantial rise in its prison population from 1.7 per thousand people in 2006 to 2.1 in 2016 (Table 9.23). These rates are also higher than the average of the European countries mentioned. As in the case of the United States, the Australian age distribution is substantially different to that of the average for the European countries. For instance, a comparison of the age distribution between Australia and Greece (the latter with an imprisonment rate equivalent to the aggregate average for the European countries of 1.2/1,000) indicates that the proportion of the Australian population aged 15–29 years of age most at risk of criminal behaviour was about 33% higher than that of Greece in 2012 (Eurostat 2017b). This would bring the Australian imprisonment rate in 2011 close to the equivalent of that of Greece. Thus, part of the difference between the lower European rates of imprisonment mentioned and those of the United States and Australia could be attributed to different age distributions of the population. However, the same might not be said about the more than double the rate of imprisonment in the United States in comparison with Australia. Accordingly, what constitutes a crime in a country is an important ingredient as well as its frequency. However, how imprisonment (and the length of it) is used by societies as a sanction can result in different prison populations in countries with a similar age distribution at risk of criminal behaviour, with cost implications.

The review of the age distribution of the prison population tends to follow now the expected pattern that peaks earlier in adult life. However, the accumulation of early flows tends add to the age of the stock, and the age-peaks tend to be in the late twenties and early thirties (Table 9.24). The comparison of the age distributions of the prison populations of Australia and the United States points to disparate experiences in the two countries that may contribute to the higher imprisonment rates in the United States. The age distribution in Australia tends to be higher in younger age groups under 40 years of age while that in the United States tends to higher above 39 years of age. The aging of the United States prison population reflects the rising median age of the United States since 1970, but it is also the result of (1) a steady increase in the rate of older adults being sentenced to prison and (2) changes enacted in the laws during 1990s that resulted in longer prison

Table 9.24 Prison population by age in Australia and the United States, 2015

Age (years)	Age group as percentage of total prison population	
	Australia	United States
Under 20	2.2	0.8
20–24	14.1	10.5
25–29	18.2	15.6
30–34	17.8	16.5
35–39	15.2	14.6
40–44	12.0	12.1
45–49	8.3	10.3
50–54	5.0	8.6
55–59	3.0	5.4
60–64	1.8	2.8
65 and over	2.4	2.4
All	100.0	100.0

Note The prison population refers to prisoners under federal and state authority regardless of where they are held. Percentages may not add because of rounding
Source ABS (2016b), Carson and Anderson (2016). Computations made by the authors

sentences. The result of these changes finds that virtually every state in the United States has seen considerable increases in the number of elderly prisoners. In Virginia, for example, 822 state prisoners were 50 years of age and over (correction services officials usually consider old age for prisoners to begin at 50 or 55 years) in 1990, about 4.5% of all inmates. By 2014, that number had grown to 7,202 or 20% of inmates (Ollove 2016). Correction departments across the United States report that health care for older prisoners costs between four and eight times what does for younger prisoners (Ollove 2016). The outcome is a larger prison population with its cost to society and when this population is ageing, the cost becomes much higher.

9.7.5 Costs of Crime

The estimation of the costs of crime to society entails difficult questions, among them the social cost of pain and the value of life. Another issue is unreported crime and the use of household surveys of victimisation based on personal interviews that by their very nature exclude homicide victims and young children. Smaller scope estimates tend to include the cost of police protection, judicial and legal processes and those of correction services that are easier to estimate from public and private expenditures. It was estimated that these costs represented the equivalent of 1.4% of gross domestic product (GDP) in the United States in 2010 (BJS 2011). The estimates of cost of crime cited by Gary Becker for 1965 amounted to about 4% but they included estimates of private security and the costs of the impact of crime that constituted about 72% of the total cost estimated for 1965. If the same relationship prevailed then the equivalent cost of crime in 2010 would be about 5% of GDP.

Estimates of government expenditure in Australia on police, court administration and corrective services in 2010 amounted to the equivalent of about 1% GDP (ABS 2012). An earlier tentative estimate for 2001 that included additional costs related to the impact of crime arrived at a total that was the equivalent of about 5% of GDP (Mayhew 2003). A more recent study estimated that both the direct and impact costs of crime in Canada in 2012 also amounted to the equivalent of about 5% of GDP (Easton et al. 2014).

Following Gary Becker's earlier assessment, it is generally accepted that the social cost of crime is greatly underestimated. The estimates have the value of their assumptions and their acceptance as actual measures of social value. They also depend on the assessment of crimes not reported that varies considerably. Nevertheless, they point to substantial material losses to society.

9.8 Deviance: Social Change and Control

Deviance from social norms can be seen as part of the process of social innovation and change. It has been seen as a means of achieving a new social order. Some of what is considered deviance are passing fads. They can also be part of youthful or even adult exploration of alternatives some of which may be adopted as new social norms. These attempts at new social order are dependent to some extent on varying social tolerance and control that influence responses to them. Cultural traits make some societies more accepting of innovation while others are more resistant to it, with different degrees of social change and sanctions. In addition, different socioeconomic considerations may make some societies feel more secure and capable of tolerating deviance while others demand and exercise more control.

However, regardless of the varying social settings, there are some acts of deviance with an impact on the safety of people and property that have been the object of formal codification as criminal behaviour. They are subject to social punishment through legal processes. There is usually a gradient of sanctioning reflecting social concern with violence and the value of property. Most offenders tend to be young males, especially in the case of crimes involving violence. Females tend to be more involved in crimes against property but at a substantially lower level. A number of reasons have been offered to explain the male predominance and the young age of offenders. Some of them relate to social expectations of males, who when they have not the means to accomplish them may lead to frustration and the use of illegal means in their attempt to achieve the aspired social status. Similarly, lower social expectations and greater control of females lead to not only lower expectations but also fewer opportunities to engage in criminal behaviour. It has been suggested that lower socioeconomic conditions tend to promote the levels of frustration, aggression and associated criminal behaviour. However, it has also been pointed out that most poor people do not become criminals, and that most people who engage on criminal behaviour during adolescence do not become adult criminals. A number of factors besides the economic environment have an impact on criminal behaviour, including major life events such as leaving school, employment, marriage and parenthood, and the quality and strength in their social engagement. Societies' mode of punishment for different types of criminal behaviour varies considerably, but all tend to use imprisonment as a sanction, especially in relation to violent crimes. Different social perceptions and capabilities have led to prison populations of various relative sizes. They may be as high as 5 prisoners per thousand people in Russia (UNODC undated) and the United States and less than 1/1,000 in Sweden (Tables 9.21 and 9.22). The association of young age with crime and imprisonment explain some of the differences but other significant factors are the use of prison as a sanction and the length of sentencing for given offenses.

Estimates of the costs of crime have been made for a number of countries. They are based on available information either on reported crime or interviews of victims through household surveys. Household surveys show that crime is considerably underreported and it is accepted that even household surveys tend to underestimate criminal activity. In addition, there are conceptual and practical difficulties in the assessment of the social value of pain and life, and other social consequences of crime. As worthy as the assumptions made, some estimates indicate that the cost of crime to be about 5% of GDP in developed countries. Although substantial, this is considered to be an underestimate of the impact of crime.

Deviance can be a positive stimulus in the process of social change but when it assumes the form of violence and appropriation of other people's property, deviance can have a significant impact on social bonds and security and have substantial social costs.

References

Australian Bureau of Statistics (ABS). (2011). *Recorded crime—Victims, 2010.* Canberra. Retrieved July 13, 2017, from www.abs.gov.au/AUSSTATS/abs@nsf/allprimaryfeatures/2A3238B5E80F7DA2CA257A15001904C2?opendocument.

Australian Bureau of Statistics (ABS). (2012). *Year book of Australia 2012.* Canberra.

Australian Bureau of Statistics (ABS). (2016a). *Recorded crime—Victims, 2015.* Canberra. Retrieved July 13, 2017, www.abs.gov.au/AUSSTATS/abs@nsf/DetailsPage/45100DO002_2015.

Australian Bureau of Statistics (ABS). (2016b). *Prisoners in Australia, 2016.* Canberra. Retrieved August 6, 2017, from www.abs.gov.au/AUSSTATS/abs@.nsf/DetailsPage/4517.02016?OpenDocument.

Australian Bureau of Statistics (ABS). (2017a). *Recorded crime—Victims, 2015–2016.* Canberra. Retrieved July 13, 2017, from www.abs.gov.au/AUSSTATS/abs@nsf/DetailsPage/4519.02015-16?OpenDocument.

Australian Bureau of Statistics (ABS). (2017b). *Australian demographic statistics, December 2016.* Canberra. Retrieved July 13, 2017, from www.abs.gov.au.

Australian Bureau of Statistics (ABS). (2017c). *Recorded crime—Offenders, 2015–2016.* Canberra. Retrieved July 17, 2017, from www.abs.gov.au/AUSSTATS/abs@nsf/DetailsPage/4519.

Australian Institute of Family Studies (AIFS). (2017). *Living together in Australia.* Retrieved July 5, 2017, from https://aifs.gov.au/facts-and-figures/living-together-australia/living-together-australia-source-data#fifteen.

Bandura, A. (1973). *Social learning theory.* New York: General Learning Press.

Bandura, A. (2001). Social cognitive theory: An agentic perspective. *Annual Review of Psychology, 2001*(52), 1–26.

Becker, G. S. (1974). Crime and punishment: An economic approach. In G. S. Becker & W. M. Landes (Eds.), *Essays in the economics of crime and punishment.* New York: Columbia University Press.

Becker, G. S. (1992). *The economic way of looking at life.* Nobel Lecture, December 9, 1992. www.nobelprize.org/nobel_prizes/economic-sciences/laureates/1992/becker_lecture.pdf.

Becker, H. S. (1955). Marihuana use and social control. *Social Problems, 3*(1), 35–44.

Becker, H. S. (1995). Outsiders. In N. J. Herman (Ed.), *Deviance—A symbolic interactionist approach.* Lanham MD: General Hall.

Bureau of Justice Statistics (BJS). (2011). *Justice expenditure and employment extracts program.* Washington DC. Retrieved May 17, 2017, from www.ojp.usdoj.gov.

Carson, E. A., & Anderson, E. (2016). *Prisoners in 2015.* Washington, DC: Bureau of Crime Statistics.

Cohen, A. K. (1955). *Delinquent boys.* New York: Free Press.

Durkheim, E. (1982). What is a social fact? In S. Lukes (Ed.) *The rules of the sociological method* [*Les regles de la method sociologique* (W. D. Halls, Trans.)]. New York: Free Press (1895).

Durkheim, E. (1984). *The division of labour in society* [*De la division du travail social* (W. D. Halls, Trans.)]. London: Macmillan (1893).

Easton, S., Furness, H., & Brantingham, P. (2014). *The cost of crime in Canada.* Vancouver BC: Fraser Institute.

Eurostat (2017a). *Crime and criminal justice statistics.* Retrieved July 16, 2017, from http://ec.europa.eu/statistics-explained/index.php/Crime_criminal_justice_statistics.

Eurostat (2017b). *Population.* Retrieved July 16, 2017, from http://ec.europa.eu/eurostat/tmg/table.do?tab+table&init+1&plugin+18&pcode+tps00002&language=en.

Federal Bureau of Investigation (FBI). (2017). *Crime in the United States 2015.* Retrieved May 17, 2017, from http://ucr.fbi.gov/crime-in-the-u.s/2015).

Gopal, N., & Marimuthu, B. (2014). A quantitative understanding of gender differentiated delinquent trends among school going adolescents in Chatsworth, Durban. *Southern African Journal of Criminology, 27*(2), 69–81.

Hirschi, T., & Gottfredson, M. (1983). Age and the explanation of crime. *American Journal of Sociology, 89*(3), 552–584.

Hirschi, T. (1995). A control theory of delinquency. In N. J. Herman (Ed.), *Deviance—A symbolic interactionist approach.* Lanham MD: General Hall.

Kaufman, J. M. (2009). Gendered responses to serious strain: The argument for a general strain theory of deviance. *Justice Quarterly, 26*(3), 410–444.

Kohlberg, L. (1981). *Essays on moral development. Vol. I: The philosophy of moral development.* San Francisco: Harper & Row.

Lanctot, N., & Le Blanc, M. (2002). Explaining deviance by adolescent females. *Crime and Justice, 29,* 113–202.

Lemert, E. M. (1995). Secondary deviance and role conceptions. In N. J. Herman (Ed.), *Deviance—A symbolic interactionist approach.* Lanham MD: General Hall.

Marwah, S. (2014). Mapping murder: Homicide patterns and trends in India—An analysis from 2000–2010. *Journal of South Asian Studies, 2*(2), 145–163.

Matza, D. (1961). Subterranean traditions of youth. *Annals of the American Academy of Political and Social Sciences, 338*(1), 102–118.

Mayhew, P. (2003). *Counting the costs of crime in Australia*. Canberra: Australian Institute of Criminology.

Merton, R. K. (1938). Social structure and anomie. *American Sociological Review, 3*(5), 672–682.

Office for National Statistics (ONS). (2016). *Incidents and rates of crime, by crime type and age of the victim. Crime survey of England and Wales*. Retrieved August 2, 2017, from www.ons.gov. uk/peoplepopulationandcommunity/crimeandjustice.

Ollove, M. (2016). Elderly inmates burden state prisons. *Stateline* (17 March 2016). Pew Charitable Trust. Retrieved November 27, 2017, from www.pewtrust.org/en/research-and-analysis/blogs/stateline/2016/03/17elderly-inmates-burden-state-prisons.

Robbins, C. A., & Martin, S. S. (1993). Gender, styles of deviance, and drinking problems. *Journal of Health and Social Behaviour, 34*(4), 302–321.

Rusche, G., & Dinwiddie, G. (1978). Labor market and penal sanction: Thoughts on the sociology of criminal justice. *Crime and Social Justice, 10*(2), 8.

Sampson, R. L., & Laub, J. H. (1992). Crime and deviance in the life course. *Annual Review of Sociology, 18*, 63–84.

South African Police Service (SAPS). (2016). *Annual crime report 2015/2016*.

Statistics Bureau of Japan (SBJ). (2016). *Japan statistical yearbook 2016*. Tokyo. Retrieved July 14, 2017, from www.stat.go.jp.

Statistics Bureau Japan (SBJ). (2017a). *Crime cases known by police by type of crime*. Tokyo: Customised tabulation.

Statistics Bureau Japan (SBJ). (2017b). *Japan statistical yearbook 2017*. Tokyo. Retrieved July 14, 2017, from www.stat.go.jp.

Statistics Canada (SC). (2017a). *Uniform crime report survey*. Ottawa: Customised tabulations.

Statistics Canada (SC). (2017b). *Estimates of population by age and sex July 1, Canada, provinces and territories*. Ottawa. Retrieved July 14, 2017, from www.statcan.gc.ca/cansim/a26?lang= eng&retrLang=eng&0001&pattern=&stByVal=1&p2=37&tabMode=dataTables&csid.

Statistics Canada (SC). (2017c). *Personal victimization incidents reported by Canadians, 2014*. Ottawa. Retrieved July 29, 2017, from www.statcan.gc.ca/pub/85-002-x/2015001/article/ 14241/tbl/tb104-eng.htm.

Steffensmeier, D. (1996). Gender and crime: Towards a gendered theory of female offending. *Annual Review of Sociology, 22*, 459–487.

Steffensmeier, D., & Haynie, D. (2000). Gender, structural disadvantage, and urban crime: Do macrosocial variables also explain female offending rates? *Criminology, 38*(2), 403–438.

Sutherland, E. H., Cressy, D. R., & Luckenbill, D. (1995). The theory of differential association. In N. J. Herman (Ed.), *Deviance—A symbolic interactionist approach*. Lanham MD: General Hall.

Swedish National Council for Crime Prevention (Bra). (2016). *Swedish crime survey 2016*. Stockholm.

Sweeney, M., Castro-Martin, T., & Mills, M. (2015). The reproductive context of cohabitation in comparative perspective: Contraceptive use in the United States, Spain, and France. *Demographic Research, 32*(5), 147–182. https://doi.org/10.4054/DemRes.2015.32.5. Retrieved July 3, 2017, from www.demographic-research.org/Volumes/Vol32/5/.

Sykes, G. M., & Matza, D. (1957). Techniques of neutralization: A theory of delinquency. *American Sociological Review, 22*(6), 664–670.

Title, C. R., & Grasmick, H. G. (1997). Criminal behaviour and age: A test of three provocative hypotheses. *Journal of Criminal Law and Criminology, 88*(1), 309–342.

Truman, J. L., & Morgan, R. E. (2016). *Criminal victimization, 2015*. Washington, DC: Bureau of Justice Statistics.

United Nations (UN). (2017). *World population prospects—The 2017 revision. Volume I: Comprehensive Tables*. New York.

United Nations Office on Drugs and Crime (UNODC). (Undated). *Total number of persons held without any sentencing decision, with a non-final sentencing decision and with a final sentencing decision*. Vienna. Retrieved August 8, 2017, from www.unodc.org.

United Nations Office on Drugs and Crime (UNODC). (2014). *Global study of homicide 2013*. Vienna.

United States Census Bureau (USCB). (2012). *Statistical abstract of the United States 2012*. Washington, DC.

United States Census Bureau (USCB). (2017*). Annual estimates of the resident population for selected age groups by sex for the United States, April 1, 2010 to July 1, 2017*. Retrieved July 17, 2017, https://facrfinder.census.gov/faces/tableservices/jsf/pages/productview.xhtml?src +bkmk.

Ventura, S. J. (2009). *Changing patterns of nonmarital childbearing in the United States*. NCHS Data Brief, 18. Hyattsville MD: National Center for Health Statistics.

World Bank (WB). (2017). *Gross domestic product per capita in purchasing power parities*. Retrieved July 7, 2017, from http://data.worldbank.org/indicator/NY.GDP.PCAP.PP.CD? locations=HR-SE.

Chapter 10
Population and Socio-economic Prospects

10.1 Socio-economic Organization in Transition

People are born and reared in a social group context—the family. This is not unique among living organisms. However, the initial longer growth-phase of humans (childhood and adolescence) makes human survival dependent on social support for a longer fraction of their life cycle. Also, this results in a long period of early socialisation and group-oriented development and behaviour (Chap. 9: Sects. 9.2–9.4). Another aspect of socio-economic organisation is concerned with survival and reproduction. The association of males with physical strength and females with reproduction led to the conventional division of labour between males and females, whereby males' activity focused on the production of most of the basic needs such as food production, shelter and protection while females concentrated on gestation, lactation and the caring of children essential to the reproduction of the species (Chap. 8: Sects. 8.1 and 8.2). Although, these features of socio-economic organisation have prevailed to a degree, they have evolved depending on circumstances and the development of new technologies in the production of basic and other human wants (Chap. 6).

Kaplan et al. (2009) proposed that human social organisation has continued to evolve. They offered four variables as change drivers in socio-economic organisation

- skill in resource production
- extent of complementarity between male and female inputs in production
- economies of scale in cooperative production
- defensibility of the means of production

They posited that skill-based production led to negative production of resources during childhood and adolescence, followed by positive production during adulthood and old age, and consequent child dependence, within a three-generation resource flow framework. The complementarity of male and female skills in production and

© Springer International Publishing AG, part of Springer Nature 2018   277
Jo. M. Martins et al., *Global Population in Transition*,
https://doi.org/10.1007/978-3-319-77362-9_10

reproduction resulted in cooperative food production and child raising and a stable family relationship of males and females. Cooperative activities led to linkages between nuclear families that involved voluntary inputs and distribution of outputs. The defensibility of inputs of production varied depending on their nature. Kaplan et al. (2009) suggested that in economies relying on foraging, skill levels depended on circumstances and type of resource production. When resources were relatively abundant the gathering required less skill and children were less dependent on their elders. The importance of the complementary role of adult males was also less distinct when resources were relatively plentiful. The scale of cooperation among foragers also varied depending on circumstances, but when hunting was involved cooperation was a more efficient mode of production and lead to cooperation among families. Equalitarian relationships prevailed in smaller scale economies. In larger scale production, leaders arose, especially if territories and communities required defensive activities. In horticultural economies, skills were important, for example in field clearing and preparation in slash-and-burn practices, or where irrigation or terracing was involved. The skills of males in preparation and female tilling of the soil and child rearing made for complementarity and cooperation between males and females. This type of resource production demanded large-scale cooperation between more than one family, as in large irrigation systems. In this case, the coordination of effort lead to the emergence of leaders and institutional mechanisms for the coordination of common efforts or communal methods of production, and resulted in less equalitarian relationships. These modes of production usually involved territorial interests that required leadership in defence activities by males. Tribal pastoralism based on domesticated livestock required skill in animal reproduction, feeding and herding. Boys could be involved in herding, and inheritance systems influenced relationships between parents and children. The complementarity of male and female roles was dependent on the size of the herd and the need for protection. Often, it was the perceived need for protection that influenced the scale of cooperation, as well as the concentration of power and the degree of equalitarian relationships. Kaplan et al. (2009) also proposed that the appearance of large scale agrarian states drastically altered the features of socio-economic organisation. Skill in the maintenance of land and production continued to be important and inheritance practices made children obliged to parents. These more stratified societies influenced the complementarity of male and female relationships, with male and female unions being affected by mating markets where the relative value of male and female was dependent on what they had to offer in the context of social hierarchy. The large scale of production and organisation was characterised by social stratification and inequality that was reflected in control by social elites to their own benefit, but that provided a degree of order and protection that contributed to varying degrees of the wellbeing of other members of society. Control and defence of resources reflected the social stratification of society and the non-equalitarian nature of relationships. Further, Kaplan et al. (2009) suggested that the four change drivers were effective in the continuing evolution of socio-economic organisation during industrialisation and in more recent economic development. They considered the shift from a land-based economy to one that relies on commercial, managerial and technological skills has led to the weakening of the land-based property elites and the rise of middle-class demands for greater social, economic and political rights. More flexible labour markets increased mobility and reduced bondage to property owners. An outcome has been the development of more skill-based economies and equalitarian political and social institutions.

10.2   Capital, Technical Change and Human Capital

The human capacity for learning from experience and their urge to innovate and to produce what is needed for survival, and other wants continue to change the source of materials and methods of production, which in turn have had an effect on the way people organise their relationships and lives. The outcome has been substantially increased production that has outpaced population growth (Chap. 1: Sect. 1.4). A perspective on economic growth is the role played by labour and capital in the process. Labour is the human capacity and effort employed in current production and capital is the resources being used on current production that are the result of past production not used in consumption. Capital can be seen as a stock affected by positive flows from investments made in productive capacity, and negative flows from wear-and-tear by use in production and obsolesce. The importance of investment and accumulated capital in economic growth was the subject of the Harrod-Domar model evolved from Keynes propositions regarding consumption, investment and income (production) (Martins et al. 2012). Investment and capital implicitly referred to physical capital in terms of equipment, buildings and infrastructure in general used as a factor of production. The compilation of aggregate estimates of national gross domestic product and income that became more generally available in the 1950s in the United States and European countries stimulated enquiries into the contributions of the factors of production to economic growth. It became apparent that the quantities of labour and capital did not account fully for economic growth and that there were other factors contributing to observed economic growth in the United States and other countries.

Solow (1957) used an aggregate production function to assess the contributions of labour and capital to economic growth, and that of technical change

$$Q = A(t)f(K, L)$$

Q   Output
K   Capital inputs in physical units
L   Labour inputs in physical units (hours worked)
A(t)   Effect of accumulated shifts over time or *technical change*

Technical change was shorthand for changes in production arising from other factors than the quantities of capital and labour. It was perceived that …*improvements in the education of the labor force, and all sorts of things will appear as "technical change"* (Solow 1957: 312). The results of the analysis for the period

1909–1949 indicated that output per worker hour about doubled and resulted in the cumulative shift in the production function by 80% in the United States. This led to the conclusion that *...about one-eighth of the total increase is traceable to increased capital per man hour, and the remainder seven-eighths to technical change* (Solow 1957: 316). Solow placed a number of caveats on his findings. Some criticisms have been made about the aggregate nature of the inputs that have varying degrees of embedded quality and differences in productivity as well as some aspects of the methodology used (e.g. Guerrien and Gun 2015). Nevertheless, the importance of factors of production other than aggregate physical capital and non-differentiated labour became recognised in understanding the rate of change in output from production, usually measured in the form of gross domestic product. From this understanding arose the concept of *human capital*. In his presidential address to the American Economic Association, Schultz (1961: 1) pointed out that *...increases in national output have been large compared with the increases in land, man-hours, and physical reproducible capital. Investment in human capital is probably the major explanation for this difference.* He identified a number of factors usually seen as consumption but that are investments that enhance human capabilities, among them:

- health services, nutrition and shelter that affect human strength, stamina, and vigour
- education at all levels, adult education and on the job training

Becker (1975) pursued the concept of human capital with an emphasis on the contributions of education and on-the-job training to economic productivity. He pointed out that earnings in the United States rose positively with skill, more capable people received more education and training than others, and that unemployment rates were inversely correlated with skill levels. Becker saw education as an investment in human capital in terms of tuition fees, supplies, transport and other expenses involved, but also in foregone income due to the time spent in education. He also noted that earnings tend to be lower at early stages of employment and that on-the-job training and skill acquisition are an investment in human capital. Further, he saw that *...one way to invest in human capital is to improve emotional and physical health. In Western countries, today, earnings are much more closely geared to knowledge than strength, but in an earlier day, and elsewhere still today, strength had a significant influence on earnings... A decline in the death rate at working ages may improve earning prospects by extending the period during which they are received; a better diet adds strength and stamina, and thus earning capacity; or an improvement in working conditions... may affect morale and productivity* (Becker 1975: 40–41).

Becker's findings of the relationship between earnings and education for the United States were found to hold for developed countries that were members of the Organisation for Economic Co-operation and Development (OECD) and for a number of developing countries (Psacharopoulos 1975). A more recent review of a large number of developing and developed countries provides evidence of the substantial return in earnings from investment in education at the micro level (Psacharopoulos and Patrinos 2004).

Analysis of the sources of economic growth in OECD countries found that education explained more in terms of economic growth than did physical capital. It also indicated that the rate of return of investments in education to economic growth was greater than the degree of return to individuals found in microeconomic studies. It was suggested that part of the difference between micro and macro findings may be attributed to the indicator for human capital (education) being a surrogate variable for other potential variables not included in the regression analysis (OECD 2003). This is supported by Schultz' and Becker's proposition that health is an important factor in enhancing human capital and its productivity and also by the observed close association between health and education (Gan and Gong 2007).

10.3 Health and Human Capital

10.3.1 Health and Cognitive Capacity

The importance of health to human capital development starts early in life and has a multigenerational dimension. Nutritional deprivation in utero has been found to result in a higher probability of lower birth weight (LBW) that in turn leads to greater likelihood of lower cognitive development and childhood chronic diseases that result in lower school attainment (Currie 2009; Nyaradi et al. 2013). It has also been shown that malnutrition during childhood has an impact on cognitive development not just during infancy but throughout childhood (Glewwe and King 2001; CDC 2014). Children who participated in a program of supplemental nutrition of women, infants and children (WIC) at nutritional risk in the United States did better in cognitive tests than children of women in a control group, even though the women in the control group had higher incomes (Currie 2009).

10.3.2 Childhood Health and Educational Achievement

Child health plays a major role in the capacity to learn and the related building of human capital. Evidence of this effect is available from a number of countries at various stages of development. In their review of the relationship between health and education, Eide and Showalter (2011) cited a number of research findings related to health and school performance. Studies of children in the United States, Canada and Norway found that higher weights at birth resulted in higher school performance and completion rates. Nutritional supplements given in early childhood in less developed countries were found to result in better cognitive test scores. This is in line with other findings of the importance of nutrition to cognitive development and school performance (Currie 2009; CDC 2014). Another facet of child health is ADHD (Attention Deficit Hyperactivity Disorder) that has been found to result in lower reading and mathematics scores and lower probability of completing high school (Eide and Showalter 2011; Currie 2009). Further, emotional and mental health problems lead to a lower probability of completion of high school and environmental pollution affects child health and, by implication, their school performance. In addition, other health shocks during childhood have an effect on physical development and educational achievement. Although the impact of acute health conditions on education performance in childhood is not clear cut, there is evidence that chronic health conditions during childhood have a significant impact on school attendance and performance (Currie 2009; Forrest et al. 2013). There is a number of parallel relationships between health, education and socio-economic status of parents. Therefore, there is often a *chicken and the egg* issue in the causal relationships between health and education of children. Research findings cited by Eide and Showalter (2011) in their review and also those cited by Currie (2009) indicate that although the socio-economic status of parents has an effect on outcomes, child health per se has an impact on learning capacity and school performance.

10.3.3   Health and Human Capital Productivity

As might be expected, lower health status in childhood results in lower probability of employment, higher incomes and days worked later in working life (Currie 2009). In addition, shocks to health during adult life have been found to affect participation in the labour force, employment and consequently earnings and productivity. The assessment of the effects of health on labour force participation has to be guarded against the possible causal relationship of work on health. Research findings that looked both at the direct and reversed relationship between health and work suggest that there is a positive relationship between health and labour force participation (Cai 2010). Health influences entry, re-entry and exit from the labour force. Research from a number of countries indicates that people with poor health tend to spend more time unemployed and have a greater chance of leaving the labour force before the conventional retirement age. This applies to mental health as well (Dewa and McDaid 2011). Health status affects the employment of males and females, both young and old. However, it seems to have a greater effect on males (Garcia-Gomez et al. 2010). In the United States, research has found that chronic health conditions result in fewer hours worked and can reduce earnings by as much as 52% for both males and females. Temporary illness was found to have no significant impact on earnings. The major losses are for males with age onset of illness when their earnings are at their peak (40–49 years) (Pelkowski and Berger 2004). A review of the impact of disease on labour market outcomes in OECD countries indicates that obesity and smoking lead to higher absence from work, and that cardiovascular, musculoskeletal diseases result in loss of working days, especially in the case of males (Devaux and Sassi 2015).

10.3.4   Life Expectancy and Healthy Life

The considerable productivity growth per head of population in the last few decades (Tables 1.19, 1.20 and 1.21) has been associated with substantial increases in life expectancy (Tables 1.12 and 4.9). However, in view of the importance of health status on human capital and its productivity, it could be asked whether the additional years of life result in more years of disability or in a healthy life that allows for potential improvements in the productivity of human capital.

Estimates of life and healthy life expectancies at birth show there has been no substantial change in the proportion of years of healthy life on average at about 88% for males and 86% for females with a longer life expectancy than males, in the world during the 26-year period of 1990–2016 (Table 10.1).

Table 10.1 Life expectancy and healthy life by income level or region, 1990–2016

Countries by income level or region	Males			Females		
	Le	HALE	HALE percent Le	Le	HALE	HALE percent Le
1990						
High income countries	72.64	64.15	88.3	79.34	68.4	86.2
Latin America and Caribbean	66.44	58.85	88.6	72.68	63.19	86.9
S'east and East Asia and Oceania	64.47	56.98	89.9	68.81	60.57	88
North Africa and Middle East	65.01	56.14	86.4	68.93	57.92	84
Sub-Sahara Africa	52.04	45.35	87.1	55.39	47.87	86.4
World	62.7	55.38	88.3	67.57	58.42	86.5
2016						
High income countries	78.27	68.58	87.6	83.48	71.61	85.8
Latin America and Caribbean	72.75	64.24	88.3	78.89	68.5	86.8
S'east and East Asia and Oceania	72.11	64.57	89.5	78.37	68.55	87.5
North Africa and Middle East	70.9	61.41	86.6	75.59	63.66	84.2
Sub-Sahara Africa	61.18	53.57	87.6	64.59	56.05	86.8
World	69.79	61.42	88	75.33	64.91	86.2

Note (Le) life expectancy years at birth. (HALE) Health life expectancy is the number of years a person on average is expected to live a healthy life taking into account years in less than full health because of disease and/or injury. High income countries include Canada, Greenland, United States, Australia, New Zealand, Brunei, Japan, Singapore, Republic of Korea and high income countries in Western Europe such as Austria and the United Kingdom. Southeast and East Asia and Oceania include countries in this region not included among the high-income countries. North Africa and Middle East include countries in Africa north of the Sahara such as Morocco, Egypt and in the Middle East such as Turkey, Saudi Arabia and Iran. Sub-Sahara Africa includes countries such as Mauritania, Senegal and South Africa
Source Hay (2017). Computations made by the authors

Table 10.2 Additional years in life expectancy and healthy life by income level or region, 1990–2016

Countries by income level or region	Expected additional years 1990–2016			
	Le		HALE	
	Males	Females	Males	Females
High income countries	5.63	4.14	4.43	3.21
Latin America and Caribbean	6.31	6.21	5.39	5.31
Southeast and East Asia and Oceania	7.64	9.56	6.59	7.98
North Africa and Middle East	5.89	6.66	5.27	5.74
Sub-Sahara Africa	9.14	9.2	8.22	8.18
World	7.09	7.76	6.04	6.49

Note See Table 10.1 for (Le) and (HALE) definitions
Source Table 10.1. Computations made by the authors

However, during the period 1990–2016, the average world increment in life expectancy of 7 years for males and 8 for females has meant an increase in the number of expected number of years in full health, with a potential for greater productivity. The number of healthy years of males and females rose by an average of about 6 years. The highest increase was in Sub-Sahara countries (average 8 years), that have the lowest average life expectancy, followed by developing countries in Southeast Asia, East Asia and Oceania (average of 6 and 8 years for males and females respectively). The lowest increase was in high income countries with the highest average life expectancy (average 4 and 3 years for males and females respectively), with also lower additions in Latin America and Caribbean (average 5 years for both sexes) (Table 10.2). These trends indicate that the number of healthy life years is rising substantially in most countries with a degree of catch-up by countries with low life expectancies and years of healthy life with potential rises in productivity. Further examination of life expectancy and healthy life years indicates that most of the increment in healthy life is below 65 years of age in the period. However, the increment in high income countries, with the longest life expectancies, tends to be strongest at the age of 65 years. Again, the greatest gains in healthy life years below the age of 65 are in Sub-Sahara countries with the lowest average life expectancy (Hay 2017).

The increments in healthy life years provide a potential for greater productivity from a fitter population but also better conditions for educational performance.

10.4   Education and Human Capital

10.4.1   Education: Investment and Returns

The importance of education and training to economic productivity was recognised by Adam Smith in his inquiry into the nature and causes of the wealth of nations

(1776). He noted the value of education and training as an investment and suggested its similarity to physical capital: ...*The acquisition of such talents, by the maintenance of the acquirer during his education, study, or apprenticeship, always costs a real expense, which is a capital fixed and realized, as it were, in his person. Those talents, as they make a part of his fortune, so do they likewise of that of society to which he belongs. The improved dexterity of a workman may be considered in the same light as a machine or instrument of trade which facilitates and abridges labour, and which, thought it costs a certain expense, repays that expense with a profit* (Smith 1970 [1776]: 377). Thus, Adam Smith saw the value of education as an investment at the cost of forsaken current consumption, but also as capital embedded in the person who acquired it. In spite of the embedded nature of education, Adam Smith recognised the social dimension of education and the gains to the society to which the individual belongs.

Although Becker, like Schultz, appreciated the value of health as part of human capital, he made special reference to education and its returns to individuals, in the form of higher earnings, after time and costs spent on education. The analysis of after-tax income of white males in 1949 in the United States indicated that earnings of those with 16 years of schooling or more could earn almost three times as much as those with only 7 or 8 years of schooling, and almost about double those with 12 years of schooling, at the age of 55–64. However, this was at the cost of lower earnings than the other two groups at 14–21 years of age, when they would be gaining additional years of schooling (Fig. 10.1).

Psacharopoulos and Patrinos (2004) cited a number of studies to arrive at the conclusion that the rate of return on education in the United States was about 10%. They also found that the rate of return of about 7–9 years of schooling was on average in the world was also 10%, with regional ranges from 7% in Europe, Middle East and North Africa to 12% in Latin America and the Caribbean. The average for OECD more developed countries was lower (8%) than in less developed countries in Sub-Sahara Africa and Latin America and Caribbean (12%).

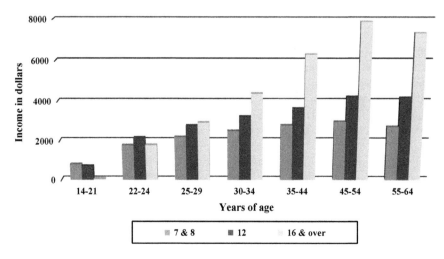

Fig. 10.1 After-tax income of white males, age and years of education, United States, 1949 (dollars)
Source Becker (1993)

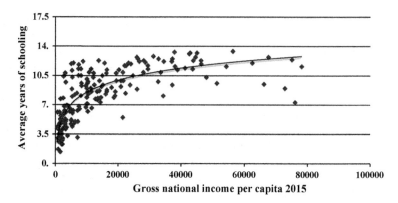

Fig. 10.2 Country average years of schooling and gross national income per head of population 2015

Note Country years of schooling are at 25 years of age and over. Qatar with a gross national income per capita of $129,916 and an average 9.8 years of schooling is not included. Gross national income per head of population is expressed in 2011 purchasing power parities (international dollars)

Source UNDP (2016)

The association between income per capita and years of schooling prevails across countries at different stages of development and geographic regions (Fig. 10.2).

Accordingly, in 2015, both males and females aged 25 years and over in countries at a very high stage of development had an average of 12 years of schooling, while countries at low stage of development had an average of 6 and 4 years of schooling respectively for males and females, or less than half, especially in the case of females. Regional differences reflected the stage of development of countries within. The differences in school attainment between males and females narrowed as the stage of development rose. However, income differences prevailed at all stages of development regardless of the negligible gap at the highest level of development (Table 10.3). This is only partly explained by differences in labour force participation (Chap. 8: Sect. 8.4.4) and reflects prevailing gendered perceptions about employment and earnings of males and females.

An analysis of the levels of education attained by adults 25 years old and over in some high and middle income countries indicates that the proportion with completed secondary and tertiary education tends to increase with income, while the proportion of adults with less than completed secondary education tends to rise as income falls (Table 10.4). Thus, as would be expected, income is not only associated with the quantum but also with the gradient of education attained.

The close association between parent income and education raises the question of possible correlation without causal significance or reversal causation between educational attainment and income. A review of research concerned with this issue shows that the weight of evidence is that education performance has an independent effect on income generation and economic growth (OECD 2010). However, because causal effects cannot be transmitted backwards in time, it is unequivocal

Table 10.3 Average years of schooling and gross national income per head of population, by sex, development stage and region, 2015

Country stage of development/region	Average years of schooling		GNI p.c.	
	Males	Females	Males	Females
Very high	12.2	12.1	50,284	29,234
High	8.3	7.8	17,384	10,214
Medium	7.8	5.6	9,131	3,314
Low	5.6	3.6	3,365	1,950
Arab States	7.6	5.9	23,810	5,455
East Asia and Pacific	8.0	7.3	14,582	9,569
Europe and Central Asia	10.7	9.9	17,547	8,453
Latin America and Caribbean	8.3	8.3	18,091	10,053
South Asia	7.8	4.9	9,114	2,278
Sub-Sahara Africa	6.3	4.5	4,165	2,637
World	8.8	7.7	18,555	10,306

Note The average years of schooling refers to males and females 25 years of age and older. (GNI p.c.) is the average gross national income of males and females in 2015, in 2011 purchasing power parities (international dollars)
Source UNDP (2016)

that the socioeconomic status of parents has an effect on the education of their children (Hauser 1971) and the returns to education of their children (Hauser 1973).

Accordingly, the assessment of the relative earnings of workers, 25 years of age or more, along the education gradient shows considerable differences in some high and middle income countries. Using the income of workers who completed upper secondary education as the standard, workers who had tertiary education earned about 50–100% more while those with less than upper secondary education earned about 20% less on average. However, the premium for tertiary education was substantially greater (200% or more) in three middle income countries in Latin America, while workers with less that upper secondary education earned less than those in high income countries with similar level of education (Table 10.5).

Educational attainment has an impact on the formation of human capital and implications to employment and earnings. It was argued by Bourdieu (1986) that educational attainment plays an important role in converting cultural capital into economic capital with direct economic benefits to individuals and society. There have been substantial gains in educational attainment in recent years of those aged 25–34 years in high and middle income countries. In the 5-year period 2010–2015, educational attainment progression was to tertiary education in high income OECD countries. In middle income countries, such as Argentina, Brazil, Indonesia and South Africa, the progression was more accentuated from primary to secondary education, but there were also gains in the completion of tertiary education (Table 10.6).

Table 10.4 Educational attainment and gross national income per capita, selected countries, 2016

Country	Educational attainment people 25 years-old and over (%)			Country GNI p. c.
	Less than upper secondary	Upper secondary	Tertiary	
United States	10	55	35	53,245
Germany	15	59	27	45,000
Australia	20	49	32	42,822
Canada	9	61	32	42,582
France	22	57	21	38,085
United Kingdom	19	44	36	37,931
Japan	...	71	29	37,268
Korea	13	53	34	34,541
Italy	40	42	18	33,573
New Zealand	27	44	32	32,870
Russia	6	64	30	23,286
Argentina	42	38	21	20,945
Mexico	59	25	16	16,383
Brazil	52	34	15	14,145
China	75	21	4	13,345
Columbia	46	30	22	12,762
South Africa	57	36	7	12,087
Indonesia	65	26	10	10,053
India	71	19	10	5,663

Note Upper secondary includes those with post-secondary but less than tertiary and short-cycle tertiary education. Tertiary education comprises those with bachelor or higher degree. (GNI p.c.) is the average gross national income per head of population in 2015, in 2011 purchasing power parities (international dollars). (…) is less than 0.5%. Country estimates of educational attainment of people 25 years of age and over are as close to 2016 as could be ascertained by the Organisation for Economic Co-operation and Development. The percentages may not add up to 100 due to rounding and overlapping categories
Sources OECD (2017), UNDP (2016)

10.4.2 Education and Employment

In addition to consistently higher earnings along the education attainment gradient, education also has an impact on the employment rate of the adult population. Employment rates of adults in OECD countries provide evidence that the employment gradient rises substantially with the level of education. Accordingly, adults (25 years-old and over) with less than completed secondary education have an employment rate of 57%, 75% with secondary education, and those with tertiary education 84%. This represents a considerable increment of 27% between those with less than completed secondary education and those with tertiary education. The employment gradient is steeper from less than secondary to secondary (18%)

Table 10.5 Relative earnings of workers by education level, selected countries, 2016

Country	Average earnings of workers 25 years-old and over education level upper secondary = 100		
	Less than upper secondary	Post upper secondary but not tertiary	Tertiary
United States	68		174
Germany	76	118	166
Australia	83	97	140
Canada	87	122	141
France	80		154
United Kingdom	76		153
Japan	78		152
Korea	72		141
Italy	77		141
New Zealand	87	114	140
Mexico	81		202
Brazil	62		249
Columbia	67		234
OECD average	78		156

Note The post upper secondary but not tertiary level of education applies only in the gradient of some countries. The earnings relate to workers 25 years of age and over. OECD are more developed countries members of the Organisation for Economic Co-operation and Development. Brazil and Columbia are not OECD member countries. Country estimates of educational attainment of people 25 years of age and over and related average earnings are as close to 2016 as could be ascertained by OECD
Source OECD (2017)

than from secondary to tertiary (9%). These differences are also experienced in some middle-income countries, although the steepness of the gradient is less accentuated (Table 10.7).

10.5   Labour Force and Employment

10.5.1   Population and the Labour Force

The labour force and its relative size depend to a great extent on the number of people of working age (Box 10.1). This in turn is the result of past and current fertility, life expectancy and stage in the demographic transition of the particular society, and also in many cases on migration (Chap. 7: Sects. 7.2–7.6). There have been substantial changes in both fertility and life expectancy during the period 1950–2015 (Chaps. 1, 3 and 4). This has resulted in considerable differences in the

Table 10.6 Educational attainment, selected countries, 2010 and 2015

Countries	Level of education attainment	Percentage 25–34 years-old		Percentage difference 2015–2010
		2010	2015	
OECD	Less than secondary	19	16	−3
	Secondary less than tertiary	45	42	−3
	Tertiary	36	42	+6
Argentina	Less than secondary	35	32	−3
	Secondary less than tertiary	46	49	+3
	Tertiary	19	19	–
Brazil	Less than secondary	47	36	−11
	Secondary less than tertiary	41	47	+6
	Tertiary	12	17	+5
Indonesia	Less than secondary	60	53	−7
	Secondary less than tertiary	31	34	+3
	Tertiary	9	13	+4
South Africa	Less than secondary	53	51	−2
	Secondary less than tertiary	37	39	+2
	Tertiary	9	10	+1

Note (OECD) is the average educational attainment of developed countries that are members of the Organisation for Economic Co-operation and Development. The percentages and differences may not add up due to rounding
Source OECD (2017)

proportions of children 0–14 years of age and people 65 years old and over, during the 65-year period, that affected the proportion of people of working age (15–64 years of age). However, these changes have not been uniform across countries at different stages of development and regions.

In the least developed countries, the proportion of children has remained about the same in 1950 and 2015 (40 and 41% respectively), in spite of a large decline in fertility. A substantial fall in fertility was also experienced by other less developed countries (where most people live), and a smaller one by more developed countries, that resulted in a decline of about 11% in the proportion of children in the two sets of countries, but from a lower base in the case of more developed countries. The proportion of children in the total population fell from 37 to 26% in other less developed, and from 27 to 16% in more developed countries. The proportion of older people remained at low levels in least developed (respectively 3 and 4% in 1950 and 2015), even though they benefited from a considerable rise in life expectancy (27 years). The change in the proportion of older people was most felt

Table 10.7 Employment rate by education level, selected countries, 2016

Country	Employment rate (%) 25 years-old and over education level			
	Less than upper secondary	Post and upper secondary but not tertiary	Tertiary	All
United States	57	69	82	73
Germany	59	81	88	80
Australia	58	78	84	76
Canada	55	74	82	76
France	51	73	85	72
United Kingdom	62	80	85	79
Japan			83	80
Korea	66	72	77	74
Italy	51	71	80	64
New Zealand	72	82	87	82
Russia	51	72	82	77
Argentina	65	73	87	73
Mexico	65	70	80	68
Brazil	65	74	83	71
Columbia	72	76	83	76
South Africa	47	62	83	56
Indonesia	71	73	85	73
OECD average	57	75	84	75

Note Figures for Japan pertain to people who have completed tertiary education and those at all levels of education. OECD are more developed countries members of the Organisation for Economic Co-operation and Development. Some middle-income countries such as Argentina, Brazil, Columbia, Indonesia, Russia, South Africa are not OECD members. Country estimates of the educational attainment of people 25 years of age and over and employment rates are as close to 2016 as could be ascertained by OECD
Source OECD (2017)

in more developed countries where it rose from 8 to 18% of the population, during the period, but the proportion also rose from 4 to 7% in other less developed countries. The outcome was that the proportion of the population of working age remained the same at 56% in least developed countries, and about the same in more developed countries (65–66%), but rose considerably in other less developed countries with a demographic bonus of 8% from 59 to 67% (Table 10.8). Thus, while least developed countries continued to have a high level of dependency on their working population, more developed countries were able to maintain a lower dependency on people of working age by exchanging higher life expectancy for lower fertility. Other less developed countries benefited from a larger proportion of their population of people in working age, with lower fertility and proportion of

Table 10.8 Global population age distribution by stage of development and region, 1950 and 2015

Country stage of development/region	Population age distribution (%)						Difference 2015–1950	
	1950			2015				
	0–14	15–64	65 and over	0–14	15–64	65 and over	TFR	Le
More developed	27	65	8	16	66	18	−1.2	14
Other less developed	37	59	4	26	67	7	−3.6	28
Least developed	41	56	3	40	56	4	−4.3	27
Africa	41	55	3	41	56	4	−1.9	23
Asia	36	60	4	25	68	8	−3.6	29
Europe	26	66	8	16	67	18	−1.1	14
Latin Am. and Caribbean	40	56	4	26	67	8	−3.7	23
North America	27	65	8	19	66	15	−1.5	11
Oceania	30	63	7	24	65	12	−1.4	17
World average	34	61	5	26	66	8	−2.4	24

Note (TFR) is the total fertility rate or the average number of children a female has during her life time. The difference is between TFR in 2010–15 and 1950–55. (Le) is the average life expectancy in years at birth. The difference is between Le in 2010–15 and 1950–55. Percentages may not add up to 100 due to rounding
Source UN (2017). Computations made by the authors

dependent children, with still a relatively low proportion of older people. Some more developed countries such as Australia, Canada, to a lesser extent the United States and some European countries, that experienced falls in their fertility and increases in their life expectancy, used migration to enhance their proportion of people of working age. Accordingly, since the 1950s, regions in more developed parts of Europe, North America and Oceania were net receivers while countries in other regions, especially Asia, Africa and Latin America and the Caribbean were net senders of international migrants (Tables 5.8 and 5.9), most of whom in labour force participation age.

10.5.2   Labour Force Participation

It has been proposed that there is a proximity effect in social networks (Festinger et al. 1968), which suggests that employment in the form of a work-based social networks affect what people do and to whom they relate. These features have an impact on living standards, social cohesion and productivity (WB 2012). A higher proportion of people of working age offers the potential for lower dependency rates. In turn, the degree of participation in the labour force influences the level of production of goods and services available to society and the productivity of the population as a whole. Earnings from employment provide means for the

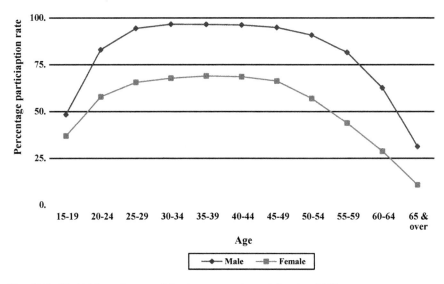

Fig. 10.3 World labour force participation rate, males and females, 2000
Note Labour force participation rate is the ratio of the number of working age who are employed or unemployed by the number of people of working age (Box 10.1)
Source Kapsos (2007)

Table 10.9 Labour force participation rates, by sex and region, 1997 and 2017

Countries by regions	Labour force participation rate (%)			
	1997		2017	
	Males	Females	Males	Females
Northern Africa	75	21	74	23
Sub-Sahara Africa	78	62	76	65
Arab States	76	18	76	21
Central and Western Asia	75	43	74	44
Eastern Asia	83	69	**77**	61
South-eastern Asia and Pacific	82	58	81	59
Southern Asia	83	34	79	29
Eastern Europe	67	52	68	53
North., South. and West. Europe	67	46	64	51
Northern America	74	59	68	56
Latin America and Caribbean	82	47	78	53
World average	79	52	76	49

Note Labour force participation rate as per Box 10.1
Source ILO (2017)

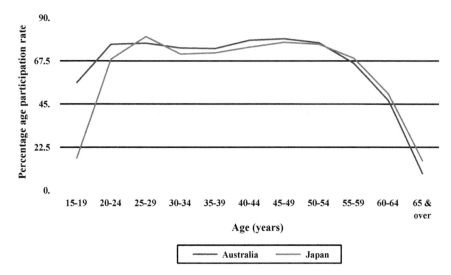

Fig. 10.4 Labour force participation rate of females by age, Australia and Japan, 2015
Source OECD (undated)

maintenance of living standards for those employed and their dependents, but also support for others through social transfers from to the unemployed and those not in the labour force. One of the gains from the investment in human capital is realised when people join the labour force. However, the growing social importance given to education means that more time is spent on it, even in developing countries (Table 10.6). This affects the age when young people join the labour force.

Labour force participation tends to rise with age from a relatively low rate at 15–19 years of age to reach its peak in the range of 35–49 years of age, and then declines to much lower rates at 65 years of age and over. The lower rates of participation in the labour force at younger ages reflect partly education and training earlier in life. The lower and declining rates in older ages arise from diminishing healthy years of life (Sect. 10.3.4), conventional retirement age at 60–64 years of age, and depreciated human capital at older ages. The participation rates of females tend to be lower throughout working age (Fig. 10.3). This is partly due to differing biological functions of male and female roles in reproduction, but also because of gendered social perceptions of the roles of males and females (Chap. 8).

The world average participation rate in the labour force of people of working age in 2017 shows a slight decline from that in 1997 for both males and females, respectively from 79 to 76% and 52 to 49. The falls were more pronounced in countries in Northern America (males −6% and females −3%) and Eastern Asia (males −6% and females −8%) (Table 10.9). The trend is for lower participation rates in countries in Europe and Northern America with social security retirement systems that apply at 60–65 years of age but also because of longer periods of education at earlier ages. The prevailing lower than average participation rates of females in Northern Africa, Arab States and Central and Western Asia are associated with cultural perceptions of the social role of females.

The effect of female association with reproduction is apparent in female labour force participation rates in Australia and Japan. Both countries have fertility rates below replacement level, especially Japan, that usually imply an older maternal age at the birth of the first child. In the two countries, female labour force participation rates rise from 15–19 years of age to peak at 25–29, then decline at 30–39 years of age, while children are raised, but participation rates rise again at 40–49 years of age, before they gradually fall like those of males at older ages (Fig. 10.4).

Box 10.1 Work, labour force and employment

The boundaries of what is considered work and other human activities are somewhat unclear and the same applies to what is understood by the labour force and employment. To provide a more consistent interpretation of these concepts the International Labour Organization (ILO 2013) has provided guidance in their use and measurement. In this context, the *reference population* is the usual residents regardless of the citizenship or legal residence. People of *working age* are those above a given age threshold involved in economic activity. This is usually 15-years of age or older. Although there is no definite upper limit, the working age is often taken to be 15–64 years of age. People *employed* are those of working age who work for a given period of time (a week or day) and are in *paid employment* or *self-employed* (whether at work or away from it). *At work* are people who have done some work for income either in cash or in kind (for paid employment), and in the case of self-employed in the form of profit or family gain in cash or kind. They also include those whose work contributed to the household income either in cash or kind. These do not comprise household members providing unpaid household services such as cooking, other household duties and caring for children or other members of the household. Nor do they include people involved in voluntary services to others. *Unemployed* people are those of working age who are without work, in the form of either paid or self-employment, and who are seeking employment during the period. The *economically active population* (EAP) are people engaged in work for the production of economic goods and services. The *labour force* or *currently active population* are people of working age who are considered either employed or unemployed. The following indicators measure some aspects of these concepts.

*EPR (%) = Number of people of working age employed * 100/Number of people of working age*

*ER_i (%) = Number of people of working age with i characteristic employed * 100/Number of people with i characteristic in the labour force*

*UR (%) = Number of people of working age unemployed * 100/Number of people in the labour force*

*UR_i (%) = Number of people or working age with i characteristic unemployed * 100/Number of people with i characteristic in the labour force*

Labour force participation relates to the proportion of people of working age who are either employed or unemployed but available to work.

LFPR (%) = (Number of people employed + Number of people unemployed)
* 100/Number of people of working age

LFPR$_i$ (%) = (Number of people with characteristic i employed + Number of people with characteristic i unemployed) * 100/Number of people of working age with characteristic i

The *gender pay gap* represents the difference between the average pay of hourly work of males and that of females.

GPG (%) = (Male average hourly earnings − Female average hourly earnings) * 100/Male average hourly earnings

Earnings inequality consists of the difference between the earnings of workers in the top and those at the bottom of the earnings distribution, such as the top and the lowest deciles.

EI $_{(9:1\ ratio)}$ = log (gross earnings of workers in the top decile/gross earnings of workers in bottom decile)

It is apparent that this ratio relates to the bottom but only to the second top decile (9th decile).

These are some of the indicators used in the measurement of participation in the labour force and nature of employment in the assessment of their characteristics.

10.5.3   Shifting Employment Sector

Employment by sector shows a substantial degree of specialisation with concentration of males in the industrial sector and females in services. However, there was a narrowing in the degree of specialisation in the period 2000–2013. This also applies in the case of agriculture where 44% of females employed worked in that sector in 2000, and 38% of males employed, the proportions narrowed down to 33 and 31% respectively in 2013 (Table 10.10).

In general, the share of employment in the agricultural sector declined, in which 40% of those employed worked in 2000 and only 32% in 2013. The proportion in industry rose slightly from 21 to 23% during that period, but the proportion employed in services increased substantially from 39 to 45%. Thus, although some increments took place in industry, most of the average fall in agriculture (9%) was associated with an increase in services (6%). The distribution of the stock of labour among the three employment sectors, over time, followed the pattern of the stages

Table 10.10 World employment by sector by sex, selected regions, 2000 and 2013

Region	Employment sector (%)					
	Agriculture		Industry		Services	
	2000	2013	2000	2013	2000	2013
Developed countries and EU	5.5	3.6	27.7	22.5	67.3	73.9
Latin America and Caribbean	26.1	20.0	25.9	27.4	48.0	52.7
South Asia	53.3	40.9	17.4	24.8	29.3	34.3
Sub-Sahara Africa	65.8	61.3	8.1	8.9	26.3	29.9
World average males	38.3	31.0	24.0	26.7	37.7	42.3
World average females	43.7	33.2	15.2	17.4	41.1	49.4
World average	40.4	31.8	20.5	23.0	39.1	45.1

Note The regions selected are in a gradient of development. (EU) are countries in the European Union. Percentages may not add to 100 due to rounding
Source ILO (2014)

of development. Four groups of countries at different stages of development illustrate this pattern. Although countries in the Sub-Sahara region experienced some shifts away from agriculture most of the decline was associated with an increase in the proportion employed in services, with only a slight rise in industry. The substantial drop in the proportion employed in agriculture in South Asia was associated with increments in industry, and to a lesser extent in services. In countries in Latin America and Caribbean the smaller proportion of those employed in agriculture was compensated by a small increase in industry and a larger rise in services. In the more developed countries members OECD and the EU (European Union), the proportions employed in both agriculture and industry fell somewhat and the only increment was in services (Table 10.10). Thus, the transfer of jobs in industry from more developed countries to less developed countries had not much impact in Sub-Sahara Africa or Latin America and the Caribbean, but was associated with a discernible rise in the proportion employed in industry in South Asia.

10.5.4   Unemployment

Although the proportions of working age populations and labour force participation are important determinants of the average productivity of societies, unemployment is also a critical issue. Unemployment is influenced by the levels of investments of varied forms, as well as economic and social organisation and functioning. The global financial crisis in the mid-2000s saw unemployment rates rise on average in the world from 5.5% in 2007 to 6.2% in 2009, and then gradually recovered to 5.8% in 2015. Nevertheless, it is estimated that the number of unemployed people was still higher in 2015 (197 million) than in 2007 (170 million) (ILO 2016a).

Table 10.11 World unemployed and labour force participation rates by region, 2000–07 and 2015

Country regions	Unemployed rate (%)		Labour force participation rate (%)	
	2000–07	2015	2000–07	2015
Northern Africa	13.4	12.1	47.4	48.2
Sub-Sahara Africa	8.1	7.4	69.8	70.2
Arab States—GCC	4.4	4.7	57.2	63.9
Arab states—Not GCC	15.5	15.2	44.7	44.3
Central and Western Asia	9.8	9.2	56.2	58.2
Eastern Asia	4.3	4.5	73.4	69.5
Southeast Asia and Pacific	6.1	4.4	70.2	69.9
Southern Asia	4.6	4.1	59.3	54.4
Northern America—Canada	7.0	6.9	66.4	65.6
Northern America—United States	5.1	5.3	65.5	62.1
Latin America and Caribbean	8.6	6.5	64.8	65.2
North., West. and South Europe	8.2	10.1	56.9	57.7
Eastern Europe	9.2	6.9	58.6	60.2
World average	6.5	5.8	NA	62.9

Note Unemployment and labour force participation rates measures as in Box 10.1. (GCC) are country members of the Gulf Cooperation Council: Bahrain, Kuwait, Oman, Qatar, Saudi Arabia and the United Arab Emirates (usually major oil producers). (Not GCC) are non-member countries of the GCC: Iraq, Jordan, Lebanon, West Bank and Gaza, and Yemen. (NA) represents not available
Source ILO (2016a)

This average pattern conceals over substantial differences in the level of unemployment and changes from before and since the global financial crisis. On average, countries in Northern Africa, Central and Western Asia, and Arab countries not members of the GCC (Gulf Cooperation Council) with unemployment rates of 9% or over remained at that level in 2015. Member countries of GCC, Eastern and South Asia, Southeast Asia and the Pacific that had lower unemployment rates remained at rates of 4–5%. Similarly, the United States regained losses in employment to achieve an unemployment rate of 5.3% in 2015. A major deviation from the downward trend in unemployment was, on average, in countries in Northern, Western and Southern Europe with an average rate rise from 8.2% in 2000–07 to 10.1% in 2015 (Table 10.11). This has been associated with a slower recovery from the global financial crisis in some large European countries such as France and Italy with unemployment rates of 10.6 and 12.1% respectively in 2015, while others such as Germany (4.6%) and United Kingdom (5.5%) achieved lower levels of unemployment (ILO 2016a).

Table 10.12 Labour productivity and earnings indices in more developed countries, 1999–2015

Index	Year			
	1999	2005	2010	2015
Labour productivity index	100.0	110.3	114.5	118.9
Labour real wage index	100.0	103.3	106.4	108.8
Difference		−7.0	−8.1	−10.1

Note The indices compiled by the International Labour Organisation refer to 33 more developed countries
Source ILO (2016b). Computations made by the authors

10.5.5 Labour Productivity, Sharing of Earnings and Inequality

Labour productivity per hour worked is a major source of economic gains in the production of goods and services and a potential source of enhancement of household income. Estimates for the period 1999–2015 show that while labour productivity in more developed countries has increased substantially labour earnings have lagged considerably (Table 10.12).

The lag in labour income has had an impact on its proportion of gross domestic product in more developed countries. Estimates for eight more developed countries in Europe, Northern America, Asia and Oceania shows that the share of labour income declined by about 4 to 6% in the 24-year period 1990–2013 from about 60 to 55%, on average, with the exception of France where the proportion remained about the same (59%) (Table 10.13).

Table 10.13 Labour income share of gross domestic product in selected more developed countries, 1990–2013

Country	Labour income share of GDP (%)					Change 2013–1990 percentage
	1990	2000	2005	2010	2013	
France	59	57	58	59	59	–
Italy	62	53	54	55	55	−7
Germany	62	61	58	57	58	−4
United Kingdom	66	61	61	62	62	−4
Canada	61	56	56	57	56	−5
United States	61	62	58	57	56	−5
Japan	66	64	60	59	60	−6
Australia	59	57	55	54	55	−4

Note (GDP) is gross domestic product
Source ILO (2015). Computations made by the authors

Table 10.14 Inequality in
labour income, selected high
and medium income
countries, during global
financial crisis, 2006 and
2010

Country	Inequality (D9/D1)	
	2006	2010
France	3.8	4.0
Italy	5.4	5.3
Germany	6.1	6.0
Sweden	3.6	4.1
United Kingdom	5.5	5.4
United States	9.5	10.6
Brazil	10.0	8.4
China	8.8	7.6
India	10.2	12.2
Indonesia	12.9	11.2
Mexico	9.5	9.1
Russia	5.7	4.6
South Africa	20.9	26.6

Note The inequality measure is based on weighted per capita
household income, taking into consideration income from other
sources than earnings from employment to measure labour
income. (D9/D1) ratio of the 9th and 1st decile (Box 10.1). The
measures for middle-income countries relate to a period about
2006–08 and 2010–12
Source ILO (2015)

During the years of the global financial crisis, changes in the degree of inequality
between the top and bottom levels of the distribution of labour income show no
consistent pattern among six high income countries. However, the overall pattern
points to substantial differences in inequality from the top to the bottom of the
distribution among these countries, in 2010, that range from about 4 times in France
and Sweden to about 11 in the United States. The inequality levels are, on average,
much higher in seven middle income countries ranging from about 8 times in China
and Brazil to 12 in India, with the exceptions of South Africa with a considerably
higher inequality of 27, and low in Russia with 5 (Table 10.14). The general trend
among these middle-income countries was for a decline in labour income inequality
during the period 2006–2010, as they might have been less affected, in degree, by
the global financial crisis than high income countries.

In addition to the degree of labour earnings inequality, there are also gaps in
earnings among people with given characteristics in the labour force. One of these
is the *gender pay gap* between the earnings of males and females already mentioned
(Chap. 8: Sect. 8.4.4). This earnings gap has been attributed to a number of factors:

- undervaluation of females' work
- workplace characteristics
- sex segregation in directing females to low paid work
- wage structure of the country with a bias in favour of males
- perception of females as economic dependents

Table 10.15 Earnings gap between males and females, selected countries, circa 2010

Country	Earnings gap between males and females employed (%)	
	Actual gender gap	Explained gender gap
France	18.0	3.3
Italy	17.1	2.5
Germany	23.1	18.6
Sweden	4.0	−12.9
United Kingdom	29.1	11.3
United States	35.8	28.2
Brazil	24.4	−10.4
China	22.9	−0.2
Mexico	21.5	6.2
Russia	32.8	−11.1

Note The estimation of the earnings gap is per Box 10.1. The explained part is proportion of the earnings gap that can be attributed to labour market characteristics. The observed negative explained gap in some countries arises from lack of knowledge of *factors that influence pay for men and women with equal experience, qualifications and other observable labour market characteristics* (ILO 2015)
Source ILO (2015)

- female employment in less labour organised sectors (ILO 2015).

Research findings indicate that some of the gap can be *explained* in terms of the characteristics of the labour market. Findings for a number of high and middle income countries indicate that labour market characteristics explain only part of the gap and that, in most cases, the earnings gap between males and females remains unexplained by those characteristics (Table 10.15)

Another inequality is the *migrant wage gap* that shows differences between earnings of migrant and national workers. They have also been ascribed to a number of factors:

- differences in levels of skill
- prejudice
- attribution of lower value to foreign-acquired education
- perception of lower needs
- under-representation in labour organisation and bargaining (ILO 2015).

As in the case of the gender earnings gap, market characteristics explain only part of the gap in earnings between nationals and migrants employed (Table 10.16). The unexplained part of the gap could be attributed to lack of knowledge about factors that could contribute to it, but might also, at least, be partly related to factors mentioned above.

Table 10.16 Earnings gap between nationals and migrants, selected countries, circa 2010

Country	Earnings gap between nationals and migrants employed (%)	
	Actual migrant gap	Explained migrant gap
France	14.9	6.0
Italy	26.7	14.6
Germany	7.4	−3.7
Sweden	8.4	−3.9
United Kingdom	8.4	0.8
Europe	17.5	6.2
Brazil	−113.8	−43.8

Note The estimation of the earnings gap follows the procedures for the estimation of earning gaps as per Box 10.1. The explained part is proportion of the earnings gap that can be attributed to labour market characteristics. The observed negative explained gap in some countries arises from lack of knowledge of factors that influence pay for nationals and migrants with equal experience, qualifications and other observable labour market characteristics (ILO 2015)
Source ILO (2015)

10.6 Productivity, Inequality and Poverty

10.6.1 Growing Global Productivity

A characteristic of human societies, throughout the ages, has been the ability to raise their productivity levels. This has been achieved through innovation in the development of tools and machines, as early capital formation, soil improvement, irrigation and fertilisers, division of labour and specialisation, and taking advantage of economies of scale depending on the size of the market. Technological change and evolved social and work organization allowed for more productive efforts but more complex, interdependent and complementary activities, that have required multigenerational investments in human capital in the form of education and skill development, and a healthier and more capable labour force, in addition to other forms of capital accumulation. The outcome has been a substantial increase in productivity per head of population (Tables 1.19, 1.20 and 1.21) and also the availability of a wider range of goods and services. This was associated with longer life expectancy, and importantly, healthier years of life, as well as increasingly higher levels of education (Tables 1.12, 1.22, 1.23 and 10.1, 10.2 and 10.3), but had a substantial impact on the environment (Tables 1.26 and 1.27, and Chap. 11). The trend in rising productivity has continued during the period 2000–2016, and the world average income per capita increased by 45% during that period, in spite of a temporary decline of about 2% during the GFC (Table 10.17) that was most felt in high income countries.

Table 10.17 World gross domestic product per capita, 2000–2016

Year	GDP p.c. International $	Index 2000 = 100
2000	10,326	100
2005	11,683	113
2007	12,663	123
2008	12,866	125
2009	12,662	123
2010	13,171	128
2015	14,739	143
2016	15,024	145

Note (GDP p.c. International $) is gross domestic product per head of population in 2011 purchasing power parities (international dollars)

Source WB (2017). Computations made by the authors

10.6.2 Life Cycle Ups and Downs

Household income and that of individuals tends to follow a hump-shaped pattern similar to the labour force participation rate (Fig. 10.3).

It starts at a low level early in life and rises to reach its peak about 45–55 years of age and then declines. Although the degree of departure from the average for all ages may change from country to country, income tends to be lower than average for all ages until the 30s and then in the 60s and older ages (e.g. Figs. 10.5 and 10.6).

This inequality is associated with years of experience and then retirement. It also reflects the number of people in the household that is lower at younger ages and later in the life of the reference person. Nevertheless, even if lower, the pattern of variation still holds after the number of people in the household is taken into consideration (Martins et al. 2012).

10.6.3 Global Income Inequality

In spite of the considerable increases in productivity worldwide, the level of income inequality per head of population prevails. In 2016, on average, people in high income countries had an income almost three times (2.88) that of the world average and people in low income countries had only one tenth of that average. Countries in East Asia and the Pacific (1.05) and Latin America and the Caribbean (0.96) had income levels about the average; the incomes of those in Northern America (3.48), Europe and Central Asia (1.93) and Middle East and Northern Africa (1.18) were above average, while countries in South Asia (0.37) and Sub-Sahara Africa (0.23) trailed well behind (Table 10.18). The substantial below average income in South Asia and Sub-Sahara Africa are only partly attributable to a lower proportion of people of working age, as they are associated with lower levels of schooling,

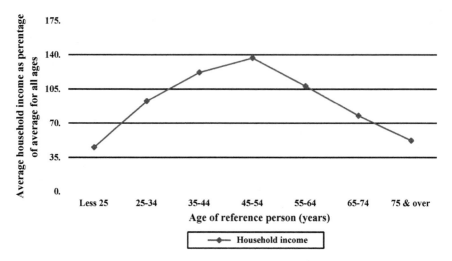

Fig. 10.5 Household income by age of reference person, United States, 2015
Note Household income for each age group is expressed as a percentage of the average household income of $69,627 for all households in 2015
Source BLS (2016). Computations made by the authors

especially in the case of females, and higher proportions of people employed in agriculture and lower proportions in industry (Tables and 10.3 and 10.10). Both point to lower levels of investment in human capital and less advanced economic organization. However, the substantial gains in education in these countries (Table 1.23) are sources of potential future enhancements. The higher rates of GDP growth per head of population in South Asia (Table 10.18) indicates a degree of catch up and income convergence.

10.6.4 Income Distribution and Inequality

The unequal distribution of income has been the subject of considerable discussion. The so-called *Pareto distribution* has sometimes been suggested as a guide of what might be a natural distribution of wealth and income that results in a stable and unequal distribution. This would imply that, say, the top 20% would have 80% of the income in society. Picketty (2014) pointed out that Pareto had only limited data on which to make this observation and that both wealth and income inequality have varied across nations and time.

There is a large range of income inequality among countries at all levels of income, even though the degree of inequality tends to be wider the lower the average income per head of population. The degree of inequality as expressed by the Gini coefficient among high income countries ranged from as low as 26% in Norway to 51% in Chile in the period 2010–15. Similarly, among middle income

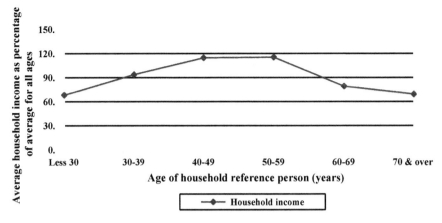

Fig. 10.6 Household income by age of reference person, Japan, 2013
Note Household income for each age group is expressed as a percentage of the average household income of ¥468,570 for all households in 2013
Source SJ (2014). Computations made by the authors

Table 10.18 World gross domestic product per capita, by income level and region, 2016

Countries by income level/ region	GDP p.c.		Annual GDP p.c. growth (%)
	International $	World average = 1.00	
High income	43,233	2.88	1.1
Middle income	10,645	0.71	2.7
Low income	1,561	0.1	1.3
Northern America	52,245	3.48	0.8
Europe and Central Asia	29,008	1.93	1.2
Middle East and Northern Africa	17,661	1.18	1.5
East Asia and Pacific	15,784	1.05	3.4
Latin America and Caribbean	14,365	0.96	−1.7
South Asia	5,621	0.37	5.5
Sub-Sahara Africa	3,440	0.23	−1.5
World average	15,024	1.0	1.2

Note (GDP p.c. International $) is gross domestic product per head of population at 2016 in 2011 purchasing power parities (international dollars)
Source WB (2017). Computations made by the authors

countries, it spread from 24% in Ukraine to 63% in South Africa, and from 32% in Mauritania to 61% in Haiti, among low income countries (Table 10.19).

An example of changes in income inequality that can take place over time is provided by data available for the United States for the 45-year period 1970–2015.

Table 10.19 Gini coefficient of income distribution, selected high, medium and low income countries, 2010–15

Country income level	Gini coefficient (%)	Percentage difference high and low coefficients
High income		24.6
Norway	25.9	
Chile	50.5	
Middle income		39.3
Ukraine	24.1	
South Africa	63.4	
Low income		28.4
Mauritania	32.4	
Haiti	60.8	

Note The Gini coefficient is a measure of inequality based on the estimation of cumulative differences, in this case of income, between a given proportion of the population and the related proportion of income. The coefficients range from zero to one. The higher the coefficient the higher the degree of inequality. In this table the coefficients are expressed as a percentage
Source UNDP (2016). Computations made by the authors

Table 10.20 Distribution of share of household income by income quintile, United States, 1970–2015

Income quintile	Share of household income by quintile (%)			
	1970	1990	2010	2015
Lowest	4.1	3.9	3.3	3.1
Second	10.8	9.6	8.5	8.2
Third	17.4	15.9	14.6	14.3
Fourth	24.5	24.0	23.4	23.2
Highest	43.3	46.6	50.3	51.1
Gini coefficient	39.4	42.8	47.0	47.9

Note Gini coefficient as per Table 10.19
Sources USCB (2000, 2016)

The degree of income inequality as measured by the Gini coefficient grew from 39% in 1970 to 48% in 2015. The proportion of total income of the bottom 40% of households fell from 15% in 1970 to 11% in 2015, while that of the top 20% rose from 43 to 51%. This meant that the share of the middle 40% also dropped from 42 to 38% during the period (Table 10.20).

This rise in inequality since the 1970s has affected a number of high income countries, even if at lower degree, such as the United Kingdom where the Gini coefficient for all households rose from 27% in 1977 to 32 in 2015/16 (ONS 2016). Circa 2013, the top 20% of households accounted for 43% of the income of all households in the United Kingdom and the bottom 20% for only 7%. Similarly, the top and bottom 20% accounted for 40 and 7% respectively in Australia, 40 and 9% in France, 38 and 9% in Germany, 36 and 9% in Sweden (OECD 2015). OECD (2015) has suggested that growing inequality among its member countries may have deleterious effects in terms of social cohesion, but also because it hinders access to education that affects investment in human capital, employment and productivity. It was also suggested that the concentration of wealth leads to greater indebtedness by the middle classes and weakens their economic security, which in turn affects economic growth. Growing inequality has also been associated with the growth of temporary and low paid jobs that lead to a lower share of labour income (Table 10.13).

10.6.5   Inequality and Poverty

One of the issues concerned with inequality is its impact on poverty. Estimates carried out by the OECD (2016) found a positive correlation between income inequality (Gini coefficient) and relative income poverty in high income countries (Fig. 10.7). The measure of relative income poverty has the advantage of being easy to estimate from more readily available income data. However, it is based on the median income. In a sense, it is a measure of central tendency rather than a measure of poverty estimated on what is the threshold for adequate living conditions in the particular country.

10.6.6   Declining Extreme Poverty

A measure of extreme poverty developed by the World Bank to overcome some of the scarcity of data based on national poverty lines is the income of $1.90 per day. In that context, extreme poverty has declined considerably in the period 1999–2013

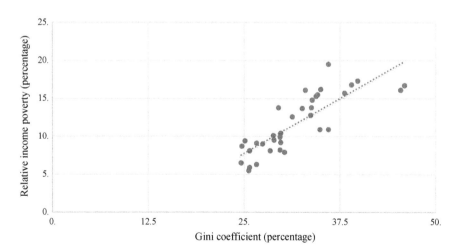

Fig. 10.7 Income inequality and relative income poverty, selected high income countries, 2015 *Note* Relative income poverty is the percentage estimated of half of the median household income. Gini coefficient as per Table 10.19 *Source* OECD (2016)

Table 10.21 World poverty ratio, 1999–2013

Year	Poverty head count ratio percentage of population		Difference $1.90–$3.20 (%)
	$1.90 per day	$3.20 per day	
1999	28.6	22.3	6.3
2005	20.8	16.9	3.9
2008	18.0	14.9	3.1
2010	15.7	13.4	2.3
2013	10.7	9.9	0.8

Note The poverty ratios are estimates of the percentage of the world population with incomes of $1.90 and $3.20 expressed in 2011 purchasing power parities
Source WB (2017). Computations made by the authors

from 29 to 11% of the world population, there was also a substantial decrease in a higher threshold of $3.20 per day (Table 10.21). This was achieved even during the GFC in middle 2000s.

Amelioration of extreme poverty was experienced across the world, especially among low and middle income countries. The largest improvement took place in East Asia and Pacific region where substantial economic growth has taken place and the poverty head count declined from 38 to 7% of the population in the period 1999–2012. Lower, but also considerable falls in extreme poverty were experienced in South Asia and Sub-Sahara Africa. However, people in these two regions continued to have the highest rates of extreme poverty among low and middle income countries, especially Sub-Sahara Africa where 43% of the population continued to live in extreme poverty (Table 10.22).

The substantial decline in East Asia and Pacific has been heavily influenced by China, with the largest country population in the world. The lesser but still extensive decline in South Asia is affected by India with the second largest country population on the planet. In the case of India, a national poverty line based on household consumption indicates that the poverty ratio declined by 15% in the 7-year period 2005–2012, from 37 to 22%. This meant that the number of people below the poverty line fell substantially from 407 million to the still large number of 269 million people (GIPC 2013).

The relative changes in poverty levels reflect investments in human capital but also degrees of social and economic organization that fostered them and in turn benefited in terms of living standards of the most vulnerable members of society.

10.7 Productivity: Priorities and Choices

10.7.1 Bare Necessities' Priority

The increases in productivity experienced, well ahead of the astounding growth in population in the 20th Century, have been associated with a decline in extreme poverty but increasing inequality in the distribution of income in some high-income

Table 10.22 Low and middle income countries poverty ratios, 1999–2012

Low and middle income countries	Poverty head count ratio $1.90 per day percentage of population			
	1999	2005	2008	2012
East Asia and Pacific	37.5	18.6	15.0	7.2
Europe and Central Asia	7.8	5.5	3.1	2.1
Latin America and Caribbean	13.9	9.9	7.1	5.6
Middle East and North Africa	4.2	3.3	2.7	n.a.
South Asia	n.a.	35.0	32.1	18.8
Sub-Sahara Africa	58.0	50.5	47.8	42.7
Average low and middle income	34.3	24.7	21.9	14.9

Note The poverty ratios are estimates of the percentage of the world population with incomes of $1.90 expressed in 2011 purchasing power parities. (n.a.) is not available
Source WB (2017)

countries (Table 10.22; Figs. 10.2 and 10.7). In view of these trends, households faced choices regarding priorities in their allocation of resources. Following Maslow's hierarchy of human needs, the priority placed on physiological needs is apparent. Accordingly, the pattern of household expenditure mirrors Engel's Law: the proportion of household expenditure on food rises as income declines (Martins et al. 2012). This general pattern prevails across and within countries.

An illustration of this pattern across countries is provided by a comparison of five countries in different regions and levels of income. The proportion of household consumer expenditure on food falls substantial from India (48%) to Malaysia (29%), Japan (21%), Australia (17%) and the United States (15%), in years circa 2011, as the average income per capita rose from $4,883 in India to $49,854 in the United States in 2011 purchasing power parities (Table 10.23). The proportion of household expenditure on food follows a similar pattern within these countries. In the United States, as average household income declined from the highest to the lowest income quintiles the proportion of household expenditure on food rose from 12 to 16% (BLS 2013). Similar increases took place in Australia, Japan and Malaysia (ABS 2011; SJ 2014; DSM 2011). In India, the average proportion spent on food rose from 43 in urban areas to 52% in rural areas, as average household consumer expenditure declined in rural households to about half of that in urban households (NSSO 2014).

10.7.2 Life Cycle Changes and Preferences

People have different attributes during the life cycle that affect what they do and the role they play in the household and society at large. They influence their participation in the labour force, household responsibilities and functions and dependency

Table 10.23 Food as proportion of household consumer expenditure and income per capita, selected countries, circa 2011

Country	Food as percentage of household consumer expenditure	GDP p.c. 2011 International $
United States	15	49,854
Australia	17	41,588
Japan	21	34,266
Malaysia	29	21,075
India	48	4,883

Note The proportion of food in household expenditure is from household expenditure surveys in the United States (2011), Australia (2009–10), Japan (2013), Malaysia (2009–10) and India (2011–12). The average for India was derived from rural and urban averages weighted for the number of households in rural and urban areas at the time of the 2011 Census. The GDP p.c. 2011 is that for 2011 in terms of purchasing power parities 2011
Sources BLS (2013), ABS (2011), SJ (2014), DSM (2011), NSSO (2014), ORG (2012), UNDP (2014). Computations made by the authors

on others. This has an impact on household income (Figs. 10.5 and 10.6), consumption levels and related expenditures.

Household expenditures according to the age of the reference person tend to follow a hump-shaped distribution of the general form

$$y = a + {}_bx - {}_cx^2$$

where y is the dependent variable household expenditure, x is the independent variable age of the household reference person, a is the intercept that may be positive or negative, b and c are the coefficients of respectively x and x^2. Data from household expenditure surveys in the United States and Australia provide examples of this pattern. The general pattern is for household expenditures on consumer items to be below the average for all ages below 25 years of age of the reference person, they rise to above average to peak at about 35 to 54 years of age and then tend to fall to below the average for all ages at 65 years of age and over (Table 10.24). The degree above and below average differs from country to country and peaks may also vary at more precise ages. However, this general pattern tends to prevail in countries, in different regions and stages of development (Martins et al. 2012).

Differences in household resources and capacities tend to promote preferences for certain types of goods and services and diminish the propensity to consume others during the life cycle. An obvious choice, in view of increasing health constraints with age, is the rising propensity to spend on medical care at older ages (Fig. 7.10). The analysis of household expenditures in the United States, Australia and Japan provide instances of the substantial propensity to spend on medical care at 65 years of age and over. In the same countries, the expenditure on clothing and footwear tends to decline at the same ages when people retire from work. The emphasis on household expenditure on housing at 30–40 years of age, at the time of

Age household reference person	Age group ratio to all ages	
	United States	Australia
Less than 25	0.624	0.865
25–34	0.945	1.036
35–44	2.17	1.196
45-54	1.204	1.235
55–64	1.235	1.028
65 and over	0.829	0.622
Average all ages	1.000	1.000

Table 10.24 Household consumer expenditure by age of reference person, United Sates 2015 and Australia, 2015–16

Note The ratios were estimated from the average household consumer expenditure on good and services in the United States (2015 yearly averages) and Australia (monthly averages for the year 2015–16)

Sources BLS (2016), ABS (2017). Computations made by the authors

family formation, is another feature of the choices made during the life cycle (e.g. BLS 2016; ABS 2017; SJ 2016). Preferences at various ages may vary somewhat, depending on culture and geographical region, but patterns are consistent with home and outward orientation at different stages of life (Martins et al. 2012).

10.7.3 Relative Affluence and Choices

Relative household affluence provides diverse scope for choices made in the consumption of good and services. In other words, the satisfaction of essential needs tends to limit household expenditure on other items. Thus, after the proportion of household expenditure on food, housing and utilities, and clothing and footwear is taken into account in India (urban households), Malaysia and United States, the remainder of the household budget for other consumer items is 38% in India, 45 in Malaysia and 50 in the United States (Table 10.25). With some variation, this pattern of household choices tends to hold across geographical areas and different stages of economic development (Martins et al. 2012).

The propensity to spend proportionately more or less on given types of consumer goods and services as income rises prevails not only across countries but also within them.

Examples from Australia, Japan and United States indicate consistent household choices for different types of consumer goods and services. Accordingly, the arc elasticity—a measure of the propensity to consume given items as income rises[1]—

---

[1]A fuller explanation of the concept and measurement of arc elasticity is provided in Martins et al. (2012), Box 8.2: 115–6.

Table 10.25 Household consumer expenditure, India, Malaysia and United States, circa 2012

Household consumer items	Consumer items as percentage of total		
	India (urban) 2011/12	Malaysia 2009/10	United States 2012
Food	42.6	29.2	15.0
Housing and utilities	12.9	22.6	30.8
Clothing and footwear	6.3	3.4	4.0
Other	38.2	44.8	50.2
All	100.0	100.0	100.0
GDP p.c. 2011 International $	4,883	21,075	49,854

Note The proportions of household expenditure for India are the average for households in urban areas, while those in Malaysia and United States are for all households. (GDP p.c. 2011 International $) is gross domestic product per head of population in 2011, at 2011 purchasing power parities (International dollars)
Sources NSSO (2014), DSM (2011), BLS (2014), UNDP (2014). Computations made by the authors

Table 10.26 Arc elasticity of selected household consumer items, Australia, Japan and United States, circa 2015

Household consumer items	Arc elasticity		
	Australia 2015/16	Japan 2015	United States 2015
Food	0.9	0.87	0.91
Housing	0.8	0.26	0.92
Alcohol beverages	1.16	0.75	1.22
Clothing and footwear	1.2	1.33	1.16
Transport	1.15	1.24	1.14
Education	1.37	1.99	1.18

Note The arc elasticity measures the propensity to consume for a given consumer item as household income rises. An arc elasticity of one indicates that the proportion spent on the given item remains constant at different levels of income. An arc elasticity of more than one means that the proportion spent on that items rises as household income increases, and less than one the inverse
Sources ABS (2017), SJ (2016), BLS (2016). Computations made by the authors

for basic goods and services such as food and housing in the three countries tends to fall as household income rises, while it increases in the case of alcoholic beverages,[2] clothing and footwear, transport and education (Table 10.26).

Similar progression is observed in less developed countries such as China. The experience in that country in 2005 was that the proportion spent by urban households on basic items such as food and housing fell as income rose, but the

---

[2]The arc elasticity for alcoholic beverages in Japan is affected by consumption of alcoholic beverages from *pocket money*, a miscellaneous item of household expenditure.

Table 10.27 Expenditure patterns of urban households by income quintiles in China, 2005

Household consumer items	Quintiles					Arc elasticity
	1st	2nd	3rd	4th	5th	
	Percentage of total household expenditure					
Food	46	42	39	36	31	0.71
Housing, dom. fuel, light and power	12	10	10	10	10	0.89
Household appliances and services	4	5	5	6	7	1.3
Clothing and footwear	9	10	11	11	10	1.06
Transport and communication	8	10	11	11	17	1.38
Medical services	7	7	8	8	7	1.00
Education and culture	12	13	14	14	15	1.13
Other	3	3	3	4	4	1.28

Note Arc elasticity as in Table 10.26. Quintiles represent household income distribution in ascending order
Source Martins et al. (2017)

proportion spent on transport and telecommunication, household appliances and services, education and culture, and clothing and footwear increased (Table 10.27).

This general progression pattern reflects both necessity and discretion afforded by varying levels of household disposable income.

10.8   Evolving and Transitional Socio-economic Development

Both technological change, including the important contribution of human capital, and related socio-economic organisation have been major factors in the substantial increases in productivity and enhanced standards of living. Major advancements in human capital have arisen from improvements in health and education embedded in people with a multigenerational dimension. Although major gaps continue to abound, substantial progress has been made in healthy living, education and training. Another feature of socio-economic development has been the growing participation of females in the formal sector of the labour force, but gaps continue to exist between the earnings of males and females, some of which have no clear explanation in terms of the characteristics of the labour market. There has also been a gap between labour productivity and earnings in more developed countries, which has led to a reduced share of labour income in gross domestic product. In spite of prevailing income inequality, an important aspect of the increase in productivity has been a reduction in the proportion and number of people living in extreme poverty in the world. Household consumer patterns are affected by income levels during the life cycle and their relationship to the hierarchy of human needs. Thus, the lower the household income the greater the proportion spent on food and other essential needs and less is left for discretionary spending on other consumer items. As household income rises the propensity to spend on food and other essentials tends to fall while the proportion of the household budget spent on such items as clothing and footwear, private transport and education tends to rise. These tendencies are found both in developed and less developed countries.

References

Australian Bureau of Statistics (ABS). (2011). *Household expenditure survey 2009–10—Summary.* Canberra.

Australian Bureau of Statistics (ABS). (2017). *Household expenditure survey 2015–16—Summary.* Canberra.

Becker, G. S. (1975). Investment in human capital: Effects and earnings. Chapter 2 (pp. 15–44). In G. S. Becker (Ed.), *Human capital: A theoretical and empirical analysis, with special reference to education.* National Bureau of Economic Research.

Becker, G. S. (1993). *Human capital: A theoretical and empirical analysis with special reference to education* (3rd ed.). Chicago: University of Chicago Press.

Bourdieu, P. (1986). The forms of capital. In J. Richardson (Ed.), *Handbook of theory and research for sociology of education* (pp. 241–258). New York: Greenwood.

Bureau of Labor Statistics (BLS). (2013). *Consumer expenditure in 2011.* BLS Reports, April 2013. United States Department of Labor. Retrieved December 18, 2017, from www.bls.gov.

Bureau of Labor Statistics (BLS). (2014). *Consumer expenditure in 2012.* BLS Reports, March 2014. United States Department of Labor. Retrieved December 18, 2017, from www.bls.gov.

Bureau of Labor Statistics (BLS). (2016). *Household expenditure survey 2015.* United States Department of Labor. Retrieved December 18, 2017, from www.bls.gov/cex/2015/combined/age.pdf.

Cai, L. (2010). The relationship between health and labour force participation: Evidence from a panel data simultaneous equation model. *Labour Economics, 17,* 77–90.

Center for Disease Control and Prevention (CDC). (2014). *Health and academic achievement.* Atlanta GA.

Currie, J. (2009). Healthy, wealthy, and wise: Socioeconomic status, poor health in childhood, and human capital development. *Journal of Economic Literature, 47*(1), 87–122.

Department of Statistics Malaysia (DSM). (2011). *Report on household expenditure survey 2009/10.* Putrajaya.

Devaux, M., & Sassi, F. (2015). *The labour market impacts of obesity, smoking, alcohol use and related chronic diseases.* OECD Health Working Papers No. 86. Paris: OECD.

Dewa, C., & McDaid, D. (2011). Investing in the mental health of the labor force: Epidemiological and economic impact of mental health disabilities in the workforce. In I. Schultz & S. Rogers (Eds.), *Work accommodation and retention in mental health* (pp. 33–51). Dordrecht: Springer.

Eide, E. R., & Showalter, M. H. (2011). Estimating the relation between health and education: What do we know and what do we need to know. *Economics of Education Review, 30,* 778–791.

Festinger, L., Schater, S., & Back, K. (1968). The spatial ecology of group formation. In H. Hyman & E. Singer (Eds.), *Readings in reference group theory and research* (pp. 268–277). New York: Free Press.

Forrest, C. B., Bevans, K. B., Riley, A. W., Crespo, R., & Louis, T. A. (2013). Health and School outcomes during children's transition into adolescence. *Journal of Adolescent Health, 52,* 186–194.

Gan, L., & Gong. G. (2007). *Estimating interdependence between health and education in a dynamic model.* Working Paper 12830. Cambridge MA: National Bureau of Economic Research.

Garcia-Gomez, P., Jones, A. M., & Rice, N. (2010). Health effects on labour market exists and entries. *Labour Economics, 17,* 62–76.

Glewwe, P., & King, E. M. (2001). The impact of early childhood nutritional status on cognitive development: Does the timing of malnutrition matter. *World Bank Economic Review, 15*(1), 81–113.

Government of India Planning Commission (GIPC). (2013). *Press note on poverty estimates, 2011–12.* New Delhi.

Guerrien, B., & Gun, O. (2015). Putting an end to the aggregate function of production… forever? *Real-World Economics Review, 73,* 99–109.

Hauser, R. (1971). *Socioeconomic background and educational performance.* American Sociological Association, Washington DC: Rose Monograph Series.

Hauser, R. (1973). Socioeconomic background and differential returns to education. In L. C. Solomon & P. J. Taubman (Eds.), *Does college matter? Some evidence on the impacts of higher education* (pp. 129–145). New York: Academic Press.

Hay, S. I. (2017). Global, regional, and national disability-adjusted life-years (DALYs) for 333 diseases and injuries and healthy life expectancy (HALE) for 195 countries and territories, 1990–2016: A systematic analysis for the Global Burden of Disease Study 2016. *Lancet, 390,* 1260–1344.

International Labour Organization (ILO). (2013). *Decent work indicators—Guidelines for producers and users of statistical and legal framework indicators.* Geneva: Second version.

International Labour Organization (ILO). (2014). *World employment trends—Trends 2014.* Geneva.

International Labour Organization (ILO). (2015). *Global wage report 2014–15.* Geneva.

International Labour Organization (ILO). (2016a). *World employment social outlook—Trends 2016.* Geneva.

International Labour Organization (ILO). (2016b). *Global wage report 2015–16.* Geneva.

International Labour Organization (ILO). (2017). *World employment social outlook—Trends for women 2017.* Geneva.

Kaplan, H. S., Hooper, P. L., & Gurven, M. (2009). The evolutionary and ecological roots of human social organization. *Philosophical Transactions of Royal Society B, 364,* 3289–3299. https://doi.org/10.1098/rstb.2009.0115.

Kapsos, S. (2007). *World and regional trends in labour force participation: Methodologies and key results.* Geneva: International Labour Organization.

Martins, J. M., Yusuf, F., & Swanson, D. A. (2012). *Consumer demographics and behaviour.* Dordrecht: Springer.

Martins, J. M., Yusuf, F., Brooks, G., & Swanson, D. A. (2017). Demographics and market segmentation: China and India. In D. A. Swanson (Ed.), *The frontiers of applied demography.* Dordrecht: Springer.

National Sample Survey Office (NSSO). (2014). *Household consumption of various goods and services in India, 2011–12.* New Delhi: Ministry of Statistics and Programme Implementation.

Nyaradi, A., Li, J., Hickling, S., Foster, J., & Oddy, W. (2013). The role of nutrition in children's neurocognitive development, from pregnancy through childhood. *Frontiers in Human Neuroscience, 7,* 97.

Office of National Statistics (ONS). (2016). *Household disposable income and inequality: Financial year ending 2015.* Retrieved December 15, 2017, from www.ons.gov.uk/peoplepopulationandcommunity/personalandhouseholddisposableincomeandinequality/financialyearending2015#main-points.

Office of the Registrar General and Census Commissioner (ORG). (2012). *Census of India 2011.* Retrieved December 18, 2017, from www.censusindia.gov.in.

Organisation for Economic Co-operation and Development (OECD). (undated). *OECD.Stat: LFS by age and sex, labour force participation rate – Indicators*. Paris. Retrieved December 7, 2017, from https://stats.oecd.org/Index.aspse?DataSetCode=LFS_SEXAGE_I_R.

Organisation for Economic Co-operation and Development (OECD). (2003). *The sources of economic growth in OECD countries*. Paris.

Organisation for Economic Co-operation and Development (OECD). (2010). *In it together, why less inequality benefits all*. Paris.

Organisation for Economic Co-operation and Development (OECD). (2015). *The high cost of low educational performance*. Paris.

Organisation for Economic Co-operation and Development (OECD). (2016). *Income distribution database (IDD): Gini, poverty and income*. Retrieved December 12, 2017, from www.oecd.org/social/income-distribution-database.hmt.

Organisation for Economic Co-operation and Development (OECD). (2017). *Education at a glance 2017*. Paris.

Pelkowski, J. M., & Berger, M. C. (2004). The impact of health on employment, wages, and hours worked over the life cycle. *Quarterly Review of Economics and Finance, 44,* 102–121.

Piketty, T. (2014). *Capital in the twenty-first century*. Translated by A. Goldhammer. Cambridge: Belknap Press of Harvard University Press.

Psacharopoulos, G. (1975). *Earnings and education in OECD countries*. Paris: Organisation for Economic Co-operation and Development.

Psacharopoulos, G., & Patrinos, H. A. (2004). Returns to investment in education: A further update. *Education Economics, 12*(2), 111–134.

Schultz, T. W. (1961). Investment in human capital. *American Economic Review, 51*(1), 1–17.

Smith, A. (1970 [1776]). The wealth of nations. In A. Skinner (Ed.). Harmondsworth: Penguin Books.

Solow, R. M. (1957). Technical change and the aggregate production function. *Review of Economics and Statistics, 39*(3), 312–320.

Statistics Japan (SJ). (2014). *Family income and expenditure survey, results of total household, 2013*. Tokyo: Ministry of Internal Affairs and Communication. Retrieved December 14, 2017, from www.stat.go.jp.

Statistics Japan (SJ). (2016). *Family income and expenditure survey, results of total household, 2015*. Tokyo: Ministry of Internal Affairs and Communication. Retrieved December 19, 2017, from www.stat.go.jp.

United Nations (UN). (2017). *World population prospects—The 2017 Revision* (Vol. I). New York.

United Nations Development Programme (UNDP). (2014). *Human development reports*. New York. Retrieved December 18, 2017, from http://hdr.undp.org/eng/content/gdp-per-capita-2011-ppp.

United Nations Development Programme (UNDP). (2016). *Human development report 2016*. New York.

United States Census Bureau (USCB). (2000*). Money income in the United States 1999*. Washington DC.

United States Census Bureau (USCB). (2016). *Income and poverty in the United States 2015*. Washington DC.

World Bank (WB). (2012). *World development report 2012*. Washington DC.

World Bank (WB). (2017). *World Bank data*. Retrieved December 11, 2017, from www.data.worldbank.org.

Chapter 11
Population and the Environment

11.1 Widening Perspectives

Population size and growth poses an ecological riddle that has persisted throughout human history. The discussion of issues has changed as understanding of the complexity of the ecological system evolves. Controversy continues to prevail when previous experience does not match current circumstances; or knowledge is lagging on the interaction of population size, human activity, its related socioeconomic organisation and their possible impact on the environment; or on the feedback loops on human life and potential survival. The 20th century experienced what Kingsley Davis (1945) described as a *population explosion:* the world's population that had grown by one half in the 50-year period 1900–1950 grew by more than two fold in the following 50 years from 1950 to 2000 (Table 1.3). This was obviously a new experience in terms of its dimensions and pace of change and concerns with population size and growth moved on. The progression has gone from fears with carrying capacity issues, such as food production and limited non-renewable resources to the impact of human activity on climate change (Table 11.1).

The Kyoto Convention on climate change of 1998 aimed to reduce the emission of greenhouse gases (GHGs), as well as other activities with a perceived impact on climate change, reflected these concerns (UN 2001). Additional commitments were made by the adoption of the Paris Agreement in 2015 (UN 2015). Discussions continue on what is the impact of human activity on climate change and potential consequences on life on Earth (IPCC 2014).

Earlier discussions of population size were often framed in terms of carrying capacity. Malthus' famous essay on population was a response to propositions on the limits to population growth by Goodwin, Condorcet, Smith and Price. Malthus was worried by carrying capacity in terms of the difference between the perceived arithmetic growth rate of food production and the geometric growth rate of population (Chap. 2: Sect. 2.5.1). Malthus' qualms were that limited food production and

© Springer International Publishing AG, part of Springer Nature 2018
Jo. M. Martins et al., *Global Population in Transition*,
https://doi.org/10.1007/978-3-319-77362-9_11

Table 11.1 Evolution of concerns with population 1940–2000s

Time	Concerns	Issues
1940–1950s	*Limited natural resources*	Inadequate food production and depletion of non-renewable resource
1960–1970s	*By-products of production and consumption*	Air/water pollution, waste disposal and radioactive/chemical contamination
1980–1990s	*Global environmental change*	Climate change, acid rain and ozone depletion
2000s	*Global environmental change*	Biodiversity, genetic engineering, deforestation, water management, migration, emerging/re-emerging diseases and globalisation

Source UN (2001)

higher fertility would result in *human misery* and *vice*. Malthus did not anticipate the decline in fertility due to the use of new contraception technology that took hold in the later part of the 20th century (Morgan 2003). Further, the population growth experienced in the 20th century was preceded by earlier improvements in food production that included the use of a wider range of crops from and land use in the New World, as well as the *Green Revolution* in the second half of the 1900s (Brown 1970).

Neo-Malthusian concerns expressed by Ehrlich (1969) and later Meadows et al. (1972) were not only about resource depletion but also the impact of pollution that was considered unsustainable. Meadows' modelling took into consideration the role of technology but gave cautionary advice: *...Faith in technology as the ultimate solution to all problems can divert our attention from the most fundamental problem—the problem of growth in a finite system—and prevent us from taking effective action to solve it* (Meadows et al. 1972: 154). They advocated *zero-population growth* or a *stationary population* as suggested by John Stuart Mill more than a century earlier (Chapter 2: Sects. 2.5.2, 2.7.3 and 2.7.4).

Ehrlich themes could be translated into a simple model of the impact of population on the environment (AAAS 2017; Sherbini et al. 2007).

$$I = P * A * T$$

I Impact on the environment
P Population
A Affluence expressed as consumption per person
T Technology.

A more specific version is

$$I = P * C * Tr * Tw * S$$

P Population
C Consumption per person

Tr   Technology resource use
Tw   Technology of waste management
S   Environmental changes for unit of resource extraction or pollution.

The model does not represent the impact on the environment. It takes resource use or pollution as surrogates for environmental harm. As in many other models, the assumptions made to calibrate each factor are real challenges, as is the interaction between each independent variable.

The Neo-Malthusian warnings caused responses from some who perceived there were vested interests by scholars dealing with *phony bad news*. For instance, Simon questioned some of the assertions made about scarcity of food and other resources, as well as the negative impact of population growth on standards of living: ...*Some publicise dire predications in the idealistic belief that such warnings can mobilize institutions and individuals to make things even better; they think that nothing bad can come of such prophecies. But we should not shrug off false bad news as harmless exaggerations. There will be a loss of credibility for real threats as they arise, and a loss of public trust in public communication* (Simon 1980: 1437).

Boserup (1965) followed a different path from the Neo-Malthusians and posited that population growth led to more intensified agricultural production and more efficient land use. Cornucopian propositions suggest that human productivity, market and production substitution will tend to avoid or compensate for resource exhaustion. The problems encountered are the result of market failures and the use of unsuitable technologies (Sherbini et al. 2007).

Some theses relate inequality among and within countries and poverty to the population impact on the environment. Poverty leads to high fertility as insurance for old age and labour. However, pressure on land leads to migration and the clearing of forests for agricultural purposes. Inequality between countries may lead to resource extraction in poorer tropical countries for the maintenance of higher consumption in more developed countries (Sherbini et al. 2007).

The Environmental Kuznets Curve (EKC) is controversial. It suggests that as economic growth takes place, environmental degradation rises but it tends to fall as economic growth continues and takes hold. This results in an inverted U-curve relationship between income per capita and environmental damage. A study of the ambient pollution levels in Mexico City and a number of other cities indicated that pollution levels peaked when economies reached the level of Mexico. The assumption was made that further economic growth led to lower pollution levels. Data and methods used have led to a range of findings from confirmation of the inverted U-curve between income and levels of pollution, while others found that it applied to some types of pollutants but not others. Other factors such as deforestation and use of different technologies for power production are variables thought to be important in the comparisons of pollution levels. Another possible factor is the international transfer of polluting industries from more to less developed countries, as economic development takes place (Stern et al. 1996; Stern 2014).

The controversial Stern (2006) review on the economic impact of climate change posed a challenge to *business-as-usual* practices (BAU) of economic activity associated with a growing population. Its dire predication of considerable economic losses under BAU and potential for change and containment at a comparatively low economic cost were the subject of both support and dispute (Box 11.1).

Box 11.1 Stern review of the economics of climate change

The Stern (2006) review of the economics of climate change was a major landmark in the discussion of the impact of human activity on climate change. Its findings and methods were supported by some and criticised by others. A basic precept of the review was that the ...*economics of climate change is shaped by the science*. This implies that economic assessment is dependent on the uncertainty of scientific knowledge at any point in time. In spite of uncertainties about the risks involved, the review arrived at the conclusion that evidence from then current scientific knowledge was that climate change was a considerable threat and would affect water and food supplies, cause health and environmental problems that would lead to flooding of coastal areas and hunger among millions of people. It stressed that people in more developed countries would be affected by the global impact of climate change, but those in less developed countries would suffer most.

Although the review dealt with other aspects of climate change, one major focus was on greenhouse gas (GHGs) emissions. It estimated that, in the year 2000, the sources of GHGs emissions were:

	Percentage
Power generation	24
Transport	14
Industry	14
Buildings	8
Other energy related	5
Energy emissions	65%
Land use	18
Agriculture	14
Waste	3
Non-energy emissions	35%
All sources	100%

This meant that about two thirds of the GHG emissions came from energy generation by technologies often based on the burning of fossil fuels such as coal and oil, for industrial and transport activities that are the foundation of industrialised economies. Based on scientific information available, it was asserted that the adoption of a business-as-usual (BAU) behaviour towards GHG emissions would lead to irreversible concentrations of carbon dioxide (CO_2), methane (CH_4), nitrous oxide (N_2O) and other greenhouse gases. That would result in rising temperatures, changes in weather patterns, ocean acidity, melting of ice sheets and glaciers, flooding of coastal and other areas, changes in crop yields and possible impact on soils and forests. The review commented on the increase in the concentration of GHGs of about 280 parts per million (*ppm*) of CO_2 equivalent (*e*) before the Industrial Revolution to the then estimated current level of 430 ppm CO_2e. It proposed that BAU would lead to 550 ppm CO_2e by 2035, with at least a 77% chance of an increase in the average world temperature of 2° Centigrade. Further, BAU could result in 550–700 ppm CO_2e by 2050, and possibly 650–1200 ppm CO_2e by 2100. It was proposed that if GHG levels in the future reached 1000 ppm CO_2e they would result in 3–10 °C warming. This was a level said to be outside human experience.

The review took the position that stabilisation of around 550 ppm CO_2e was possible and desirable with appropriate mitigation and adaption measures. It assessed that lack of action would lead to an annual 5% loss of gross domestic product (GDP), and that if wider range of risk and damage was considered, the estimate might be at least 20% of GDP. While, it was estimated that the cost of intervention to limit concentration levels at 550 ppm CO_2e would cost about 1% of GDP. It was implicit that the longer the period of inaction the higher the remedial cost.

The stabilisation process envisaged that annual emissions of GHGs would be reduced to about 60–80% of then current levels. This would involve the decarbonising of the power generation sector by 60% by 2050. A related issue was the reduction of deforestation, improved agricultural practices and the development of carbon capture and storage. Further, the review advocated the practice of placing a price on carbon emissions to provide incentives for the adoption of effective technologies and practices, and possibly provide revenue for the implementation of mitigation action.

Stern's findings were the object of criticism on scientific and economic grounds by a number of scientists and economists (e.g. Carter et al. 2006). An issue raised was the scientific basis of the report that relied to some extent on the Intergovernmental Panel on Climate Change (IPCC) to which some objected. It was contended that much of the information used relied on model estimates rather than actual measurements, and that the review was selective in their choices from the wide range of options. Criticism was levelled at the association between levels of CO_2 accumulation and rises in temperatures that critics found too high and not based on actual measurement. The review was also seen to gloss over the possibility of lower population growth than that it used for the year 2100, with implications for consumption levels and population densities. Other criticisms relate to the lack of acknowledgement of technological change that inevitably would take place in agriculture and other modes of production that would have an impact on both food supply and emissions of GHGs. As the scientific base of the economic assessment was deemed flawed, the economic findings were found deficient. Further, criticisms were levelled at the economic analysis and assessment itself. It was asserted that the costs of damages in a BAU situation were exaggerated and that the costs of mitigation were too low. The selection of the rate of discount and method of its use in the assessment were deemed to be inappropriate, and that the use of different discount rates would, of course, result in different economic assessments. Both the review and its critics stimulated efforts to clarify and further the extent of relevant scientific knowledge and the ethical and other issues involved in the economic impact of climate change.

11.2   Environmental Conundrum: Population and Economic Growth

A crucial issue is the inevitable growth in population during the 21st century and the objective of raising the living standards of the largest proportion of the world's population who live in less developed countries. Population growth rates have declined since 1970s (Table 1.7), and they are projected to fall further to the year 2100 (Table 1.15). The projected increase of more than 4,000 million people in the period 2010–2100 is attributed mostly to population momentum generated by the population explosion of the 20th century (Table 11.2). The projection indicates that population momentum will have a negative effect on population growth in more developed countries, as the population transition experienced by them affected their

Table 11.2 Contributions to world population growth by demographic component

Demographic component	Percentage contribution of demographic components population increase 2010–2100 country development stage		
	More developed	Less developed	World
Momentum	−5.2	33.9	26.9
Mortality	11.5	17.4	16.3
Fertility	−23.9	21.7	13.8
Migration	21.1	−4.3	–
All	3.3	68.6	56.9

Note The projected additions to population could be expressed by the equality $\Delta P = P_y + P_{mor} + P_f + P_{mig}$. ($\Delta P$) is the increase in population; (P_y) is the increase in population due to population momentum (age distribution that affects birth and death rates); (P_{mor}) is the increase in population due to declining mortality; (P_f) is the increase in population due to fertility above replacement level; (P_{mig}) is the increase in population due to net migration
Source Andreev et al. (2013)

age distribution with a consequent decline in fertility, only partly compensated by migration from less developed countries and lower mortality. Population momentum will be the single major component of population growth in less developed countries, and the major driver in the world's population growth during the 21st century.

Past population growth has demanded larger food production to maintain and improve levels of nutrition, especially in developing countries where most people live. This has been associated with deforestation and land use for agriculture that impacted on the role of forests as carbon sinks. The Green Revolution that helped to increase the production of food required higher use of fertilisers and insecticides that if not managed adequately can have deleterious effects on water quality, animal and human health. Efforts to raise food production have also affected fishing and, in some cases, depleted fish stocks. Thus, growth in food production for a larger number of people has posed environmental issues. In addition to greater agricultural and fishing activity, there have also been rises in the level of and changes in the type of industrial production, as the basis of economic development to maintain and raise living standards. The Industrial Revolution and coupled technological changes relied to a great extent on the substitution of human brawn and animal strength by other forms of energy. A synthesis of this complex development attributed to Earl Cook has been described by Livi-Bacci (2017: 23): hunters and gatherers (starting with the emergence of modern humans between 300,000 and 200,000 ago) consumed about 5,000 calories per capita, which increased to about 12,000 calories per capita with the agricultural revolution (between 10,000 and 6,000 years ago) and increased to at least 70,000 per capita following the industrial revolution (between 200 and 150 years ago), and, which, in some contemporaneous now exceeds 200,000 calories per capita. As suggested by the immense increase that came with the industrial revolution, these forms of energy increasingly entailed the burning of fossil fuels, such as coal and oil products. Thence, an association between the growth in gross domestic product (GDP) and energy production, that is in turn linked with the burning of fossil fuels and the accumulative emission of greenhouse gases, mostly carbon dioxide (CO_2). These associations have led to a new formulation of the Ehrlich's IPAT proposition known as the *Kaya identity*:

$$F = P \ * \ (GDP/P) \ * \ (E/GDP) \ * \ (F/E) = P \ * \ g \ * \ e \ * \ f$$

F   global emissions of CO_2
P   global population
GDP   global gross domestic product
E   global energy production.

In this context, (GDP/P) is GDP per capita or (*g*), (E/GDP) is the *energy intensity* of GDP (*e*) and (F/E) is the *CO_2 intensity* of energy production (*f*). The equality can be reduced to

$$F = P * (GDP/P) * (F/GDP) = P * g * h$$

(F/GDP) is the *carbon intensity of GDP (h)* that is the combined effect of both the *energy intensity of GDP (e)* and the *carbon intensity of energy production (f)*.

The equality can also be expressed in terms of proportional growth rates:

$$r(F) = r(P) + r(g) + r(h)$$

r (F)   rate of growth of F
r (P)   rate of growth of P
r (g)   rate of growth of (GDP/P)
r (h)   rate of growth of (F/GDP).

(Raupach et al. 2007)

It is important to state the obvious: carbon is an essential element in animal and plant life and carbon dioxide is a greenhouse gas that keeps atmospheric conditions for life on the planet. However, the critical question is one of balance, as too much of an essential element may have harmful effects. Among other things, as might be expected, Raupach et al. (2007) found that in 2004 the level of energy used per head of population was considerably higher in more than less developed countries, including China and India. This was reflected in the greater energy intensity of GDP (*e*) in more developed countries. In general, the carbon efficiency of energy production tended to be higher in more than less developed countries. Nevertheless, one result of the substantially higher GDP per capita (*g*) in more than less developed countries was that: more developed countries with about 20% of the population (*P*) accounted for 59% of emissions (*F*). It was estimated that emissions rose substantially in more developed countries during the period 1980–2004, in spite of slow growth in population, reductions in the energy intensity of GDP (*e*), and stable carbon intensity of energy (*f*), because of the rapid GDP per capita (*g*) growth during the period. In most of the less developed countries, population and GDP per capita growth resulted in large emissions growth that was higher than the growth in GDP per capita. China and India showed some improvement in energy intensity of GDP (*e*). Nevertheless, China with a low rate of population growth and India with a higher one both experienced a high level of growth in emissions from growth in GDP per capita and the high carbon intensity of GDP (*h*).

The outcome of these trends was that in 2004, more developed countries contributed to most of the emissions but least to their rate of growth, while less developed countries with a lower proportion of total emissions had a much higher rate of emission growth. In the context of the cumulative nature of CO_2 emissions from anthropogenic activity from the burning of fossil fuels and land use since the Industrial Revolution, it was estimated that about half of the emissions have been stored in land and ocean as carbon sinks, the remaining other half has accumulated in the atmosphere. In spite of the growing rate of emissions by less developed countries, it was estimated that they have contributed only about one quarter (23%)

of the accumulated CO_2 emissions since the Industrial Revolution, while more developed countries were responsible for about three quarters (77%).

The estimates of GHG emission in 2010 by sector (Fig. 11.1) show the growing importance of industry in comparison with the estimate made by the Stern review (Box 11.1), the impact of industrial growth in less developed countries, and the continuing importance of transport both at national and international levels.

These earlier warnings of the lack of success in reducing CO_2 emissions from energy and other forms of production and transport, and the continuing accumulation of carbon in the atmosphere were confirmed by the Intergovernmental Panel on Climate Change (IPCC)'s fifth assessment revision (AR5) (2014). The IPCC estimated that anthropogenic greenhouse gases emissions in CO_2 equivalent rose by 80% in period 1970–2010 and that 76% of GHG emissions were in the form of CO_2. Further, it found that GHG emissions reached their highest level ever in the decade 2000–2010. It pointed out that the small reduction of emissions in more developed countries in 2000–2010 were due to the transfer of production and related emissions to less developed countries for products consumed in more developed countries. Accordingly, the rise in GHG emissions in less developed countries arose not only from their own rise in consumption but also partly by the growing export of products for consumption in more developed countries. Concerns with climate change have led to the setting of targets for reductions in GHG emissions postulated to keep the rising of world temperatures within 2 °C. This has been designated as the *decarbonisation* of energy production associated with GDP per capita (p.c.). Inevitable additions to the world's population during the 21st century, proposed growth in GDP p.c. to improve living standards in less developed countries, the bond between GDP p.c. and energy use and the carbon intensity of energy production raise important issues: how the goal of keeping GHG emissions

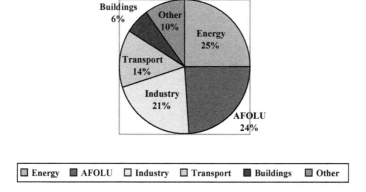

Fig. 11.1 World greenhouse emissions by sector, percentage, 2010
Note The total world greenhouse gases emissions were estimated as 49 Gt CO_2 equivalent in 2010; (Gt) is giga tons, (giga) is 10^9; (CO_2 equivalent) are emissions of CO_2 and other greenhouse gases, such as methane (CH_4) and nitrous oxides (N_xO) converted into CO_2 global warming potential over 100 years; (FOLU) are emissions from agriculture, forests and other land use
Source IPCC (2014)

in line with the target of containing the world temperature within 2 °C can be achieved. These issues have *intergenerational* and *inter-country* dimensions. The first arises from the gap between the time that benefits from higher GDP p.c. are felt and the time that it takes for the accumulation of GHG emissions to impact on climate. The second is an upshot from the inequality of standards of living that prevail among countries, and even within countries.

The higher standard of living of current and future generations reflect investments in infrastructure and human capital made by people who lived in the past and contributed to the accumulation of GHG emissions. However, they are in the past and the current generation who benefits from them cannot compensate them. Another question is whether the current generation should pay for the cost of reducing GHG emissions for the benefit of future generations. This is the crux of the issue and if no significant action takes place under BAU conditions, as the IPCC findings indicate, GHGs will continue to accumulate beyond the set target to keep world's temperature within the 2 °C margin of increase by the year 2100.

Another question is: while more developed countries enjoy the gains of past and current higher GHG emissions, why should people in less developed countries constrain their GDP p.c. growth coupled with increases in energy use and emissions. Their constraint would diminish the rate of global GHG accumulation at a cost to themselves but the benefit would be felt globally, including by people in more developed countries.

Further, gains from the production of goods and services that add to GHG accumulation may accrue to given individuals, corporations and countries, but the impact of the accumulated emissions affects not only them but others who may not have shared in the gains from the emissions. This is similar to the old proposition of the privatisation of gains and socialisation of costs. It is also akin to the nature of *public goods* in economics, where the actions of some individuals benefit others who did not contribute to them, thus giving rise to so called *free riders*. Markets cannot deal with such issues that are labelled *market failures* that include equity issues, especially if the intergeneration dimension is considered.

The IPCC (2014) suggested that ...*Climate change is a global commons problem... Because the GHG emissions of any agent (individual, company, country) affect every other agent, an effective outcome will not be achieved if individual agents advance their interests independently of others. International cooperation can contribute by defining and allocating rights and responsibilities with respect to the atmosphere...* (IPCC 2014: 38).

11.3 Environment Domains and Human Activity

Human survival depends on land, water and air endowments: the three domains of the environment. This dependency entails an interactive relationship: people benefit from their activity and use of the domain endowments but this very same activity results in changes to the environment. These changes have feed back loops on

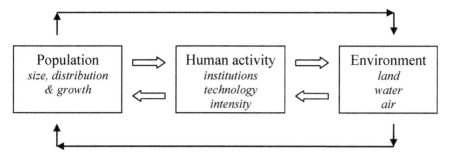

Fig. 11.2 Population, environment and human activity
Source Adapted from Hunter (2001)

people that affect their way of living and quality of life, such as the deleterious effects of wastes on people, contamination of the air they breathe from pollution, and possible climate change (Fig. 11.2).

Some of the consequences of human activity on land, water and air use have been documented and some of their effects on people have also been established. Nevertheless, as stated, there continues to be limited knowledge of the relationships between human activity and the environment and potential consequences for both the environment and people. In addition to the limited scientific knowledge, there is insufficient relevant measurement of the nature and intensity of the impact of human activity on the environment. The IPCC (2014) report of its fifth assessment revision (AR5) lists some of these shortcomings. Nevertheless, there is evidence of the import of population growth and human activity to changes in land, water and air. It is apparent that population growth is a major factor in the changes of the environment. However, the major driver is the growth in the level of human activity as per GDP growth: the world's population increased by more than 2 times from 1950 to 2000 (Table 1.5) but the world's GDP rose 7 fold in the same period (Table 1.19), or about 3 times more than the increase in population.

11.4 Population, Land and the Environment

11.4.1 Land Use: Agriculture and Forests

Agriculture is the human activity that uses the largest proportion of land: 38% in 2014. The proportion of land used by agriculture increased somewhat since 1990 (37%) while that of forest declined by about the same proportion from 32 to 31% (Table 11.3). This reflected continuing deforestation, but at a lower rate than observed in the past. Earlier deforestation took place mostly in temperate climates in Europe, Asia and North America, as forests were converted to agricultural purposes that were later reversed in some cases, such as in Europe. More recently,

Table 11.3 World land use by type, 1990–2014

Land use	Percentage of all			
	1990	2000	2010	2014
Agriculture	37.0	38.1	37.4	37.7
Forest	31.6	31.2	30.9	30.8
Other	31.4	30.7	31.7	31.5
All	100.0	100.0	100.0	100.0

Note (Other) was estimated as the residual after the proportions of agriculture and forest estimated by FAO were summed; there is the possibility that some land can be used for more than one purpose
Source FAO (2017a). Computations made by the authors

deforestation has taken place mostly in tropical forest areas, like those of Brazil, Indonesia and Nigeria (Sherbini et al. 2007).

The analysis of land use by region for the period 1990–2014 reveals an uneven pattern in the change of land use for agricultural purposes (Table 11.4). A substantial proportional increase took place in Asia (+5%) with smaller proportional increments in Africa (+1%) and Americas (+1%), but there was a considerable proportional decline in Europe (−8%) and Oceania (−7%). The additions in the proportions of land use for agriculture in Africa and Americas were partly due to losses in the proportions of forests. Nevertheless, forest losses were almost double the gains of agriculture. This indicates that there are other factors in the losses by forests that may involve logging for timber, fuel and other purposes. Asia's proportional increment in land use for agriculture was well above the losses in the proportion of forests. This may be due to land used for more than one purpose or additions from land previously employed for other purposes. The decrease in the

Table 11.4 World land use by type and region, 1990–2014

	Percentage of all					
	Africa	Americas	Asia	Europe	Oceania	World
1990						
Agriculture	36.8	30.5	48.2	29.1	56.9	37.0
Forest	23.8	43.4	20.5	37.8	20.8	31.6
Other	39.4	26.1	31.3	33.1	22.3	31.4
All	100.0	100.0	100.0	100.0	100.0	100.0
2014						
Agriculture	38.2	31.7	53.2	21.2	49.5	37.7
Forest	21.2	41.1	19.1	45.9	20.4	30.8
Other	40.6	27.2	27.7	32.9	30.1	31.5
All	100.0	100.0	100.0	100.0	100.0	100.0

Note (Other) was estimated as the residual after the proportions of agriculture and forest estimated by FAO were summed; there is the possibility that some land can be used for more than one purpose; there is also the question of the high land use in Oceania, mostly Australia; This might arise by quasi pastoral use of desert lands and decline in that classification
Source FAO (2017a). Computations made by the authors

proportion of land for agriculture in Europe matches closely the gains in forests. The changes in the proportion of land use for agriculture in Oceania took place without much change in the proportion of land used for forests. The substantial decline in the proportion used for agriculture in Oceania might have risen by discontinuing the use of quasi desert land in Australia for grazing.

Although not as substantial as in the past, the continuing deforestation in some regions of the world, not entirely compensated by forest gains in Europe, reduces capacity to use forests as carbon sinks for growing GHG emissions and adds to emissions by the burning and other disposition of fallen trees (Bredemeier 2002).

A major source of additional agricultural production is the use of non-organic fertilizers and pesticides. Accordingly, the global use of nitrogen, phosphate and potash fertilisers increased in the period 2002–2014. There are substantial regional differences in fertiliser use. Africa with more traditional agricultural practices employs the lowest levels of non-organic fertilisers, while Asia with emphasis on rice cultivation has the largest application of all three types of fertilisers. In addition to the high rate of use, Asia also has the largest rate of growth in the use of fertilisers by hectare (Table 11.5). The improved yields from the non-organic fertilisers have increased food production for the growing population but they have had an environmental cost. The use and overuse of non-organic fertilisers and pesticides has had an effect on water pollution and the enrichment of freshwater by inorganic nutrients that have resulted in excessive algae growth (eutrophication), as well as the loss of wildlife and plant biodiversity (AAAS 2017).

Another aspect of agricultural production is irrigation, especially in Asia (Table 11.6). Most of the additions to agricultural land in the last few decades have

Table 11.5 World non-organic fertiliser use by region, 2002–2014

Year	Fertiliser use kilograms per hectare					
	Africa	Americas	Asia	Europe	Oceania	World
Nitrogen						
2002	11.3	44.8	86.0	43.7	26.0	53.9
2014	14.5	59.0	113.2	52.0	35.3	68.8
Percentage change	28.3	7.1	31.7	7.3	12.3	5.9
Phosphate						
2002	4.3	22.2	34.4	13.6	30.2	22.5
2014	5.5	30.2	49.4	12.0	28.7	29.5
Percentage change	27.9	36.0	43.6	−11.8	−5.0	31.1
Potash						
2002	2.0	22.2	21.3	17.5	7.6	17.4
2014	2.3	28.9	36.9	14.2	5.8	23.8
Percentage change	15.0	30.2	73.2	−18.9	−23.7	36.8

Source FAO (2017a); computations made by the authors

Table 11.6 World agricultural land specifically equipped for irrigation by region, 1990–2014

Region	Percentage of agricultural land specifically equipped for irrigation		
	1990	2000	2014
Africa	1.0	1.2	1.4
Americas	3.8	4.0	4.3
Asia	12.4	11.8	14.2
Europe	5.1	5.5	5.6
Oceania	0.4	0.6	0.8
World	5.3	5.8	6.8

Source FAO (2017a)

been for irrigated crops (FAO 2011). A feature of the rise of irrigated land is the use of ground water that is difficult to replenish. It was estimated that agriculture consumes about 70% of all fresh water resources (FAO 2014).

Irrigation of marginal lands has placed pressure on water resources and has had an impact on soil degradation and salinization. For instance, this has been a major environmental problem in the Murray-Darling basin in Australia: acid sulphate soils, algal blooms and possible climate change have been identified as major problems in that basin as the result of irrigation (MDBA 2014).

The rise in food production and associated technologies resulted in substantial increases in GHG emissions from agriculture in the period 1970–2014 (Table 11.7). Growth in emissions was particularly high in Asia, the Americas and Africa, with an actual decline in Europe that reduced the proportion of its land dedicated to agriculture (Table 11.4). Asia with the world's largest proportion of people to feed also had the largest share of emissions. However, its share of emissions from agriculture was lower than its proportion of the world's population in 2014. The Americas and Oceania shares of emissions were substantial larger than their

Table 11.7 World greenhouse emissions from agriculture by region, 1970–2014

Year	Emissions CO$_2$e Gigagrams					
	Africa	Americas	Asia	Europe	Oceania	World
1970	289,063	836,367	1,173,408	807,185	149,823	3,255,846
1990	569,253	1,092,086	1,715,571	988,718	207,111	4,572,738
2010	794,509	1,302,315	2,258,577	572,990	149,094	5,077,485
2014	833,533	1,322,447	2,313,435	588,317	188,071	5,245,823
Percentage 2014						
Emissions	15.9	25.2	44.1	11.2	3.6	100.0
Population	16.2	13.4	59.9	10.0	0.5	100.0
Increase 2014						
1970 = 1.000	2.884	1.581	1.972	0.729	1.255	1.611

Note (Gigagram) is 10^9 grams. (CO$_2$ e) are emissions of carbon dioxide (CO$_2$) and other greenhouse gases, such as methane (CH$_4$) and nitrous oxides (N$_x$O) converted into CO$_2$ global warming potential over 100 years. Population as at 2015
Source FAO (2017a), UN (2017). Computations made by the authors

fractions of the world population. Africa and Europe shares were closely related to their proportions of the world's population (Table 11.7). Although agriculture is not the major source of GHG emissions, it makes a substantial contribution to the accumulation of GHGs in the atmosphere. Particular aspects of agricultural emissions are those from livestock. It was estimated that yearly emissions from livestock accounted for 14% of the global anthropogenic GHGs in CO_2 equivalent. While CO_2 from livestock made up 5% of the global anthropogenic CO_2 emissions, methane (CH_4) emissions represented 44% of the global total, and emissions of nitrous dioxide (N_2O) from livestock made up 53% of global emissions (FAO 2013). The use of nitrogen in crop production has also added to nitrous dioxide emissions with an effect on soil and water quality, as well as the atmosphere (FAO 2003).

Continuing deforestation is mostly for crop and livestock purposes but also for paper and other wood-based products. In addition, millions of people continue to rely on wood burning as a source of fuel for domestic cooking and heating. These have a direct effect on the environment from the release of CO_2 from the burning of vegetation and other processes, but there is also a loss of the size of the carbon sink provided by shrinking forests. Forests provide a degree of soil stability and water retention that are lost with deforestation that may result in soil erosion and loss of ground water, especially in areas with unstable soils. Further, deforestation tends to be associated with a loss of biodiversity of plants and animals that have forests as their habitat (FAO 2009).

11.4.2   Land Use: Mining

Mining makes a major contribution to industrialisation and economic growth. It provides much of the raw materials for the manufacture of commodities and fossil fuels for the energy required for industrial production, transport and domestic use. Building infrastructure of the socioeconomic system has relied on large input of cement and steel. Their production is based on mining of lime and other cement components and iron ore, and requires high energy levels usually provided by burning fossil fuels, such as coal.

As in the case of agricultural production, mining and the raw materials extracted come at an environmental cost. They are different but significant both in the case of underground and surface mining. Environmental costs occur during exploration, operation and after mine closure. During exploration, heavy vehicles and drilling equipment need usually to gain access that leads to land clearing for roads and site preparation. This may also involve the burning of covering vegetation and GHG emissions. Both in underground and surface mining, miners usually need to reach below the watertable and pump out and store ground water. There may also be the release of methane that could be used for power production but is often released into the atmosphere. Further, mineral ores constitute only a small proportion of the soil that is removed, especially in the case of open mining. It has been estimated that 60% of the soil extracted for iron ore is wasted, 70% in the extraction for manganese, and more than 99% for tungsten, zinc and gold (AAAS 2017). These waste piles are usually accumulated close by the mining site. Both the water reservoirs and the waste piles created may contain toxic substances that leak and result in the contamination of streams and soil cover, with deleterious consequences to animal life and vegetation. Milling, leaching and other methods of ore improvement usually entail the release of toxic materials with detrimental effect on the environment. The refining of ores, as in copper smelters, can also result in environmental problems that affect human health, other life and agricultural production (Borregaard and Dufey 2002).

11.4.3   Population Growth, Industrial and Service Production

Agriculture and mining have been basic in rising living standards of the growing global population. Some of their outputs are used for direct household consumption. However, most of mining and a significant proportion of agricultural outputs are inputs for industrial processes and rely heavily on transport and other services, for their final use as items for household consumption or investments in infrastructure. The level of human activity as expressed by gross domestic product indicates that most of the global GDP is related to industrial and service production (WB 2017a). As in previous times since the Industrial Revolution (Table 1.20), global GDP rose substantially faster than population in the period 2001–2015, and GDP per head of population about doubled during that 14-year period. The rate of growth per head of population in middle income countries, such as China and India, was considerably higher (7% p.a.) than that of low income countries (4% p.a.) and about double that of high income countries (3% p.a.) (Table 11.8).

The growth in industrial production and supporting transport demanded greater energy supplies that increased by more than two fold. Most of the increase in energy supply to support industrial and other human activity was fed by fossil fuels that made up 80% of the fuels used in 2014. In the period 1973–2014, both coal

Table 11.8 World gross domestic product by country income level, 2001 and 2015

Country income level	GDP p.c.		2015 GDP p.c. 2001 = 1.000	GDP p.c. yearly growth percentage
	2001	2015		
Low	894	1,636	1.830	4.3
Middle	4,318	10,902	2.635	6.9
High	28,821	45,758	1.588	3.3
World	8,196	15,675	1.913	4.6

Note (GDP p.c.) is the average gross domestic product per head of population in international dollars, purchasing power parities 2011
Source WB (2017b); computations made by the authors

Table 11.9 World total primary energy supply by fuel type, 1973 and 2014

Fuel type	Percentage of TPES		Percentage change 2014 − 1973
	1973	2014	
Oil	46.2	31.3	−14.9
Coal	24.5	28.6	4.1
Natural gas	16.0	21.2	5.2
Biofuels and waste	10.5	10.3	−0.2
Nuclear	0.9	4.8	3.9
Hydro	1.8	2.4	0.6
Other	0.1	1.4	1.3
All: million tonnes of oil equivalent	6,101	13,699	124.5

Note (TPES) Total primary energy supply is all energy production including international marine and aviation fuel bunkers; it is expressed in terms of the gross calorific value of million tonnes of oil equivalent (Mtoe)
Source IEA (2016). Computations made by the authors

(+4%) and natural gas (+5%) increased their proportion of the larger global fuel supply, while there was a major decline in the proportion of oil (−15%) (Table 11.9).

Although more developed countries (OECD) continued to have the largest total primary energy supply (TPES) (38%) of a much greater global supply in 2014, a major feature of the increase in energy supply was the decline in their proportion of energy supply since 1973 (OECD −23%). This was partly due to the transfer of manufacturing of commodities consumed in more developed countries to less developed ones (Sect. 11.2). The substantial increase in China's proportion of energy supply (+15%) was associated with its continuing high rate of growth in the output of manufactured goods for both domestic and for export to other markets. Similar factors influenced the significant rise in the proportion of energy supply in other Asian countries (Table 11.10).

The *energy intensity of GDP* growth and the *carbon intensity of energy* resulted in the doubling of the global CO_2 emissions from fuel combustion in the period of 1973–2014. In line with the changes in the shares of all fuels combusted, the proportion of CO_2 emissions from oil declined considerably (−16%) while those of coal (+10%) and natural gas (+5%) rose (Table 11.11).

As would be expected from the pattern in TPES, the share of CO_2 emissions from fuel combustion in more developed countries (OECD) continued be the largest (37%) in 2014 while that of China's (28%) was the second major share of global emissions of CO_2. Other Asian countries (12%) and Non-OECD countries in Europe and Eurasia (8%) had the other largest shares of the global CO_2 emissions. But while the share of Non-OECD countries declined sharply (−8%) that of other Asian countries increased by almost the same proportion (9%) during the period 1973–2014. This followed the pattern of change experienced in TPES. It is apparent that China's share of CO_2 emissions was substantially higher than their proportion

Table 11.10 World total primary energy supply by region, 1973 and 2014

Region	Percentage of total primary energy supply		Percentage change 2014 − 1973
	1973	2014	
OECD	61.3	38.4	−22.9
China	7.0	22.4	15.4
Asia (excluding China)	5.5	12.7	7.2
Non-OECD in Europe and Eurasia	15.5	8.2	−7.3
Non-OECD in Americas	3.5	4.7	1.2
Africa	3.4	5.6	2.2
Middle East	0.8	5.3	4.5
Bunkers	3.0	2.7	−0.3
All: million tonnes of oil equivalent (Mtoe)	6,101	13,699	124.5

Note Total primary energy supply (TPES) is all energy production including international marine and aviation fuel bunkers; it is expressed in terms of the gross calorific value of million tonnes of oil equivalent (Mtoe); (OECD) are more developed countries that are members of the Organization of Economic Cooperation and Development; bunkers relate to fuel supplies for international marine and aviation transport

Source IEA (2016). Computations made by the authors

Table 11.11 World carbon dioxide emissions from fuel combustion by fuel type, 1973 and 2014

Fuel type	Percentage of total CO_2 emissions		Percentage change 2014 − 1973
	1973	2014	
Oil	49.9	33.9	−16.0
Coal	35.6	45.9	10.3
Natural gas	14.4	19.7	5.3
Other	0.1	0.5	0.4
All: millions of tonnes (Mt)	15,458	32,385	109.5

Note (Other) includes bunkers for international marine and aviation transport; emissions exclude non-energy emissions; (CO_2) is carbon dioxide; (Mt) is millions of tonnes

Source IEA (2016); computations made by the authors

of total primary energy supply. The inverse applied to more developed countries (OECD) (Table 11.12). This points to possible differences in the carbon intensity of energy supplies in more developed countries and China and consequent different impact on the environment.

In addition to CO_2 emissions, industrial and transport have also added to the emissions of other GHGs such as methane (CH_4) and nitrous oxides (N_xO) that have a deleterious effect as they mix with moisture in the air and waterways. Growing industrial activity also produce chemical and other wastes that contaminate soil and waterways and eventually the oceans (AAAS 2017).

Table 11.12 World carbon dioxide emissions from fuel combustion by region, 1973 and 2014

Region	Percentage of total CO_2 emissions		Percentage change 2014 − 1973
	1973	2014	
OECD	66.6	36.6	−30.0
China	5.7	28.2	22.5
Asia (excluding China)	3.0	11.8	8.8
Non-OECD in Europe and Eurasia	15.9	7.6	−8.3
Non-OECD in Americas	2.5	3.6	1.1
Africa	1.8	3.4	1.6
Middle East	0.8	5.3	4.5
Bunkers	3.7	3.5	−0.2
All: millions of tonnes (Mt)	15,458	32,385	109.5

Note (Other) includes bunkers for international marine and aviation transport; emissions exclude non-energy emissions; (CO_2) is carbon dioxide; (Mt) is millions of tonnes
Source IEA (2016). Computations made by the authors

11.4.4   Population Growth and Urbanization

As stated earlier (Chap. 6), population growth has been associated with increasing urbanisation to a stage that more than half of the world's population now live in urban areas. Urbanization provides many economies of scale that can be beneficial. Greater population densities can reduce the land footprint of the growing population; it can provide better transport and lower the burning of fossil fuels per head of population through mass public transport. It can also supply a range of facilities to be used by a larger number of people than in rural settings (UN 2001). Much of the population growth in urban agglomerates arises from migration attracted by opportunities created by industrialisation. A major issue is that rapid growth in urban population may not be matched by commensurate investment in infrastructure and facilities to provide adequate living conditions and may also result in the growth of urban slums (Chap. 6: Sect. 6.7) with an effect on the quality of soil, water and air. Transport and other emissions in large cities have resulted in smog in megacities such as Los Angeles, Beijing and many other urban centres that affect not only air quality but also the health of human and other life (UN 2001).

11.4.5   Population Growth and Biodiversity

Although there are different definitions and measurement techniques, it is clear that biological diversity has declined substantially in the past 50 years (Committee on International Science's Task Force on Global Diversity, 1989). Swanson (1995: 48–49) argues that the main cause of loss of biodiversity can be attributed to the influence of human beings on the world ecosystem. He claims that human beings have deeply altered the environment, and modified the territory, exploiting the species directly (hunting and fishing), changing the biochemical cycles and transferring species from one area to another of the planet. Swanson (1995: 48) goes on to argue that the loss of biological diversity is not a natural process, but, rather, a socioeconomic one. The natural course of evolution is towards diversity, but the socioeconomic course of evolution is towards uniformity, especially in agriculture. As such, another aspect of the environmental conundrum (Sect. 11.2) presents itself in the form of the loss of biological diversity due to the mass production of food and other commodities, the appropriation of land for agriculture, mining, industrial and service production, and urbanization.

11.5 Population, Water and the Environment

11.5.1 Sources and Distribution of Water in the World

Most of the planet is covered by water. It is the natural habitat of a variety of living species. It is also essential to species living on land including humans. Most of the water is in oceans that cover about 70% of the world's surface (FAO 2014). Oceans are the source of 96% of the water in the world. Another 1% of the world's water is saline in ground water and lakes. Fresh water constitutes only 3% of all water. Most fresh water is stored in glaciers, ice caps and permanent snow cover (69%), with about a third (30%) in ground water and 1% in other sources (Table 11.13).

Precipitation in a variety of modes, such as rain and snow is the major source of renewable fresh water. Most of the annual precipitation on land is absorbed by forests and other landscapes (56%) and a smaller proportion by agriculture (5%).

Table 11.13 World sources of water, circa 2017

Sources	Percentage	
	All water	Fresh water
Oceans, seas and bays	96.5	
Other saline water (ground water and lakes)	1.0	
Saline water	97.5	
Fresh water	2.5	
Glaciers, ice caps and permanent snow cover		68.7
Ground water		30.1
Other fresh water (lakes, rivers, ground ice, permafrost, soil moisture, atmosphere, swamp water and biological water)		1.2
All sources	100.0	100.0

Source FAO (2017b). Computations made by the authors

The rest (39%) is the renewable fresh water available to humans and the environment. Precipitation is rather uneven in different regions of the world. The Americas experience the highest rate of precipitation, especially Latin America and the Caribbean. In 2013, the Americas had 46% of the world's renewable fresh water resources for 30% of the land surface. Asia has a diverse volume of fresh water resources with high precipitation in the tropical areas of Southern and Eastern Asia and low in the dry desert areas in the Middle East. It has the lowest average volume of renewable fresh water resources per head of population. Africa has a relatively low average precipitation but a diverse distribution of renewable freshwater resources from the Northern Africa desert areas to the tropical areas of East Equatorial Africa. Europe has a lower rate of precipitation than Africa, especially in the large area of the Russian Federation. However, the European more temperate climate tends to compensate for higher evaporation in other regions. Oceania land mass (mainly Australia), is mostly desert. It has the lowest average precipitation and only 2% of the world's renewable freshwater resources per year with 6% of the planet's land area. This results in substantial differences in the rates of renewable fresh water resources per person in various areas of the world (FAO 2017b).

A potential source of fresh water is desalination. About 50% of desalinated water is produced in countries in the Arabian Peninsula with substantial reserves of oil and capacity to produce the required energy. Another 10% of desalinated water is produced in the United States. However, 44 countries are landlocked without potential access to this source of fresh water (FAO 2017b).

A harmful type of precipitation is acid rain. Industrial emissions of sulphur dioxide (SO_2) and nitrogen oxides (N_xO) and agricultural emissions of nitrogen and ammonia (NH_3) combine with moisture in the atmosphere and fall on land and water in the form of rain, snow, sleet or hail. The same type of emissions can also be dropped in the form of particles or combine with air moisture as haze. Acid rain and other forms of acid depositions can harm vegetation, and result in acidic water in rivers and lakes that affect fish and other living organisms. It is also known to affect the health of humans (EC 2017).

11.5.2 Fresh Water Use

People need clean fresh water to stay alive and sanitation to be healthy. Yet, in 2010 some 11% of people in the world were without clean drinking water. Sanitation was also a problem for a substantial proportion of the world's population (FAO 2014).

Most fresh water is used for agriculture (70%) and industrial (19%) purposes (Table 11.14), and only 5% is used for direct human consumption (FAO 2011). As stated, irrigation has been the major source of growth in agricultural production to feed a larger population. However, it has placed pressure on ground water that has resulted in waterlogging and salinization of soil in some cases (FAO 2014). Fertilisers and pesticides associated with irrigation (e.g. paddy rice) have led to both

Table 11.14 World water withdrawal by major use and region, 2003

Region	Water withdrawal by sector percentage of total withdrawal			Total water withdrawal km^3 p.a.	Water withdrawal percent IRWR
	Municipal	Industrial	Agriculture		
Africa	10	4	86	215	5
Americas	16	35	49	790	4
Asia	9	9	82	2,451	20
Europe	16	55	29	374	6
Oceania	17	10	73	26	3
World	11	19	70	3,856	9

Note (IRWR) is internal renewable water resources: surface and ground water; (km^3 p.a.) is cubic meters per year
Source FAO (2011)

soil degradation and runoffs that have contaminated fresh water flows and flows to the sea (AAAS 2017).

11.5.3   Population Growth, Mangroves and Estuaries

One of the features of population growth and urbanization has been the occupation and/or land filling of mangroves and estuaries. Mangroves provide hinterland protection from storms and their waters are rich in nutrients and provide considerable quantities of fish and seafood. Their destruction has removed their protective nature and their use as rice-paddy and fish farming has also impacted on the environment (Sherbini et al. 2007; FAO 2016).

11.5.4   Population Growth and Fishing

Although agriculture has been the major source of food for the larger world population, fisheries and aquaculture have made a substantial contribution to food stocks. It has been estimated that the world average consumption of fish per head of population doubled from 9.9 kg in 1960 to 20 in 2014. Fish production growth of 3.2% per year in the period 1961–2013 was well ahead of the rate of population growth (FAO 2016). Fish captured from marine and inland fisheries rose by 4% in the period 2009–2104, while fish from marine and inland aquaculture production increased at much more by 33%. Thus, most of the additional fish production came from aquaculture in that period (Table 11.15).

People in Asia consumed almost three quarters of the world's fish supplies for human consumption (70%), and had the second highest rate of 23 kgs of fish per head of population, after Oceania with 25 kgs but only 1% of global fish

Table 11.15 World fisheries and aquaculture production, 2009–2014

Production type	Percentage of total		Increase
	2009	2014	2009 = 1.000
Capture	61.8	55.9	1.035
Aquaculture	38.2	44.1	1.325
Total (million tonnes)	145.9	167.2	1.146

Source FAO (2016). Computations by the authors

consumption. Europe (22 kg per capita) and North America (21 kgs per capita) followed. Countries in Latin America and the Caribbean (9 kgs per capita) and Africa (10 kgs per capita) had substantial lower levels of fish consumption (Table 11.16).

Fish production from marine fisheries has stabilised since the 1990s because of declining fish stocks due to over fishing in some areas, such as the fishing of cod in the Northwest Atlantic and the decline of one third of the in fish caught in the Mediterranean and Black Seas in the period 2007–2014. It has been assessed, the proportion of fish stocks within biological sustainable levels declined from 90% in 1974 to 69 in 2013, and that the proportion at those at unsustainable level rose from 10 to 31% of fish stocks. Fish stocks considered underfished amounted to only 11% of the total in 2013 (FAO 2016). Thus, overfishing of marine fisheries has reduced fish stocks as a source of food for a growing population, at least for some time while marine fisheries recover from past fishing practices. Aquaculture appears to provide a key to future increments in fish production.

11.5.5 Human Activity and Warming of the Oceans

In addition to other depositions in the oceans from agriculture and industrial production, the oceans have been functioning as carbon sinks for anthropogenic CO_2 emissions. It has been assessed that most of the emissions from energy generation

Table 11.16 World fish for human consumption by region, 2013

Region	Percentage consumption	Consumption per capita kgs per year
Africa	7.7	9.8
North America	5.4	21.4
Latin America and Caribbean	4.1	9.4
Asia	70.3	23.0
Europe	11.7	22.2
Oceania	0.7	24.8
World	100.0	19.7

Source FAO (2016). Computations made by the authors

in the period 1970–2010 have been accumulated in the oceans. A consequence of the accumulation of CO_2 has been the warming of ocean waters. Ice sheets in Greenland and possibly Antarctica have lost some of their mass and sea levels have risen. Further, CO_2 stored in the oceans has increased the acidity of sea water (IPCC 2015). These changes have had an effect on the role that oceans play in the world climate. It has been suggested that oceans capacity to absorb CO_2 has declined as emissions have increased (Raupach et al. 2014).

11.6   Population, Air and the Environment

A major effect of human activity and industrialisation has been the substantial increment in the emission of greenhouse gases. Some of which were absorbed in carbon sinks in land and oceans, but a substantial proportion were added to the atmosphere. As indicated earlier, some GHG emissions may fall on land and water either as dry precipitations or as acid rain that affects animal and plant life, soil and water quality. GHG emissions from human activity have about doubled from 27 giga (10^9) tonnes of CO_2 equivalent (GtCO_2e) in 1970 to 49 GtCO_2e in 2010. The proportion of CO_2 emissions from the combustion of fossil fuels and industrial processes that constituted 55% of GHG emissions in 1970 increased to 65% in 2010, while the shares of the total emissions of methane and CO_2 from agriculture, forests and other land use (FOLU) declined (Table 11.17).

As it is now the established pattern of industrial development, GHG emissions declined in high income countries from 53% of the global emissions in 1970 to 38% in 2010, while those of upper middle income countries with the highest rates of industrial growth rose from 22 to 37% during the same period (Table 11.18).

Table 11.17 World total anthropogenic greenhouse gas emissions by group of gases, 1970–2010

Greenhouse gases	Percentage of total				
	1970	1980	1990	2000	2010
CO_2 from fossil fuels and industrial processes	55	58	59	62	65
Methane	19	18	18	16	16
CO_2 FOLU	17	15	16	13	11
Nitrous oxide	8	8	7	7	6
Fluorinated gases	...	1	1	1	2
Total GHG emissions GtCO_2e per year	27	33	38	40	49
Average annual percentage increase in period from previous date		2.0	1.4	0.6	2.2

Note (CO_2) is carbon dioxide; (Methane) is CH_4; Nitrous oxide is (N_2O); (Fluorinated gases) are gases such as hydrofluorcarbons (HFCs), perfluorcarbons (PFCs), sulphur hexafluoride (SF_6) and nitrogen trifluoride (NF_3); (FOLU) is agriculture, forests and other land use; (GtCO_2e) is giga (10^9) tonnes CO_2 equivalent
Source IPCC (2014)

Table 11.18 World total anthropogenic greenhouse gas emissions by country income level, 1970–2010

Country income level	Percentage of total			Percentage change 2010 − 1970
	1970	1990	2010	
Low	11.7	9.3	6.9	−4.8
Lower middle	12.4	14.5	16.0	3.6
Upper middle	21.5	25.9	37.0	15.5
High	52.6	48.4	37.9	−14.7
Bunkers	1.8	1.6	2.2	0.4
Total GHG emissions GtCO$_2$e per year	27	38	49	

Note (GtCO$_2$e) is giga (10^9) tonnes of CO_2 equivalent
Source IPCC (2014)

At issue is the rising volume of GHG emissions in recent decades in spite of the Kyoto Convention and their cumulative effect in the atmosphere. It is posited that anthropogenic GHG emissions have an impact on the world's temperature and climate, in addition to the mentioned acidification of soil and oceans. Under BAU conditions, it has been estimated that the GHG concentration in the atmosphere will exceed the proposed target of 450 ppm of CO_2 equivalent by 2030. A market-oriented proposal is to place a price on carbon. This would increase the marginal cost of carbon above the private marginal cost and stimulate a shift to lower use of carbon intensive practices in energy production and other activities (IPCC 2014). Other abatement and adaption suggestions have been made but BAU seems to have prevailed in recent decades, as expressed in the increase in the use of coal for energy production. This is the challenge faced especially by less developed countries that are increasing their industrial output not just for domestic consumption but also for export to more developed countries.

11.7   Some Technology, Institutional, Market and Policy Issues

11.7.1   Public and Private Interests

One of the issues faced by society is the potential difference between individual and social interests. Some related conceptual ideas were raised by Hardin (1968) in an article entitled *The tragedy of the commons*. His approach has been criticised but some features of the *commons* concept have been used in relation to environmental degradation. It suggests that much of the environmental domains such as land, water and air are in public ownership. This places individuals at a moral hazard in relation to the environmental management. It might be costlier to individuals to control emissions and wastes from their activities than to use free or quasi free public commons for their emissions and wastes. Therefore, individuals might have no interest in the impact of their emissions and wastes that end up in land, water and air in public property.

Accordingly, it might be economically rational for individuals and corporations to continue the degradation of soil, contamination of rivers, lakes, estuaries and seas, and emissions that affect air quality at no cost to themselves, against the costs that they might incur in the use of either cleaner technologies or management of emissions and wastes from their activities. This is an issue that can be addressed by public policies and regulation, but may not be…

11.7.2   Market Prices, Resources and Technology

A similar issue arises from the market price of resources and the relative costs to individuals of dirtier or cleaner technologies. The relative abundance and price of different types of fuels might encourage the use of either coal or natural gas in energy production. These prices do not take into consideration the relative environmental impact of either coal or natural gas in energy production and the price paid by consumers per unit of energy.

The use of a particular technology may also depend on the cost of related equipment (upfront costs) and running costs at the unfettered market prices. However, this price may not take into consideration social costs arising from environmental impact of the particular technology. This applies to agriculture as well as manufacture and service production, and private use of goods and services. This is currently one of the issues in the use of fossil fuels, solar and other technologies in energy production. Again, this a matter that can be addressed by public policies concerned with market incentives and signals, innovation and technology change, and investment support.

11.7.3   Institutional and Cultural Features

Institutional inertia is a major factor in dealing with the environmental impact of the inevitable future population growth and desirable improvements in living standards in developing countries. Among other things, adherence to current practices in agriculture may hinder the efficiency of agricultural production to feed the projected increase in population. FAO has suggested that land tenure should be changed, as well as the relationship between land and water management institutions. It also recommended greater access to credit by small land owners to facilitate enhancement investments in more efficacious agricultural practices that currently are affected by *insecure land tenure, lack of incentives, lack of access to markets or appropriate technologies and use of marginal lands* (FAO 2011: 5).

A variation on interests and the *commons* is the *intergenerational burdens* in dealing with current environmental management practices and the costs and future benefits or losses (WB 2010). Should current cohorts pay for the costs of mitigation that will have most impact in the future? Or should future cohorts suffer from the lack of management by past generations?

These are also questions of public policy that may not be resolved at national level and might require international cooperation, as the contamination of air and water resources have a tendency to cross borders from the country of origin, as demonstrated by acid rain in North America and Northern Europe, and the haze in Malaysia and Singapore from the burning of forests in Indonesia.

References

American Association for the Advancement of Science (AAAS). (2017). *AAAS atlas of population and environment*. Retrieved August 11, 2017, from http://atlas.aaas.org.

Andreev, K., Kantarova, V., & Bongaarts, J. (2013). *Demographic components of future population growth*. Population Division, Technical Paper No. 2013/3. New York: United Nations.

Borregaard, N., & Dufey, A. (2002). *Environmental effects of foreign investment versus domestic investment in the mining sector in Latin America*. Paris: OECD.

Boserup, E. (1965). *The conditions of agricultural growth*. London: Earthscan.

Bredemeier, M. (2002). Anthropogenic effects on forest ecosystems at various spatio-temporal scales. *Scientific World Journal, 2*, 827–841. Retrieved September 1, 2017, from https://doi.org/10.1100/tsw.2002.129.

Brown, L. R. (1970). *Seeds of change*. New York: Praeger Publishers.

Carter, R. M., de Freitas, C. R., Goklany, I. M., Holland, D., Lindzen, R. S., Byatt, I., et al. (2006). The Stern review: A dual critique. *World Economics, 7*(4), 165–232.

Committee on International Science's Task Force on Global Biodiversity. (1989). *Loss of biological diversity: A global crisis requiring international solutions*. Washington, D.C: National Science Foundation.

Davis, K. (1945). The world demographic transition. *Annals of the American Academy of Political and Social Sciences, 237*, 1–11.

Ehrlich, P. (1969). *The population bomb*. New York: Ballantine.

Environment Canada (EC). (2017). *Environment and climate change Canada*. Retrieved September 6, 2017, from www.ec.gc.ca/air/default.asp?lang=en&n=7E5E9F00-1#wsD5D8B879.

Food and Agriculture Organization (FAO). (2003). *World agriculture: Towards 2015/2030—An FAO perspective*. London: Earthscan Publications Ltd.

Food and Agriculture Organization (FAO). (2009). *State of the world's forests 2009*. Rome.

Food and Agriculture Organization (FAO). (2011). *The state of the world's land and water resources for food and agriculture—Managing systems at risk*. New York: Earthscan.

Food and Agriculture Organization (FAO). (2013). *Tackling climate change through livestock—A global assessment of emissions and mitigating opportunities*. Rome.

Food and Agriculture Organization (FAO). (2014). *FAO statistical yearbook 2013*. Rome.

Food and Agriculture Organization (FAO). (2016). *The state of world fisheries and aquaculture*. Rome.

Food and Agriculture Organization (FAO). (2017a). *FAOSTAT*. Retrieved August 31, 2017, from www.fao.org/faostat/en.

Food and Agriculture Organization (FAO). (2017b). *AQUASAT*. Retrieved September 5, 2017, from www.fao.org/nr/water/aquastat/didyouknow/index.stem.

Hardin, G. (1968). The tragedy of the commons. *Science, 3869,* 1243–1248.

Hunter, L. M. (2001). *The environmental implications of population dynamics.* RAND.

Intergovernmental Panel on Climate Change (IPCC). (2014). *Climate change 2014 mitigation of climate change.* Cambridge: Cambridge University Press. Retrieved August 22, 2017, from http://ipcc.ch/report/ar5/wg3/.

Intergovernmental Panel on Climate Change (IPCC). (2015). *Climate change 2014—Synthesis Report.* Geneva. Retrieved September 8, 2017, from www.ipcc.ch/pdf/assessment_report/ar5/syr/SYR.

International Energy Agency (IEA). (2016). *Key world energy statistics.* Paris. Retrieved September 10, 2017, from www.iea.org.

Livi-Bacca, M. (2017). *A concise history of world population* (6th ed.). Chichester: Wiley.

Meadows, D. H., Meadows, D. L., Randers, J., & Behrens, W. W. (1972). *The limits to growth.* London: Pan Books.

Morgan, S. P. (2003). Is low fertility a twenty-first-century demographic crisis? *Demography, 40* (4), 589–603.

Murray-Darling Basin Authority (MDBA). (2014). *Environmental challenges and issues—The Basin.* Retrieved May 27, 2014, from www.mdba.gov.au/about-basin-envirnent/challenges-issues.

Raupach, M. R., Marland, G., Ciais, P., Le Quere, C., Canadell, J., Klepper, G., et al. (2007). Global and regional drivers of accelerating CO_2 emissions. *Proceedings of the National Academy of Sciences, 104*(24), 10288–10293. Retrieved August 21, 2017, from www.pnas.org/cgi/doi/10.1073/pnas.0700609104.

Raupach, M. R., Gloor, M., Sarmiento, J. L., Canadell, J. G., Frolicher, T. L., Gasser, T., et al. (2014). The declining rate of atmospheric CO2 by land and oceans sinks. *Biosciences, 11* (3453–3475). Retrieved August 21, 2017, from https://doi.org/10.5194/bg-11-3453-2014.

de Sherbini, A., Carr, D., Cassels, S., & Jiang, L. (2007). Population and the environment. *Annual Review of Environmental Resources, 32,* 345–375.

Simon, J. L. (1980). Resources, population, environment: An oversupply of false bad news. *Science, New Series, 208*(4451), 1431–1437.

Stern, D. I., Common, M. S., & Barbier, E. B. (1996). Economic growth and environmental degradation: The environmental Kuznets curve and sustainable development. *World Development, 24*(7), 1151–1160.

Stern, D. I. (2014). *The environmental Kuznets curve: A primer.* CCEP Working Paper 1404. Canberra: Australian National University.

Stern, N. (2006). *Stern review: The economics of climate change.* London: Her Majesty's Treasury.

Swanson, T. (1995). Uniformity in development and the decline of biological diversity. In T. Swanson (Ed.), *The economics and ecology of biodiversity decline* (pp. 41–53). Cambridge: Cambridge University Press.

United Nations (UN). (2001). *Population, environment and development—The concise report.* New York.

United Nations (UN). (2015). *Adoption of the Paris agreement.* Framework Convention on Climate Change.

United Nations (UN). (2017). *World population prospects: The 2017 revision. Volume I: Comprehensive tables.* New York.

World Bank (WB). (2010). *World development report 2010.* Washington, DC.

World Bank (WB). (2017a). *World development indicators.* Retrieved September 10, 2017, from http://data.worldbank.org/data-catalog/world-development-indicators.

World Bank (WB). (2017b). GDP per capita, PPP. Retrieved September 10, 2017, from http://data.worldbank.org/indicator/NYGDP.PCAP.PP.CD?end=2015&start=2001.

Chapter 12
The Future and Its Challenges

> *It has been said that the great question is now at issue, whether man* [and woman] *shall henceforth start forwards with accelerated velocity towards illimitable, and hitherto unconceived improvement, or be condemned to a perpetual oscillation between happiness and misery, and after every effort remain still at an immeasurable distance from wished-for goal.*
>
> Thomas Robert Malthus (1798)

12.1 Inevitable Future Population Growth

12.1.1 Alternatives and Pathways of Population Change

Population momentum will ensure that the world population will continue to grow throughout the 21st century. But by how much? is an important question. The United Nations projection of population at constant fertility rates results in a population of 10,942 million by 2050 and 26,329 million by 2100. The lesser, but still impressive, medium projection generates a population of 9,772 and 11,184 million people by 2050 and 2100 (Table 1.15). This lower projection will still raise the world population since 2015 by about one third by 2050 and by more than one half by 2100. These projections will increase the world population density that was 54 people per km^2 in 2015 to 72 and 82 people per km^2 respectively in 2050 and 2100 (Table 1.18).

The medium projection leads to a variety of population characteristics in the world regions depending on their individual stages of the population transition. Accordingly, this projection results in different patterns of growth and changing proportions of regional populations of the world total.

The population of Europe that has experienced a decline in fertility in past decades is expected to continue to have fertility below replacement level. It would consequently experience a loss in population and make up a smaller proportion of the world population from 10% in 2015 to 7 and 6% in 2050 and 2100.

© Springer International Publishing AG, part of Springer Nature 2018
Jo. M. Martins et al., *Global Population in Transition*,
https://doi.org/10.1007/978-3-319-77362-9_12

The opposite would take place in Africa where fertility would continue to be well above replacement level until 2100 and population growth would continue to be high, even if the rate of growth were to decline towards 2100. The population of Africa, which constituted 16% of the world total in 2015, would increase its share to 26 and 40% of the total in 2050 and 2100 respectively.

The projected pattern in Asia and Latin America and the Caribbean reflects the continuing decline in fertility from just above replacement level in 2015 to below it in the following decades. Momentum would lead first to a rise and then, as it wanes, to a fall in their populations. The proportion of Asia's population of the world total would fall from 60 to 54% from 2015 to 2050, and then further to 43% in 2100. Similarly, the population of Latin America and the Caribbean would also grow in absolute number from 2015 to 2050 and then fall by 2100, but its proportion of the world population would keep on declining from 9% in 2015 to 8 and then 6% in 2050 and 2100.

The projection for Northern America and Oceania with fertility around replacement level, but with significant contributions by immigration to population growth, would be for continuing population growth, but their proportion of the world population would remain at about 5% in the case of Northern America and less than 1% in Oceania (Tables 1.16 and 1.17).

Patterns and timing of change in China and India, with the two largest populations in the world, play a major role in the Asian context and in the world, as they constituted about a third of the world's population in 2015. China's population given its early decline of fertility below replacement level is projected to experience continuing population losses by the 2040s. The projection for India, given fertility above replacement level until the 2020s, is not projected to start losing population until the 2060s (UN 2017).

The different growth pathways of the world regions will lead not only to changes in population size and pressure on land and other resources but also have implications for differences in age distribution, dependency ratios and labour force participation potential. These differences will have an impact on the capacity to produce basic and other commodities and maintenance or enhancement of living standards (Chaps. 7 and 10).

12.1.2   Feeding the Growing Population

One of the challenges faced by future population growth is the provision of basic needs such as food and water. Two aspects are apparent, one arises from population growth and the other from increases in consumption per head of population by developing countries to catch-up with more developed countries. As important as other regions are, the analysis of the size and patterns of population growth point to two regions: Asia and Africa. Indications are that income per head of population in Asia will continue to grow while it is uncertain, but likely, that that incomes in Africa will not grow as fast and remain below average, at least for some decades.

Consequently, future demand for food in Africa might be in line with population growth, while in Asia there may be increases in consumption per head of population and shifts from vegetable to animal sources of protein (OECD-FAO 2017). In Asia, China and India will be at different stages of their demographic and economic transitions with different demands at various times.

Water for human use is a major concern. As abundant as it appears, less than 1% of the world's water can be used for human needs. Fresh water supplies are subjected to competing use in food production, industry and waste disposal. Water availability per head of population is projected to fall by 50% by 2050. Falling water availability and population growth are bound to lead to a precarious situation (UNDP 2006).

Land and water are two major sources of food. After the increase in land use for agricultural purposes from the 1960s to 1990s, concerns about the consequences of deforestation have been associated with a decline in the clearing of forests for agricultural purposes, in some cases there has been a reduction in land use for agriculture due to urbanization, aforestation and desertification. This means that increases in yields of crops and higher productivity in other agricultural activities will have to supply the additional food production needed for the growing future population. Review of crop yields shows that there are substantial lags in yields in both Asia and Africa and that the use of existing methods could increase yields substantially to provide additional food in the future (OECD-FAO 2017). However, a limiting factor may be the mentioned availability of water. Agriculture accounts for 70% of global water use by humans, and more than 90% in the world's less developed countries. Thus, it has been suggested that current rates of water use and growth in agricultural production to feed the larger population may result in a fresh water supply crisis (UNWAP 2015).

As indicated earlier, when income per head of a population rises there is a propensity for changes in food preferences. For instance, in India there is a tendency to increase the consumption of dairy products in preference to cereals, while in China the propensity is for higher consumption of meat and fish. These shifts reflect no only local physical conditions and climate but also cultural differences. Another influence on the growth of food production, within the constraints of existing land use for agricultural purposes, is competition from cultivation for industrial purposes such as the production of cotton and other crops such as sugar, maize and cassava for biofuel production (OECD-FAO 2017).

Fishing has been a major source of food. Over-fishing has led to a decline in the rate of growth of captured fish production (Chap. 11: Sect. 11.5.4). An alternative that has already taken hold is an increase from aquaculture that is envisaged to become larger than captured fish production (OECD-FAO 2017).

The potential in food growth is not without its risks. The substantial use of irrigation in agricultural production has been associated with salinization and soil degradation, and other environmental impacts, such in the case of the Murray-Darling area in Australia and rice cultivation in Vietnam. The same applies to the overuse of fertilisers and emissions from agriculture (Chap. 11: Sect. 11.4.1; OECD-FAO 2017).

12.1.3   Settlement of the Growing Population

The substantial growth in population in coming decades presents a challenge as to what mode of settlement will be adopted. The United Nations envisages that most of the population growth in the 21st Century will be concentrate in urban areas, while population in rural areas is projected to decline from about 3.4 billion people in 2015 to 3.2 billion in 2050 (UN 2014a). In the two major growth regions of Africa and Asia, it is projected that most people will become urban dwellers by 2050. The urban population of Africa will rise from 40% of the total population in 2015 to 56% in 2050. The urban proportion of the total population in Asia will also increase from 48 to 64% in the 35-year period 2015–2050. The projected trend is for the relatively lower population growth regions to add to the already high proportion of their urban population in 2015 (Table 12.1). In Asia, it is projected that 76% of China's population will live in urban settlements by 2050 and 50% in India. In Africa, 67% of Nigeria's population is projected to live in urban settlements at that time (UN 2014b).

A feature of the projected growth in urban living is that the number of megacities with more than 10 million people will increase to 41 in 2050 from 29 in 2015 (UN 2014a).

There are perceived advantages in urban living with its potential economies of scale, diverse labour markets and easier access to education and health services. The corollary is the required investments in infrastructure to provide adequate water and sanitation, and services for the collection and safe disposal of wastes, as well transport and energy. In the past, lags in these services in fast growing urban settlements have resulted in large proportions of urban dwellers having to live in slum conditions, such as the *favelas* of Rio de Janeiro and the *kampungs* of Jakarta. As a result, about 30% of the urban population in developing regions lived in slums in 2014. These have carried with them public health problems, degradation of the soil, rivers and sea and other environmental damages (Chap. 6: Sect. 6.7).

Table 12.1 World urbanization prospects by region, 2015–2050

Region	Percentage of population in urban settlement		Change 2015 − 2050%
	2015	2050	
Africa	40	56	16
Asia	48	64	16
Europe	74	82	8
Latin America and Caribbean	80	86	6
Northern America	82	87	5
Oceania	71	74	3
World	54	66	12

Source UN (2014b). Computations made by the authors

Therefore, the projected rapid urbanisation in Africa and Asia, and to a lesser extent in other regions, carries with it the challenge of addressing past neglect, as well as more adequate investments in infrastructure and urban services.

The growth of larger urban conurbations will add to the problems of coordination and to the already complex governance of urban areas. They entail not only identification of matters that need to be addressed and responsibilities, but also decision-making and implementation frameworks that are adequate to mobilise and allocate relevant resources, and to bring about acceptable living conditions. Another dimension of governance is the fostering of social cohesion and opportunity for participation in both the identification of issues to be resolved and their implementation.

12.1.4 Energy for a Growing Population

A feature of economic development and industrialisation has been the substitution of human and animal power by energy generated from other sources. Although, hydro and nuclear sources have played a role, energy generation has relied mostly on the burning of fossil fuels for electrical power and transport. Oil, coal and natural gas have accounted for more than 80% of the total primary energy generation in recent decades. They also contributed to about 90% of carbon dioxide emissions in 2014, especially coal that accounted for 46% of carbon dioxide emissions for 29% of energy supply at that time (Chap. 11: Sect. 11.4.3).

The International Energy Agency (IEA 2017) has estimated that the demand for energy in the world will increase by 30% from 2016 to 2040. This is on the assumption that the world economies will grow on average by 3.4% per year and population growth will be in accordance with the United Nations medium projections. In general, it is predicted that two thirds of the additional energy use will take place in developing countries. A large proportion of this is related to the envisaged growing demand in India where energy use is projected to rise from 11% of the world total in 2016 to 18% in 2040. It is estimated that this addition is the equivalent of the current European Union's energy use. Another major contribution to the growth in demand is the additional use in China that is estimated to be the equivalent of the current United States' energy use.

A number of developments influence future sources and modes of energy production. One of these is the recent lowering of the cost of photovoltaic (PV) panels by 70% and of batteries by 40% and their greater source of energy in India and China. This development has relevance to other major users of energy such as the United States (IEA 2017). It has been suggested that rooftop PV systems in the United States could generate the equivalent of 40% of electricity use in 2016 (Castellanos et al. 2017).

Another development is the increasing use of natural gas with lower emissions than coal or oil, as well as improvements in the efficiency of production, distribution and use of energy. Other trends are the larger use of wind power production

Table 12.2 World primary energy supply by fuel type and scenario, 2016–2040

	Percentage of total primary energy demand			2040 difference new policies and sust. dev.
	2016	New policies 2040	Sustainable development 2040	
Coal	27	22	13	+9
Oil	32	27	23	+4
Gas	22	25	25	–
Nuclear	5	6	10	−4
Hydro	3	3	4	−1
Bioenergy	1	10	11	−1
Other renewables	2	6	14	−8
World TPED (mtoe)	13,760	17,584	14,084	+3,500

Note (New policies) figures are estimates of the outcome of countries agreement to changes in fuel types and modes of generation. (Sustainable development) figures are those in line with the United Nations Sustainable Development goals. (TPED) is total primary energy demand. (mtoe) means millions of tonnes of oil equivalent
Source IEA (2017)

in the European Union, further rises in the use of bioenergy in Brazil, and the foreseen greater number of electric cars. In this context, one example is the decision to phase out gasoline and diesel powered cars in the United Kingdom and France by 2040 (IEA 2017).

New policy scenarios would lead to an increase in the proportion of natural gas (+3%), bioenergy (+9%) and other renewables (+4%), and a decline in the proportion of use of coal (−5%) and oil (−5%) between 2016 and 2040. However, this would fall short of changes needed to meet the United Nations sustainable development goals by 2040 that require substantial reductions in the overall production of energy from the new policies scenarios (by 3,500 million tonnes of oil equivalent) and lowering of the proportions of coal (−9%) and oil (−4%) fuels and a rising proportion of other sources of energy production (Table 12.2). Thus, the challenge of providing energy for both population and economic growth, and reducing the impact on the environment continues to be troublesome and a possible threat to the future of the planet.

12.1.5   Commons: Private and Public Interests

The continuing tussle within and among countries concerning the abatement of emissions from energy production reflects a more general issue of the conflict that can arise between private and public interests. This operates within and across country boundaries and on the commons of the atmosphere and the oceans, and at times across generations (Hardin 1968). Thus, private gain of some may become a loss for the many across groups in society, geographical areas and time. The Intergovernmental Panel on Climate Change (IPCC 2014) stated that emissions arising from the interests of any individual, organisation or country have an impact on the common atmosphere and will affect the welfare of others and also that of future generations (Chap. 11: Sect. 11.2). This conflict of interests applies to other areas of human activity such as other forms of pollution and waste disposal. It is also of relevance to other human enterprise where market failures lead to deleterious outcomes and require cooperation among individuals and countries. An example is the overfishing of cod in the Grand Banks of Newfoundland that led to the collapse of these cod fisheries in the 1990s (Myers et al. 1997). The conflict can be seen as another aspect of the prisoners' dilemma of *defecting* or *cooperating* mentioned by Dawkins (2006) in the context of genetic success. Although *defecting* might be the rational decision for an individual, it results in prejudicial outcomes for the group, while *cooperating* leads to outcomes that benefit all in the group.

12.2 Evolving Roles, Inequalities, Lags and Gaps

12.2.1 Evolving Roles and Activity

Evolving social and economic activity has and should continue to have an impact of the roles of males and females in the family, the economy and society. As fertility declines in developing countries, where most people live, and female participation in the formal labour force rises, the stereotype roles of males specialising in production and females in reproduction and caring will need to evolve. Also, the increasing mechanisation and automation of production will diminish the relevance of the relatively greater physical strength of males in production (Chap. 8). This presents the challenge to male and female roles in terms of household and social decision-making, hours of work at a job and at home to be in more harmony with the changed circumstances. Education continues to play an important role in empowering females and enhancing their human capital in the labour market, society and within the household.

The increasing use of power devices by both males and females and changes in the nature of work towards more sedentary occupations (Chap. 10) pose a challenge to human ability to keep physically fit while changing the nature of their work.

Longer periods spent in education early in life and longer life spans after conventional retirement age, and the trend towards independent living (Chaps. 7 and 10) raise a number of issues. One of them is the growing number of people living in one-person households, either due to later family formation or to widowhood from the longer survival of females. Longer years spent in education by a larger proportion of young people will affect the dependence of adolescents and young adults either on their families or social support and possibly lead to later family formation. Another issue is the role of people after the conventional retirement age. The age of retirement was set at a time when average life expectancy was relatively low in more developed countries. The expected life expectancy of males in more developed countries was 62 years in 1950–1955 and that of females 67 years. The respective life expectancies were 75 and 82 years in 2010–2015 and are expected to be 82 and 86 years in 2045–2050 (UN 2017). Although the retirement age has been changed in some countries, the change has been only a fraction of the rise in life expectancy (OECD 2017). The role of older people in society and their engagement in social and economic activity in accordance with their changed capacity is another riddle faced by society. With the development of new technologies, especially in more developed countries, the way that society supports older people will further evolve away from familial to private or public support systems.

12.2.2 Lags and Gaps

Much progress has been made in recent decades in advancing the human condition and the quality of human capital in terms of health and education. Nevertheless, very large lags indicate great opportunity to enhance the lives of people in middle and lower income countries. The difference in maternal mortality of 17 deaths per hundred thousand live births in high income countries and 495 in low income countries is an indication of the nature of the challenge faced. Similarly, infant mortality in low income countries at 60 per thousand live births lags well behind that of 5 in high income countries. The same large differences apply in the case of child mortality under the age of 5 years (Table 12.3). These lags prevail not only among countries with different levels of income, they also occur in high income countries. An example is the substantial disparity in the rate of infant mortality between indigenous and non-indigenous people in a number of high income countries. In 2015, the infant mortality rate of Australian Indigenous people at 7 per thousand live births was about twice that of 3 per thousand of the non-indigenous Australians (ABS 2016). Similarly, the infant mortality rate of American Indians and Alaska Natives in 2014 was 8 per thousand of live births compared to 6 per thousand of all races in the United States (USDHHS 2017). A similar lag existed between the infant mortality of Canadian Indigenous people at 10 per thousand live births in 2004–2006 and that of Non-Indigenous at 4 per thousand (SC 2017).

Another challenge to be met is the rate of malnutrition of children that affects both their physical and intellectual development. The proportion of the children affected varies from 3% in high income countries to 38 in low income countries (Table 12.4).

A subject of direct relevance to malnutrition is the provision of adequate sanitation facilities that enhance the retention of nutrients. Only 28% of the population in low income countries and 52% in low middle income countries had access to

Table 12.3 World maternal, infant and under 5 years of age mortality by country income level, 2015

Country income level	Maternal mortality ratio	Infant mortality rate	Under 5 years of age mortality rate
Low	495	60	90
Low middle	253	44	59
Upper middle	55	15	18
High	17	5	6
World average	216	35	48
Difference highest and lowest	478	55	94

Note Maternal mortality ratio is the number of mother deaths per 100,000 live births. Infant mortality rate is the number of infant deaths under one year of age per thousand live births. Under 5 years of age mortality rate is the number of child deaths under the age of five years per thousand of children of that age. Infant and under 5 years of age mortality rates are the average for the years 2010–2015

Sources UN (2017), WB (2016). Computations made by the authors

Table 12.4 World prevalence of child malnutrition and stunting by country income level, 2008–2014

Country income level	Percentage prevalence child malnutrition, stunting
Low	38
Low middle	34
Upper middle	8
High	3
World average	24
Difference highest and lowest	35

Note The prevalence is the percentage of children under 5 years of age and in years in the period 2008–2014, depending on information available

Source WB (2016)

improved sanitation facilities in comparison with 96% in high income countries (Table 12.5), in line with the gradient of malnutrition (Table 12.4).

In spite of the progress made in high and middle income countries (Table 10.6), another area with substantial lags among countries with different income levels is education, as illustrated by the literacy rates of adolescents and young adults. The level of youth literacy ranged from 68% in low income countries to 100% in high income countries in the period 2005–2014 (Table 12.6).

At a more fundamental level, one of great challenges to be faced is the abatement or eradication of extreme poverty. The substantial improvements experienced in recent decades in reducing extreme poverty ($1.90 per person and day) from 34 to

Table 12.5 World access to improved sanitation by country income level, 2015

Country income level	Percent population
Low	28
Low middle	52
Upper middle	80
High	96
World average	68
Difference highest and lowest	35

Note The prevalence is the percentage of children under 5 years of age and in years in the period 2008–2014, depending on information available
Source WB (2016)

Table 12.6 World youth literacy rate by country income level, 2005–2014

Country income level	Youth literacy rate percentage
Low	68
Low middle	86
Upper middle	99
High	100
World average	91
Difference highest and lowest	32

Note Youth literacy rate is the percentage of youth 15–24 years of age who meet literacy standards or reading and writing. The figures relate to the period 2005–2014, depending on information available
Source WB (2016)

15% of the world population leaves a lag between an average of 2% of the population in Europe and Central Asia to 43% in Sub-Sahara Africa. People living in extreme poverty in Sub-Sahara Africa and South Asia constituted 78% of the people living in extreme poverty in the world (Table 10.22).

Some important gaps between males and females also pose some substantial challenges. These include the gap in the level of education between males and females, especially in medium and low income countries in Sub-Sahara Africa, South Asia and the Arab States (Table 10.3). Unexplained gaps also defy justification in the lower earnings of females than males in high and middle income countries (Table 10.15).

Another important gap is access to contraception that in Sub-Sahara Africa is only 28% compared with 69% in European countries (Table 8.8).

These lags and gaps point to inequalities in human endowments and opportunities to enhance living conditions that would bring human condition to a much higher level in future decades.

12.3 Asymmetries and Sharing of Productivity Gains

12.3.1 Asymmetry in Age Distribution

An inevitable consequence of varying rates of past and projected fertility is substantial differences in age distribution and proportion of working age people in countries at different stages of the demographic transition (Table 10.8). Thus, while some countries such as those in Africa will have a potential demographic bonus, in terms of a high proportion of people of working age, others in Europe will be affected by deficits in people of working age to support a higher proportion of older people. Worker migration from lower to higher income countries has been a feature of past decades, but the dimensions of the deficits in high income countries are bound to increase. Cultural barriers have been a source of social stress in receiving countries and brain drain has resulted in losses of human capital in sending countries (Chap. 5). The management of this asymmetry among countries at different levels of economic development will be a challenge to be faced by both receiving and sending countries.

12.3.2 Intergenerational Transfers

The inevitable ageing of populations in high and middle income countries will increase the dependency of old people on the working population (Table 7.16). The old age dependency ratios of Germany and Japan are projected to rise substantially from already high ratios of respectively 32 and 43% in 2015 to 54 and 71% in 2050. But more fundamental changes are projected in Brazil from 11 to 37%, China from 13 to 44%, Korea from 18 to 66% and Thailand from 15 to 61% over the same period (UN 2017). The maintenance of adequate living standards will require substantial fiscal transfers from working age people to old-age people in such

Table 12.7 Public expenditure on pensions, selected countries, 2015–2050

Country	Public expenditure on pensions percentage GDP		Difference percentage GDP 2050 − 2015
	2015	2050	
Germany	10.0	12.5	+2.5
Korea	2.6	5.2	+2.6
Brazil	9.1	16.8	+7.7
China	4.1	9.5	+4.4
OECD average	8.9	9.5	+0.6

Note GDP is gross domestic product
Source OECD (2017). Computations made by the authors

countries. While countries such as Germany and Japan have been addressing the fiscal issues involved, these are new challenges for countries that in the past have had low old age dependency. Accordingly, it has been estimated that public expenditures on pensions will rise substantially even in Germany to 12.5% of GDP in 2050 from 10.0% in 2015. The increment in Korea will be of similar dimension, but the proportion of GDP will double from 2.6 to 5.2% during that period. Similarly, the increase in China will be from 4.1 to 9.5%, and that in Brazil will be more substantial from 9.1 to 16.8% (Table 12.7).

12.3.3 Asymmetry in Sharing of Productivity Gains

The economic transformation taking place from technological change and associated productivity gains have been associated with asymmetry in the sharing of productivity gains (Table 10.12). This has led to greater inequality in earnings and share of labour income associated with growth in low paid jobs. OECD (2010) has pointed out that this trend will prejudice further opportunities for investments in human capital and have a deleterious effect on social cohesion. This asymmetry is another challenge faced by societies in their endeavour to enhance the quality of life and equity among their people.

12.3.4 Asymmetry Between Socioeconomic and Political Development

Technological development of the means of communication, transfer of manufacturing from higher to lower income countries, greater international exchange of goods and services, and the spread of economic interests of corporations across the globe, have created an asymmetry between political institutions at national level and the increasing global nature of economic activity and interdependencies. This has led to major gaps in the coordination of national and international relationships. It is also apparent in efforts to deal with individual interests of corporations and countries and those of the global population. The lack of agreement on how to deal with the quality of the common seas and air shared by all is an important illustration of this asymmetry.

12.4 Experiences and Challenges

The ground-breaking experience of the last century in population growth and transition will continue to provide population momentum and new experiences in the 21st Century. Many of the issues to be addressed are not new. They are not just about the production to meet the needs of the growing population, but they are concerned, to a great extent, with social organisation and the distribution of the products of human activity. In a way, it is like the difference between the attainment of knowledge and its beneficial application.

The substantial growth in human productivity has not led to the eradication of poverty or elimination of inequalities in standards of living, but made these differences more conspicuous, as information about them became more readily available. In addition, the rise in productivity has been associated with environmental contamination and degradation that national governments have had difficulty in managing. Partly, this is because economic development and organisation have become increasingly interdependent in a more global construct, without commensurate political institutions and decision-making processes to deal with the sharing of gains and management of the commons.

References

Australian Bureau of Statistics (ABS). (2016). *Deaths, Australia, 2015*. Canberra.

Castellanos, S., Sunter, D. A., & Kammon, D. M. (2017). Rooftop solar photovoltaic potential in cities: How scalable are assessment approaches? *Environmental Research Letters, 12*, 1–6.

Dawkins, R. (2006). *The selfish gene*. Oxford: Oxford University Press.

Hardin, G. (1968). The tragedy of the commons. *Science, 162*, 1243–1248.

Intergovernmental Panel on Climate Change (IPCC). (2014). *Climate change 2014 mitigation of climate change*. Cambridge: Cambridge University Press. Retrieved August 22, 2017, from http://ipcc.ch/report/ar5/wg3/.

International Energy Agency (IEA). (2017). *World energy outlook 2017*. Retrieved January 2, 2018, from www.iea.org/weo2017/.

Myers, R. A., Hutchings, J. A., & Barrowman, N. J. (1997). Why do fish stocks collapse? The example of cod in Atlantic Canada. *Ecological Applications, 7*(1), 91–106.

Organisation of Economic Co-operation and Development (OECD). (2010). *In it together, why less inequality benefits all*. Paris.

Organisation of Economic Co-operation and Development (OECD). (2017). *Pensions at a glance 2017*. Paris.

Organisation of Economic Co-operation and Development & Food and Agriculture Organization (OECD-FAO). (2017). *OECD-FAO agricultural outlook 2017–2026*. Paris.

Statistics Canada (SC). (2017). *Rate of adverse birth outcomes, by Indigenous identity, singleton births, Canada, 2004 through 2006*. Retrieved January 11, 2018, from www.statcan.gc.ca/pub/82-003-x/2017011/article/54886/tbl/tbl02-eng.hmt.

United Nations (UN). (2014a). *World urbanization prospects: The 2014 revision highlights*. New York.

United Nations (UN). (2014b). *World urbanization prospects: The 2014 revision*, CD-ROM edition. New York. Retrieved March 5, 2017, from www.esa.un.org/undp/wup/index.hmt.

United Nations (UN). (2017). *World population prospects—The 2017 revision—Volume I: Comprehensive tables*. New York.

United Nations Development Programme (UNDP). (2006). *Human development report 2006*. New York.

United Nations Water Assessment Programme (UNWAP). (2015). *World water development report 2015*. Colombella.

United States Department of Health and Human Services (USDHHS). (2017). *Infant mortality and American Indians/Alaska Natives*. Retrieved January 11, 2018, from https://minorityhealth.hhs.gov/omh/browse.aspx?lvl=4&lvlid=38.

World Bank (WB). (2016). *World development indicators 2016*. Washington, DC.

Printed by Printforce, the Netherlands